SHAKESPEARE SURVEY

ADVISORY BOARD

SHAKESPEARE SURVEY

AN ANNUAL SURVEY OF

SHAKESPEARE STUDIES AND PRODUCTION

46

EDITED BY

STANLEY WELLS

CAMBRIDGE
UNIVERSITY PRESS

Published by the Press Syndicate of the University of Cambridge
The Pitt Building, Trumpington Street, Cambridge CB2 1RP
40 West 20th Street, New York, NY 10011–4211, USA
10 Stamford Road, Oakleigh, Melbourne 3166, Australia

First published 1994

Printed in Great Britain at the University Press, Cambridge

A cataloguing in publication record for this book is available from the British Library

ISBN 0 521 45027 6 hardback

Shakespeare Survey was first published in 1948. Its first
eighteen volumes were edited by Allardyce Nicoll. Kenneth
Muir edited volumes 19 to 33.

EDITOR'S NOTE

Volume 47 of *Shakespeare Survey*, which will be at press by the time this volume appears, will have as its theme 'Playing Places for Shakespeare'. Volume 48, on 'Shakespeare and Cultural Exchange', will include papers from the 1994 International Shakespeare Conference; the theme of Volume 49 will be '*Romeo and Juliet* and its Afterlife'.

Submissions should be addressed to the Editor at The Shakespeare Institute, Church Street, Stratford-upon-Avon, Warwickshire CV37 6HP, to arrive at the latest by 1 September 1994 for Volume 48 and 1 September 1995 for Volume 49. Pressures on space are heavy; priority is given to articles related to the theme of a particular volume. Please either enclose postage (overseas, in International Reply coupons) or send a copy you do not wish to be returned. All articles submitted are read by the Editor and at least one member of the Editorial Board, whose indispensable assistance the Editor gratefully acknowledges.

Unless otherwise indicated, Shakespeare quotations and references are keyed to the modern-spelling Complete Oxford Shakespeare (1986).

Review copies of books should be addressed to the Editor, as above. In attempting to survey the ever-increasing bulk of Shakespeare publications our reviewers inevitably have to exercise some selection. We are pleased to receive offprints of articles which help to draw our reviewers' attention to relevant material.

S. W. W.

CONTRIBUTORS

JOHN ASTINGTON, *University of Toronto*
CATHERINE BATES, *Peterhouse, Cambridge*
KENNETH C. BENNETT, *Lake Forest College*
WILLIAM C. CARROLL, *Boston University*
THOMAS CLAYTON, *University of Minnesota*
LAWRENCE DANSON, *Princeton University*
MARGRETA DE GRAZIA, *University of Pennsylvania*
MICHAEL DOBSON, *University of Illinois at Chicago*
JULIET DUSINBERRE, *Girton College, Cambridge*
MICHAEL HATTAWAY, *University of Sheffield*
PETER HOLLAND, *Trinity Hall, Cambridge*
DAVID LINDLEY, *University of Leeds*
RUSS MCDONALD, *University of North Carolina*
ROBERT B. PIERCE, *Oberlin College, Ohio*
NIKY RATHBONE, *Birmingham Shakespeare Library*
ANN THOMPSON, *Roehampton Institute*
MARTIN WIGGINS, *The Shakespeare Institute, University of Birmingham*
H. R. WOUDHUYSEN, *University College, London*

CONTENTS

ILLUSTRATIONS

SHAKESPEARE AND SEXUALITY

ANN THOMPSON

Sexuality must not be thought of as a kind of natural given which power tries to hold in check, or as an obscure domain which knowledge tries gradually to uncover. It is the name that can be given to a historical construct: not a furtive reality that is difficult to grasp, but a great surface network in which the stimulation of bodies, the intensification of pleasures, the incitement to discourse, the formation of special knowledges, the strengthening of controls and resistances, are linked to one another, in accordance with a few major strategies of knowledge and power.

The history of sexuality supposes two ruptures if one tries to center it on mechanisms of repression. The first, occurring in the course of the seventeenth century, was characterized by the advent of the great prohibitions, the exclusive promotion of adult marital sexuality, the imperatives of decency, the obligatory concealment of the body, the reduction to silence and mandatory reticences of language. The second, a twentieth-century phenomenon, was really less a rupture than an inflexion of the curve: this was the moment when the mechanisms of repression were seen as beginning to loosen their grip; one passed from insistent sexual taboos to a relative tolerance with regard to prenuptial or extra-marital relations; the disqualification of 'perverts' diminished, their condemnation by law was in part eliminated; a good many of the taboos that weighed on the sexuality of children were lifted.

Michel Foucault, *The History of Sexuality*, volume 1 (1976), translated by Robert Hurley (Penguin, 1990), pp. 105–6 and p. 115.

'Sexuality' is a fashionable and controversial topic today, not just in literary studies but throughout the whole range of the humanities and social and behavioural sciences. It is both a new topic and an interdisciplinary one. This is explicitly recognized by the University of Chicago Press which publishes a periodical called the *Journal of the History of Sexuality*, now in its second year, which claims to cover relevant areas 'from incest to infanticide, from breast-feeding and women's sexuality to female prostitution, from pornography to reproductive politics, and from the first homosexual rights movement to AIDS'. Advertising for the journal stresses the marked increase in scholarship in the history of sexuality in the past decade, and points out that publications have been widely scattered across traditional subject boundaries in social, political and cultural studies. It is evident from the list of topics cited that this explosion of interest relates to the coming together of three current modes of academic discourse: feminism, post-Freudian psychoanalysis, and homosexual or gay studies. A modest amount of time spent browsing in any bookstore, library or even publisher's catalogue will demonstrate how much work is being done in all of these fields.

In *Making Sex: Body and Gender from the Greeks to Freud*, Thomas Laqueur claims that 'Sometime in the eighteenth century, sex as we know it was invented',[1] but he argues that this 'invention' depended on the cultural reorientation that went on during the Renaissance

---

[1] (Cambridge, Mass., 1990), p. 149.

period when there occurred a shift in perception from a one-sex model of humanity to a two-sex model: that is, instead of seeing the female body as a lesser (inverted) version of the male body, people began to see it as its incommensurable opposite. The early modern period does seem to feature heavily in histories of sexuality. As my second quotation from Foucault suggests, our twentieth-century focus on sexuality can perhaps be seen as a result of the loosening of the mechanisms of repression, while our interest in the seventeenth century can be seen as an attempt to investigate the supposed point of the imposition of those mechanisms. The strong influence of Foucault on literary critics (especially new historicists) has made it seem inevitable that the debate about sexuality is conducted primarily in terms of knowledge and power; despite Laqueur's investigation of the history of the disappearing female orgasm, it seems almost quaint these days to associate sexuality with pleasure.

Shakespeare studies have of course been affected by these debates. 'Shakespeare and Sexuality' was the topic of the twenty-fifth International Shakespeare conference at Stratford-upon-Avon in August 1992, and this volume of *Shakespeare Survey* includes several of the papers delivered at the conference. It was a controversial topic from the start: when it was proposed by the Advisory Committee at the previous conference in 1990, one delegate immediately objected and said 'Why can't we call it "Shakespeare, Love and Marriage?"' During the conference itself more than one person complained to me in similar terms: 'Can't we stop talking about sex and talk about romance?' A female scholar from India confided that she had not dared to put the topic on her application for funding which would be seen by her male colleagues. Several women complained that male speakers took the topic as an excuse to talk in overly self-indulgent ways about two obsessions, women's bodies and male sexual anxiety.

Nevertheless, the papers given at the confer-

ence and the debates that went on around them reflected the 'state of the art' in this field in interesting ways. I do not feel it is appropriate to attempt either a complete retrospect of work on 'Shakespeare and Sexuality' or a detailed account of the conference. Rather, I propose to draw out what seem to me to be a number of key concerns of the past decade under some fairly broad general headings: 'Feminism', 'Men in Feminism and Gay Studies', 'The Boy Actor' and 'Language'.

FEMINISM

In the preface to *Making Sex* Thomas Laqueur says that he could not have written the book 'without the intellectual revolution wrought by feminism since World War II and especially during the last twenty years'. Certainly in Shakespeare studies there can be no doubt that feminist criticism has been enormously influential in putting issues of sexuality and sexual difference on to the critical agenda. In his 1991 annotated bibliography of *Shakespeare and Feminist Criticism*, Philip C. Kolin covers four hundred and thirty-nine items from the publication of Juliet Dusinberre's *Shakespeare and the Nature of Women* in 1975 to his cut-off point in 1988.[2] While all these books and essays could be seen to relate to the question of sexuality in the broadest sense, Kolin lists just thirty-eight items under 'sexuality (female)' in his subject index and eighteen under 'sexuality (male)', of which only thirteen are different from those listed under 'sexuality (female)'. A quite surprisingly high proportion of these, in fact about half, authored by both men and women, deal with the topic of male anxiety about female sexuality – the speakers at Stratford were not unusual in their concentration on this issue. Other topics which recur, but less frequently, are sexual stereotyping, sexuality (and sexism) in the

---

[2] (New York and London, 1991). Dusinberre's book was published in London.

reproduction and reading of Shakespeare, and ambivalence about male sexuality and the issue of homoeroticism.

The focus on male anxiety testifies to the prevalence of psychoanalytical approaches, especially in feminist criticism from North America. A strong tradition can be traced from *Representing Shakespeare: New Psychoanalytic Essays* edited by Murray M. Schwartz and Coppélia Kahn in 1980[3] through Kahn's own *Man's Estate: Masculine Identity in Shakespeare*,[4] Marjorie Garber's *Coming of Age in Shakespeare*,[5] David Sundelson's *Shakespeare's Restoration of the Father*[6] and Kay Stockholder's *Dream Works: Lovers and Families in Shakespeare's Plays*[7] to Janet Adelman's *Suffocating Mothers*[8] and Valerie Traub's *Desire and Anxiety: Circulations of Sexuality in Shakespearean Drama*[9] (both published in 1992). At times earlier contributions to this approach have been attacked for exhibiting an ahistorical essentialism (see, for example, Kathleen McLuskie's essay 'The Patriarchal Bard: Feminist Criticism and Shakespeare: *King Lear* and *Measure for Measure*'),[10] but it has provided us with many valuable insights into Shakespeare's treatment of infantile sexuality, family relationships, the formation of sexual identity, male bonding, misogyny, the fear of cuckoldry and other related issues.

The subtitle of Valerie Traub's book, *Circulations of Sexuality in Shakespearean Drama*, is, as she explains, a deliberate allusion to Stephen Greenblatt's *Shakespearean Negotiations* which was subtitled *The Circulation of Social Energy in Renaissance England*.[11] Greenblatt's work in that book as well as in his earlier *Renaissance Self-Fashioning*[12] has been an important influence on all critics who have examined the issue of individual identity in the early modern period, but there has been some tension between feminist critics and new historicist critics with the former accusing the latter of treating issues of sexuality almost entirely in terms of power to the exclusion of gender: see Lynda E. Boose, 'The Family in Shakespeare Studies; or – Studies in the Family of Shakespeareans; or –

The Politics of Politics',[13] Carol Thomas Neely, 'Constructing the Subject: Feminist Practice and the New Renaissance Discourses'[14] and my own 'Are There Any Women in *King Lear*?'[15] In this respect, the work of Michel Foucault, in *The History of Sexuality* and especially in *Discipline and Punish: The Birth of the Prison*,[16] has perhaps had an overly negative effect on our definitions of early modern sexuality. At the same time one should in fairness record that feminists have been accused of introducing a new kind of Puritanism into the discourse of sexuality.

Feminist critics have often objected to negative views of Shakespeare's female characters. They have argued that the plays are less sexist than the theatrical and critical traditions which continually reproduce them. Barbara Mowat pointed out in 1977 the discrepancy between Shakespeare's women and the way they are perceived by male characters,[17] and other feminist critics have shown that male directors and critics are all too likely to agree with male characters – to take as it were Hamlet's view of Gertrude rather than Shakespeare's. Irene Dash has used stage history to demonstrate, in *Wooing, Wedding and Power: Women in Shakespeare's Plays*,[18] how regularly women's roles

---

[3] (Baltimore, 1980).
[4] (Berkeley, 1981).
[5] (London, 1981).
[6] (New Brunswick, N.J., 1983).
[7] (Toronto, 1987).
[8] (London, 1992).
[9] (London, 1992).
[10] In *Political Shakespeare* edited by Jonathan Dollimore and Alan Sinfield (Manchester, 1985), pp. 88–108.
[11] (Oxford, 1988).
[12] (Chicago, 1980).
[13] *Renaissance Quarterly*, 40 (1987), 707–42.
[14] *English Literary Renaissance*, 18 (1988), 5–10.
[15] In *The Matter of Difference* edited by Valerie Wayne (Hemel Hempstead, 1991), pp. 117–28.
[16] Translated by Alan Sheridan (New York, 1979).
[17] 'Images of Women in Shakespeare's Plays', *Southern Humanities Review*, 11 (1977), 145–57.
[18] (New York, 1981).

have been distorted and limited in productions, often with the effect of reducing a robust interest in sexuality to the more coy attitudes thought of as feminine by later ages. In her paper in the present volume Juliet Dusinberre argues that editors have performed the same 'softening' service by underestimating the amount of sexual innuendo in Rosalind's speech.[19] As long ago as 1957 Carolyn Heilbrun argued that Gertrude had been misunderstood and wrongly condemned by male critics;[20] Linda T. Fitz explored a similar phenomenon in 'Egyptian Queens and Male Reviewers: Sexist Attitudes in Antony and Cleopatra',[21] and Jacqueline Rose has argued in 'Sexuality in the Reading of Shakespeare: Hamlet and Measure for Measure' that the 'problems' in those plays relate to the sexual anxieties of male critics and their determination to hold female desire responsible for any breakdown in moral or aesthetic order.[22]

MEN IN FEMINISM AND GAY STUDIES

There has clearly been a male response to feminist criticism in the publication of a number of books dealing directly with men's relationship to it: see for example Men in Feminism edited by Alice Jardine and Paul Smith[23] and Engendering Men: The Question of Male Feminist Criticism edited by Joseph Boone and Michael Cadden.[24] The work of many male critics is listed in Kolin's annotated bibliography of Shakespeare and Feminist Criticism though not all of them would necessarily describe themselves as feminists. One critic who has explicitly engaged with what it means to write as a male feminist is Peter Erickson whose Patriarchal Structures in Shakespeare's Drama provides a clear and at times grim analysis of the sexual politics of the plays.[25] In his recent Rewriting Shakespeare, Rewriting Ourselves Erickson discusses in an afterword his own project which 'involves undoing the automatic, apparently given, equation between Shake-

speare as white male author and myself as white male critic'.[26]

At the same time, there has been a growing interest in the history and construction of homosexuality and lesbianism. Did they even exist in the modern sense in the Renaissance period? The issue has been explored by James M. Saslow in 'Homosexuality in the Renaissance: Behavior, Identity, and Artistic Expression'[27] and by Alan Bray in Homosexuality in Renaissance England.[28] Literary scholars have also been contributing to this debate: Eve Kosofsky Sedgwick's Between Men: English Literature and Male Homosocial Desire[29] invigorated discussion by distinguishing between homosociality and homosexuality and locating male homoerotic desire in the specific social context of patriarchal heterosexuality. She discussed Shakespeare's Sonnets which are an inevitable focus of attention in this context, despite Margreta de Grazia's brave attempt in her paper in this volume to locate the 'scandal' elsewhere.[30] While the eighteenth century did its best, as Michael Dobson demonstrates below,[31] to eliminate the tricky question of Shakespeare's own sexuality altogether, a

---

[19] See below, pp. 9–21.

[20] 'The Character of Hamlet's Mother', Shakespeare Quarterly, 8 (1957), 201–6. When Heilbrun reprinted this as the first essay in her collection Hamlet's Mother and Other Women (New York, 1990), pp. 9–17, she commented in the Introduction that as a critic of Shakespeare in 1957 'I was a feminist waiting for a cause to join' (p. 2).

[21] Shakespeare Quarterly, 28 (1977), 296–316.

[22] In Alternative Shakespeares edited by John Drakakis (London, 1985), pp. 95–118.

[23] (London, 1987).

[24] (London, 1991).

[25] (Berkeley, 1985).

[26] (Berkeley, 1991), p. 169.

[27] In Hidden From History: Reclaiming the Gay and Lesbian Past edited by Martin Duberman, Martha Vicinus and George Chauncey Jr (New York, 1989), pp. 90–105.

[28] (London, 1982). See also Bruce R. Smith's Homosexual Desire in Shakespeare's England (Chicago, 1992).

[29] (New York, 1985).

[30] See below, pp. 35–49.

[31] Pp. 137–144.

twentieth-century scholar like Joseph Pequigney in *Such is My Love: A Study of Shakespeare's Sonnets* tries to put it back, claiming a specifically homosexual identity for the author and deploring the way that most commentators neglect or dispose of the issue.[32] Such an identity today (or, more precisely, such an implied commitment to specific erotic practices) is of course overshadowed by the history of AIDS which makes the association between desire and death grimly literal.

Other related areas of debate have been the differences between Marlowe and Shakespeare in this respect (see Marilyn J. Thorssen, 'Varieties of Amorous Experience: Homosexual and Heterosexual Relationships in Marlowe and Shakespeare',[33] and Joseph A. Porter, 'Marlowe, Shakespeare, and the Canonization of Heterosexuality'[34]), and the question of homoeroticism in *The Merchant of Venice* where the Antonio/Bassanio/Portia triangle has been read as a struggle between homosexual and heterosexual love (see Seymour Kleinberg, '*The Merchant of Venice*: The Homosexual as Anti-Semite in Nascent Capitalism',[35] Keith Geary, 'The Nature of Portia's Victory: Turning to Men in *The Merchant of Venice*',[36] and Karen Newman, 'Portia's Ring: Unruly Women and Structures of Exchange in *The Merchant of Venice*'.[37])

There has been far less written about lesbianism, though Valerie Traub has recently explored the question of homoerotic desire from a lesbian angle, especially in her chapters on 'Desire and the Differences it Makes' and 'The Homoerotics of Shakespearean Comedy' in *Desire and Anxiety*.[38] Making use of feminist film criticism on the 'male gaze' and the positioning of the audience in relation to screen representations, she argues eloquently for an eroticism which does not flow directly from gender identity and is not limited to the binary homosexual/heterosexual opposition. (See also her more recent essay on 'The (In)Significance of "Lesbian" Desire in Early Modern England'.[39])

THE BOY ACTOR

Male homosexual desire in the Renaissance period is often represented as something which involves an age difference if not a sex difference: it is seen as the desire of adult men for 'boys', and the use of such terms for the younger partner as 'ganymede', 'catamite' and 'ingle' all testify to this. The boy actor of women's parts has been the focus of considerable interest to gay critics as well as to feminist critics in recent years. At the same time a more general interest in transvestism as a widespread social phenomenon not exclusive to the Renaissance is shown in two recent books by prominent Shakespearian critics: Marjorie Garber's *Vested Interests: Cross-Dressing and Cultural Anxiety*,[40] and Jonathan Dollimore's *Sexual Dissidence: Augustine to Wilde, Freud to Foucault*,[41] which has a chapter on 'Cross-Dressing in Early Modern England'. In the light of this it is perhaps surprising that there has not yet been a major new book on the boy actor, but at least two scholars, Juliet Dusinberre and Stephen Orgel, are working on such projects. In fact we still know extraordinarily little about the actual performers, their lives and careers, but we can argue, both from the texts themselves and from secondary material (notably the attacks on the immorality of the stage), that this particular dramatic convention gave rise to a number of debates about

32 (Chicago, 1985).
33 In *Human Sexuality in the Middle Ages and Renaissance* edited by Douglas Radcliff-Umstead (Pittsburgh: University of Pittsburgh Publications on Middle Ages and Renaissance, 1978), pp. 135–52.
34 *South Atlantic Quarterly*, 88 (1989), 127–47.
35 *Journal of Homosexuality*, 8 (1983), 113–26.
36 *Shakespeare Survey* 37 (1984), 55–68.
37 *Shakespeare Quarterly*, 38 (1987), 19–33.
38 As cited in n. 9 above.
39 In *Erotic Politics: The Dynamics of Desire in the Renaissance Theatre*, edited by Susan Zimmerman (New York and London, 1992), pp. 150–69.
40 (London, 1992)
41 (Oxford, 1991).

sexual identity, sexual difference and sexual transgression.

Several scholars working in this area have discussed cross-dressing as a real-life social phenomenon in Renaissance England as well as a theatrical practice. They have investigated the social and religious background and the possible relationships between women wearing men's clothes on the streets and men wearing women's clothes on the stage. Such work includes Juliet Dusinberre's section on 'Disguise and the Boy Actor' in chapter 4 of *Shakespeare and the Nature of Women*,[42] Lisa Jardine's chapter on 'Female Roles and Elizabethan Eroticism' in *Still Harping on Daughters*,[43] Mary Beth Rose's essay on 'Women in Men's Clothing: Apparel and Social Stability in *The Roaring Girl*',[44] Laura Levine's 'Men in Women's Clothing: Anti-theatricality and Effeminization from 1579 to 1642',[45] Jonathan Dollimore's 'Subjectivity, Sexuality and Transgression',[46] Stephen Orgel's 'Nobody's Perfect: Or Why Did the English Renaissance Stage Take Boys for Women?'[47] and Jean E. Howard's 'Crossdressing, the Theatre, and Gender Struggle in Early Modern England'.[48]

Others have concentrated more specifically on the immediate dramatic effects of the convention: such work includes Paula S. Berggren's 'The Woman's Part: Female Sexuality as Power in Shakespeare's Plays',[49] Kathleen McLuskie's 'The Act, the Role, and the Actor: Boy Actresses on the Elizabethan Stage',[50] Mary Free's 'Shakespeare's Comedic Heroines: Protofeminists or Conformers to Patriarchy?',[51] Matthew H. Wikander's '"As secret as maidenhead": The Profession of the Boy-Actress in *Twelfth Night*',[52] Phyllis Rackin's 'Androgyny, Mimesis, and the Marriage of the Boy Heroine on the English Renaissance Stage'[53] and Lorraine Helms's 'Playing the Woman's Part: Feminist Criticism and Shakespearean Performance'.[54]

A central issue of debate about the boy actor has been over whether the convention empowers women, by allowing female char-acters to adopt freedoms denied them in a patriarchal culture, or whether in the end the disguises serve only to reaffirm the sexual hierarchy. On the more positive side, critics such as Dusinberre, Berggren, and Rackin (as well as Catherine Belsey in 'Disrupting Gender Difference: Meaning and Gender in the Comedies'[55]) see at least the possibility for an escape from the constraints of femininity, an opening up of rigid gender distinctions, a playfulness with ideas of androgyny. On the negative side, critics such as Free and Howard reject the view of Shakespeare's heroines as proto-feminists and argue that cross-dressing on the stage was not in fact a strong site of resistance to traditional assumptions about gender. In this context, more than one critic has contrasted Shakespeare's use of the boy-disguised-as-a-girl-disguised-as-a-boy in *As You Like It* and *Twelfth Night*, usually arguing that Rosalind is empowered by her disguise while Viola is trapped by hers: see Nancy K. Hales' 'Sexual Disguise in *As You Like It* and *Twelfth Night*'[56] and Valerie Traub's chapter on 'The Homo-erotics of Shakespearean Comedy' in *Desire and Anxiety*.'[57] Peter Erickson on the other hand has interpreted both the ending and the epilogue in

---

[42] (London, 1975).
[43] (Brighton, 1983).
[44] *English Literary Renaissance*, 14 (1984), 367–91.
[45] *Criticism*, 28 (1986), 121–43.
[46] *Renaissance Drama*, 17 (1986), 53–81.
[47] *South Atlantic Quarterly*, 88 (1989), 7–29.
[48] *Shakespeare Quarterly*, 39 (1988), 418–40.
[49] In *The Woman's Part: Feminist Criticism of Shakespeare* edited by Carolyn Ruth Swift Lenz, Gayle Greene and Carol Thomas Neely (Urbana, 1980), pp. 17–34.
[50] *New Theatre Quarterly*, 3 (1987), 120–30.
[51] *Shakespeare Bulletin*, 4 (1986), 23–5.
[52] *Comparative Drama*, 20 (1986), 349–62.
[53] *PMLA*, 102 (1987), 29–41.
[54] In *Performing Feminisms* edited by Sue-Ellen Case (Baltimore, 1990), pp. 196–206.
[55] In *Alternative Shakespeares* edited by John Drakakis (London, 1985), pp. 166–90.
[56] *Shakespeare Survey 32* (1979), 63–72.
[57] As cited in n. 9 above, pp. 122–44.

As You Like It as means of containing and even eliminating female power.[58]

Surveying this necessarily selective run of references, it seems surprising that two participants in the debate have seen fit to scold feminist critics for neglecting the issue: they are James L. Hill, in '"What, are they children?": Shakespeare's Tragic Women and the Boy Actors'[59] and P. H. Parry in 'The Boyhood of Shakespeare's Heroines'.[60] Hill argues that the relatively straightforward roles given to the women in the tragedies could reflect Shakespeare's awareness of the limitations of the boy actors as much as his actual views of real women, while Parry stresses that the original audience must always have been fully aware of the male actors under the female costumes. In the light of this last remark it is interesting that Juliet Dusinberre queries in 'As *Who* Liked It?' below whether women in the plays' original audiences responded any more positively to the boy actors than women did to the recent all-male production of *As You Like It* by the Cheek by Jowl company.[61] (Some women I spoke to after this paper said that *they* had liked the production well enough, but others had felt excluded, particularly by the ending.)

LANGUAGE

If sexuality is socially constructed, it is also, and necessarily on the English Renaissance stage, verbally constructed. Language itself, as feminist linguistics has shown, is far from being gender-neutral. Male/female stereotypes are built into everyday language use as well as into more elaborated literary contexts. In *Literary Fat Ladies: Rhetoric, Gender, Property*[62] Patricia Parker explores the sexual politics of Shakespeare's plays through an analysis of their rhetorical structures, arguing that the 'women are words, men deeds' cliché gave rise to an anxiety about effeminization associated with linguistic excess or 'fatness': Hamlet associates impotence with talking like a drab. Specific tropes such as *hysteron proteron*, *dilation* and *delation*, are seen as

moulding the gender hierarchy in *King Lear* and the destruction of Desdemona in *Othello* respectively. Women's supposed lack of verbal self-control is associated with other kinds of 'fluency' or 'leakiness' by Gail Kern Paster in 'Leaky Vessels: The Incontinent Women of City Comedy',[63] while in his paper in this volume, Russ McDonald contrasts what he sees as the generally 'masculine' language of Shakespeare's tragedies with the more 'feminine' language of the late romances, associating the gender stereotypes with the genres themselves.[64]

Men arguably control language, in the plays as in real life. In '"The Blazon of Sweet Beauty's Best": Shakespeare's *Lucrece*', Nancy Vickers shows how female characters such as Lucrece, Desdemona and Innogen can become victims of the *blazon*, the elaborated verbal description of a woman's beauty, a trope which originates in the male imagination and functions in situations of male rivalry.[65] (An excellent reading of *The Rape of Lucrece* in a shortened version prepared by Russell Jackson during the Stratford conference, performed by the Royal Shakespeare Company actors Samantha Bond and Paul Jesson, emphasized for me how firmly patriarchal the story is, beginning with men arguing over the virtues of their wives and ending with men arguing over who has the right to revenge the dead heroine.) To somewhat similar effect, though in relation to a very different text, Carol Cook claims in 'The Sign and Semblance of Her Honor: Reading

---

58 As cited in n. 25 above, pp. 24–5, 34.
59 *Studies in English Literature*, 26 (1986), 235–58.
60 *Shakespeare Survey 42* (1989), 99–109.
61 See *Shakespeare Survey 45* (1993), 128–130.
62 (London, 1987).
63 *Renaissance Drama*, 18 (1987), 43–65.
64 See below, pp. 91–106.
65 In *Shakespeare and the Question of Theory*, edited by Patricia Parker and Geoffrey Hartman (London, 1985), pp. 95–115.

Gender Difference in *Much Ado About Nothing*' that 'what is at stake is a masculine prerogative in language, which the play itself sustains'.[66] The contest in 'phallic wit' between Beatrice and Benedick contributes in the end to the survival of the masculine ethos. Women can play with words but men own them.

Some critics have been more optimistic about the possibility of a more positive feminine use of language. Deborah T. Curren-Aquino argues in 'Toward a Star that Danced: Woman as Survivor in Shakespeare's Early Comedies' that the women in these plays have more adaptable verbal skills than the men.[67] Taking a comparable line on Isabella and Helena in 'Speaking Sensibly: Feminine Rhetoric in *Measure for Measure* and *All's Well That Ends Well*', Christy Desmet nevertheless concedes that the women are finally consigned to silence in a male world.[68] Paradoxically, as Philip C. Kolin notes in the Introduction to his annotated bibliography of *Shakespeare and Feminist Criticism*, many studies of women's distinctive language in the plays have in fact focused on their silence.[69]

Sometimes, however, Shakespeare's women speak when male critics and directors would prefer them to be silent, and this is especially evident when they talk about sexuality. I have already mentioned Juliet Dusinberre's discussion of the suppression of 'rudeness' in Rosalind's language: for years that character's explanation of her moodiness in 1.3 – 'some of it is for my child's father' – was prudishly emended to 'some of it is for my father's child'. George

Bernard Shaw revealed himself to be a true Victorian when he remarked of Beatrice that 'In her character of professed wit she has only one subject, and that is the subject which a really witty woman never jests about, because it is too serious a matter to a woman to be made light of without indelicacy'.[70] In *Wooing, Wedding and Power* Irene Dash points out that the part of the sexually outspoken Princess in *Love's Labour's Lost* has often been severely abbreviated, both on stage and in expurgated editions, in a series of attempts to save her from 'vulgarity' and to make her speech more 'ladylike' by post-Renaissance standards.[71] In his paper in this volume William C. Carroll discusses the issue of female sexuality and linguistic obscenity – an area which still poses problems for editors.[72]

We are not always entirely easy talking about sexuality even today, and we don't always know if we are getting the tone right, but at any event, as I hope I have shown, the topic 'Shakespeare and Sexuality' has generated a great deal of language, both spoken and written, witty and serious, and this volume is unlikely to be the last word on it.

---

66 *PMLA*, 101 (1986), 186–202.
67 *Selected Papers from the West Virginia Shakespeare and Renaissance Association*, 11 (1986), 50–61.
68 *Renaissance Papers 1986* (1987), 43–51.
69 As cited in n. 2 above, p. 42.
70 In *Shaw on Shakespeare*, edited by Edwin Wilson (Harmondsworth, 1969), p. 156.
71 As cited in n. 18 above, pp. 14–20.
72 See Carroll below, pp. 107–19.

AS *WHO* LIKED IT?

JULIET DUSINBERRE

Bernard Shaw wrote on 4 October 1897 that the Shakespearian producer Augustin Daly 'was in full force at the Islington Theatre on Monday evening last with his version of "As You Like It" just as I don't like it'.[1] Surprisingly, the reaction of many people in the late twentieth century to this most actable of plays is often one of disappointment. The actress Juliet Stevenson, who played Rosalind in 1985, complained of productions which offered '"a rural romp in an Arden full of polystyrene logs"' and protests: 'I'd always suspected that there's a much more dangerous play in *As You Like It*.'[2] The 1990 Cheek by Jowl all-male production was greeted ecstatically by both male actors and male critics: Adrian Lester's Rosalind was voted 'sexy' and exciting. Men liked it. But what about women? If a woman's voice was raised in the critical debate, I missed it. In the past, of course, there would have been no such voice, except from the reminiscences of a few celebrated actresses. How different our theatrical records might have been had Elizabeth Pepys scribbled in the margin next to her husband's account of *A Midsummer Night's Dream* as the most ridiculous and insipid play he ever saw in his life: 'Sam didn't like it but I thought it was great, very sexy.'

What *did* the numerous women in Shakespeare's audience like? The Elizabethans considered theatre-going to be unavoidably erotic,[3] and in anti-theatrical literature it was feared the boy actor would arouse homoerotic fantasies.[4] But what, in that case, would the fantasy life of the women in the audience look like?

In *As You Like It* Rosalind finds herself in a script supplied by men which she rewrites as the play progresses.[5] She becomes, more than any other heroine, the author of her own drama. The idea of a woman's writing a part for herself which she liked better than those written by men is present in one of the works Shakespeare certainly used for *As You Like It*.

When Shakespeare sought a name for his

---

[1] *Dramatic Opinions and Essays*, reprinted in Gāmini Salgādo, *Eyewitnesses of Shakespeare* (Sussex, 1975), p. 167.

[2] Quoted in Carol Rutter, *Clamorous Voices: Shakespeare's Women Today* (London, 1988), p. 97.

[3] Stephen Orgel, 'Nobody's Perfect: Or Why Did the English Stage Take Boys for Women?', *The South Atlantic Quarterly*, 88 (Winter, 1989), 7–29; p. 17.

[4] Jonathan Dollimore, *Sexual Dissidence* (Oxford, 1991), p. 293; Lisa Jardine, *Still Harping on Daughters: Women and Drama in the Age of Shakespeare* (Sussex, 1983), p. 9; see Kathleen McLuskie, 'The Act, the Role and the Actor: Boy Actresses on the Elizabethan Stage', *New Theatre Quarterly*, 3:10 (1987), 120–30.

[5] Jean Howard, 'Crossdressing, The Theatre, and Gender Struggle in Early Modern England', *Shakespeare Quarterly*, 39 (1988), 419–40; p. 435, sees Rosalind in various ways as acting out 'the parts scripted for women by her culture', where I want to argue that she rewrites those scripts. Nelly Forman, 'The Politics of Language: Beyond the Gender Principle', in Gayle Greene and Coppélia Kahn, eds., *Making a Difference: Feminist Literary Criticism* (London, 1985), p. 73, notes that 'while sex is an anatomical fact, sexuality is culturally devised; it is the manner in which society fictionalizes its relationship to sex and gender roles'.

hero he rejected Lodge's Rosader in favour of the much more dashing 'Orlando' of Ariosto's romance, the *Orlando Furioso*, translated into English in 1591 by the Queen's godson, Sir John Harington. At the beginning of Canto 37 Ariosto has a conventional address to worthy ladies, regretting that they are underrated by jealous male writers and have no chance to write their own praises and thus redress the balance:

> Though writers in time past were not your frends,
> The present time shall make you large amends.

Harington added three lines of his own:

> Yet in this age, so learn'd are some of you,
> So well acquainted with the noble muses,
> You could your selves, remedie such abuses.[6]

Women could rewrite the record in truer vein, as they liked it. This was probably intended as a compliment to the Queen, to whom the translation is dedicated. But it contrasts with the dedication of Lodge's *Rosalynde* 'To the Gentlemen Readers'.[7] Harington had begun his translation by offering Elizabeth's ladies the bawdy Canto 28, a tale of women's desires satisfied despite men's attempts to control them. The Queen sent him away with a flea in his ear to translate the rest of the poem, which he did, embellishing its eroticism.[8]

I want to argue that the fictions of sexuality conjured up in *As You Like It* draw some of their vitality from the complex relationship which existed for more than a quarter of a century between Harington and the Queen, an interaction captured in the play in the relation between Rosalind and two Shakespearian inventions, Touchstone and Jaques. The orientation of *As You Like It* towards women as inventors of the fictions in which they must play a part, and as recipients of those fictions, suggests that Harington, as courtier, translator, wit, ladies' man, is a central part of the play's frame of reference. His presence in the play gives Shakespeare's pastoral an edge within the politics and fictions of 1599[9] which casts light

on its original courting of danger, and on its special address to women in the audience. Harington's second literary work was also aimed at a female readership: the notorious treatise printed in 1596 on his invention of the water-closet, entitled *The Metamorphosis of Ajax*.

The work which gave Harington the authority to offer this frank discussion of how to make great Elizabethan houses smell sweeter was Rabelais' *Gargantua and Pantagruel*, of which Harington was an ardent admirer, quoting, imitating, and annotating the work in his own tract. Early editors of Shakespeare saw Rabelaisian echoes in *As You Like It*[10] but were at a loss to explain or develop these perceptions, perhaps partly because *The Metamorphosis of Ajax*, a source of regal discontent when it first

---

6 Ariosto, *Orlando Furioso*, in English Heroical Verse by John Harington Esquire (imprinted at London by Richard Field, 1591), Canto 37: 7, 8.

7 Geoffrey Bullough, *Narrative and Dramatic Sources of Shakespeare*, vol. 2 (London, Henley, and New York, 1964), p. 159.

8 Sir John Harington, *An Apologie* [for *The Metamorphosis of Ajax*, printed simultaneously] in *Sir John Harington's A New Discourse of a Stale Subject, called The Metamorphosis of Ajax*, ed. by Elizabeth Story Donno (London, 1962), p. 256: 'The whole work being enjoyned me as a penance by that saint, nay rather goddesse, whose service I am devoted unto. And as for the verses before alledged, they were so flat against my conscience, that I inserted somewhat, more then once to qualifie the rigour of those hard speeches.' Townsend Rich, in *Harington & Ariosto* (New Haven, 1940), pp. 56–7, prints Harington's plate to the offending Canto 28, to which representations of three copulating couples have been added to Ariosto's original, suggesting that Harington was not afraid that its eroticism would really offend the Queen (pp. 56–7). Rich considers Harington's addition to the text, above, was intended as a compliment on the Queen's learning (p. 80).

9 Sukanta Chaudhuri, *Renaissance Pastoral and its English Developments* (Oxford, 1989), pp. 25, 57, for the political and social allusiveness of Renaissance pastoral; *see also* Edward I. Berry, 'Rosalynde and Rosalind', *Shakespeare Quarterly*, 31 (1980), 42–52; p. 52.

10 The Variorum *As You Like It*, ed. Horace Howard Furness, vol. 8 (Philadelphia, 1890), pp. 39, 161. Warburton noted verbal echoes between Touchstone's dialogue with Corin and Rabelais' *Tiers Livre*.

appeared, seemed to Victorian scholars too disgusting to investigate. Elizabeth herself felt it proper to express discontent; Robert Markham wrote to Harington in 1598:

Your book is almoste forgiven, and I may say forgotten; but not for its lacke of wit or satyr . . . The Queen is minded to take you to her favour, but she sweareth that she believes you will make epigrams and write *misacmos* again on her and all the Courte; she hath been heard to say, 'that merry poet her godson, must not come to Greenwich, till he hath grown sober and leaveth the Ladies sportes and frolicks'.

For this work, as for the *Orlando*, women were Harington's best audience.[11]

A critic has recently argued that the subversive and iconoclastic character of Rabelais' text speaks to women because women's writing is always subversive.[12] Harington uses Rabelais as a text to subvert high culture, copying Rabelais' mockery of authorities, his obscenity, his determination to reinstate the body at the centre of discourse. This determination underlies *As You Like It*, whether in Touchstone, retorting to Rosalind's: 'O Jupiter, how weary are my spirits!' with the tart: 'I care not for my spirits, if my legs were not weary' (2.4.1–3), or Rosalind herself: 'Men have died from time to time, and worms have eaten them, but not for love' (4.1.100).[13] The world of high male literary culture constantly receives a shot in the arm from a competing fiction. Seeing evidence of Orlando's passion engraved on every bark and hearing that Celia has actually met her love in the forest, Rosalind cries: 'Alas the day, what shall I do with my doublet and hose! What did he when thou sawest him? What said he? How looked he? Wherein went he? What makes he here? Did he ask for me? Where remains he? How parted he with thee? And when shalt thou see him again? Answer me in one word.' Celia retorts: 'You must borrow me Gargantua's mouth first, 'tis a word too great for any mouth of this age's size' (3.2.214–21). The reference does not seem to me to come from folk tales of the giant Gargantua, but from a network of

associations with Rabelais' iconoclastic work, which was well known by Ben Jonson and by a number of writers in the 1590s.[14] Rabelais' book of *Gargantua* casts light on *As You Like It*'s special renegotiation of its own inherited narratives, and particularly on the fictions with which it surrounds the whole area of women's desire.

At the end of *Gargantua* the hero builds his own special abbey, a place which is to be the antithesis of the monasteries he has known, with their vows of poverty, chastity and obedience, and their old-fashioned education which has left him more ignorant than it found him. The Abbey of Thelema which completes the book of *Gargantua* is a Utopian fantasy of freedom: *thelema* is the Greek word used in the New Testament for 'will' and for the freedom attendant on recognizing the new will of God, as set forth in Paul's Epistle to the Galatians:

Now that faith is come, we are nomore under the scolemaster. For ye all are the children of God by the faith in Christ Jesu . . . Here is nether Jewe ner Gent[il]e: here is nether bonde ner fre: here is nether man ner woman, for ye are all one in Christ Jesu.[15]

---

11 Sir John Harington, *Nugae Antiquae*, vol. 2 (London, 1779), pp. 287–8.

12 Carol Bellard-Thomson, 'Rabelais and Obscenity: A Woman's View', in Helen Wilcox *et al.*, eds., *The Body and the Text* (New York: Harvester Wheatsheaf, 1990), p. 174.

13 In Rutter, *Clamorous Voices*, pp. 110–11, Juliet Stevenson describes how she wanted to deliver Rosalind's speech '"men have died from time to time, and worms have eaten them, but not for love"'. She explains that the director, Adrian Noble, wanted to play it mournfully, but that her Rosalind was being much more iconoclastic: '"These romantic myths persist, but they are lies."' Stevenson concludes: 'It was one of those examples when you find in a rehearsal room that the male and female experience of loving are in some ways different.'

14 Huntington Brown, *Rabelais in English Literature* (Cambridge, Mass., 1933), pp. 31–70 and Appendix A; *see* Agnes Latham, ed., *As You Like It*, Arden edition (London and New York, 1975), p. 71.

15 *The Byble: that is/the holy Scripture of the Olde and New Testament*, trans. Myles Coverdale ([Cologne or Marburg?], 1535); M. A. Screech, *Rabelais* (London, 1979), p. 188.

Thelema, an abbey for men and women, is built on a doctrine of perfect liberty. Inscribed over its door is the motto: FAY CE QUE VOUDRAS: Do what thou wilt.[16] As you like it. Arden, for all its pastoral echoes, is conceptually in harmony with the ideals of the Abbey of Thelema, in which those who enter are wealthy, free and chaste – not as celibates, but as people who will in due course marry and go back to a world they will transform through their new vision of concord between man and woman.[17] In the creation of the Abbey Rabelais enshrines his own loathing of the excesses of monasticism and of its false ideals of virtue. Its transforming powers allow its inmates to develop along the lines of their own liberal and virtuous natures. To this extent the Abbey of Thelema offers an illuminating gloss on the transformative power of Arden and its ability to suggest a new vision of life when the exiled court returns from the Forest.

If Rabelais' presence in *As You Like It* depended solely on a general congruence between the vision of Arden and of the Abbey of Thelema, the connection might seem, despite the way in which 'FAY CE QUE VOUDRAS' resonates on the curious throwaway title of Shakespeare's play, to say no more than that Shakespeare's pastoral world draws on various Utopian fantasies. But the connections in the play with Rabelais' narratives are more particular, and surround especially the figures of Touchstone, Jaques, and even to some extent Orlando.[18] I want to suggest that Rabelais' subversive work informs *As You Like It* through the connecting medium of the Queen's godson, Sir John Harington.

At various points in critical history Harington has been a favoured candidate for the original of Jaques.[19] I don't want to revive that empirical investigation. In the *Tiers Livre* the Fool Triboulet is eulogized by Panurge with an extravagance which recalls Jaques' fascination with Touchstone. Certainly connections exist on a level of covert allusion to the water-closet work, *The Metamorphosis of Ajax*. Harington

plays on his name, Jack; Jaques is greeted by Touchstone as 'good Monsieur What-ye-call't' (3.3.66). When Harington was knighted by Essex after the Irish expedition (to the Queen's rage) a contemporary source spoke of Sir Ajax Harington.[20] The curious charged relation between Jaques and Rosalind in *As You Like It* makes better sense if seen in the context of a prolonged sparring match between Harington and the Queen. 'Rosalind is your love's name?'

---

[16] *Gargantua*, in *Les Oeuvres den François Rabelais*, vol. 1 (Lyon, 1573), p. 87: 'En leur reigle n'estoit que ceste clause, FAY CE QUE VOUDRAS. Parce que gens libres, bien nez, bien instruits, conversans en compagnies honnestes, ont par nature un instinct & orguillon, qui toujours les pousse à faits vertueux, & retire de vice, lequel ils mommoient honneur.'

[17] M. A. Screech, *The Rabelaisian Marriage* (London, 1958), pp. 27–9.

[18] Walter Kaiser, *Praisers of Folly* (London, 1964), p. 14, notes that Ariosto's Orlando belongs in the special category of 'the fool in love, which is an entire tradition in itself. "En enamorado simple", as Don Quixote (a kind of one himself) calls him.' Vestiges of this character remain with Shakespeare's Orlando, as Jaques recognizes: 'By my troth, I was seeking for a fool when I found you', but Orlando turns the insult: 'He is drowned in the brook. Look but in, and you shall see him' (3.2.279–82). Touchstone himself is, by the end of the play, a Fool in love. Harington possessed a text entitled *Orlando Foolioso* which might refer to the character of the Fool in love. W. W. Greg, *Dramatic Documents for the Elizabethan Playhouses*, vol. 1 (Oxford, 1931), p. 176, reads Harington's title as a reference to the 'bad' Quarto reprint (1599) of Greene's *Orlando Furioso*.

[19] Bullough, *Sources*, vol. 2, p. 154 n. 1; Latham, *As You Like It*, p. xlviii. Detailed arguments in favour of Harington occurred in an interesting series of letters in the *TLS* for 1929, from B. H. Newdigate (3 and 10 January 1929) and R. H. Gunther (17 January). Andrew Gurr, *Playgoing in Shakespeare's London* (Cambridge, 1987), pp. 97–8, quotes a letter from Harington to Robert Cecil in 1605: 'That the world is a stage and we that live in it are all stage players ... I playd my chyldes part happily, the scholler and students part to neglygently, the sowldyer and cowrtyer faythfully, the husband lovingly, the countryman not basely nor corruptly ... Now I desyre to act a Chawncellors part hollyly.'

[20] Ian Grimble, *The Harington Family* (London, 1957), p. 130, notes that Harington is named as Sir Ajax Harington in the Calendar of State Papers.

enquires Jaques languidly of Orlando; hearing an assent, he observes: 'I do not like her name.' Orlando retorts: 'There was no thought of pleasing you when she was christened' (3.2.258–62). There *was* presumably thought of pleasing Elizabeth when she stood godmother to the infant Jack Harington.

However, Touchstone, more than Jaques, is the medium of the play's Rabelaisian vision. Elizabeth allowed Harington a Fool's licence in her court, but each of his literary works exceeded that prerogative and his favour at court alternated with prolonged spells in the country, where he cultivated his own pastoral myth.[21] Harington actually calls himself a 'touchstone' in an epigram he wrote in 1589 to his wife, on the birth of their first child, when he gave her a diamond ring:

The touch will try this Ring of purest gold
My touch tryes thee, as pure though softer mold.
That metall pretious is, the stone is true,
As true, and then how much more pretious you?[22]

Touchstone's loyalty to his mistress contrasts in *As You Like It* with the patterns of betrayal and corruption which characterize Duke Frederick's court: 'He'll go along o'er the wide world with me', remarks Celia (1.3.131). Sir John Harington wrote in his dedication of the *Orlando* to Elizabeth that 'your gracious favours have bene extended in my poore familie even to the third generation'. Sir John's mother, Isabella Markham, had been Elizabeth's maid of honour at Hatfield. Both Harington parents were in the Tower with Elizabeth in 1554; she became godmother to their first son. In 1575 the Queen sent the fourteen-year-old 'Boy Jacke' the text of her milkmaid speech on her right to celibacy: 'I do thys, because thy father was readye to sarve and love us in trouble and thrall.'[23] Harington senior had in 1550 translated Cicero's *De Amicitia* under the title *The Booke of Freendship*, a meditation on how to know true friends which is reminiscent of Duke Senior's sense of true friendship in the exiled court in Arden. The Harington family metal

21 Harington wrote in February 1599 of the extreme danger he was in on his return from Essex's disastrous Irish expedition: 'After I had been there but an hour, I was threatened with the Fleet; I answered poetically, that coming so late from the land-service, I hoped that I should not be prest to serve in her Majesty's fleet in Fleet-Street. After three days every man wondered to see me at liberty' (*Nugae Antiquae*, vol. 2, p. 25). In 1601 he was still in trouble, having been knighted by Essex, and the tart message came from the monarch: 'Go tell that witty fellow, my godson, to get home; it is no season now to "foole it here". I liked this as little as she dothe my knighthood, so tooke to my bootes and returned to the plow in bad weather' (*Nugae Antiquae*, vol. 2, p. 65). In old age Elizabeth seemed to weary of his jesting, though perhaps not of his devotion to her: 'Her Majestie enquirede of some matters whiche I had written, and as she was pleasede to note my fancifulle braine, I was not unheedfull to feede her humoure, and reade some verses, whereat she smilede once, and was pleasede to saie, when thou doste feele creepinge tyme at thye gate, these fooleries will please thee lesse; I am paste my relishe for suche matters' (Harington to his wife, 27 December 1602, *Nugae Antiquae*, vol. 2, p. 79).

22 Sir John Harington, *Epigrams* (1600), bound in the *Orlando Furioso*, in a fine scribal manuscript which the author sent to his mother-in-law, with a letter signed in autograph. The one quoted is the first in the collection. See R. H. Miller, 'Sir John Harington's Manuscripts in Italic', *Studies in Bibliography*, 40 (1987), 101–6. Some of Harington's Epigrams were published in 1615 (after his death in 1612) and a full collection in 1618, reprinted in John Harington, *Epigrams 1618* (Menston, 1970). The one quoted, *Of a pointed Diamond given by the Author to his wife, at the birth of his eldest sonne*, is in B1ᵛ, but various minor textual variations exist, which I prefer not to incorporate as the 1600 version has holograph corrections and is presumably therefore the way Harington wanted it.

23 The text of the speech, together with the Queen's note to Sir John Harington, is reprinted in *Nugae Antiquae*, vol. 2, p. 70. Harington senior wrote to the Bishop of Winchester from the Tower in 1554 that both he and his wife Isabella [neé Markham] suffered with Elizabeth in her imprisonment: 'My wyfe ys her servante and doth but rejoyce in thys owre miserie, when we looke with whome we are holden in bondage' (*NA*, vol. 3, p. 178). Harington senior's translation of Cicero: *The Booke of Freendship of Marcus Tullie Cicero* is reprinted in Ruth Hughey, *John Harington of Stepney: Tudor Gentleman* (Columbus, Ohio, 1971). To compound the Harington family connection with Touchstone is the curious coincidence that Harington senior's first wife, Esther, illegitimate daughter of Henry VIII (described in documents as 'base-born'), is in some of the records named not Esther, but Audrey (Hughey, p. 17).

had indeed been tried on the touchstone of adversity and had been found true. Around the turn of the century Harington may have translated Petrarch's *De Vita Solitaria* as *The Prayse of Private Life*, converting Petrarch's text into a covert dialogue with himself, on whether he is happier at the court or in the country, a dialogue which Touchstone conducts with the shepherd Corin.[24]

Touchstone's utterances in *As You Like It* connect at various levels the play's fictions and Rabelais' Abbey of Thelema. One of the characteristics of Thelema is the different status accorded to time from that of a traditional monastery in which the hours are marked by bells: 'It was decreed that in this new structure there should be neither Clock nor Dial ... For, (said Gargantua), the greatest losse of time, that I know, is to count the hours' – 'La plus vraye perte dut temps qu'il sceust, estoit de conter les heures.'[25] 'There's no clock in the forest' (3.2.295). Except, it might be said, for Touchstone's dial, which causes Jaques to crow like chaunticleer for exactly an hour. In an epigram which Harington wrote criticizing his mother-in-law for being late for dinner, he stops his little son in the middle of grace, but his mother-in-law retorts:

Say on my boy (saith shee) your father mocks,
Clowns and not Courtiers use to go by clocks,
Courtiers by clocks said I and Clowns by Cocks.[26]

On the title page of the Ariosto translation Harington is pictured with his dog and his pocket dial.

Harington was a passionate playgoer, who possessed in his library a large collection of quarto editions, including most of Ben Jonson's plays and eighteen of Shakespeare's, three in duplicate.[27] He wrote an essay called *A Treatise on Playe* [1595?] in which he argued for the wise influence of comedy on the audience.[28] He circulated about fifty of his epigrams in manuscript in the 1590s. In one Epigram he describes telling a friend about how he was praised for the Ariosto translation:

He disapprov'd the purpose many wayes,
And with this proverbe prov'd it labour lost:
Good Ale doth need no signe, good Wine no
bush,
Good verse of praisers, needs not passe a rush.

Present in these lines are Shakespearian senti-

---

24 *The Prayse of Private Life*, in Sir John Harington, *Letters and Epigrams*, ed. Norman Egbert McClure (Philadelphia, 1930). McClure's ascription of the work to Harington has been challenged in favour of Samuel Daniel (*TLS*, 4 Sept., 1930), but the evidence remains somewhat inconclusive. The author – whether Harington or Daniel – writes of the country dweller: 'He envieth noe man, nor hateth any bodie, but contente with his fortune, holdeth himself secure' (p. 331), continuing two pages later: 'Content he is with his owne, and more doth not desire.' The treatise reminds the reader of the scene between Touchstone and Corin both verbally, in the use of the words 'solitary' and 'private', and in its dialogue structure which is more pronounced than in Petrarch's original (see Jacob Zeitlin, ed., *The Life of Solitude of Francis Petrarch* (Illinois, 1924).

25 *Gargantua*, vol. 1, p. 81ᵛ: The translation is from Thomas Urquhart and Peter Le Motteux, *The Lives, Heroic Deeds & Sayings of GARGANTUA & His Son PANTAGRUEL by* DR FRANCIS RABELAIS, vol. 1 (London, 1921), p. 161. Urquhart's translation of Books I and II was published in 1653, and Book III in 1693. Motteux's Books IV and V were published in 1694.

26 *Epigrams* (1600) printed in the *Orlando Furioso*. The manuscript poem quotes a child's utterance which is written in the child's hand, and may have been the work of the son born in 1589, who would have been ten in 1599, the probable date of *As You Like It*. For Harington's dial, see Newdigate, Letter to *TLS*, 10 January 1929.

27 F. J. Furnivall, 'Sir John Harington's Shakespeare Quartos', *Notes and Queries*, 7th Series 9 (17 May 1890), 382–3. E. K. Chambers, *The Elizabethan Stage*, vol. 3 (Oxford, 1923), p. 183, notes that when Harington listed his collection of quarto plays in 1610 he possessed exactly 'six-sevenths of the complete output of the London press'. In 1606 Harington wrote to Mr Secretary Barlow of theatricals at court: 'I have much marvalled at these strange pageantries, and they do bring to my remembrance what passed of this sort in our Queens days; of which I was sometime an humble presenter and assistant but I neer did see such lack of good order, discretion, and sobriety, as I have now done' (*Nugae Antiquae*, vol. 2, p. 129).

28 *A Treatise on Playe*, in *Nugae Antiquae*, vol. 2, p. 160.

ments, the title of a Shakespearian comedy, and the proverb which Rosalind evokes in her Epilogue: 'If it be true that good wine needs no bush, 'tis true that a good play needs no epilogue.'[29] In another epigram a competition between the author and another poet is resolved by a third writer, who prefers the second poet's sonnets to Harington's epigrams: 'Their sugred taste best likes his likresse senses.'[30] Are these Shakespeare's 'sugred Sonnets' (Francis Meres' celebrated epithet)?[31] Despite the food for speculation these examples offer, I want to suggest only Shakespeare's awareness of the curious amalgam of interests for which Harington stood: his *Apologie of Poetrie* which prefaces his translation of Ariosto, the *Orlando* itself,[32] and his fascination with Rabelais manifested in *The Metamorphosis of Ajax*. In *As You Like It* these concerns function within the play as channels through which criticism of Elizabeth's fictions of sexuality can be mediated.

Harington's interests inform the scene in *As You Like It* in which Touchstone, overheard by Jaques, courts Audrey. The Fool quotes Ovid, whose name peppers the margin of Harington's Ariosto translation; Shakespeare's Fool then launches into a disquisition on poetry and lying.[33] I believe that Shakespeare had Harington's *Apologie of Poetrie* (Preface to the *Orlando Furioso* translation) in mind rather than Sidney's. The celebrated reference apparently to Marlowe, fits Harington's own discontent in *The Metamorphosis of Ajax*, that his own 'writings now lay dead'.[34] 'When a man's verses cannot be understood, nor a man's good wit seconded with the forward child, understanding, it strikes a man more dead than a great reckoning in a little room. Truly, I would the gods had made thee poetical' (3.3.9–13). There seems, notes the editor of the Arden edition, to be some unexplained bawdy reference here.[35] A man defends poetry against lying, writes erotic verses to ladies, laments that they are no longer talked about, and sets his mind to disposing of the great reckonings of feasting courtiers into wholesome little rooms.

[29] *Epigrams 1618*, 'Of his translation of Ariosta', D2. Oddly enough, the *envoi* to Harington's *Apologie of Poetrie* which prefaces the *Orlando* is couched in terms which bring Rosalind's address to her audience to mind: 'But now to conclude, I shall pray you all that you have troubled your selves to reade thus my triple apologie, to accept my labors, and to excuse my errors, if with no other thing, at least with the name of youth (which commonly hath need of excuses) and so presuming this pardon to be granted, we shall part good frends.'

[30] Harington, *Epigrams 1618*, Epigram 37, sig. C2. The epigram is not printed with the 1600 manuscript collection, not necessarily because it had not been written, but because those epigrams are almost all domestic in their frame of reference.

[31] *Francis Meres' Treatise 'Poetrie'*, ed. Don Cameron Allen (Illinois, 1953), p. 76: 'His sugred Sonnets among his priuate friends.' Meres gives Harington as the source of the 'sugar' metaphor: 'As Rubarbe and Sugarcandie are pleasant & profitable: so in poetry ther is sweetnes and goodnes M. John Haring [*sic*] in his Apologie for poetry before his translated Ariosto' (p. 67). Meres commends Harington's translation of Ariosto together with Golding's Ovid (p. 82).

[32] Rich, *Harington and Ariosto*, p. 50, believes that Harington had a manuscript copy of Sidney's *Apology for Poetry* to hand when he wrote his own version.

[33] Ben Jonson, 'Conversations with William Drummond', in C. H. Herford and Percy Simpson, eds., *Ben Jonson* (Oxford, 1925–52) vol. 1, p. 133: 'That when Sir John Harrington desyred him to tell the Truth of his Epigrames, he answered him that he loved not the Truth, for they were Narrations and not Epigrams.' The editors suggest (vol. 1, p. 153 n. 38) that Harington retaliated with an epigram to Momus (Jonson?) 'That his Poetrie shall be no fictions, but meere truths':

But read to carpe, as still hath been thine use,
Fret out thine heart to search, seek sift and pry,
Thy heart shall hardly give my pen the ly.

Harington possessed copies of nine of Jonson's plays, including all those associated with the war of the theatres.

[34] Donno, *Sir John Harington, An Apologie*, p. 211: 'Some supposed, that because my writings now lay dead, and had not bene thought of this good while ... so I wold send my Muse abroad.'

[35] Latham, p. xxxiv. If one is tempted to stir the muddy waters of the purge offered by Shakespeare to Ben Jonson in the second part of *The Return from Parnassus* (IV.ii.1716), one might interject the figure of the author of *The Metamorphosis of Ajax*:

As Sheldon's letter to Harington said, there was no real disjunction between the works: 'If you can but tell a homilie tale of this in prose as cleanlie, as you have told in verse a baudie tale or two in Orlando mannerlie, it maie passe among the sowrest censurers verie currantlie.'[36] Through Harington Rabelais' subversion of inherited texts enters Shakespeare's comedy.

I have spent some time on this connection because *As You Like It* seems to me to rewrite the record of female desire so that women want to read it. The agent of rewriting is Rosalind. This dominant heroine with, in the end, magical skills, creates the parameters within which the danger of Shakespeare's play can be recovered, because she is so closely identified in the play with Elizabeth I,[37] a relationship pointed by the covert presence in the text of the Queen's godson. The Queen's mythology and history inform the texture of the play.

Shakespeare's Rosalind shares her name not only with the heroine of Lodge's romance, but with the great lady of Spenser's *Shepheardes Calender* who has broken Colin Clout's heart, for whom he is still lamenting in the April eclogue in which he celebrates Elisa. 'Rosalinde' as spelt by Spenser with the final 'e' is an anagram of ELISADORN: Elisa adorned, as she is in Colin's song of praise to the 'Queene of Shepheardes'.[38] E. K.'s gloss states that the name Rosalinde hides one of the most illustrious in the land, worthy 'that she should be commended to immortalitie for her rare and singular vertues' and comparable to Petrarch's Laura. In 1590 Raleigh, in his commendatory sonnet to *The Faerie Queene*, envisages Petrarch weeping at the approach of the Faerie Queene through whom Laura herself is consigned to oblivion.[39] The Queene of Shepheardes in Spenser's fourth Eclogue in *The Shepheardes Calender* is connected by Spenser to Virgil's fourth Eclogue which will see the return of the Golden Age.[40] What are the Duke's followers doing in Arden? They 'fleet the time carelessly, as they did in the golden world' (1.1.112–13). Shakespeare has surrounded

Rosalind with the Queen's iconography.[41] Elizabeth's personal mythology is to some extent present in Lodge's *Rosalynde*. When Ganymede in Lodge's romance relinquishes her

---

Few of the university [men] pen plaies well, they smell too much of that writer *Ovid*, and that writer *Metamorphoses*, and talke too much of *Proserpina & Juppiter*. Why heres our fellow Shakespeare puts them all downe, I and *Ben Ionson* too. O that *Ben Ionson* is a pestilent fellow, he brought up *Horace* giving the Poets a pill, but our fellow Shakespeare hath given him a purge that made him beray his credit.

(J. B. Leishman, ed., *There Parnassus Plays* (1598–1601) (London, 1949), p. 337.) A purge was not in this period the same as an emetic (delivered in *Poetaster*). Harington is a constant presence in the *Parnassus* plays (*see* Leishman, pp. 151, 263–5, 340).

36 Donno, *The Metamorphosis of Ajax*, pp. 57–8.
37 Leah Marcus, 'Shakespeare's Comic Heroines, Elizabeth I, and the Political Uses of Androgyny', in Mary Beth Rose, ed., *Women in the Middle Ages and the Renaissance: Literary and Historical Perspectives* (Syracuse, 1985), pp. 143, 149.
38 Roy Strong, *The Cult of Elizabeth* (London, 1977), pp. 46–55, cites many examples of Sir John Davies's acrostics with the name Elizabeth. I am indebted to Louis Adrian Montrose's brilliant analysis of Elizabeth's use of the pastoral motif in her maintenance of power, in '"Eliza, Queen of shepheardes", and the Pastoral of Power', *English Literary Renaissance*, 10 (1980), 153–82, although Montrose, surprisingly, does not discuss Rosalind in *As You Like It* in this context.
39 *The Shepheardes Calender*, in R. Morris, ed., *The Complete Works of Edmund Spenser* (London, 1873), p. 456; *The Faerie Queene*, ed. by Thomas P. Roche, Jr (Harmondsworth, 1978), p. 19.
40 Montrose, '"Eliza, Queen of shepheardes"', p. 160; *see* also L. Staley Johnson, 'Elizabeth, Bride and Queen: A Study of Spenser's April Eclogue and the Metaphors of English Protestantism', *Spenser Studies*, 2 (Pittsburg, 1981), 75–91.
41 Harington was heartbroken at the Queen's death in 1603: 'Here now wyll I reste my troubled mynde, and tende my sheepe like an Arcadian swayne, that hathe lost his faire mistress; for in soothe, I have lost the beste and fairest love that ever shepherde knew, even my gracious Queene; and sith my good mistress is gone, I shall not hastily put forthe for a new master' (*Nugae Antiquae*, vol. 2, p. 226). His sorrow puts one in mind of Lear's Fool; *see also* Henry Chettle's call to Shakespeare to join other poets in a pastoral lament for Elizabeth in *Englandes Mourning Garment* (Printed at London by U.S. for Thomas Millington [1603]).

disguise (at her father's request) the narrator exclaims that 'she seemed *Diana* triumphing in the Forrest: upon her head she wore a chaplet of Roses, which gave her such a grace, that she looked like *Flora* pearkt in the pride of all her flowers'.[42] Lodge's Ganymede here seems to anticipate Perdita as Queen of the sheep-shearing 'poor lowly maid, / Most goddess-like pranked up' (*The Winter's Tale*, 4.4.9–10), a shepherdess who is in reality a royal princess. The choice of the *persona* of Ganymede in both Lodge's romance and in Shakespeare's play suggests a model not of 'homosexual flirtation' but of dynastic symbolism, as in the Medici revision of the myth in the late sixteenth century.[43] The presence of an earlier generation in *As You Like It* in Duke Senior and his court, gives the play its own dynastic framework. Its retrospective glow seems to conjure up the euphoric mood of hope of Elizabeth's own exile from court under Mary, and implicitly to contrast the joyous adversities of the past with the disillusion and uncertainty of the late 1590s.

At the heart of *As You Like It* is a challenge, inherent in Rosalind's own role, to Elizabeth's elaborately constructed fictions of chastity and desire. Harington was himself bound up with Rosalind's interrogation of Elizabeth's own myths. In 1575 Elizabeth had bidden her young godson ponder her speech to Parliament on her celibacy: 'As if I were a milkmaide wyth a pale on my arme, wheareby my pryvate person might be a littel set by; I wolde not forsake my poore and single state, to match with the greatest Monarche.'[44] The fruit of Harington's ponderings was *A Tract on the Succession to the Crown (AD 1602)* in which he implicitly queried Elizabeth's evasion of the issue of her succession: 'To make the world thinke she should have children of hir owne, she entertained till she was fiftye years of age mentions of marriage.' He also criticized the notion that chastity meant celibacy, and, in the court of his time, was a compliment for women not for men: 'But I doubte how to prayse these thinges, and how this wanton age of ours will brooke to

have a man praised for chastitie.'[45] Through the Harington connection in *As You Like It* Shakespeare insinuates Rabelais into the play's web of associations, giving Rosalind the dangerous role of challenging the cultural myths and stories used by Elizabeth for her own maintenance of power. This challenge involves in *As You Like It* an awareness of the vernacular in its associations not only with radical Protestantism, but, historically, with the world of women.

Rabelais stands, within the framework of Evangelical Humanism, for the triumph of the vernacular over the classical languages. The championing of the mother-tongue was part of the Protestant challenge to monasticism, and the vernacular was very early on associated with Elizabeth in her vital role as Protestant princess, thus linking her with the world of the 1530s in which Rabelais' work was censored. Rabelais' *Tiers Livre* (1546) is dedicated to the spirit of Marguerite of Navarre, whose *Miroir de L'Ame Pécheresse* Elizabeth had translated into English and given to her ardently Protestant stepmother, Katherine Parr. Marguerite's work had in 1533 enjoyed the brief distinction of being considered heretical for quoting the scriptures in the vernacular.[46] Mikhail

---

42 Bullough, *Sources*, vol. 2, p. 252; Leah Scragg, *The Metamorphosis of Gallathea* (Washington, 1982), p. 82.

43 Orgel, 'Nobody's Perfect', p. 22; James M. Saslow, *Ganymede in the Renaissance* (New Haven and London, 1986), pp. 143, 165, 172, 174.

44 *Nugae Antiquae*, vol. 3, pp. 178, 314–15. The milkmaid passage appears in two separate places in the *Nugae Antiquae* suggesting that Harington extracted it for particular note from the original.

45 Sir John Harington, *A Tract on the Succession to the Crown (AD 1602)*, ed. Clements R. Markham (London, 1880), pp. 40, 86–7.

46 Elaine Beilin, *Redeeming Eve* (Princeton, 1987), p. 67; Johnson, 'Elizabeth, Bride and Queen', p. 80, notes that one of the Queen's accession pageants pictures two hills: 'One was rocky and contained a withered tree; the other was green and flourishing and contained a fresh, green tree. The first hill was called *Ruinosa Respublica* and the second, *Respublica bene iustituta*. After seeing this tableau, Elizabeth received the Bible in English, being assured that she could avoid the barrenness of the one hill by taking the book.'

Bakhtin has observed that the radical laughter of Renaissance writing is ignited at the juncture of the battle between the official language of Latin and the vulgar vernacular.[47] Harington incorporated into the text of *The Metamorphosis of Ajax* the text of the Black Sauntus which his father set to music under Tallis's instruction for the amusement of Henry VIII, who used to sing it. It contains the refrain, 'Lingua canant vernacula.'[48] Elizabeth I became the lodestone of a movement to aggrandise the vernacular and make it worthy to stand alongside the classical languages. But this is not precisely the way in which either Harington or Rabelais thinks of the vernacular.

For both writers the vernacular is itself subversive. Rabelais uses the vernacular not as a dignified tool, but as an undignified one, as a means of undermining the pretensions of the Church, the Law, education, scholars who can spout Latin but who can't see beyond their own noses. Harington was conscious that Ariosto was himself a vernacular writer in a woman's mode, the romance, and that his tutor at Cambridge would have been horrified to see him wasting all that good instruction in Latin and Greek on a paltry Italian bauble.[49] Harington's joke in *The Metamorphosis of Ajax* about being a courtier well learned in *latrina lingua* offended Elizabeth, but is true to the spirit of the Black Sauntus which her father relished. Rabelais' vernacular brings into the book, as does *The Metamorphosis of Ajax*, subjects which high culture leaves outside its covers.

In *As You Like It* Rosalind's witty vernacular, like Beatrice's, seems to mock the literary stories from which the play itself is derived, just as Rabelais mocks in *Gargantua* the transmission of learned male Humanism through the official language of Latin. Rosalind's language is sometimes authentically Rabelaisian: 'I would thou couldst stammer, that thou mightst pour this concealed man out of thy mouth as wine comes out of a narrow-mouthed bottle – either too much at once, or none at all. I prithee, take the cork out of thy mouth, that I may drink thy

tidings' (3.2.194–9). Bottles, mouths, corks and women have their own chain of associations in Rabelais, quite apart from their connection with intoxicating liquor.[50] Rosalind's odd reference to Pythagoras: 'I was never so berhymed since Pythagoras' time that I was an Irish rat, which I can hardly remember' (3.2.172–4) makes more sense in the Gargantuan context. Rabelais declares in his Prologue that his book will be full of Pythagorean allegory.[51] Shakespeare translates the high-culture male pastoral world into a setting more accessible to women by allowing Rosalind to rewrite the fictions

---

[47] Mikhail Bakhtin, *Rabelais and His World*, trans. Helen Iswolsky (Bloomington, 1984), p. 72.

[48] Harington had already sent the text and the music to Burleigh in 1595: 'This verse is called *The Blacke Sauntus, or Monkes hymne to Saunte Satane*, made when Kynge Henry had spoylede their *synginge*. My father was wont to say, that Kynge Henry was used in pleasante moode to sing this verse; and my father, who had his good countenance, and a goodlie office in his Courte, and also his goodlie Esther to wife, did sometyme receive the honour of hearing his own songe, for he made the tune which my man Combe hath sent herewith; having been much skilled in musicke which was pleasing to the King, and which he learnt in the fellowship of good Maister Tallis, when a young man' (*Nugae Antiquae*, vol. 2, p. 83). The text Harington then incorporated into *The Metamorphosis* (see Sir John Harington, *A New Discourse of a Stale Subject, called The Metamorphosis of Ajax*: Written by Misacmos, to his friend and cosin Philostilpnos (At London: Printed by Richard Field, 1596), Bviii *verso*.

[49] Sir John Harington, *An Apologie of Poetrie*, Preface to the *Orlando Furioso* (1591). In 'The Life of Ariosto' which Harington wrote at the end of the *Orlando Furioso* he said that Ariosto wrote in Italian rather than in Latin because 'he had a desire (as most men have) to enrich their owne language with such writings, as may make it in more account with other nations' (p. 417).

[50] Natalie Zemon Davis, 'Women on Top: Symbolic Sexual Inversion and Political Disorder in Early Modern Europe', in Barbara A. Babcock, *The Reversible World* (Ithaca and London, 1978), names Gargantua's mother as an 'unruly' woman (p. 158), and remarks of Rosalind that 'though she later gives herself to Orlando in marriage, her saucy counsel cannot be erased from the real history of the courtship' (p. 161).

[51] Screech, *The Rabelaisian Marriage*, pp. 123–7, demonstrates Rabelais' elaborate use of Pythagorean numerology in *Gargantua*.

which seem to surround her.[52] In doing so she opens the play world to the women in the audience.

The *Orlando Furioso* predicates female cruelty as a spur to male desire. Shakespeare's Rosalind retells that story when, as Ganymede, she conjures up for Orlando the vision of a Rosalind modelled on Ariosto's Angelica, for whose love the original Orlando went mad. Ganymede implies to Orlando that Rosalind's giddiness will match that of Ariosto's romantic heroine. Shakespeare's Orlando is dizzied by this vision of female caprice: 'I would not have my right Rosalind of this mind, for I protest her frown might kill me.' But Shakespeare's Rosalind cannot take the cue of the cruel lady; she murmurs instead: 'By this hand, it will not kill a fly.' Her tenderness turns to direct invitation: 'But come, now I will be your Rosalind in a more coming-on disposition; and ask me what you will, I will grant it' (4.1.102–6).[53] Rabelais in the Abbey of Thelema mocks the idea that the relation of men and women should be predicated on fictions of cruelty and denial. Rosalind's interchanges with Orlando seem to query the denials of Elizabeth's own personal narrative.

Thelema might have provided a more fruitful model for the Elizabethan court than the elaborate fictions of chastity and desire which surround Britomart in *The Faerie Queene* Book III. But the liberty of Thelema looks dangerously like conformity,[54] and its rationalism in some ways like a classic Aristotelian reassertion of reason over passion. The Abbey of Thelema may spell the liberty which Celia and Rosalind seek to embrace: 'Now go we in content, / To liberty, and not to banishment' (1.3.136–7). Steven Mullaney points out brilliantly that the flight to Arden which offers freedom to Rosalind offers also freedom to the theatre in 'the marginal and ambivalent domain of London's Liberties.'[55] But Rosalind in disguise does not underwrite Thelema's concept of casual amity between men and women. She does not embrace the egalitarian relationships of

Thelema any more than she accepts the romantic structures of Ariosto's romance. Through the *persona* of Ganymede she consistently rewrites *all* the narratives she has inherited.

Shakespeare's heroine ultimately rewrites the Queen herself, a figure uneasily locked in her own fictional marriage to her country, denying desire while exploiting its inventions. Shakespeare suggests in this play that desire in women is not inordinate lust, but nor is it harmonious friendship. In *As You Like It* Shakespeare acknowledges, in a way that the fiction of the Abbey of Thelema does not, the realities of passion as evasive of self-discipline. Passion is dangerous; it thrives not on liberty but on repression. The energy of the play derives from a constant oscillation, centred mainly in Rosalind herself, between repression and expression, from which powerful fantasies of sexual desire are generated, and circulate through the entire theatre, revitalizing both players and audience.

In a theatre where Rosalind was automatically played by a boy I believe that far from

---

52 Allen, *Francis Meres' Treatise 'Poetrie'*, p. 76: 'As *Epius Stolo* said, that the Muses would speak with *Plautus* tongue, if they would speak Latin; so I say that the Muses would speake with *Shakespeares* fine filed phrase, if they would speake English.' This rewriting of the record in order to make it more accessible can also be paralleled in Harington's embellishments to the manuscript he owned of Sidney's *Arcadia*. P. J. Croft, 'Sir John Harington's Manuscript of Sir Philip Sidney's *Arcadia*', in Stephen Parks and P. J. Croft, *Literary Autographs* (Los Angeles, 1983), p. 68, argues that Harington's interventions in the text, as in his own translation of Ariosto, aim 'to "lower the tone", to inject some ordinary humor – and ordinary human tenderness – into a work whose heroic tone tends to exclude the ordinary'.

53 Helena Faucit, Lady Martin, *On Some of Shakespeare's Female Characters* (Edinburgh, 1891), p. 271, observed that she could never say '"I do take thee, Orlando, for my husband" ... without a trembling of the voice, and the involuntary rushing of happy tears to the eyes, which made me to turn my head away from Orlando.'

54 Screech, *Rabelais*, p. 190.

55 Steven Mullaney, *The Place of the Stage* (Chicago and London, 1988), pp. 20–5.

arousing primarily homoerotic fantasies, she would have been much closer to women in the audience than Rosalind necessarily is once she is played by a woman. In Shakespeare's theatre the boy actor shared his social status with the women in the audience who watched him enact the heroine.[56] The real boy actor feigning womanhood might have been more beguiling in the part of Rosalind, so often disappointing to modern audiences – men and women – because the part was so carefully written to reflect the boy's apprenticed state.[57] He is, after all, just a moony youth, given power within the theatre, just as the women who watch him also experience a power and a freedom not allowed to them outside its walls. To the boy actor the part of Rosalind must have offered an experience of control comparable to the playing of the old role of Boy Bishop (prohibited under Henry VIII),[58] which allowed the boy momentarily to preside over his elders and betters. Beneath Rosalind's control of her world in the play is an enactment of revolt in which the boy actor participates.

Ellen Terry wrote: 'To act, you must make the thing written your own. You must steal the words, steal the thought, and convey the stolen treasure with great art.'[59] This is, surprisingly, the language of contemporary feminism: steal language, remarks Hélène Cixous, and then you can fly (*voler*).[60] The boy playing Rosalind steals the language of the adult male scoffing at women: makes it his own by describing himself; and flies by releasing desires which float into the theatre audience and are shared by the women who watch him.

The play ends with Rosalind in the Epilogue in the role of magician. Elizabeth herself was conceived of in her Progresses as a magical presence.[61] But Rosalind is also a playwright, a youthful version of Prospero, abandoning the book in which she has rewritten so many male narratives, begging men and women alike to read the structures of their own desires into the feigning of the poet. Hoping that the play may please, but first of all, that it may please

women.[62] At this point Rosalind offers her most daring rewriting of Lodge's *Rosalynde*, which ends, as it began, addressing Gentlemen Readers and giving to Gerismond, the heroine's father, the stage-management of the marriages.[63] In *As You Like It* that role is Rosalind's. Furthermore Rosalind in the Epilogue spurns confinement to gender, appearing before the audience in that supremely unstable essence which the play has created,[64] in which

56 Gurr, *Playgoing in Shakespeare's London*, pp. 53–65; Orgel, 'Nobody's Perfect', p. 8; Jean E. Howard, 'Scripts and/versus Playhouses: Ideological Production and the Renaissance Public Stage', *Renaissance Drama*, 20 (1989), 31–49.

57 Lesley Anne Soule, 'Subverting Rosalind: Cocky Ros in the Forest of Arden', *New Theatre Quarterly*, 6:26 (1991), 126–36; p. 128.

58 Montrose, '"Eliza, Queen of shepheardes"', p. 163, for the relation of the Boy Bishop to pastoral inversion.

59 Ellen Terry, *Four Lectures on Shakespeare*, ed. Christopher St John (London, 1931), p. 15. Terry wrote: 'Don't believe the anti-feminists if they tell you, as I was once told, that Shakespeare had to endow his women with virile qualities because in his theatre they were always impersonated by men! This may account for the frequency with which they masquerade as boys, but I am convinced it had little influence on Shakespeare's studies of women. They owe far more to the liberal ideas about the sex which were fermenting in Shakespeare's age. The assumption that "the woman's movement" is of very recent date – something peculiarly modern – is not warranted by history. There is evidence of its existence in the fifteenth century' (p. 81).

60 'The Laugh of Medusa', in Elaine Marks and Isabelle de Courtivron, eds., *New French Feminisms* (London, 1981), p. 258: 'It's no accident that *voler* has a double meaning.'

61 Montrose, '"Eliza, Queen of shepheardes"', p. 170.

62 Richard Levin, 'Women in the Renaissance Theatre Audience', *Shakespeare Quarterly*, 40 (1989), 165–74; p. 168; Phyllis Rackin, 'Androgyny, Mimesis, and the Marriage of the Boy Heroine on the English Renaissance Stage', *PMLA*, 102 (1987), 113–33; pp. 124–5.

63 Bullough, *Sources*, vol. 2, p. 256.

64 Laura Levine, 'Men in Women's Clothing: Antitheatricality and Effeminization from 1579 to 1642', *Criticism*, 28 (1986), 121–43; p. 128. Rosalind's epilogue seems to have caused comment even in Shakespeare's theatre, and appears to be parodied in the Induction which Marston added to *The Malcontent* in 1604. Sly

stories are constantly generated and altered, but not finished.[65]

In *As You Like It* Shakespeare allows his heroine to move through inherited narratives of desire commenting on the peculiarities of the male imagination. For Rosalind the language of desire insists, as Harington had insisted in *The Metamorphosis of Ajax*, on reinstating the body at the centre of culture. Rosalind offers women, as Harington had offered women readers of his *Orlando*, the opportunity to rewrite the record. The implied accusation, that the Queen had not rewritten the male narrative, nor created fictions of sexuality which could speak to women, gave the play in the troubled late 1590s its edge of danger. In Elizabeth's politically empowering fictions desire could resolve itself only into sterility.

The deferral implied in Rosalind's adieu does no doubt transfer the promise of the past, as Elizabeth's own reign had ultimately done, into the realm of fantasy. But that fantasy of deferred satisfaction, voiced by the boy who must when the speech is over return to the role of apprentice, speaks particularly to women, for whom the satisfaction of desire involved, in Shakespeare's society at least, so much dwindling into wives, mothers, dependants. *As You Like It*, far from creating closure, ends by releasing into the auditorium an eroticism constantly open to revision by women. *Fay ce que voudras*: a message for women rather than for men, at least in Shakespeare's time, where women knew only too well that *As You Like It* meant as men liked it, everywhere except in the theatre.

pretends to make an extempore prologue (printed in quotation marks): '"Gentlemen, I could wish for the women's sake you had all soft cushions: and gentlewomen, I would wish that for the men's sakes you had all more easy standings"' (John Marston, *The Malcontent*, ed. by Bernard Harris (London, 1967), p. 14: Induction, pp. 128–30; this reference to Shakespeare's play has not, to my knowledge, been noted. On a bawdy level the gentlemen here seem to be ladies and the ladies gentlemen. The reference is particularly interesting as evidence of the play's being performed in the public theatre probably some time in 1603, so that the Epilogue would have been fresh in Marston's mind.

[65] Since writing this essay I have read Alan C. Dessen, 'Shakespeare on Stage: Resources and Images: Shakespeare in 1990', *Shakespeare Quarterly*, 42 (1991), 214–24; p. 215, in which the author asks whether larger casts create unwarranted closures in the play's narratives: 'Whose images are to be most prized? As *who* likes it?'

MALVOLIO AND THE EUNUCHS: TEXTS AND REVELS IN *TWELFTH NIGHT*

JOHN ASTINGTON

Fashionably enough, the central farcical scene of *Twelfth Night* concerns an act of reading. What Malvolio reads and how he reads it have significant connections both with other events in the play, and with the wider world of seventeenth-century English society. The letter he finds invites him to join the festive rituals of love – to disguise himself, to smile, and to become a wooer, on the expectation of ending the revelling with epithalamium and marriage. This model for human conduct – the argument of romantic comedy – is in fact endorsed by a secondary text hidden within the first, as we shall see. But Malvolio, reading the words eagerly in the light of his predisposition, sees no subtleties, let alone the gaping trap. The festival in which he has already begun to take part is not the affirmative and sustaining one he imagines, but a punitive, defaming, mocking ritual aimed at him, his pride, pretensions, and authority. His reading – or misreading – marks his entry to a festive world, and festivals, like texts, are ambiguous. Particularly his treatment at the hands of the plotters forms a suggestive inverse ritual to set against those patterns which are traced by the energies of misplaced and baffled erotic desire, eventually untangled and fulfilled.

In the last scene of the play Feste finally delivers Malvolio's letter, excusing himself with the observation that 'madman's epistles are no gospels'. One could say that Malvolio's mistake has been to fall into the trap of taking a mad epistle for gospel, but here Olivia is not to be diverted by Feste's attempt to superimpose a theatrical style on plain sense: Orsino's recognition that 'This savours not much of distraction' echoes her own. Earlier in the play, Toby has pre-empted another plain reader, Viola, by rewriting Sir Andrew's challenge and by avoiding committing it to paper: 'this letter, being so excellently ignorant, will breed no terror in the youth. He will find it comes from a clodpoll'. In the course of the play we have, then, two epistles which are gospels, in so far as their sense, or lack of it, is revealed in their style, and one which is dressed as a dish of poison, devilish and heretical.

Malvolio, if he is indeed a 'kind of puritan', should have had some experience in the interpretation of difficult or ambiguous writings, but he capitulates so absolutely to the apparent sense of a text that even Maria is amazed at his extreme folly: 'Yon gull Malvolio is turned heathen, a very renegado, for there is no Christian that means to be saved by believing rightly can ever believe such impossible passages of grossness.' Something has been wrong, clearly, with Malvolio's Puritan discipline, if he can fall so easily for 'some obscure epistles of love', taking the shadow for the substance in such an unguarded manner. In doing so, of course, he is unconsciously aping his betters, and it is the deluded Olivia who is readiest to understand and forgive him, pointedly comparing his case with hers twice in the play. Not that she is aware of her own delusion, however. She confidently assumes she is an accomplished reader of texts, and of bodies as texts, when she dismisses the first chapter of Orsino's heart, which Viola proposes as *her* gospel: 'O, I have read it. It is heresy.'

The revenge of foolery and holiday on Malvolio is motivated by his repressive and humourless sense of order, and by his self-conceit, but the terms of his humiliation are very deliberately chosen: not only is he made to transgress class barriers, but he is translated into a lover, about which role there is something deeply and fundamentally inappropriate. Malvolio's initial rule over the celibate, mourning household of Olivia is sterile and deathly. Sad and civil, he is customarily dressed in suits of solemn black, and he marks himself all too clearly as an enemy to the life of comic energy: his first line in the play invokes the pangs of death. Olivia's own brooding on death, however affected it may be, aligns her sympathetically with Malvolio's gloomy order: the entirely imaginary affection that Maria invents has at least a germ of plausibility about it. But Malvolio is valued by Olivia as a servant precisely because he appears to be passionless, 'Unmovèd, cold, and to temptation slow', a defender not only of wit, manners, and honesty, but of honesty in its sexual sense, a symbolic guardian at Olivia's gates. As a classically constructed blocking character, Malvolio *inamorato* is punished by the passion he apparently denies.

By the beginning of the box-tree scene, the treasons have already been planted in his mind, which is running on marriage: 'Having been three months married to her, sitting in my state – ... Calling my officers about me, in my branched velvet gown, having come from a day-bed where I have left Olivia sleeping.' Dreams of power and luxury, therefore, accompany the relatively sober, yet preposterous 'married to her'; indeed the fantasy of high social rank runs slightly ahead of dreams of sexual indulgence. Married in his mind, he encounters the fateful epistle, the very letters of which drip with concupiscence.[1] The style of the text he reads is a clever mixture of obliquity and directness, fustian riddles, grandiloquence, and minor rhetorical flourishes with a rather dated air. The prose begins with a clear warning – 'If this fall into thy hand, revolve' – and immediately passes to an apparently clear statement – 'In my stars I am above thee' – followed by a fugal development on the theme of greatness, which Malvolio is naturally disposed to hear with pleasure. Within the famous tripartite clause, thrice repeated in the course of the play, there lurks, perhaps, another warning for the truly virtuous. That is to say that the construction of this part of the epistle is remarkably close to gospel. In the nineteenth chapter of the Gospel according to St Matthew, Christ has been drawn by the Pharisees into a discussion of divorce and marriage. The complexities of morality and law lead the disciples to think that perhaps 'it is not good to marry'. In the King James Bible, Christ replies as follows:

11 But hee said vnto them, All men cannot receiue this saying saue they to whom it is giuen.

12 For there are some Eunuches, which were so borne from their mothers wombe: and there are some Eunuches, which were made

---

[1] A further interpretation of Malvolio's chosen letters has been suggested by Leah Scragg: '"Her C's, her U's, and her T's: Why That?": A New Reply for Sir Andrew Aguecheek', *RES* 42 (1991), 1–16. Her suggestion that the line may have some reference to cutpurses has an interesting incidental bearing on my argument in this essay: see below.

Eunuches of men: and there be Eunuches, which haue made themselues Eunuches for the kingdome of heauens sake. He that is able to receiue it, let him receiue it.

Christ's words, he twice warns, are not to be understood by everyone, and the terms of his analogy are in many respects puzzling, but the evident centre of his meaning is that true greatness is not of this world, and that sexuality may be a bar to finding it. If Maria has intended this gospel text to serve as an allusive reflection beneath the surface of her epistle, the sense of the phrases begins to shimmer with opposites and distinctions: physical loss and spiritual gain, greatness and littleness (deficiency), fertility and sterility.

Malvolio has been offered an oblique warning about the futility of his marriage, if not a veiled insult, but fails to catch either. He would not, however, have known the gospel in the Authorized Version, and any kind of Puritan would have been most likely to be familiar with the Geneva Bible. The 1560 text translates the crucial verse in Matthew in a slightly different way:

For there are some chaste, which were so borne of (their) mothers bellie: and there be some chaste, which be made chaste by men: and there be some chaste, which haue made them selues chaste for the kingdome of heauen.[2]

The effect of 'chaste' is a good deal blander, and implies choice rather than compulsion or accident, although the second clause becomes puzzling in this respect. But the marginal glosses, a chief feature of the Calvinist bibles, leave the reader in no doubt over the sense in the first instance: 'the worde signifieth (gelded) and they were so made because they shuld, kepe the chambers of noble women: for they were iudged chaste.' Malvolio, keeper of the chamber to Olivia, certainly wishes to be judged chaste, but is far from deeming himself unable to marry, from recognizing his own incapacity. The gloss on those that make themselves chaste, or who achieve chasteness, might

we say, explains the phrase as a positive effect of grace, and of an effort of free will rather than negative self-abnegation or mutilation: Christ's phrase refers to those 'Which haue the gift of cōtinēce, & vse it to serue God with more free libertie.' And perhaps because the connection between chastity and godliness has an unfortunately Papist slant, the final sentence of the verse, Christ's second *caveat*, receives the following gloss: 'This gift is not commune for all men, but is verie rare, and givē to fewe: therefore men may not rashly absteine from marriage.' The Puritan reading of the text, finally, is to endorse the argument of comedy. This is made particularly clear in Calvin's own commentary on these verses. Speaking of the disciples' uncertainty, he writes, perhaps rather surprisingly:

But why do they not think on their side how hard was the bondage of their wives? Simply because they are thinking only of themselves and their own convenience and are not motivated by the mind of the flesh that they forget others and want only themselves to be considered. Their ungodly ingratitude betrays itself that they reject this wonderful gift of God out of fear of one inconvenience or out of boredom. According to them it would be better to flee marriage altogether than to tie oneself to a perpetual bond of fellowship. But if God instituted marriage for the common welfare of the human race, it is not to be rejected because it carries with it some things which are less agreeable.[3]

The world must be peopled, and the will of God followed. Malvolio may therefore have some sense of the buried text, but without necessarily reading it as being directed against marriage; God, or 'Jove', as he may have more innocuously become by the time of the Folio text, seems to be overseeing the whole affair,

---

[2] This translation is superseded by the 1582 (*et seq.*) Geneva New Testament, which gives the word as 'eunuches', and in every other respect is very close to the King James version. The Bishops' Bible (1568) uses 'chaste'.

[3] *A Harmony of the Gospels Matthew, Mark and Luke*, trans. T. H. L. Parker (Edinburgh, 1972), p. 248.

including the interpretative spirit with which the sense of the words is received. Malvolio's reading of the letter, which he imagines to be free of 'imagination', could therefore be said to be a parody of the tendency of Puritan interpretation to read ambiguous texts in the direction of a theological programme, or to invoke the will of God to endorse personal predilections.

Godliness may render a man unfit for marriage, but the Geneva glosses also warn that 'Some by nature are vnable to marie, and some by arte'; 'The worde Eunuche is a generall word, and hath diuers kindes under it, as gelded men and bursten men.' By extension, one might say that the metaphoric application of physiological circumstances, Christ's starting point, hath divers kinds under it.[4] Malvolio's spiritual sterility renders him unfit for comic marriage, whatever his physical potency may be. More importantly to the rituals of comedy, the gulling which is initiated in the box-tree scene is an extended episode of humiliation. Induced to declare himself no eunuch by nature, Malvolio then puts himself at risk of being made one by art. His self-exposure, capture, imprisonment, and binding – the entire course of his 'bafflement' – is not only the well-recognized expulsion of repressive order from festival and holiday, but an act of sexual degradation – a displaced gelding, through which Malvolio is emasculated by the laughter of the sexually united pairs:

> Maria writ
> The letter, at Sir Toby's great importance,
> In recompense whereof he hath married her.
> (*Twelfth Night*, 5.1.359–61)

Yet however absurd the holy duty of marriage may seem in Malvolio's case – and it is not so much that the world has no need of more Malvolios as that he is contemplating marriage with the wrong person and for entirely the wrong reasons – it is extremely important to the play as a whole. 'If anyone imagines', says Calvin, 'that it is to his advantage to be without a wife and so without further consideration

decides to be celibate, he is very much in error. For God, who declared that it was good that the woman should be the help meet for the man, will exact punishment for contempt of his ordinance. Men arrogate too much to themselves when they try to exempt themselves from their heavenly calling.'[5] The solemnity of God's punishment may be out of place in a comedy, as may the name of God itself, but the sense of 'heavenly calling' in sexual union is precisely in key with the magical happiness towards which the romantic comedies move. Resistance against this movement, or surprised acquiescence in it, is generally expressed with reference to purely natural or pagan forces, as when Viola speaks to Olivia about her beauty.

> Lady, you are the cruell'st she alive
> If you will lead these graces to the grave
> And leave the world no copy.   (1.5.230–2)

Or when, at the end of the same scene, Olivia gives in to something beyond her own power to resist:

> Fate, show thy force. Our selves we do not
>   owe.
> What is decreed must be; and be this so.
>   (1.5.300–1)

It is Olivia who most resists her obligation to marry by taking on a vow to what she imagines are higher things. Her withdrawal from the world is cast in the language of religious observance.

---

[4] That the text was read literally as well as metaphorically is demonstrated by its citation in the discussions over the Essex divorce case in 1614. George Abbot, Archbishop of Canterbury, quoted the passage as clear 'warrant' for annulment of marriage. King James, arguing against too narrow a definition of 'inability', denied that Christ's categories of male impotence were prescriptive. See *The Narrative History of King James* (London, 1651), pp. 95, 102. I am grateful to Professor Leslie Thomson for drawing my attention to this material.

[5] *Harmony*, p. 249.

... like a cloistress she will veilèd walk,
And water once a day her chamber round
With eye-offending brine –   (1.1.27–9)

But the form of the observance, as Feste points out, is really without a religious object, an empty fetish like that of abjuring the sight and company of men, 'as if celibacy contained some meritorious service – just as the Papists imagine it is an angelic state. But all Christ intended', Calvin says of making oneself a eunuch for the kingdom of heaven's sake, 'was that the unmarried should set the aim before them of being more ready for the exercises of religion if they are freed from all cares. It is foolish to imagine that celibacy is a virtue, for this is no more pleasing to God in itself than fasting is, nor does it deserve to be reckoned among the duties required of us.'[6] The 'divinity' the disguised Viola brings to Olivia shows her the vanity of withdrawing from the world. False and true divinity continue to pursue each other, with ironic effect, throughout the play. Immediately following the scene in which a false priest catechizes the desperate Malvolio, Olivia marries the dream she has loved since the fifth scene of Act I.

> If you mean well
> Now go with me, and with this holy man,
> Into the chantry by. There before him,
> And underneath that consecrated roof,
> Plight me the full assurance of your faith,
> That my most jealous and too doubtful soul
> May live at peace.   (4.3.22–8)

The wonderful gift of God is celebrated in a religious ceremony which the seemingly arbitrary forces of nature, imagination, and sheer chance have helped bring about. The 'peace' Olivia looks forward to is precisely what has eluded Malvolio at the end of the play – but his symbolic and structural roles are very different from hers.

Viola's loss of a brother does not lead *her* to a cloistered withdrawal from the world, but she does pursue concealment, and specifically proposes a disguise which will remove her from the responsibilities of sexuality: 'Thou shalt present me as an eunuch to him.' She makes herself a eunuch not for the kingdom of heaven's sake but to gain some advantage over the forces of time and occasion, both of which eventually give her the peace they give Olivia. The exotic nature of Viola's proposed role, however, is unlikely to render her unobtrusive: in a Christian climate the eunuch was both freakish and foreign, specifically Turkish, as the Captain recognizes in his acknowledgment of Viola's request. Eunuchs might be fascinating in themselves as human types, but certainly by virtue of being involved in the mythologized fantasy world of Turkish sexuality. No more is made of the oddity of Viola's disguise – she is no Castrucchio, as Orsino's Illyria is not Volpone's Venice – but she retains a troublingly provocative physical presence, constantly drawing attention to her appearance from Orsino, Malvolio, Feste, and chiefly from Olivia. Disguise, and hence denial of sexual identity in her case, is a 'wickedness' as much as it is creative and liberating. It liberates, in fact, only for so long, and time first draws the knot of confusions tighter before untangling it. Olivia's claim on her as a husband, which she is able to corroborate with priestly authority, threatens first Viola's death and then the loss of the man she loves. So, once the appearance of Sebastian has begun to resolve the paradoxes, we have Viola's insistence, echoed by Orsino, that she resume her own clothes: 'Do not embrace me' she tells her brother, and the prohibition is implicitly extended to her future husband. As she is a man – or a eunuch – she is not ready to give herself to anyone.

Viola's superfluous disguise in Act 5 is matched by that of the humiliated Malvolio, still wearing the ludicrous costume he has been gulled into assuming by his reading of the letter – point devise, the very man. The 'notable shame' he has undergone has included his

---

[6] *Harmony*, p. 249.

parading in the clothes and demeanour of an aspiring lover – a sexual role quite out of keeping with his peevish, repressed, sterile self-regard. One of the roles of festival customs, modern social historians agree, was to enforce communal order as much as temporarily to subvert it. David Underdown has described the clash in seventeenth-century English society between the cohesive function of festival and the godly order of those with a new vision of and programme for social organization:

The division in the English body politic which erupted in civil war in 1642 can be traced in part to the earlier emergence of two quite different constellations of social, political, and cultural forces, involving diametrically opposite responses to the problems of the time. On the one side stood those who put their trust in the traditional conception of the harmonious, vertically integrated society – a society in which the old bonds of paternalism, deference, and good neighbourliness were expressed in familiar religious and communal rituals – and wished to strengthen and preserve it. On the other stood those – mostly among the gentry and middling sort of the new parish élites – who wished to emphasize the moral and cultural distinctions which marked them off from their poorer, less disciplined neighbours, and to use their power to reform society according to their own principles of order and godliness.[7]

The church ale – at which cakes and ale were the traditional fare – was one typical site of this conflict. An ancient parish tradition – a kind of communal picnic with drinking, as well as piping, dancing, and sometimes dramatic activity – its function was to bring the parishioners together in a festive money-raising activity to support the parish's charitable works. To the Puritan eye this praiseworthy end was entirely vitiated by the displays of unrighteousness the feast gave rise to. From about the time of *Twelfth Night* onwards there are numerous instances from across the country of festal customs being used against local Malvolios, in the course of which the representatives of authority were both mocked and, in extreme cases, physically assaulted.

Violence is in fact an entirely traditional ingredient of many forms of game and festival, and hence could give further cause to the godly to suppress festive customs. The liminal and group-bonding functions of football games with neighbouring villages, for example, are noted by Underdown: ''Tis no festival unless there be some fightings' is a contemporary saying he quotes (p. 96). Personal or communal rivalries and disputes could therefore be sorted out – more or less symbolically – under the cover of festival licence. In *Twelfth Night* it is Sir Toby who is the lord of *violent* misrule, and he is perhaps not uncharacteristic of enthusiastic seventeenth-century revellers in that during his final appearance in the play he is both drunk and bleeding. The particular contest he has just lost, begun in jest and ended in earnest, is with a young stranger over his apparent sexual invasion into territory Toby may regard as his to defend, if not to bestow. However ironically, he has promised Olivia to Sir Andrew, and his oath to his gull earlier in the play is made on the physical manifestations of his own manliness: 'If thou hast her not i'th' end, call me cut' (2.3.180–1). Once Cesario shows some fighting spirit, male prowess is at stake: 'Come, my young soldier, put up your iron. You are well fleshed ... Nay then, I must have an ounce or two of this malapert blood from you' (4.1.37–43).

Malvolio's heated imaginings about Olivia in the letter scene give rise to a string of violent stage-whispers from the box-tree – 'O for a stone-bow to hit him in the eye!'; 'Fire and brimstone!'; 'Bolts and shackles!' (a premonition of Malvolio's punishment); 'Shall this fellow live?'; '... does not Toby take you a blow o' the lips, then?'; 'Out scab'; 'Marry, hang thee brock'; '... I'll cudgel him, and make him cry "O!"' After this, Malvolio is perhaps lucky to undergo the relatively lenient treatment he gets, although it is certainly a

---

[7] *Revel, Riot and Revolution* (Oxford, 1985), p. 40.

fairly frequent tendency in modern stagings of the play to emphasize the physical punishment in the revellers' teasing of him in 3.4, and since the eighteenth century the pain and privation of the dark house scene have often been stressed, to the degree that Malvolio has seemed on the edge of being mad indeed. His binding – promised by Sir Toby in 3.4 – is not usually seen. He leaves the stage free, and while on Shakespeare's stage he may have been entirely invisible in 4.2, these days we tend to see an anguished face and beseeching, clutching hands as he pleads with Sir Topas and Feste. In any event, in fictional terms he must be free enough to write his letter, and when he re-emerges into the world of light he doesn't usually bear about him signs of his bondage (the far commoner stage tradition is for him to have straw sticking to his hair and clothes). Yet he is still dressed in his lover's garb, as I noted above, usually sadly muddied and ripped in performance, to signal the trials of constancy. The absurd costume, Maria's fantastical invention, includes the restricting bonds of the cross garters, which soon after he has put them on are already making him 'sad':

This does make some obstruction in the blood, this cross-gartering, but what of that?   (3.4.19–21)

The Grocer's Wife from *The Knight of the Burning Pestle* could tell him; there are dangers in putting on silly costumes: 'I'll see no more else indeed, la: and I pray you let the youths understand so much by word of mouth; for I tell you truly, I'm afraid o' my boy. Come, come, George, let's be merry and wise. The child's a fatherless child; and say they should put him into a strait pair of gaskins, 'twere worse than knot-grass; he would never grow after it' (2.92–8).[8] The innocently lubricious sense of 'grow', typical of the Wife's chatter, alerts us to one element of Malvolio's shaming: his binding is a symbolic sign of his impotence, of his having been made a festival eunuch. I think he should keep his cross garters obediently tied until he finally hobbles off to seek revenge.

I want to return to the rituals of sexual humiliation, but first to explore a second violent festive practice which has frequently been noted in commentary on the play, as seeming in some way to stand for the treatment of Malvolio. The previously unannounced Fabian enters the play in 2.5 as a further resentful victim of Malvolio's war on holiday pastimes: he has been 'brought ... out o' favour with my lady about a bear-baiting here'. 'To anger him', Toby replies, 'we'll have the bear again, and we will fool him black and blue'. Once again the promised violence happens only symbolically – Malvolio is not beaten up as is Captain Otter (as bear) by his wife (as dog) in Jonson's *Epicoene* – but we are reminded at this moment of the strong connections between festival and brutal punishment, and the evident need to give vent to disruptive and aggressive tendencies even in the midst of celebrations which affirmed the strength and mutual support of the community. Malvolio's bearishness remains in that he sees his tormentors as a 'pack' – hounds rather than people – at the end of the play.[9] The violent accompaniments of festive activity are everywhere apparent in the social world surveyed by David Underdown: bear and bull baitings are the invariable entertainments at church ales. While one may have been attendant on feasting – the bull was baited before being butchered – the other patently was not. That the actual torturing of animals, whatever symbolic function it may have been recognized to carry, could itself take a symbolic form in festival is proved by an intriguing reference Underdown cites from Somerset in 1603, involving some trouble while someone was 'playing Christmas sports in a bear's skin' (p. 60). Such a winter-time activity – very reminiscent of Lanthorn Leatherhead's reported

---

8 Francis Beaumont, *The Knight of the Burning Pestle*, ed. S. P. Zitner (Manchester, 1984).

9 See, e.g., Ralph Berry, '"Twelfth Night": The Experience of the Audience', *Shakespeare Survey 34* (1981), 111–19.

feats in *Bartholomew Fair* (3.4. 126–28) – may have as much to do with *The Winter's Tale* as with *Twelfth Night*, but the ritualized hunting that is expressed in animal baiting, and the deliberate arousal, in the case of cock-fighting, for example, of competitive sexual aggression in the animals, reveal an ambivalent fascination with purely physical power and instinctive drive as forces which must be celebrated, yet punished.[10] Jonson, once again, more directly incorporates festive baitings and huntings into his comic structure, and his plays are to that extent crueller than Shakespeare's. Volpone's direct address to the audience following his sentence by the court – 'This is called mortifying of a fox' – reminds us of the festive custom of hunting a fox or other small animal indoors, within the hall at a feast, frequently involving killing it by driving it into the fire. One of the fox's sins in *Volpone*, of course, is lust. The totemic sexual rituals associated with hunting and killing the stag, however, are clear enough in Shakespeare's work. The festive song in *As You Like It* is an anthem of male prowess and anxiety – the lusty horn is given to the victor as a sign that he is a potential victim of forces which lie outside his direct control. Falstaff's ritual punishment for lust at the end of *The Merry Wives of Windsor* is suffered in the disguise of a male deer – he is symbolically pinched and burnt, rather than actually butchered and cooked. Falstaff's dis-horning, George Turberville tells us, exactly follows the English practice of dismembering the stag after the kill; following the removal of one sign of the deer's maleness, 'before that you go about to take off his skynne, the fyrst thing that must be taken from him, are his stones which hunters call his doulcettes'. These form part of 'the dayntie morselles which appertayne to the Prince or chief personage on field'.[11] In Beaumont and Fletcher's *Philaster* the cowardly and lustful Pharamond has paid the woodmen for the dowcets and head of a slain deer (4.2) – that he evidently needs them as aphrodisiacs hardly commends his unassisted sexual powers. Fol-

lowing the scenes of actual hunting in the fourth act, Pharamond becomes the human quarry of a popular riot in the fifth, when the citizens, like Laertes' Danish supporters, mutiny to reinstate Philaster. The language with which they threaten him deliberately recalls the hunting terms of Act 4, and his proposed punishment mockingly strips him of manhood.

PHARAMOND
Gods keep me from these hell-hounds.
I CITIZEN
Shall's geld him, Captain?
CAPTAIN
No, you shall spare his dowcets, my dear donsels; as you respect the ladies let them flourish. The curses of a longing woman kills as speedy as a plague, boys.
I CITIZEN
I'll have a leg, that's certain.
2 CITIZEN
I'll have an arm.
. . .
2 CITIZEN
He had no horns, sir, had he?
CAPTAIN
No, sir, he's a pollard; what wouldst thou do with horns?
2 CITIZEN
O, if he had, I would have made rare hafts and whistles of 'em; but his shin bones if they be sound shall serve me. (5.4.53–74)[12]

Symbolic hunting therefore carries within it a potential for sexual shaming and degradation. Pharamond and Falstaff are both punished for lust by public exposure, and Malvolio's treatment clearly has something of a similar purpose, although it certainly lacks the direct physical violence the two former figures suffer. At least this is so in the text; there is a *theatrical* tradition of varying degrees of physical torture of Malvolio by Feste in 4.2. Malvolio's punish-

---

[10] See François Laroque, *Shakespeare's Festive World* (Cambridge, 1991), pp. 47–8.
[11] *The Noble Arte of Venerie* (London, 1575), p. 127.
[12] Francis Beaumont and John Fletcher, *Philaster*, ed. A. Gurr (London, 1969).

ment is to be 'propertied', but largely to be forgotten, removed, and 'baffled' until his incandescent entry into Act 5. He is certainly punished for excess, but punished by deprivation, and his physical powerlessness in the dark house is perhaps to remind him of his unsuitability for the preposterous role he has taken on. A born eunuch, in Christ's terms, he is absurdly unfitted for the position of comic wooer and bridegroom.

The impotent lover, in body, mind, and social conduct, is a stock figure of erotic comedy. The absurdly enamoured father, the old man, the stupid heir, the pretentious braggart, the rake, all are variant threats to the union of the true lovers, and they must be outwitted, exposed, or otherwise removed in the course of the plot. In Jonson's *Bartholomew Fair* the egregious ninny Cokes, the contracted bridegroom of the witty but powerless Grace Wellborn, loses his fiancée to Quarlous in the liberating chaos of a festival atmosphere. He also loses his money, but in having his purse cut – twice – he is symbolically gelded of the manhood he so ineptly represents. He half recognizes what has happened to him in the words he addresses – mistakenly – to Overdo: 'Cannot a man's purse be at quiet for you, i' the master's pocket, but you must entice it forth, and debauch it?' (3.5.213–14), while Wasp scornfully tells his charge 'now you ha' got the trick of losing, you'd lose your breech, an't 'twere loose' (ibid. 221–3).[13] Cokes, though he hardly cares in the regressively childish festive world he has entered, is symbolically shamed and neutered. His fascination with the puppets, babies, and trash is a complete identification – he, like the puppet Dionysius, has no sex. It is Jonson's disciple Richard Brome who writes the frankest version of what appears to be a submerged theme of festival and comedy when in his 1639–40 play *The Court Beggar* a doctor is held down across a table and threatened with castration at the hands of a 'Sowgelder' (4.2). His protests remind the audience of the dangerous uproar of popular holidays:

You dare not use this violence upon me
More rude than rage of Prentices.[14]

The gelding turns out to be a 'counterfeit plot' – partly a deliberate degradation in revenge for the doctor's prior actions, and partly to scare him into confessing that the patient he is attending is, like Antonio in *The Changeling*, a sham madman. The scene could therefore be taken simply as a particularly risqué piece of farce used to enliven a rather creakily episodic plot, yet the larger question remains of why this particular action may have occurred to Brome as being suitable to a comedy filled with spurious and defective wooers.[15]

Nothing quite so specifically humiliating or violent turns up in the court records of pre-Restoration England, although there is a good deal of material connected with disorders and outrages arising from popular rituals of sexual control.[16] The usual individual target for the community to direct its displeasure over aberrant sexual conduct was likely to be a woman; the whore, the adulteress, the scold, all suffered ritual mockery, exposure, and varyingly violent degrees of punishment. Yet the ceremonies which marked such disapproval –

---

13 Ben Jonson, *Bartholomew Fair*, ed. E. A. Horsman (London, 1960).

14 *The Dramatic Works of Richard Brome*, 3 vols. (London, 1873), vol. 1.

15 For a political reading of the play see Martin Butler, *Theatre and Crisis 1632–1642* (Cambridge, 1984), pp. 220–8. The aberrant sexual behaviour in the play might be said to be a further manifestation of the madness and corruption Butler locates as its organizing themes.

16 An incident related in a letter by Robert Gell to Sir Martin Stuteville in July 1628 concerns violent revenge for rape at the siege of La Rochelle. Ten men of the town dressed up as women to lure the guilty soldiers of the besieging army, who then 'were so received that all to save their lives yielded unto yᵉ young men, and went into the town, where, beeing most severely and barbarously punished, they were sent back to glory in the camp of their exploit, for which they were never again fitted'. *The Autobiography and Correspondence of Sir Simonds D'Ewes, Bart.*, ed. J. O. Halliwell, 2 vols. (London, 1845), vol. 2, p. 201.

ridings, parades, rhymes, lampoons, duckings, and so forth – were by no means directed at women alone. The man who suffered himself to be cuckolded or beaten was likely to be a target of mockery as an unmanly man, a man who couldn't wear the breeches. One particularly widespread custom, which has a literary record that stretches at least from Samuel Butler to Thomas Hardy, was the skimmington, a wild processional ride involving disguise, rough music, and, as Martin Ingram has written, 'mocking laughter, sometimes light-hearted, but often taking the form of hostile derision which could, on occasion, escalate into physical violence'.[17] The ritual is clearly related to symbolic hunting, and indeed could feature participants dressed in horns or animal skins. If the custom arose to mock unconventional sexuality or deviant behaviour within a marriage its scope could be far wider, as Ingram explains:

While female domination and immorality were the characteristic pretexts for ridings, there were other occasions. A simple form of riding was sometimes used in a holiday context in 'trick or treat' games, and to punish people who refused to join in the festivities or who in other ways offended the holiday spirit. At Chichester in 1586, a game of 'tables' on New Year's Eve was rudely interrupted when 'William Brunne who then played the part of a lord of misrule came in . . . and said that that game was no Christmas game and so perforce took [one of the players] . . . from thence and made him ride on a staff to the High Cross.' The use of ridings to punish people who would not give money to Lords of Misrule on holidays was denounced by Philip Stubbes. Unfortunately, when refusal to take part in festivities (or, worse still, attempts to suppress such festivities) were based on Puritan principles, such ridings were apt to become distinctly less light-hearted and more elaborate. John Hole, the Puritan constable of Wells, discovered this to his cost in 1607. Hole and his associates tried to suppress the city's May games, which had been organised on a particularly grand scale that year in order to raise money for the repair of St Cuthbert's church. Hole's interference raised a storm of opposition, and he and his friends were savagely derided in a series of

spectacular ridings performed before thousands of people.   (Ingram, pp. 170–1)

The John Hole case, which was surveyed by C. J. Sisson in Lost Plays of Shakespeare's Age as long ago as 1936, is particularly suggestive about the treatment given Malvolio by the revellers of Twelfth Night. Hole, like Malvolio, set out to oppose holiday revels on principle; the revellers' revenge was character assassination, as Hole was accused of adultery with another godly objector to the festival, the delightfully named Mrs Yard. None of the surviving lampooning verses make what one would think to be the obvious jokes about hole and yard (suitably inverted in good festival fashion), but Hole is simultaneously accused of lechery and impotence, like Malvolio doubly mocked for sexual ambition and incapacity. Particularly the exposure of the Wells killjoys by theatricalizing them – staging them in disguises and caricatured paintings – by making them join, in effigy at least, the very celebrations they have tried to stop, reveals a direct relationship between festive rituals and the comic structure of such plays as Twelfth Night. In the play Malvolio is more subtly tricked into staging himself as a parodic festival figure – a grotesquely inept embodiment of the energy celebrated in holidays, and as such a betsy, a guy, a Jack-a-Lent, a cockshot man, at whom people can hardly forbear hurling things. Death, darkness, sterility, and ill luck are heaped on his back, and laughed out of the play.

His scapegoat function has frequently been remarked on, but one theoretical defence of festive customs, presumably including the shaming rituals, was that they were restorative and socially cohesive. The exhibition of conflict or aberrance under the special conditions of holiday licence would lead, with luck, to

---

[17] 'Ridings, Rough Music and Mocking Rhymes in Early Modern England', in Popular Culture in Seventeenth-Century England, ed. B. Reay (London, 1985), pp. 166–97: p. 168.

resolution and rehabilitation. Thus those accused as rioters at Rangeworthy near Bristol in 1611 defended themselves by pointing out that communal feasting was for 'the refreshing of the minds and spirits of the country people, being inured and tired with husbandry and continual labour ... for preservation of mutual amity, acquaintance, and love ... and allaying of strifes, discords and debates between neighbour and neighbour'. This sounds remarkably like the spirit of Fabian's plea to Olivia not to let retributive justice inappropriately be applied to holiday jests:

> Good madam, hear me speak,
> And let no quarrel nor no brawl to come
> Taint the condition of this present hour,
> Which I have wondered at. In hope it shall not,
> Most freely I confess myself and Toby
> Set this device against Malvolio here
>
> ...
>
> How with a sportful malice it was followed
> May rather pluck on laughter than revenge
> If that the injuries be justly weighed
> That have on both sides passed.   (5.1.352–65).

But the victims of the Rangeworthy riot, a Puritan constable and his followers who were beaten when they tried to arrest musicians and dancers, did pursue their case through the courts, and hence we happen to know about the incident. David Underdown holds up this obscure rural scuffle as an emblem of a changing world: 'The Rangeworthy revel is thus a classic example of Jacobean cultural conflict. Rituals appropriate to a traditional society, enshrining ancient values of custom and good neighbourhood, were attacked by people in authority who put individual piety, sobriety, and hard work above the older co-operative virtues' (p. 63).

Malvolio refuses Fabian's open hand. He has, after all, been most notoriously abused, and excluded from achieving greatness in any sense. Donald Sinden's entertaining account of playing the part ends with his invocation of the bitterness of Malvolio's humiliation and disappointment. There is nothing for him

following his exit, Sinden suggests, save suicide.[18] Yet surely only a particularly sensitive, late-Romantic Malvolio would be snuffed out by a device. I think the seventeenth-century man is heading for his lawyer, and Star Chamber.

To return, finally, to texts, it is worth noting that mock preaching was a recurrent element in popular revels, particularly those with a satiric thrust against a local community figure. Such was the play which Sir Edward Dymock had performed at his house in Kyme, Lincolnshire, in August 1601, and which guyed Henry, Earl of Lincoln. Following the play proper one John Cradock preached a mock sermon in a black gown and cap; a witness said that he wore 'A counterfeat beard, and standing in a pulpitt fixed to the maypole on kyme greene, havinge a pott of ale or beare hanginge by him in steade of a hower glasse.' The costume sounds remarkably like that of Sir Topas, but the performance was evidently a good deal more elaborate, though entirely in key with Feste's excellent fooling. Cradock 'did represent the person of a Minister or Priests, and did ... utter ... "The Marcie of Musterd Seed and the blessing of Bullbeefe and the peace of Pottelucke be with you all. Amen."'[19] Cradock's spoof text for the sermon, from 'The 22 chapter of the book of Hitroclites', led to a series of improbable romance tales and jests, possibly with further parodic reference to the formulae of the liturgy and scripture. Some years later in Wiltshire a drunken revel included the preaching from the pulpit within the parish church of a mock sermon on the text of 'the one and twentieth chapter of Maud Butcher and the seventh verse' (Ingram, p. 166). Mockery of

---

[18] *Players of Shakespeare*, ed. P. Brockbank (Cambridge, 1985), p. 66.

[19] N. J. O'Conor, *Godes Peace and the Queenes* (Cambridge, Mass., 1934), pp. 108–26: pp. 119–20. The Dymock episode is discussed at length by C. L. Barber: *Shakespeare's Festive Comedy* (Princeton, 1959), chapter 3.

ecclesiastical authority and liturgical frameworks for mock heroics may be thought particularly Rabelaisian revels, but they were evidently equally English, and survived to the years when they might be employed to deride Puritan earnestness. If they did not appear overtly in plays licensed for the public stage, that should not surprise us. The subtler parodic text Maria includes in the spurious letter is at once a test of Malvolio's reading, a word to the wary, and a libel on his sexuality; as such it lies entirely within the English festival tradition.

THE SCANDAL OF SHAKESPEARE'S SONNETS

MARGRETA DE GRAZIA

Of all the many defences against the scandal of Shakespeare's Sonnets – Platonism, for example, or the Renaissance ideal of friendship – John Benson's is undoubtedly the most radical. In order to cover up the fact that the first 126 of the Sonnets were written to a male, Benson in his 1640 *Poems: Written by Wil Shake-speare. Gent.* changed masculine pronouns to feminine and introduced titles which directed sonnets to the young man to a mistress. By these simple editorial interventions, he succeeded in converting a shameful homosexual love to an acceptable heterosexual one, a conversion reproduced in the numerous reprintings of the 1640 *Poems* up through the eighteenth century. The source for this account is Hyder E. Rollins's authoritative 1944 variorum Sonnets, the first edition to detail Benson's pronominal changes and titular insertions.[1] Subsequent editions have reproduced his conclusions, for example John Kerrigan's 1986 edition which faults Benson for inflicting on the Sonnets 'a series of unforgivable injuries', above all 'a single recurring revision: he emended the masculine pronouns used of the friend in 1 to 126 to "her", "hers", and "she"'.[2] With varying degrees of indignation and amusement, critical works on the Sonnets have repeated the charge.

The charge, however, is wrong. Benson did not attempt to convert a male beloved to a female. To begin with, the number of his alterations has been greatly exaggerated. Of the seventy-five titles Benson assigned to Shake-speare's sonnets, only three of them direct sonnets from the first group of the 1609 Quarto (sonnets 1–126) to a woman.[3] Furthermore, because none of the sonnets in question specifies the gender of the beloved, Benson had no reason to believe a male addressee was intended. As for the pronominal changes, Rollins himself within nine pages of his own commentary multiplies the number of sonnets 'with verbal changes designed to make the verses apply to a woman instead of a man' from '*some*' to '*many*'.[4] Rollins gives three examples as if there were countless others, but three is all there are and those three appear to have been made to avoid solecism rather than homoeroticism. In only one sonnet are pronouns altered, though even there not uniformly. In sonnet 101, masculine pronouns are emended to feminine in lines 9, 11, and 13 ('Because *she* needs no praise wilt thou be dumb?'; 'To make *her* much

---

[1] *A New Variorum Edition of Shakespeare: The Sonnets*, 2 vols. (Philadelphia, Pa. and London, 1944), vol. 2, p. 20, n. 1. Sidney Lee in his introduction to a 1905 facsimile of the Sonnets noted Benson's changes but without itemizing them or speculating on Benson's motives: *Shakespeare's Sonnets: Being a Reproduction in Facsimile of the First Edition* (Oxford, 1905), pp. 57–8.

[2] *The Sonnets and A Lover's Complaint* (Middlesex and New York, 1986), p. 46.

[3] Benson gives the title 'Selfe flattery of her beautie' to sonnets 113–15, 'Upon receit of a Table Booke from his Mistris' to sonnet 122, 'An intreatie for her acceptance' to sonnet 125. See Rollins, vol. 2, pp. 20–1 for a list of Benson's titles.

[4] Cf. Rollins, pp. 20 and 29.

outlive a gilded tomb'; 'To make *her* seem, long hence, as *she* shows now'), but the masculine (or neutral) pronoun is retained in line 5 ('"Truth needs no colour with *his* colour fix'd"').[5] Benson apparently wished to avoid a possible confusion between Truth and the beloved by altering the gender of the latter. In sonnet 104, 'friend' is emended to the more conventional 'love' but again apparently out of formal rather than moral considerations: the 'fair love' of sonnet 104 is thereby made consistent with the twice repeated 'my love' of sonnet 105, the sonnet with which it is grouped (along with sonnet 106) to form a single poem entitled 'Constant Affection'. The only other alteration may also be stylistic: the emendation of sonnet 108's nonce 'boy' to the frequently repeated 'love' avoided the anomaly of a single sonnet addressed to a boy.[6]

Indeed the 1640 collection hardly seems concerned with covering up amatory poems to males. The very first fourteen lines printed in the 1640 *Poems* contain eleven male pronouns, more than any other sonnet, in celebrating an emphatically male beauty. If Benson had wished to censure homoerotic love, why did he not omit the notoriously titillating master–mistress sonnet (20)? Or emend the glamorizing sonnet 106 that praises the beloved – in blazon style, part by part – as the 'master' of beauty? Or the sexually loaded sonnet 110 that apologizes to a specifically male 'god in love' for promiscuity of a decidedly 'preposterous' cast?[7] The same question applies to the numerous sonnets in which references to a male beloved as 'my love', 'sweet love', 'lover', and 'rose' are retained.

It is not Shakespeare's text, then, that has been falsified by Benson but rather Benson's edition that has been falsified by the modern tradition.[8] The question is, why has so patent an error not been challenged before? Certainly it is not for scarcity of copies: while only twelve copies exist of the original 1609 Sonnets, there are that many of the 1640 *Poems* in the Folger Library alone.

I wish to propose that modern treatments of the Sonnets have displaced onto Benson a singularly modern dilemma: what to do with the inadmissible secret of Shakespeare's deviant sexuality?[9] Benson is described as having put an end to that dark secret in the most radical way imaginable, by altering the sex of the beloved and thereby converting an ignominious homosexual passion into a respectable (albeit still adulterous) heterosexual one. In attributing such an act and motive to Benson, modern criticism curiously assumes – indeed posits – the secret it then reviles Benson for concealing. Quite simply, Benson's alleged act of editorial suppression presupposes something in need of suppression: there *must* be something horrible at the heart of the sonnets – the first 126 of them – to compel such a dire editorial manoeuvre.

I have dwelled on Benson only parenthetically to set the factual record straight. My real interest is not in factual error but in the kinds of cultural imperatives that motivate such errors. I see Benson's error as a glaring instance of the need to bury a shameful secret deep within the Sonnets. The need was not Shakespeare's. It has been rather that of Shakespeare criticism which for the past two centuries has been repeating variants of the repression it obsessively ascribes to Benson. This repression has, as I will proceed

---

5 Benson (London, 1640).

6 The only other sonnet referring to the beloved as 'boy' (sonnet 126, 'O thou my lovely boy') was with seven others dropped from the 1640 collection, perhaps by accident.

7 See Stephen Booth's gloss to sonnet 110, lines 9–12, pp. 356–7 as well as to sonnet 109, lines 9, 10, 13, 14, pp. 352–3 in *Shakespeare's Sonnets* (New Haven, Conn. and London, 1977).

8 For accounts of how Benson's printing-house and editorial practices have also been maligned, see Josephine Waters Bennett, 'Benson's Alleged Piracy of *Shakespeares Sonnets* and of Some of Jonson's Works', *Studies in Bibliography*, 21 (1968), pp. 235–48. See also Margreta de Grazia, *Shakespeare Verbatim: The Reproduction of Authenticity and the 1790 Apparatus* (Oxford, 1991), p. 49, n. 1, pp. 163–73.

9 On the hysterical response to this problem in modern readings of the Sonnets, see Peter Stallybrass, 'Editing as Cultural Formation: The Sexing of Shakespeare's Sonnets', *Modern Language Quarterly*, 54, (March, 1993), 91–103.

to argue, produced the very scandal it would deny. At the same time, it has overlooked the scandal that *is* there, not deep within the text but right on its surface.

I

This has been the case from the time the Sonnets were first edited: by Edmond Malone in his 1780 edition.[10] Or, to be more precise, from the time the Sonnets were first *not* edited: by George Steevens who reprinted the 1609 Sonnets in a collection of early quartos in 1766 but refused to edit them for his 1793 edition of Shakespeare's complete works. While he could justify their publication as documents, he refused to honour them with an editorial apparatus, the trappings of a classic.[11] Though he maintained that it was their literary defects that disqualified them, his response to sonnet 20 points to something more visceral: 'It is impossible to read [it] without an equal mixture of disgust and indignation.'[12] Surely it is this kind of aversion that prompted his condemnation of Malone's decision to edit them: Malone's 'implements of criticism, like the ivory rake and golden spade in Prudentius, are on this occasion disgraced by the objects of their culture'. For Steevens, Malone's attempt to cultivate such soiled objects as the Sonnets defiled the tools of editing. It was Steevens then and not Benson who first attempted to conceal the scandal of Shakespeare's dirty sexuality, not by changing pronouns but by reproducing the Sonnets in the form of a dusty document rather than of a lofty classic.

Malone, by providing the Sonnets with a textual apparatus in 1780 and then by including them in the canon proper in his 1790 edition of Shakespeare's Plays and Poems achieved precisely what Steevens had dreaded: he elevated the Sonnets to the status of literature. But the filth that embarrassed Steevens remained – remained to be covered up. In fact, as we shall see, Malone's major editorial ambition in regard to the Sonnets – to establish the connection between the first person and Shakespeare[13] – made the cover-up all the more urgent: if the Sonnets were in Shakespeare's own voice, what was to be done with the fact that the majority of them expressed desire for a young male?

Malone's driving project of identifying the experience of the Sonnets with Shakespeare's own is evident in all his major editorial interventions. Unlike Benson who expanded their contents to accommodate the experience of all lovers by giving them generic titles, Malone limited them so that they applied exclusively to Shakespeare.[14] His first step was to restrict the Sonnets to two addressees by introducing a division after sonnet 126. With only two beloveds, the task of identifying particulars could begin. First the young man was identified on the assumption that he was the same as the dedication's Mr W. H. Other identifications followed suit: of persons, time, things, circumstances. The dedicator's T. T. was Thomas Thorpe, Spenser was the rival poet, the 'now' of the sonnets was early in Shakespeare's career, the gift referred to in 122 was a table-book given to Shakespeare by his friend, sonnet 111's 'publick means, which publick manners breeds', referred to Shakespeare's own lamentable ties to the theatre, the unfaithful lover of sonnet 93 was Shakespeare's own wife. All of these efforts to give particularity to the Sonnets contributed to Malone's project of personalizing them. His attempts to identify their abundant deictics, what Benveniste has called 'egocentric markers' – their hes and shes, thous and yous, this's and thats, heres and theres – fastened the

---

10 *Supplement to the Edition of Shakespeare's Plays Published in 1778 by Samuel Johnson and George Steevens*, 2 vols. (1780), vol. 2.

11 *Twenty of the Plays of Shakespeare*, 4 vols., ed. George Steevens (1766).

12 Quoted by Rollins, vol. 1, p. 55.

13 See de Grazia, p. 154.

14 See de Grazia, pp. 155–6.

Sonnets around Shakespeare's 'I'.[15] Thus the experience they recorded could be recognized as that which Shakespeare lived.

The identification proved, as might be anticipated, highly problematic, for there was one connection that could not be allowed: as Malone's own division emphasized, most of the sonnets were addressed to a male. At each of the three points where Malone insisted upon the division at 126, circumlocutions betrayed his unease: although he referred to the addressee of the second group as a 'lady' and 'female', the addressee of the first group was no man or male, but rather 'this person', the majority of the sonnets are '*not* addressed to a female'.[16] The unspeakable, that 126 sonnets were addressed to a *male*, remained literally unspoken; at the same time, the basic division according to the beloved's gender proclaimed it.

Within the text too, Malone had to dodge the implications of his own specification, indeed whenever any of the first 126 sonnets were explicitly erotic or amatory. Footnotes then must strain to distance Shakespeare from their content, as did the note to the notorious sonnet 20: 'such addresses to men, however indelicate, were customary in our author's time, and neither imported criminality, nor were esteemed indecorous' (p. 207). Even more belaboured was Malone's rationalization of Shakespeare's references to himself as the 'lover' of the male youth. Here, too, it is not Shakespeare who offends, but rather the custom of his age: and the customary offence was even then not at the level of conduct but at the level of speech. It was 'Such *addresses* to men', '*expressions* of this kind', as well as 'the general *tenour* of the greater part of them' that were 'common in Shakespeare's time, and ... not thought indecorous' [my emphasis] (pp. 219–20). For Malone, nothing separated his present from Shakespeare's past more than the 'strange' custom among men of *speaking* of other men as their 'lovers'.[17] The offence was linguistic and literary and not behavioural; to censure the Sonnets would, therefore, be as 'unreasonable'

as faulting the plays for violating Aristotle's *Poetics* – an anachronistic *literary* judgement (p. 207). Thus for Malone the greatest difference between his late eighteenth-century and Shakespeare's late sixteenth-century was that in Shakespeare's time, male/male desire was a manner of speaking and not doing, whereas in Malone's more enlightened time it was neither: not done, not even spoken of (hence his repeated euphemisms and circumlocutions).

There is another remarkable instance of how Malone embroils himself in his own editorial commitments. While wanting to read the Sonnets as personal poems, he must impersonalize what his edition foregrounds as their most salient feature: that most of them are addressed to a young male. His longest footnote stretching across six pages pertains to sonnet 93, 'So shall I live supposing thou art true', a sonnet on sexual jealousy. He fastened on this sonnet in full conviction that Shakespeare, in the Sonnets as well as in the plays, wrote with particular intensity on the subject of jealousy because he himself had experienced it; it was his 'intimate knowledge' of jealousy that enabled him to write on the subject 'more immediately *from the heart*' (p. 266). Malone avoids the scandal that Shakespeare experienced sexual jealousy for a boy by a 'Bensonian' changing of Shakespeare's *boy* to Shakespeare's *wife*, thereby violating his own ascription of the first 126 sonnets to a male, or rather 'not a female'. This weird displacement freed Malone to talk comfortably about Shakespeare's sexual experience – in heterosexual (Shakespeare as cuckold) rather than homosexual terms (Shakespeare as pederast). A digression on his wife's infidelity

---

[15] For the profusion of deictics in the Sonnets, see Joel Fineman, *Shakespeare's Perjured Eye: The Invention of Poetic Subjectivity in the Sonnets* (Berkeley, Los Angeles, London, 1986), pp. 8–9, p. 311, n. 6.

[16] *The Plays and Poems of William Shakespeare*, 10 vols. (1790; facs. rpt, New York, 1968), vol. 10, pp. 191, 265, 294. Subsequent references to this volume will appear in text.

[17] On 'lover', see Booth, p. 432.

provided the additional benefit of justifying the adulterous liaison that the second group of sonnets recorded – Shakespeare was unfaithful to his wife because she had first been unfaithful to him. Realizing the danger of such inferences, Steevens (in the notes he contributed to Malone's edition) attempted to block it by insisting that the poem reflected not Shakespeare's *experience* but his *observation*, an impersonal rather than a personal relation (pp. 266–8). Malone stuck fast to his position, finding grounds for Shakespeare's experience of jealousy in documents, anecdotes, and the plays themselves.

James Boswell the younger, when he completed Malone's edition of *The Plays and Poems* in 1821, sided with Steevens, ruling Malone's conviction as 'uncomfortable conjecture'.[18] The judgement was unusual for Boswell, for throughout the twenty-one volume edition he rarely contradicted his friend and mentor. Yet his comments on the Sonnets opposed Malone with astonishing frequency. Indeed it would be fair to say that Boswell dismantled all of the connections Malone had worked so hard to forge between the Sonnets and Shakespeare's experience. The reason is clear: Boswell wanted to counteract the impression that Malone's 1780 edition, reissued in 1790, had produced: it is 'generally admitted that the poet speaks in his own person' (p. 219). Boswell, in the preliminary and concluding remarks with which he bracketed Malone's edition, as well as in scattered internal notes, attempted to stifle all autobiographical possibilities, beginning with Malone's opening identification of 'the individual to whom they were principally addressed, and the circumstances under which they were written'. The Sonnets could not have been addressed to any real nobleman for none, according to Boswell, would have tolerated such effeminizing verse. Any 'distinguished nobleman' would have taken offence at the 'encomiums on his beauty, and the fondling expressions' appropriate only to a 'cocker'd silken wanton' (p. 219). Thus such amorous

language could not have been 'customary' between men in Shakespeare's time, as Malone had insisted, for it would have implied that men were effeminate. For Boswell, male desire for males could not have been an acceptable way of even speaking, even back then. For him, male/male desire existed nowhere (in England anyway), not in Shakespeare's past, not in his own present; not in language, not in deed. It was sheer make-believe: what Boswell terms, not unsalaciously, 'effusions of fancy ... for the amusement of a private circle' (p. 220).

To establish their status as 'fancy', Boswell must sever all the connections Malone had forged between the Sonnets and Shakespeare's life. And so he does, one by one: Shakespeare was as young as thirty-four or at most forty-five when writing the sonnets so how could it be he who is represented as old and decrepit in several sonnets? Of course, it is not the association with old age (or with the theatre) that disturbed Boswell, but the logical extension of *any* connection: 'If Shakespeare was speaking of himself in this passage, it would follow that he is equally pointed at upon other occasions' (p. 220). More specifically, if it was Shakespeare who was old then it was also he who was 'grossly and notoriously profligate', the perpetrator of '"harmful deeds"', whose '"name had received a brand"', and whose reputation suffered from the '"impression which vulgar scandal stamped upon his brow"'. Such identifications were, Boswell insisted, absurd, for among the extant biographical materials 'not the slightest imputation [was] cast upon his character'. This is not surprising, for Malone and Boswell in their *New Life of Shakspeare* had rejected as factually inaccurate the numerous scandalous anecdotes that had cast him in the shady roles of poacher, adulterer, and carouser.[19]

---

[18] *The Plays and Poems of William Shakespeare* (1821; facs. rpt, New York, 1966), vol. 20, p. 309. Page references to this volume will henceforth appear parenthetically in text.

[19] For Malone's invalidation of the inculpatory anecdotes, see de Grazia, pp. 104–7, pp. 135–41.

If Boswell found any fault at all in Shake-speare, it was for his 'selection of topics', his representation in any form of male/male desire. But Boswell legitimized this choice by attributing it to Shakespeare's altogether admirable 'fondness for classical imitation' (p. 221). Boswell now is at last able to name the unspeakable topic, though only in simultaneously disavowing it: and not in his own words, but in words properly removed from his own by quotation marks and from standard English by sixteenth-century old spelling. The quotation is from Webbe's *Discourse of English Poetrie* that defends Virgil's second eclogue by insisting that the poet 'doth not meane ... any disordered loue, or the filthy lust of deuillish Pederastice' (p. 221).[20] Boswell keeps a clean distance from the 'filthy' object as if afraid of dirtying his ivory rake and golden spade. Having dismantled all of Malone's connections, Boswell can conclude with a discussion of the Sonnets' literary merits, the only relevant consideration after they have been wrenched from toxic reality and consigned to innocuous fancy.

I have discussed the Malone (1780, 1790) and the Malone/Boswell (1821) editions because it is with them that the modern history of the Sonnets begins, and since no full edition of the 1609 Quarto was printed prior to Malone's, that belated history can be considered their *only* history.[21] They have the further importance of having established the two critical approaches that have repeated themselves for two centuries now – sometimes ingeniously, sometimes hysterically: (1) Malone's – the Sonnets are about Shakespeare but not as a lover of young men or, (2) Boswell's – the Sonnets are not about Shakespeare or anything else, especially not about Shakespeare as a lover of young men. Though these approaches are antithetical and mutually exclusive, it must be stressed that both are motivated by the same urgency to deny Shakespeare's desire for a male.

In this regard the history of the Sonnets' reception provides a stunning example of the phenomenon Jonathan Dollimore has recently identified: the centrality of homosexuality in a culture that denounces it.[22] The denial of homosexuality in the Sonnets has produced the two polarized approaches by which they have been traditionally read for two centuries. Furthermore, what has been denied (by evasions, displacements, circumlocutions, suppressions, abstractions, etc.) has slipped into the text itself producing (as if from the Sonnets themselves) an hermeneutical interior capable of concealing a sin, a crime, a pathology. The unspeakable of Sonnets criticism has thus become the unspoken of the Sonnets – to the exclusion of, as has yet to be seen, what they quite forthrightly say.

II

I now wish to turn to one of Malone's major editorial acts, his division of the sonnets into two gendered groups, 126 to a young man, the remaining twenty-eight to a woman. The division has been generally accepted. It seems, after all, quite obvious: none of the first 126 sonnets are addressed explicitly to a woman and none of the remaining twenty-eight are addressed explicitly to a male. *Explicitly* is the key word, for what Malone's clear-cut division has obscured is the astonishing number of sonnets that do *not* make the gender of the addressee explicit.[23] Shakespeare is exceptional among the English sonneteers (Sidney, Spenser, and Daniel, for example) in leaving the beloved's

---

[20] Boswell corrects Webbe for referring to the eclogue as the sixth ('by a slip of memory, or the printer's mistake') when it should be the fourth (p. 221). Bruce R. Smith situates this eclogue in Renaissance pastoral in 'The Passionate Shepherd', *Homosexual Desire in Shakespeare's England: A Cultural Poetics* (Chicago and London, 1991), pp. 79–115.

[21] The 1609 Sonnets were reprinted but without an apparatus by Bernard Lintott in 1711 and by George Steevens in 1766.

[22] *Sexual Dissidence: Augustine to Wilde, Freud to Foucault* (Oxford, 1991).

[23] See Booth's scrupulous account of the division, p. 430.

gender unspecified in so many of the sonnets: about five-sixths of them in the first 126 and just less than that in the collection entire. The uncertainty of the beloved's gender is sustained by other types of ambiguity, most notoriously in the 'master-mistress' sonnet 20, but also in sonnet 53 in which the youth is described as a paragon of both masculine and feminine beauty, of both Adonis and Helen; similarly, a variety of epithets recur that apply to either sex: rose, friend, love, lover, sweet, fair.

The little evidence we have of how the Sonnets were read before Malone strongly suggests that the first 126 sonnets were not read as being exclusively to a male. Benson assumed that the sonnets were to a female unless otherwise specified, as the titles he assigned to his groupings indicate.[24] So too did the numerous eighteenth-century editors who reprinted Benson: Gildon (1723) referred to them as 'being most to his Mistress' and Sewell (1725) believed them to have been inspired by 'a real, or an imaginary Lady'.[25] Independent of Benson, there is further and earlier evidence. Gary Taylor has discussed five manuscript versions of sonnet 2 from the early decades of the seventeenth century with the title 'To one that would die a maid';[26] there is also a 1711 reprint of the 1609 quarto that describes the collection as '154 Sonnets all of them in Praise of his Mistress.'[27] The eighteenth-century antiquarian William Oldys who possessed a copy of the quarto assumed that some of the first 126 sonnets were addressed to a female, and George Steevens defended his logic: 'From the complaints of *inconstancy*, and the praises of *beauty*, contained in them, [the Sonnets] should seem at first sight to be addressed by an inamorato to a mistress'.[28] Malone's preliminary note announcing the division at 126 literally prevented such a 'first sight', precluding the possibility open to earlier readers of assuming the ungendered sonnets to a female.

This is not, however, to say that Malone got it wrong: clearly no sonnets are addressed to a female in the first 126 and none to a male

(except Cupid) in the subsequent twenty-eight. Just as clearly, the poet abandons the young man in 126 and declares his allegiance to a mistress in 127 and the formal irregularities (twelve pentameter lines in couplets) may punctuate that shift.[29] Nor is there any reason not to take 144's announcement – 'Two loves I have': 'a man right fair' and 'a woman, colour'd ill' – at face value. Some kind of binary division appears to be at work.[30] The question is whether that division is best described in terms – or *only* in terms – of gender difference: in terms, that is, of the object choices that have lent themselves so readily to the modern distinction between homosexuality and heterosexuality.[31]

For that construction of desire – as Foucault's expansive history of sexuality as well as Alan Bray's concentration on the Renaissance have demonstrated[32] – depended on a construal of the body and of the psyche that postdated Shakespeare, like Malone's edition itself, by

---

[24] Rollins aligns the 1640 titles with the 1609 sonnet numbers, vol. 2, pp. 21–2.

[25] See de Grazia, p. 155, n. 57.

[26] 'Some Manuscripts of Shakespeare's Sonnets', *Bulletin of The John Rylands University Library*, 68, 1 (1985), 217.

[27] Bernard Lintott, *A Collection of poems in Two Volumes ... Being all the Miscellanies of Mr William Shakespeare, which were Publish'd by himself in the Year 1609 ...*, 2 vols.

[28] Malone and Boswell, p. 306.

[29] In the 1609 quarto, the irregularity is rendered typographically conspicuous by two sets of empty brackets in place of the final couplet.

[30] On the possibility that the Sonnets were organized according to a tripartite structure (152 Sonnets, 2 Anacreontics, a Complaint) based on generic rather than gender difference following the model of Daniel, Spenser, Lodge, and others, see John Kerrigan's Introduction to *Sonnets*, pp. 13–14 and the bibliographic references on p. 66.

[31] On the taxonomy of 'homo' and 'hetero', see Eve Kosofsky Sedgwick, *The Epistemology of the Closet* (Berkeley and Los Angeles, 1990).

[32] Michel Foucault, *The History of Sexuality*, vol. 1: *An Introduction*, trans., Robert Hurley (New York, 1978) and Alan Bray, *Homosexuality in Renaissance England* (London, 1982).

about two centuries. It may then be that Malone's overly emphatic division of the Sonnets into male/female appears more in keeping with the cultural preoccupations at the turn of the eighteenth century than of the sixteenth. It may be symptomatic of a much later emphasis on sexual differentiation, one that has been fully charted out recently in Thomas Laqueur's *Making Sex: Body and Gender from the Greeks to Freud*.[33]

According to Laqueur, 'Sometime in the eighteenth century, sex as we know it was invented.'[34] What he means by this bold pronouncement is that until then there was essentially one sex rather than two. According to the classical or Galenic model, the female possessed an inverted, interior, and inferior version of male genitalia; as countless anatomical drawings attest, the uterus was imagined as an inverted scrotum, the vagina an inverted penis, the vulva an inverted foreskin. Reproductive processes as well as parts were also on par, so that conception required orgasm from both male and female. Not until the eighteenth century were male and female typically divided into two discrete sexes with distinct reproductive parts and processes: hence the invention of 'sex as we know it'. The shift is reflected in an array of verbal and graphic representations: the construction of a different skeleton for women than for men; anatomical drawings representing incommensurate reproductive structures rather than homologous ones; the division of formerly shared nomenclature into male and female so that once ungendered sperm, testicles, and stones are gendered male and differentiated from female eggs and ovaries. In short, a reproductive biology was constructed based on *absolute* rather than *relative* difference. It is only then, Laqueur notes, that the expression 'opposites attract' is coined, suggesting that 'natural' sexual attraction is between unlikes rather than likes.[35]

As Laqueur points out, this reconstrual removed sexuality from a vast system of metaphysical correspondences based, like society

itself, on hierarchical order and situated it firmly in the body or 'nature'. That a woman was previously imagined to possess less perfected versions of male genitalia legitimized her subordination to man. Biology thus upheld social hierarchy. Once difference was grounded in the body rather than in metaphysics, once male and female anatomy was perceived as incommensurate rather than homologous, then sexuality lost its 'social' bearings and became instead a matter of 'nature'. As Laqueur insists repeatedly, and as his characterization of the shift as an *invention* rather than as a *discovery* suggests, the change represents no empirical or scientific advance – 'No discovery or group of discoveries dictated the rise of the two-sex model'[36] – but rather a cultural and political reorientation. Malone's division of the Sonnets may best be understood in the context of this reorientation.

There is another shift that strangely corresponds to both Malone's twofold division and biology's two-sex model, and it occurs at roughly the same point in time. In eighteenth-century grammars and discussions of grammar, a new attention to linguistic gender binaries appears. The hierarchy preserved in the one-sex model had also applied in questions of grammatical agreement: male gender prevailed over female because it was the 'more worthy' gender. In his popular rhetoric (1553), Thomas Wilson considered natural order violated when women preceded men in a syntactic construction, since man was clearly the dominant gender. In his official Latin Grammar (1567), William Lyly assumed the same principle in explaining that an adjective describing both a male and female noun must agree with the male ('Rex et Regina Beati') because 'The masculine

---

33 (Cambridge, Mass. and London, 1990).

34 P. 149. Laqueur notes the agreement of Michel Foucault, Lawrence Stone, and Ivan Illich in identifying the late eighteenth century as the point at which human sexuality was reconceptualized, p. 5 and n. 14.

35 P. 152.

36 P. 153.

gender is more worthy than the feminine.'[37] In the eighteenth century, however, this ontological and grammatical hierarchy has ceased to be self-evident. And the reason appears to be that grammar now looks to biology rather than to metaphysics for its lead. New discoveries in biology are brought to bear on grammar, so that it is maintained that the discovery that plants have sexes introduced inconsistency into classical grammar's classification of plants as neuter.[38] In highly gendered languages like German, a general rethinking of conventional grammatical gender occurs. In English that possesses no conventional grammatical gendering, the problem took a more focused form. Towards the end of the eighteenth century, the first call for an epicene or gender-neutral pronoun is heard, in response to what is only then perceived as a problem: what to do with constructions like '*everyone* should go to *his* place' where a female and male antecedent is represented by the male 'his'.[39] As in biology, grammar can no longer assume an hierarchical relation between male and female to justify the predominance of male gender.

It is not only in relation to the third person that hierarchy disappears; in English, it had also by the start of the eighteenth century disappeared from the second person. In standard English, *thee/thou* had been dropped in favour of *you*, collapsing the complexly nuanced range of distinctions based on class relations. It is curious that Malone, who took great pride in noting philological difference in Shakespeare's age, ignored the second person pronoun while focusing on the third. Several recent critics, however, have discussed it, noting that the first 126 sonnets vacillate between *you* and *thou*, while the second twenty-eight consistently stick to *thou*.[40] Their explanations have been varied, contradictory and incomplete; the highly complex code remains unbroken. What can be ventured, however, is that the unwritten rules governing second person usage in the Renaissance were social and hierarchic.[41] They originated in social rank, though clearly com-

plicated by a calculus of differentials that included age, gender, education, experience, race, ethical worth, emotional stake, etc.[42]

This is not to propose a new division, the first 126 to 'you/thou' the next twenty-eight to 'thou'[43] – but rather to suggest that gender difference is not the *only* way to differentiate the Sonnets' 'Two loves'. There are other forms of otherness that the Malonean or modern tradition has ignored. Sexual difference is only one differential category in these poems, class is another, so is age, reputation, marital status, moral probity, even physical availability. In each of these categories, the poet is more like the mistress than like the youth; love of like

---

37 *A Short Introduction of Grammar* (London, 1530), p. 47.

38 See Dennis Barron, *Grammar and Gender* (New Haven, Conn., 1986) p. 35.

39 Ibid. pp. 190–1.

40 See G. P. Jones, 'You, Thou, He or She? The Master–Mistress in Shakespearian and Elizabethan Sonnet Sequences', *Cahiers Elisabéthains* 19 (1981), 73–84 and Andrew Gurr, 'You and Thou in Shakespeare's Sonnets', *Essays in Criticism*, 32 (1982), 9–25. Arthur F. Marotti is sensitive to the tonal effects of such position-alities in his discussion of how Shakespeare's artistry can compensate for his inferior social rank, in 'Love is not Love: Elizabethan Sonnet Sequences and The Social Order', *English Literary History*, 49 (1982), 413–16.

41 On the origins of the distinction between *tu/vos* in Latin and *thou/you* in English, see R. Brown and A. Gilman, 'The Pronouns of Power and Solidarity', in T. A. Sebeok, ed., *Style in Language* (Amherst, Mass., 1960), pp. 253–76.

42 The same perplexing instability of address characterizes another male/male couple divided by rank, not to mention age, experience, and size: Falstaff and Hal, who shift constantly from one form to the other as they uneasily jockey for position in a relationship characterized by jockeying, a relationship in which male/male erotic desire is, as Jonathan Goldberg has recently argued, not entirely absent, 'Hal's Desire, Shakespeare's Idaho', forthcoming in *Henry IV*, ed. Nigel Wood (Open University). I wish to thank him for letting me read the typescript.

43 Sonnet 145 is the sole exception which substitutes 'you' for 'thou', in the interest of preserving rhyme: 'I hate, from hate away she threw, / And sau'd my life saying not you'.

would, therefore, incline him more to the mistress than the boy. It is because Joel Fineman's awesome *Shakespeare's Perjured Eye: The Invention of Poetic Subjectivity in the Sonnets* limits difference to sexual difference that its argument is so troubling. For more relentlessly and consequentially than any one since Malone, Fineman has emphasized the distinction between male and female; indeed, it is fundamental to his Lacanian account of the constitution of subjectivity. The rupturing transition required by this account occurs, for Fineman, in the move from homosexual love of the same to heterosexual love of the other, from the ideal specularity of the youth to the false linguistics of the mistress, a move that readily translates into the Lacanian break from the imaginary into the symbolic. In short, Fineman bases what may be the vastest claim ever made for the Sonnets – that they invent poetic subjectivity for the western tradition – on sexual difference, on that rupturing but constitutive transition from a like and admired object to an unlike and loathed one.[44] Yet in light of the biological and grammatical phenomena we have been attending, Fineman's construal of sexual difference is premature. The 'Invention of Poetic Subjectivity' he attributes to Shakespeare must await 'the invention of sex' Laqueur sees as an eighteenth-century phenomenon. Until male and female can be seen as two discrete sexes rather than variants on one sex, how can subjectivity be constituted in the break between the two?

It is because Fineman overstresses the gender division at sonnet 126 that his study might be seen as the culmination of the Malonean tradition. Focus on male/female difference lends itself too readily to a psychosexuality that excludes the psychosocial. If social distinctions like class or even age were introduced, for example, the entire Lacanian progression would be turned on its head, for the poet would experience the youth's aristocratic otherness *before* the mistress's bourgeois sameness, his extreme junior *before* his approximate peer.

How, then, would it be possible to make the transition Lacanian subjectivity requires from imaginary identification to symbolic dislocation? I've put the burden of two centuries of criticism on Fineman's massively difficult book in order to make a very simple point: tradition has postulated (and concealed) in the Sonnets a sexual scandal that is based in the personal abstracted from the social, on a biology of two-sexes rather than on an epistemology of one-sex, on a division according to a gendered third person rather than a ranked second person. As I will show in the remainder of this paper by turning – at long last – to the Sonnets themselves, this has been a mistake ... so *big* a mistake that the real scandal has been passed over.

III

The ideological force of the imperious first line of the Sonnets has gone virtually unnoticed: 'From fairest creatures we desire increase.'[45] In the first seventeen poems which have traditionally (and rather preciously) been titled the procreation sonnets, there can be no pretence of *fair* being either an abstract value like the

---

[44] The book's overinvestment in gender binaries raises troubling political and hermeneutic questions. Its argument that subjectivity is attained through the renunciation of the imaginary realm of homosexual sameness bears a disturbing resemblance to a pseudo-Freudianism that perceives homosexuality as stunted or incomplete development. It also requires that sonnets 1–126 be read as univocal and 127–52 as equivocal, though Fineman later revises this programme by maintaining that equivocation is present in both groups, though only latently in the first.

[45] The Sonnets will henceforth be quoted from the facsimile of the 1609 *Shake-speares Sonnets* printed in Stephen Booth's edition. Lars Engle has recently discussed this first line as inaugurating the Sonnets' concern with 'human value in time', but without noting the specific class inflection of this value, 'Afloat in Thick Deeps: Shakespeare's Sonnets on Certainty', *Publications of the Modern Language Association*, 104 (1989), 832–43.

Platonic Good or a disinterested one like the Kantian Beautiful. *Fair* is the distinguishing attribute of the dominant class, not unlike Bourdieu's *taste* that serves both to distinguish the dominant class and, by distinguishing it, to keep it dominant.[46] The first seventeen sonnets urging the fair youth to marry and beget a son have an open and explicit social function: to reproduce, like an Althusserian state apparatus, the *status quo* by reproducing a fair young man, ideally 'ten for one' (6). The preservation of the youth preserves his aristocratic family line, dynasty or 'house': 'Who lets so faire a house fall to decay?' (13). If such houses are allowed to deteriorate, the social formation would itself be at risk: hence the general (and conservative) desire to increase 'fairest creatures' and to convince those privileged creatures that the repair of their 'beautious roofe' should be their 'chiefe desire' (10). Were these houses and roofs *un*fair, there would be no cultural imperative to maintain them, just as there is none to reproduce *unfair* (homely) persons: 'Let those whom nature hath not made for store, / Harsh featurelesse, and rude, barrenly perish' (11); while the youth is 'much too faire, / To be deaths conquest and make wormes thine heire,' (6) the 'Harsh, featureless, and rude' can return to dust unlamented. 'Increase' is to be desired only from those whom Nature has 'best indow'd' with 'bountious guift' (11); and those gifts are not simply physical or spiritual riches but the social and material ones that structure society from the top. For this reason, it is only the fair lineaments of fair lineages that should be reproduced for posterity – 'Thou shouldst print more, not let that coppy die.'

Underscoring the social concerns of this first group is their origin in pedagogical materials designed to cultivate fair young men. As has long been noted, these sonnets derive from Erasmus' 'Epistle to persuade a young gentleman to marriage', Englished in Thomas Wilson's widely influential 1553 *The Arte of Rhetorique*.[47] The treatise was used in schools as a rhetorical exercise in persuasion. Languet

repeated it in a letter to the young Sidney and Sidney in turn echoed it in his *Arcadia*, that consummate expression of aristocratic ethos. The treatise's tropes and arguments attained commonplace status, as is suggested by the seventeenth-century popularity of the sonnet that deploys the most of them, sonnet 2, copies of which survive in twelve early manuscripts.[48] It seems likely, then, that these opening sonnets would have evoked the pedagogical context which prepared fair young men to assume the social position to which high birth entitled them. The 'private friends' among whom according to Francis Meres these sonnets circulated as well as the patron to whom the collection is ostensibly dedicated can be assumed to have recognized this rhetoric as a blueprint for reproducing the fair values of the dominant class.[49]

Shakespeare's 'Two loves' relate to this opening set piece quite explicitly: after sonnet 17, it is through his own poetic *lines* rather than the youth's generational *loins* that fair's lineaments are to be reproduced, fair's lineage

---

46 Pierre Bourdieu, *Distinction: A Social Critique of the Judgement of Taste*, trans. Richard Nice (Cambridge, Mass., 1984).

47 For the influence of this epistle on Shakespeare and others, see Rollins, *Variorum* I, p. 7 and II, p. 192, T. W. Baldwin, *The Literary Genetics of Shakespeare's Poems and Sonnets* (Urbana, Ill., 1950), pp. 183–5, and Katharine M. Wilson, *Shakespeare's Sugared Sonnets* (London and N.Y., 1974), pp. 146–67.

48 See Taylor, pp. 210–46.

49 This is not to say that the Sonnets unequivocally reproduce aristocratic value. As Thomas M. Greene points out, the thrift and husbandry urged upon the young man in the first seventeen sonnets is decidedly bourgeois ('Pitiful Thrivers: Failed Husbandry in the Sonnets', *Shakespeare and the Question of Theory*, ed. Patricia Parker and Geoffrey Hartman (N.Y. and London, 1985, pp. 230–44.) Furthermore, the socially inferior poet (sonnets 25 and 110) by taking on the youth's responsibility for reproducing fair in effect assumes aristocracy's genetic privilege: his inky poetic lines preempt the youth's fair genealogical ones: 'His beautie shall in these blacke lines be seene' (63).

extended.[50] The fair line ends, however, at 127 with the shocking declaration that 'now is blacke beauties successive heire'. As if a black child had been born of a fair parent, a miscegenating successor is announced, one who razes fair's lineage ('And Beautie slandered with a bastard shame') and seizes fair's language ('beauty hath no name') – genealogy and etymology. Desire inverts its object at this breaking point: from an embodiment of a social ideal to an embodiment of a social atrocity. In praising the youth's fair lineaments, social distinction had been maintained; in praising the mistress's dark colours, social distinction is confounded. This reverses the modern ranking of the 'Two loves' that has found one unspeakable and the other simply regrettable. For the love of the youth 'right fair' which tradition has deemed scandalous promotes a social programme while the love for the mistress 'collour'd ill' which tradition has allowed threatens to annihilate it.

This is a sign, I think, that there is something misleading about the male/female categories by which Malone divided the collection: they too easily slip into the post-Enlightenment categories of homosexual and heterosexual which provoke responses that are precisely the inverse of what the Sonnets themselves call for. I would like to propose instead that the two groups be reconsidered under rubrics available in the period, appearing in E. K.'s note to the *Shepherdes Calendar* defending Hobbinol's passion for young Colin Clout on the grounds that 'paederastice [is] much to be preferred before *gynerastice*, that is the love that inflameth men with lust toward womankind'.[51] Unlike homosexual and heterosexual, the terms better correspond with Shakespeare's 'better' and 'worser' loves, his pederastic love of a boy ('my lovely Boy', 126) and gynerastic love of a womb (the irresistible 'waste of shame', 129).[52] As E. K. specifies, pederastic love is 'much to be preferred' over gynerastic, and the Sonnets demonstrate why: because it does not imperil social distinction.

Indeed the poet's main task in the first group is to protect those distinctions, a task that takes the specific form of preserving the youth's lineaments from Time's disfigurations. Shakespeare's 'pupill pen' is in contest with 'Times pensel' (16). In his own verse lines, he would transcribe the youth's fair features before 'confounding Age' unfairs them by cross-hatching his physiognomic lineaments with 'lines and wrincles' (63), cancelling or deleting the youth's fair copy, rendering him thereby 'featurelesse' like those consigned to perish barrenly – as if to make him indistinguishable from the 'Harsh' and 'rude'. In the gynerastic group, however, it is not Time but Lust that threatens distinction. Lust mars not through the sharp incisions of Time's stylus – its pen-knife – but through the obscuring adulterations of 'a woman colour'd ill'. While Time's deadly scriptings disfigure what is seen, Lust's murky adulterations confound what is known. Once a black mistress preempts the fair youth, a whole range of epistemological distinctions collapse: between black and fair (131, 132) to be sure, but also between truth and lies (138); private and

---

50 For the semantic and homonymic connections between lines and lineaments, see William Empson, *Seven Types of Ambiguity* (New York, 1947), pp. 54–5, cited by Booth, p. xiii. For the line/loin resonances, see Additional Notes to Booth's 1978 edition, p. 579.

51 Kerrigan brings E. K.'s gloss to bear on the Sonnets to conclude that the Sonnets register a 'profound homosexual attachment of a scarcely sensual, almost unrealized kind', p. 51; Stephen Orgel comments briefly on the psychological and legal advantages of 'paederastice' over 'gynerastice' in 'The Boys in the Back Room: Shakespeare's Apprentices and the Economics of Theater', unpublished manuscript. See also Smith's discussion of the quote in relation to Virgil and Spenser, pp. 95–8.

52 On the identification of woman with womb, see Richard Verstegan: 'And as Homo in Latin doth signifie both man and woman, so in our toung the feminyne creature also hath as we see the same of man, but more aptly in that it is for due distinction composed with womb, *she being that kynde of mann that is wombed*, or hath the womb of conception, which the man of the male kynd hath not', *The Restitution of Decayed Intelligence* (Antwerp, 1605), p. 194.

public (137); first person and second, first person and third (135–6); past, present, and future (129); is and is not (147), worst and best (150), angel and friend (144). In the first group, though aging himself ('Beated and chopt with tand antiquitie' (62), the poet sets himself up as Time's adversary, his own glamourizing lines counteracting Time's disfiguring marks; in the second group, however, Lust and Will are familiars rather than adversaries, so much so that Will is literally synonymous with Lust in 135 and 136, and Lust personified blurs into Will's person in 129. Pederasty's 'Pupil Pen' reinscribes the pedagogical ideal with which the Sonnets begin; while the gynerastic 'waste of shame' adulterates even the most black and white distinctions.

This is not to say that love of the youth is altogether 'of comfort'. The majority of the sonnets to him register intense longing, humiliation, loss felt and anticipated, betrayal, and even worse, self-betrayal – all the result, perhaps, of a cultural overinvestment in 'fairest creatures'. Yet the cost is nothing in comparison with what gynerasty exacts.[53] As the promiscuous womb threatens social order, so too gynerasty threatens psychic stability. Will himself takes on the hysterical attributes of the womb that obsesses him, in the breathlessly frantic copulatives of 129, in the semantic confusions listed above which in sonnet 147 he calls 'mad mans' discourse. There could be no more shocking manifestation of his hysteria than sonnet 136 in which every word could be said to signal his desire, homonymically or synonymically.[54] This maniacal repetition is audible in 'Will, will fulfill the treasure of thy loue, / I fill it full with wils, and my will one', but it is present in all the sonnet's phonetic variables as well, reducing their signification to the tautological deadlock of 'Will wills will'. Nor is Will ever released from this uterine obsession; like all men in sonnet 129, he does not know how to avoid the sulphuric pit (144), how 'To shun the heauen that leads men to this hell' (129); hence the fatal return in the final two Anacreontics to

his mistress's genital 'eye', her inflammatory and unquenchable 'Well'.[55]

But the real horror of gynerasty is social and general rather than personal and particular. Edgar in *Lear* contemns Goneril's royal womb adulterated by the bastard Edmund as 'indinguish'd [sic] space of Womans will'.[56] It is precisely this failure of discrimination that characterizes the dark lady's sexual capacity, as is evidenced by her indiscrete admission of Wills. In these sonnets it is not only common names that lose distinction, but also proper. Men named Will are indistinguishable: Will Shakespeare would be among them, and perhaps Will of the dedication's Mr W. H., and perhaps the mistress's husband is also Will, but what difference does it make when Will like *Homo* (like 'sausie Iackes' too) is a common name to all?[57] Repeatedly in these sonnets the indiscriminate womb is contrasted with that exclusive treasured 'place' or 'viall' (6) in which the youth's purely aristocratic seed would be antiseptically distilled or 'pent in walls of glasse'

---

53 Stephen Orgel, in commenting on the 'all but axiomatic' love of men for boys in the period, refers to the Sonnets as evidence that 'the problem of sex between men involves a good deal less anxiety' than between men and women, 'The Boys in the Back Room: Shakespeare's Apprentices and the Economics of the Theater'.

54 No special case has to be made for 'loue' or 'loue-sute' as synonyms for will, and Booth's commentary supports the equivalence of the sonnet's other nouns ('soule', 'things of great receit', 'stores account', 'treasure', 'number', 'one', 'nothing', and 'none'), pp. 469–73. Verbs also relate to lust: 'come' to climax; 'check' to its deferral; 'knows', 'proves', 'recko'ned' to forms of carnal knowing; 'fulfill' and 'fill' to orgasm; 'is admitted' and 'hold' to sexual entry. Adjectives express sexual desirables – 'sweet', 'great', 'blind' – and adverbs modify the sexual act, 'so near', 'thus farre', 'with ease'.

55 On eye as vulva, see Booth, p. 521.

56 *The Tragedie of King Lear*, The Norton Facsimile *The First Folio of Shakespeare*, prepared by Charlton Hinman (New York, 1968), TLN 2724.

57 Paul Ramsey notes that 22½ per cent of all Englishmen were named Will at the end of the sixteenth century, *The Fickle Glass: A Study of Shakespeare's Sonnets* (New York, 1979), p. 23.

(5). The 'large and spacious' place that is the focus of desire in the second group is no such discerning 'seuerall plot': it is 'the wide worlds common place' (137) and primarily an incontinently liquid one – 'the baye where all men ride' (137) and 'sea all water, [that] yet receiues raine still' (135) – in which all distinctions of blood bleed into one another.

As the law itself under Elizabeth confirmed by more severely prosecuting fornication between men and women than between men, nothing threatens a patriarchal and hierarchic social formation more than a promiscuous womb. By commingling blood-lines, it has the potential to destroy the social fabric itself. The gynecrasty of the Sonnets, then, needs to be considered in terms of the range of sexual practices Alan Bray has foregrounded (among them, bestiality, adultery, rape, and prostitution) that were in the period termed 'sodomy' and associated with such crimes against the state as sorcery, heresy, and treason.[58] There is good reason, therefore, to credit Jonathan Goldberg's recent suggestion that in Renaissance terms, it is Shakespeare's sonnets to the dark lady rather than those to the young man that are sodomitic.[59]

The dark lady's indiscriminate womb images social anarchy no less than Lear's invocation of cosmic cataclysm: 'all germains spill at once'.[60] The germains spill serially in the mistress rather than all 'at once', but with the same helter-skelter randomness, *including those of the fair youth*, so that his noble seed is intermixed with that of common 'sausie Iackes' (128) and of unnumbered intercoursing 'Wills'.[61] The patriarchal dream of producing fair young men turns into the patriarchal nightmare of a social melting pot, made all the more horrific by the fact that the mistress's *black* is the antithesis not just of fair but of *white*. Tradition has been ever slower to entertain the possibility that these poems express desire for a black woman rather than desire for a boy. But the important work that is being done on England's contact with Africa and on its cultural representations of that

contact is making it increasingly difficult to dissociate in this period blackness from racial blackness – black from blackamoor – promiscuity from miscegenation, especially in a work that begins by arguing for the perpetuation of pure fair blood.[62]

This paper began with one traditional error and ends with another. The first was minor, an erroneous representation of Benson's publishing efforts. The last, however, is quite major. The scandal in the Sonnets had been misidentified. It is not Shakespeare's desire for a boy; for in upholding social distinctions, that desire proves quite conservative and safe. It is Shakespeare's gynerastic longings for a black mistress that are perverse and menacing, precisely because they threaten to raze the very distinctions his poems to the fair boy strain to preserve. As with the Benson falsification, it is the motive behind the error that is worth thinking about. And I will end by doing so.

Since the eighteenth century, sexuality has been seen in biological and psychological terms rather than social.[63] Perversion, therefore, is seen as pathological rather than subversive. But in a period in which the distribution of power and property depended on orderly sexuality, it remained imperative that sexuality be understood and judged in social terms. The

---

[58] See Smith, esp. pp. 41–53 and Jonathan Goldberg, *Sodometries: Renaissance Texts, Modern Sexualities* (Berkeley, 1992), pp. 18–23.

[59] 'Hal's Desire, Shakespeare's Idaho'.

[60] *The Tragedie of King Lear*, TLN 1663.

[61] The promiscuous dark lady is not unlike Spenser's miscegenating Acrasia ('bad mixture') who razes the estates of her noble lovers in *FQ*, Bk. II, 12.

[62] On the racial inflections of fair/dark and black/white in the early modern period, see Ania Loomba, *Gender, Race, Renaissance Drama* (Manchester and New York, 1989), pp. 42–5 and Kim Hall, 'Unacknowledged Things of Darkness', Ph.D. thesis, Univ. of Pennsylvania, 1990.

[63] This paragraph owes much to Dollimore, pp. 236–40 et passim.

48

social consequences of sexual arrangements (whether male–female marriages or male–male alliances) and derangements (male–female adultery or male–male sodomy) was too basic to allow them to become merely personal matters – to become, that is, what they have become in modern sexual discourse: the precondition of personal identity. Modern readings of the Sonnets (the only kind we have) have skewed the relation of Shakespeare's 'Two loves' to conform with this classification. The result is quite topsy-turvy: readings of the young man sonnets have concealed a personal scandal that was never there; and readings of dark mistress sonnets have been blank to the shocking social peril they promulgate. A category mistake lies at the bottom of this odd hermeneutic: the Sonnets' 'Two loves' have been misclassified, the 'love of comfort' avoided as abnormal and unnatural and the 'love of despaire' countenanced as normal and natural. This essay has argued that a reclassification is in order according to a different system altogether, one that would replace the personal categories of normalcy and abnormalcy with the social ones of hierarchy and anarchy – of desired generation and abhorred miscegenation.

WEAVING AND WRITING IN *OTHELLO*

CATHERINE BATES

Iago tells tales, tall tales. He fabricates a story – Desdemona's adulterous liaison with Cassio – and then relies upon his own ingenuity and the propensity of those around him to be persuaded by the internal logic of his comedic narrative: 'the knave is handsome, young, and hath all those requisites in him that folly and green minds look after; a pestilent complete knave, and the woman hath found him already' (2.1.245–7).[1] His few, well-placed innuendos are fully dramatized in Othello's imagination, testifying to all the powers of suggestion as his words translate into action. And, although Iago's story-line is enacted in the play's performance, Shakespeare images it throughout the play quite literally. That is to say, he stresses the literariness, the sheer wordiness of Iago's narrative. Cassio's actions are thus 'an index and obscure prologue to the history of lust and foul thoughts', a text which Othello's 'unbookish jealousy must conster' (2.1.257–8; 4.1.101). Rapt, Othello looks on while Iago 'begins the story', and is so mesmerized by the tale that he too rewrites his wife: 'Was this fair paper, this most goodly book, / Made to write "whore" upon?' (4.1.130–1; 4.2.71–2). As he moves through the play, Othello's ensign displays a sign of love which, as he declares himself, 'is indeed but sign' (1.1.157). Unlike the 'certaine signes' of the Spenserian text, however, which direct the reader toward 'matter of iust memory', Iago's sign is detached, aberrant, free-floating, mischievous, confounding – leaving one character after another to ask (as we might) 'What *is* the matter?'[2]

To suggest that Shakespeare invests the act of story-telling with extraordinary potency in this play is not in itself, of course, to say anything new. But it will be the argument of this essay that Shakespeare's *representation* of narrativity, his treatment and choice of narrative sources, and the imagery with which he surrounds narration can be shown to illuminate the play's central concerns. In his essay on the essential narrativity of *Othello*, Stephen Greenblatt writes that 'Iago's constant recourse to narrative ... is both the affirmation of absolute self-interest and the affirmation of absolute vacancy; the oscillation between the two incompatible positions suggests in Iago the principle of narrativity itself, cut off from original motive and final disclosure.'[3] Iago's story is substance-less. There is nothing to it, both in

---

1 All references to Shakespeare are to *The Riverside Shakespeare*, ed. G. Blakemore Evans (Boston: Houghton Mifflin, 1974).

2 Spenser, *The Faerie Queene*, 2.Proem.4; 1. All references to Spenser are to the *Variorum* edition, ed. Edwin Greenlaw, Charles G. Osgood, F. M. Padelford, 8 vols. (Baltimore: Johns Hopkins University Press, 1932–8). For the question, 'What is the matter?', see *Othello*, 1.1.83; 1.2.38; 1.3.58; 2.3.164; 4.1.49; 4.2.98; 4.2.114; 5.1.50; 5.2.47; 5.2.105; 5.2.259. Through Iago's interventions, the matter in this play is 'mangled', 1.3.173.

3 Stephen Greenblatt, *Renaissance Self-Fashioning From More to Shakespeare* (Chicago: University of Chicago Press, 1980), pp. 236–7.

the ease with which he deceives, and in the way in which he conjures something out of nothing and then relies for his devastating effect on the innate belief in the logic of the storyline as it unfolds and (seemingly miraculously) fulfils the very expectations it has been set out so carefully to raise. It is story-telling for story-telling's sake, and I would like to suggest that what Greenblatt sees as the fundamental *oscillatoriness* of Iago's function puts us in mind of the busy, itchy, implicitly sexual back-and-forth of the weaver's shuttle as it flies to and fro in its narrative exercise.

For, as the weaver of a word-net, Iago brings together a whole series of strands which betray, in the very metaphors we use to describe and account for narrative, the ancient semantic overlap between weaving and writing. The word 'text' derives, after all, from the Latin *texere*, 'to weave'. Thus any text is, by definition, a woven thing, a textile, an enfolded and unfolding surface with an imaginative texture of its own. 'Discourse', from *discurrere*, suggests, as Hayden White writes, 'a movement "back and forth" or a "running to and fro"', moving like a shuttle between alternative ways of encoding reality, cultural and individual.[4] The weaving metaphor thus underlies even the most primary conception of narrativity, and gives rise to a host of related images.[5] Thus 'subtle' (an important word for a play like *Othello*, as we shall see) derives from the Latin *sub tela*, 'under a net'. When Spenser writes of Arachne's 'subtile net' and 'subtile web', or Marvell of Cromwell 'twining subtle fears with hope, / He wove a net of such a scope', their readers would have been expected to pick up the multiple strands of association which the etymological awareness of their lines expresses.[6]

It is with such a net, of course, that Iago captures Othello. Like that earlier word-spinner, Richard III, Iago is the 'labouring spider [who] / Weaves tedious snares to trap mine enemies', the 'bottled spider / Whose deadly web ensnareth' those about him.[7] So, with his 'little ... web', Iago sets out to catch

Cassio, taking advantage of Othello's already 'enfetter'd' soul to 'make the net / That shall enmesh them all' until all the 'credulous fools are caught' (2.1.168; 2.3.345, 361–2; 4.1.45). Spider-like, Iago sits in the centre of the play spinning fictions that have the power to destroy for all their slightness and invisibility. 'Hypocrisie is woven of a fine small thred, / Subtler, then *Vulcan's* Engine', Ferdinand warns his sister in *The Duchess of Malfi*.[8] And Iago's hypocrisy – his playful, irresponsible, gruesome separation of signs from their signifieds – weaves a web of words that is all outside, quite substance-free, and, like Vulcan's net, trifling and airy-light.

Indeed, it is the image of Vulcan's net which draws together the various semantic and thematic strands of this essay. For Iago is a skilful workman: he fabricates in the sense that he produces a fabric, an artefact of human devising; but he also fabricates in the sense that he makes something up, he lies. 'Fabricate' is etymologically related to 'forge' – both the blacksmith's instrument for fashioning metal, and his action in forging, in hammering it out – as, of course, Vulcan the blacksmith works at his smithy. And, by the same semantic develop-

---

[4] Hayden White, *Tropics of Discourse: Essays in Cultural Criticism* (Baltimore: Johns Hopkins University Press, 1978), p. 3.

[5] As, for example, 'yarn', from OE *gearn*, thread; also 'rhapsody', from Greek *rhaptein*, to sew, *ôidê*, a song.

[6] Spenser, *The Faerie Queene*, 2.7.28, 2.12.77; Marvell, 'An Horatian Ode upon Cromwell's Return from Ireland', lines 49–50, in *Andrew Marvell: The Complete Poems*, ed. Elizabeth Story Donno (Harmondsworth: Penguin, 1972), p. 56. One of the subtle things about *Othello* is that the word 'subtle' is never used of those for whom it would be most appropriate. But, as Iago projects Cassio as a 'subtle knave', and Othello Emilia as a 'subtle whore', they reveal themselves to be under the very net of their own deceitful devising (2.1.242; 4.2.21).

[7] *Richard III*, 1.3.241–2; *2 Henry VI*, 3.1.339–40.

[8] *The Duchess of Malfi*, 1.1.347–8, in *The Complete Works of John Webster*, ed. F. L. Lucas, 4 vols. (London: Chatto and Windus, 1927).

ment as the word 'fabricate', the forging of an artefact – a chain or a net – came by extension to mean the contriving, devising, inventing, making up of *anything*. Hence forgeries. Iago and Vulcan are thus related in their activity. Vulcan's forge produces the invisible net that catches Mars and Venus; Iago's workmanship, even subtler than Vulcan's engine, produces a forgery that will 'enmesh them all'.

Largely about subtlety (in its various senses), *Othello* is, then, a highly subtle play, not least in the way it alludes so inescapably, yet so delicately, to its most obvious mythic prototype – the story of Mars and Venus, caught *in flagrante* under the net (*sub tela*) that Vulcan made: 'the suttlenesse and slight thereof was such, / It followed euery little pull and closde with euery touch.'[9] Invisible to the naked eye, lighter and slighter than cobwebs, Vulcan's net nonetheless tricks the two (who thought, as the saying goes, to dance in a net unseen), exposing them to the ridicule of the gods.

As a military general who finds himself upon Cyprus – Venus' isle – we can scarcely avoid attributing to Othello's situation a profound archetypal significance. He is a Mars disarmed, a soldier who finds his occupation mysteriously gone, and a man who, like his own men, curiously misinterprets this very feminine place as a 'warlike isle' (2.1.43; 2.3.57) – an ominous misnomer for an island which has welcomed Desdemona to its shores as a second Aphrodite, another queen of love:

> O, behold,
> The riches of the ship is come on shore!
> You men of Cyprus, let her have your knees.
> Hail to thee, lady! and the grace of heaven,
> Before, behind thee, and on every hand,
> Enwheel thee round!   (2.1.82–7)

And not only is Cyprus mythically associated with the female. Within the specific space and time of the play the island is given over to revelry, to carnival, to all the parodying, travestying freedom of the holidayish, one-off, comedic form: 'It is Othello's pleasure, our noble and valiant general, that ... every man

put himself into triumph; some to dance, some to make bonfires, each man to what sport and revels his addiction leads him ... All offices are open, and there is full liberty of feasting from this present hour' (2.2.1–10). The atmosphere on Cyprus that fatal, festive night is one of free play and rule-breaking – the traditional arena for the principle of disorder, fragmentation, rebelliousness, and topsy-turvidom that the grotesque always represents.

As Othello is caught, like Mars, with 'trifles light as air', so too his otherwise separate roles become hopelessly entangled. For, identified (as we have seen) primarily with the guilty lover (Mars) who is caught by Iago's web (Vulcan's engine), Othello is also, of course, identified with the jealous husband (Vulcan himself). Othello's presentation thus undergoes a confusing conflation. Othello falls prey to Iago's story-telling because he is himself a story-teller, a man whose tale seduces Desdemona and has the power, according to the Duke, to win all the daughters of Venice. And, as Othello the story-teller is persuaded by another's story, so he undergoes that process of condensation so familiar in literature and dreams, and becomes the teller told, the seducer seduced, the beguiler beguiled, the spell-binder spell-bound. As the jealous husband who guiltily betrays his own wife, Othello becomes (like Antony or Amphialus) another of those Renaissance heroes of the self-divided, self-defeating, ultimately self-murdering predicament. His hitherto controlled, contained, compartmentalized identity breaks down, changed utterly, in this terrible female place.

Shakespeare's allusions to the story he would have found most easily in Ovid thus lend this play a rich mythic resonance, although the allusions are – like Vulcan's net – subtle. Presented with an image of a soldier and his lover on the island of Venus it is impossible to escape

---

[9] *The xv bookes of P. Ouidius Naso, entytuled Metamorphosis* (1567), trans. Arthur Golding, sig. G5^v.

the text's implied inference, its reference back to a more ancient though familiar story. And, although we cannot say that it is explicitly stated, we are nonetheless invited to make the connection, to pick up the threads of a poetic tradition for ourselves. I labour the point because, in a play that so insistently collapses identities in on themselves, so our roles as readers and spectators are also implicated and embroiled by this fine-spun net. Shakespeare throws over us the web of textual reference, leaving us entangled, enmeshed in knots of allusion and metaphor which threaten to perplex the more we try to unravel them.

Shakespeare's text is thus as much of a net as Vulcan's or Iago's. It is, after all, a story, a tissue of other stories. And, in the self-consciousness of its own story-telling, *Othello* links up with its source in Ovid in a more subtle way, perhaps, than might at first have been supposed. For, when we turn to the fourth book of the *Metamorphoses*, from which the story of Mars and Venus comes, we find that Ovid too has collapsed his categories, and bound tale and telling in a particularly suggestive way.

This part of the *Metamorphoses* opens with the daughters of Minyas who, contravening the order to put aside their work and join in the celebratory rites of the new god, Bacchus, stay at home and spin. As they work on their looms the women entertain each other with stories, and Ovid repeatedly and explicitly links their handiwork with their narratives. As the women draw out their strands of wool and wind them around their fingers, so they spin their stories, one by one. And each story itself, produced out of this industrious, female activity, spins round and round with its own self-reflecting wit, the spinning women weaving into their tales image after image of weaving. Thus Pyramus and Thisbe (the first tale) are killed through a misinterpretation of that fatal textile, Thisbe's bloodied veil. Mars and Venus (the second tale) are, as we have seen, adulterously caught in Vulcan's net. As the story continues, Apollo is made to suffer a similar fate for informing on

their adultery, and, in that doubling back which we are beginning to see as characteristic of this theme, the story unfolds to reveal the entangler himself entangled. Made by the vengeful Venus to fall hopelessly in love with an earthly maiden (Leucothoë), Apollo is reduced to adopting the lowliest role when (disguised as her mother) he approaches his beloved while she works (like the girl who is narrating her story) on her spinning. Leucothoë sits by the lamplight with her twelve maid-servants busily drawing threads through her whirling spindle – an instrument which suggestively falls from her trembling fingers when the god reveals his maleness. And, although he enjoys her, Apollo falls victim to female jealousy when another of his mistresses, now spurned, in turn informs on him. Leucothoë is buried alive by her irate father and transformed into an incense bush before Apollo can enjoy her again. This story ended, the daughters of Minyas busily continue their spinning as they listen to a third – the tale of Salmacis' desire for Hermaphroditus, son of Venus and Mercury. Unable to make the maidenly boy love her, Salmacis twines herself around his naked body like a snake around its prey or ivy round a tree-trunk, or, implicitly, like the thread around the fingers of her narrator.

The story of Mars and Venus is not simply of importance to *Othello* in its obvious parallelism with Shakespeare's plot, therefore, but also because of the very nature of its telling. It lies embedded in a group of stories each of which turns around the metaphor of weaving, twining, trapping, and *in* each of which these motifs themselves reflect the active spinning they both accompany and represent. It is only natural that *Othello*, a text so aware of the potency of story-telling, should betray a consciousness of its own narration, and its re-telling of an older story which is itself bound up with the crafted act of making – with poetry.

Moreover, in Ovid's text, the image of women spinning together is exclusively and axiomatically female: an environment which, in its privacy and interiority, explicitly sets itself apart from maleness, from the bacchanalian rites going on outside. It represents a world in which men can only enter in disguise – in skirts. And although the daughters of Minyas cannot, in the end, withstand the greater power of the male god whose rites they ignore (appropriately, their looms are transformed into vines, their threads into tendrils, their purple wool into grapes) yet there is in their transgressive, rebellious, independent stance a kind of power. Repressed, domesticated, kept indoors, the emblematic enclave of spinning women invokes the full potency of their weaving – unravelling the bonds of male power through their disobedient story-telling as effectively as Venus captures Apollo or as Philomel later implicates her violator. Like Philomel, these silenced, unheeded women find ways to give expression through what Sophocles (in an arresting phrase, reported by Aristotle) called 'the shuttle's voice'.[10] The phrase describes Philomel's tapestry, an inanimate, crafted object, indeed, a 'text', that speaks (in Sophocles' double metonymy) both for itself and for its ravished maker.

In its age-old association with the female, weaving thus carries with it a freight of signifying power – the projected utterance of the otherwise silenced; the unchallengeable speaking voice of the tongueless. Weaving becomes speaking, textile becomes text, as the women's handiwork subtly catches, unties, and re-constitutes the narrative threads of their reality.

In Book IV of the *Metamorphoses*, then, Ovid not only invokes this image of weaving, working women. *He shows women weaving weaving into their stories while they weave.* Acutely conscious of its own origin and narrativity, his text approximates most closely at this point to what Bakhtin might have termed 'novelistic' discourse – multilayered, perspectival, and relative. It is not enough to take each story as a separate, rounded-off, completed entity, for each one is so manifestly embedded in its own making and in the environment of its production. As we have seen, the narratives of Pyramus and Thisbe, Venus and Mars, Salmacis and Hermaphroditus interweave their own individual and internal images of binding into a larger construct, one story following another as their narrators relentlessly twist threads beneath their fingers. We are all too aware of the tellers, of what is going on around the act of story-telling. Consequently, no one tale can be separated from its point of origin, from the dense network of allusion and reference it both constitutes and reflects. And, as the multitude of threads mounts up, so it becomes more and more difficult to conceive of the story-line in terms of singleness. Indeed, as each of the daughters of Minyas embarks on her chosen tale, she tantalizingly refers to a whole host of other stories that she *could* tell. Each girl eventually decides on one only after turning several other possibilities over in her mind. Out of the copiousness of possibilities, the infinite number of tales they could tell, comes a dizzying sense of heteroglossia, of avenues kaleidoscopically opened up though not explored. And, although Bacchus eventually intervenes (transforming the women into bats, their looms into vines), there is until this point an almost frantic sense of the unstoppability of their work. As one story merges into another, one level of narrative blends into the next, we are faced with a vision of 'endlesse worke', an unfinishable discourse that threads on and on, over and over, round and round.[11] Bakhtin's description of the novelistic form best characterizes this exciting, alarming prospect: 'an indeterminacy, a certain semantic openendedness, a living contact with unfinished, still-evolving, contemporary reality (the openended present)'.[12]

It is against such open, continuate, heteroglot

---

[10] Aristotle, *On the Art of Poetry*, trans. Ingram Bywater (Oxford; Clarendon Press, 1920), p. 59.

[11] Spenser, *The Faerie Queene*, 4.12.1.

[12] Mikhail Bakhtin, *The Dialogic Imagination*, trans. Caryl Emerson and Michael Holquist (Austin: University of Texas Press, 1981), p. 7.

discourse that Bakhtin contrasts the epic: 'the national heroic past: it is a world of "beginnings" and "peak times" in the national history, a world of fathers and of founders of families, a world of "firsts" and "bests"'. Unlike the irredeemably relative novelistic mode, the register of the epic is superlative. For Bakhtin 'there is no place in the epic world for any openendedness, indecision, indeterminacy. There are no loopholes in it through which we may glimpse the future; it suffices unto itself, neither supposing any continuation nor requiring it.'[13]

Within the associative worlds of Ovid and Shakespeare, novelistic and epic translate into two modes of utterance – two modes perceived to be (and quite clearly distinguished as) female and male. For the turning discourse of the daughters of Minyas deliberately sets itself against a male authority. And, in Shakespeare's play, Othello finds his natural epic mode, his tendency toward completed, closed-off narrative, strangely out of place. A latter-day Aeneas, Othello recounts his life-story – easily to the initially clubbable, comfortably receptive Brabantio, but less easily to Desdemona: a woman who was, by his own account, constantly distracted away from his compelling narrative by the apparently more compelling 'house affairs' (1.3.147). Indeed, until he has her as a captive audience, Othello has disconcertedly found himself delivering his grand tale to Desdemona shopkeeper-like, 'by parcels' (1.3.154). No Dido, Desdemona evidently found her day-to-day household duties just as important as the Moor's epic tale. It is only he who interprets her as frantically dispatching her work so as to come back breathless and curious for more. And it is not until he takes the initiative to pin down this busy woman and unfold his story that Othello (as he confesses himself) succeeds in wooing her:

> Which I observing,
> Took once a pliant hour, and found good means
> To draw from her a prayer of earnest heart
> That I would all my pilgrimage dilate. (1.3.150–3)

With its associations of compliance, plying a needle, and folding (from French, *plier*), Othello's adjective 'pliant' here unconsciously betrays his recognition of more female ways of speaking. Like the humbled Hercules, Othello has become a spinster, a needlewoman, in his need to 'draw' Desdemona out, to unthread her.

Bakhtin constantly writes of the 'straightforwardness' of the epic mode, and its canonicity, linearity, unyieldingness are well reflected in the bullishness of Othello's assertive storytelling. In the singleness of his story-line and purpose Othello pays allegiance to the traditional, humanistic definition of narrative excellence as expressed, in this example, by Ben Jonson: 'Our style should be like a skeine of silke, to be carried, and found by the right thred, not ravel'd and perplex'd; then all is a knot, a heape.'[14] In attempting to thread his way through increasingly complicated experience, Othello's predicament calls Theseus to mind, groping his way out of the labyrinth by means of a single thread. In contrast to this singleness, the traditionally apian metaphor of direct utterance, Othello finds himself the victim of a spider – or rather of a web-like encircling, multi-directional discourse which, in adopting 'female' modes of narrativity (digressiveness, openendedness, continuity) is, to him, utterly baffling.

It is with this perceived 'female' mode that Lyly and Sidney provocatively ally themselves in their fictions. The *New Arcadia* presents itself as 'this idle work of mine, which I fear (like the spider's web) will be thought fitter to be swept away than worn to any other purpose'.[15] Lyly's *Euphues and his England* (1580) begins its prefatory letter 'To the Ladies' with the story of

---

[13] Ibid. pp. 13, 16.

[14] From *Discoveries*, in *Ben Jonson*, ed. C. H. Herford, Percy and Evelyn Simpson, 11 vols. (Oxford: Clarendon Press, 1925–52), vol. 8, 624.

[15] Sir Philip Sidney, *The Countess of Pembroke's Arcadia (The New Arcadia)*, ed. Victor Skretkowicz (Oxford: Clarendon Press, 1987), p. 506.

how 'Arachne hauing wouen in cloth of Arras, a Raine-bow of sundry silkes, it was obiected vnto hir by a Ladie more captious then cunning, that in hir worke there wanted some coulours.'[16] Styling themselves in this way, the fictions of Sidney and Lyly challenge the very humanist principles of serious, teleological writing that they invoke, placing themselves on one side of that quintessentially Renaissance dichotomy between humanist and courtly. As texts avowedly and self-advertisingly addressed to women, the *New Arcadia* and *Euphues and his England* situate themselves within a courtly mode of utterance which had been characterized in the tradition of the *questione d'amore*. Countless fifteenth and sixteenth-century texts invoke the recreative and festive scenario of men and women who gather together to analyse and anatomize questions of love and sexuality, a scene Shakespeare himself presents in Act 2, scene 1 as Cassio, Iago, Emilia, and Desdemona idly pass the time on the Cyprus shore. It was the essence of these courtly dialogues to argue each question on every side, and to postpone resolution or decision in favour of a more openended, composite truth. While academic or judicial inquiry might aspire to conclusion, the courtly modes in which the *Arcadia*, *Eupheus*, and *Othello* have a share resist completion and continue to debate their issues to and fro. It was the freedom of this style of dialogic utterance that struck Sir Thomas Hoby as he translated the form's most famous prototype, *The Book of the Courtier*: 'Both Cicero and Castilio professe, they follow not any certaine appointed order of precepts or rules, as is used in the instruction of youth, but call to rehearsall, matters debated in their times too and fro in the disputation of most eloquent men and excellent wittes.'[17] For Hoby, courtly discourse is a form which marks itself off from more visibly straightforward, pedagogical, rule-bound methods, and he alludes in his 'too and fro' to the busy activity of the shuttle, conflating the movement of feminine talk with the movement of feminine work.

As a site of endlessly fascinating, anxiety-inducing concern, the confrontation of these two modes (male/female, humanist/courtly, bee/spider) reappears over and over again in Renaissance texts. Spenser's *Amoretti* sonnet 23 is just one example:

> *Penelope* for her *Vlisses* sake,
> Deuiz'd a Web her wooers to deceaue:
> in which the worke that she all day did make
> the same at night she did againe vnreaue:
> Such subtile craft my Damzell doth conceaue,
> th'importune suit of my desire to shonne:
> for all that I in many dayes doo weaue,
> in one short houre I find by her vndonne.
> So when I thinke to end that I begonne,
> I must begin and neuer bring to end:
> for with one looke she spils that long I sponne,
> and with one word my whole years work doth
>   rend.
> Such labour like the Spyders web I fynd,
>   whose fruitlesse worke is broken with least
>   wynd.[18]

As Othello becomes entangled in a net, so Spenser's male poet finds himself caught in the apparently winding illogicality of female behaviour. Penelope is introduced as an icon of wifeliness, weaving her tapestry explicitly for her husband's sake, 'her wooers to deceaue'. But far from identifying himself with this fortunate husband, or even (less happily, but still consistently) with the endlessly frustrated suitors, the poet instead sees himself as another *Penelope*, as someone who takes 'many dayes' to weave this text. Indeed, there is a hint that the poet even imagines his own voice to be 'the shuttle's voice', and himself to be the very tapestry itself, the work which Penelope patiently unravelled at the end of each day. The

---

[16] *The Complete Works of John Lyly*, ed. R. Warwick Bond, 3 vols. (Oxford: Clarendon Press, 1902), vol. 2, p. 8.

[17] Baldassare Castiglione, *The Book of the Courtier*, trans. Sir Thomas Hoby, ed. W. H. D. Rouse (London: Dent, 1928), p. 3.

[18] Spenser, *Amoretti* 23, in *The Minor Poems* (*Variorum* edition), vol. 2, p. 204.

poet's will to ending, to completion, to resolution, to conquest, is thus frustrated at its very origin, until he horrifiedly finds himself, not a bee, but a spider, spinning around himself the wild, encircling threads of failure.

In his *A Lover's Discourse*, Roland Barthes links the Penelope-figure, the archetypal weaving woman, with a hidden, unvoiced male fear:

Historically the discourse of absence is carried on by the Woman: Woman is sedentary, Man hunts, journeys; Woman is faithful (she waits), man is fickle (he sails away, he cruises). It is Woman who gives shape to absence, elaborates its fiction, for she has time to do so; she weaves and she sings; the Spinning Songs express both immobility (by the hum of the wheel) and absence (far away, rhythms of travel, sea surges, cavalcades). It follows that in any man who utters the other's absence *something feminine* is declared; this man who waits and who suffers from his waiting is miraculously feminized.[19]

The implication behind Barthes' words is that man goes away leaving woman behind. He 'sails away, he cruises' *precisely so as to be absentee*, to have his own presence missed and lamented, and thus get around the fear of missing anything himself. The feminine spinning songs, the texts expressive of absence, are seen, then, to touch at some level on the castration complex, and to emblematize the fear that lies at the heart of any distinction between 'male' and 'female' utterance. Man will do anything – travel vast distances, undergo the most terrible trials – in order not to face the loneliness and dreadfulness of his hidden fear. And the tapestry, that image of female conniving, is all the time a projection of this anxiety.

In his epic wandering Othello is the epitome of the absent hero, the Ulysses whose adventures take him far from home. Yet it is not his absence but his existence back at the hearth that Shakespeare's play explores. And, as Othello's great seductive tale, his 'travel's history' (1.3.139) subversively contains its own 'ravelling', so the single-threaded narrative of his life is symbolically undone by the homely, domesticated world to which he has returned.

Incapable of leading him out of the labyrinth, Othello's skein of silk is, in Jonson's image, ravelled, perplexed, knotted, and heaped. Neither spider nor bee, he approximates rather to that favourite Renaissance emblem of self-entanglement – the silk-worm – a creature which, as Montaigne wrote, 'uncessantly goeth turning, winding, building and entangling her selfe in hir owne worke'.[20]

In another essay, Montaigne gives expression to that common clustering of male prurience, anxiety, and vulnerability which, I have been suggesting, we can see in *Othello*. In the essay on cripples, he turns his attention to lameness in women:

I would have saide, that the loose or disjoynted motion of a limping or crooke-backt Woman, might adde some new kinde of pleasure unto that businesse or sweet sinne, and some un-assaid sensuall sweetnesse, to such as make triall of it: but I have lately learnt, that even ancient Philosophy hath decided the matter: Who saith, that the legs and thighs of the crooked-backt or halting-lame, by reason of their imperfection, not receiving the nourishment, due unto them, it followeth that the Genitall parts, that are above them, are more full, better nourished and more vigorous. Or else, that such a defect hindring other exercise, such as are therewith possessed, do lesse waste their strength and consume their vertue, and so much the stronger and fuller, they come to *Venus* sports. Which is also the reason why the Graecians described their Women-Weavers, to bee more hotte and earnestly-luxurious, than other Women: Because of their sitting-trade, without any violent exercise of the body. What cannot we dispute of according to that rate? I might likewise say of these, that the same stirring which their labour, so sitting doth give them, doth rouze and sollicite them, as the jogging and shaking of their Coache, doth our Ladies.[21]

---

[19] Roland Barthes, *A Lover's Discourse*, trans. Richard Howard (London: Jonathan Cape, 1979), pp. 13–14.

[20] Montaigne, 'Of Experience', in *The Essayes of Michael, Lord of Montaigne*, trans. John Florio, 3 vols. (London: Dent, 1910), vol. 3, p. 325.

[21] Montaigne, 'Of the Lame or Crippel', ibid. vol. 3, pp. 287–8.

It is a wonderfully disingenuous passage, attesting to all the anxiety of the male for the sedentary, spinning woman, whose activity is perceived to be a surrogate for proper, husbandly sex as obviously as the distaff substitutes for the phallus. Moreover, the twists and turns of Montaigne's logic betoken the author's profound discomfiture as he alternately confronts and turns aside from the image of weaving he has himself described. For his associations of auto-eroticism, self-sufficiency, and productivity follow on immediately from an account of how the Amazons crippled male babies in order to ensure their subordination: 'In that feminine common-wealth of theirs, to avoyde the domination of men, they were wont in their infancy to maime them, both their armes and legges and other limmes, that might any way advantage their strength over them, and make onely that use of them, that we in our World make of our Women.'[22] It is a nervous, twitchy performance. For, as the Amazons cripple male children, maiming their arms and legs (and tremblingly unnameable 'other limmes'), so Montaigne in effect cripples women as a general category, of use only as sexual objects. Yet the act of *dis*abling (Montaigne's crippling of women, the Amazons' maiming of male children) couples with the act of *en*abling (Montaigne's sarcasm, women's sexual pleasure) to produce the kind of logical toing and froing typical of the very 'feminine' mode Montaigne tries to suppress.

In the same way, Shakespeare sets up Othello to confront the source of his anxiety in his over-heated and unstable responses to that eminently housewifely woman, Desdemona. There is an abiding sense of the domestic in this play, of the private, female realm lurking just behind the wings, a mysterious world of ongoing and self-justifying activity from which Desdemona comes and to which she returns. The public world of the play attempts to turn its back on this inner space, but characters are constantly being called out from within – from their private chambers and bedrooms – in order to face the hurly-burly of the street, until a powerfully imagined interior world intrudes itself on the action. For a play devoted to soldiers and soldiering, there is a curiously persistent emphasis on this hidden, household space. Othello takes to describing his former life in terms of his present situation:

> But that I love the gentle Desdemona,
> I would not my unhoused free condition
> Put into circumscription and confine
> For the sea's worth. (1.2.25–8)

Much rests on Othello's 'but'. For what he is describing as his own is the domesticated, house-bound existence of a woman: he *is* circumscribed, confined, housed. His acute sensitivity to the thresholds of Desdemona's honour later in the play (the point of entry at which countless thousands have enjoyed her body) collapses the female body within its containing space (the home) until Othello ends up experiencing for himself a kind of psychological rape. Othello protests too much. When he reassures the Senate of his continued professionalism as a soldier, he promises that

>   when light-wing'd toys
> Of feather'd Cupid seel with wanton dullness
> My speculative and offic'd instruments,
> That my disports corrupt and taint my business,
> Let housewives make a skillet of my helm.
> (1.3.268–72)

Yet, in effect, this is exactly what happens to Othello. Humiliated by Iago's plots and plans, he finds that his helmet has been transformed into a saucepan, while his epic grandeur becomes as poignant and unbearable as Don Quixote's.

Iago too constantly attempts to set himself apart from this threateningly banal world of feminine activity. In the opening scene he edgily dismisses Cassio as a man who 'never set a squadron in the field, / Nor the division of a battle knows / More than a spinster' (1.1.22–4).

---

[22] Ibid. p. 287.

For him, all that the best woman (including his wife) is good for is 'To suckle fools and chronicle small beer' (2.1.160). In this context, the semantic slippage from 'housewife' to 'hussy' is asking to happen, as indeed it does – twice. Women, says Iago, are 'Players in your huswifery, and huswives in your beds' (2.1.112). Bianca is an everywoman, exposing in the openness of her trade the secret wish that lurks in every female heart: 'A huswife that by selling her desires / Buys herself bread and clothes' (4.1.94–5). For Iago, domestic science translates simply into an economics of desire.

Even more than the other women of the play, Desdemona is located within the interior, domestic space of the household – that object of male surveillance and scrutiny that is yet so elusive of their control. Addressing the murdered Desdemona in the final scene, Gratiano informs us of Brabantio's death: 'Thy match was mortal to him, and pure grief / Shore his old thread in twain' (5.2.205–6). And, although he cannot bring himself to make the connection explicit, Gratiano here invests Desdemona's innocent, housewifely spinning with the dreadful finality of the Fates.

In the midst of his crazed, agonized jealousy, Othello makes a similar connection, remembering that Desdemona is a needle-woman, 'So delicate with her needle!' (4.1.187). Yet her busy, plying needle becomes a synecdoche for Othello's fear as it imitates Desdemona's own erotic 'turning' in her husband's fevered imagination: 'you did wish that I would make her turn. / Sir, she can turn, and turn; and yet go on / And turn again' (4.1.252–4).

As Peter Stallybrass writes, 'turning becomes a figure for her inconstancy: as she can turn to him, so she can lie to him or turn to the arms of another man'.[23] But the critic's words could be suggestively altered, perhaps, so as to read: 'turning becomes a *trope* for her inconstancy'.

For, to Othello, not only Desdemona's movements but her very figures of speech and turns of phrase body forth her feared unfaithfulness. It is precisely in her troping, in her perceived reluctance to submit to masculine modes of singleness and straightforwardness, that Desdemona appears to her husband – turning, troping, tropical, foreign, exotic, and erotic.

It is no accident then that the two 'texts' or woven things that appear in *Othello* – the handkerchief and the wedding sheets – are redolent of female associations. The handkerchief, that magic web passed down from sibyl to Egyptian sorceress to mother to wife, becomes a massive projection of the fears anciently bound up in the weaving metaphor. And the wedding sheets where Othello meets his end are another such externalization. It is from amongst these sheets that the dying Othello appeals for the last time for a return to the safe, traditional, single mode of epic utterance – the single thread which he continues to hope will lead him out of the hateful, fateful labyrinth of his anxiety.

The act of re-telling promises to order experience, and to re-integrate the events of the play. Yet this is made ironic not only by the play's insistence from the very beginning on the disturbing and destructive power of story-telling, but also by the fact that the tale inevitably disintegrates and fragments as each spectator, each member of the audience departs and goes a separate way. Like Penelope's tapestry, the text that held together for a few hours on the stage is rent, unravelled, undone, to be endlessly reconstituted and re-woven with every successive performance through time.

---

[23] Peter Stallybrass, 'Patriarchal Territories: The Body Enclosed', in *Rewriting the Renaissance: The Discourses of Sexual Difference in Early Modern Europe*, ed. Margaret Ferguson, Maureen Quilligan, and Nancy Vickers (Chicago: University of Chicago Press, 1986), p. 137.

'THAT'S SHE THAT WAS MYSELF': NOT-SO-FAMOUS LAST WORDS AND SOME ENDS OF *OTHELLO*

THOMAS CLAYTON

I

To those for whom Shakespeare's plays still have value as works of dramatic and poetic art that move and enlighten the receptive, the last words of his tragic protagonists and other major characters should be of special interest and importance as momentous and definitive, because they evidently were for Shakespeare, whether composing or revising, and beginning quite early on, in *Richard III* and *Richard II*, for example; but they seem to take on special resonance and significance in the later tragedies, notably A. C. Bradley's Big Four, and also *Antony and Cleopatra* and *Timon of Athens*.[1]

II

Shakespeare constructed the ending of *Othello* in such a way that Desdemona and Othello both expire on the terminal note of a single heroic couplet, each concerned primarily and affectionately with the other. Othello's last lines have been noticed often enough, and Desdemona's, too, especially in recent years; but they have seldom been attended to in any detail and their significant complementarity has apparently gone unnoticed, no doubt partly because 'Soft you, a word or two ... And smote him thus' – Othello's 'last great speech', in T. S. Eliot's phrase – has come so to dominate almost every kind of commentary on the endplay.[2] But the complementarity was evidently deliberate, not fortuitous, and this seems to be Shakespeare's first dramatic and dialogical expression *in*

extremis of special endplay effects of the kind inchoate in *Hamlet* and extended further in *Othello* and further still in *King Lear* and *Antony and Cleopatra*, the latter three of which match a dying protagonist with a dead loved one. It is of interest also because in *Othello* the lines speak for themselves in a way almost independent of variations in performance. In the later plays the same intense yearning is expressed in ways that *must* be conveyed substantially in action as well as, perhaps as much as, in words: the actor's Lear *himself* must somehow, somewhere, 'look there, look there'; and Cleopatra must make her way between the world of worms whose kingdoms are clay, and the real or fancied Elysium 'where souls do couch on flowers' and Antony had anticipated that their 'sprightly port [would] make the ghosts gaze' (4.15.51, 52).[3]

---

[1] I am indebted to R. W. Dent, Jay L. Halio, Jongsook Lee, George Sheets, Kari Steinbach, and Virginia Mason Vaughan for valuable comments and suggestions; and to the Graduate School of the University of Minnesota for a grant in aid of research.

[2] 'Shakespeare and the Stoicism of Seneca', *Selected Essays*, new edn (New York, 1950), p. 110.

[3] For discussion of related terminal dialogue and action in *King Lear* and *Antony and Cleopatra*, see Thomas Clayton, '"Is this the promis'd end?" Revision in the Role of the King', *The Division of the Kingdoms: Shakespeare's Two Versions of 'King Lear'*, ed. by Gary Taylor and Michael Warren (Oxford, 1983), pp. 121–41; and '"Mysterious by This Love": The Unregenerate Resurrection of Antony and Cleopatra', *Jadavpur University Essays and Studies III, Special Issue: Festschrift in Honour of S. C. Sengupta*, ed. by Jagannath Chakravorty (Calcutta, 1982), pp. 95–116.

At least since Thomas Rymer, two conflicting Othellos have persisted, the sympathetic Noble Moor that I take to be Shakespeare's, and the other one, 'loving his own pride and purposes' and given to evasions 'with a bombast circumstance', an Othello malformed and perpetuated by racial bigotry beginning in the play itself with these phrases of Iago's. In the nineteenth century, when travesties were in high fashion, there was at least one mocking minstrel-show *Othello* and a lame and lengthy travesty of this popular target. Subsequently liberated from overt *racial* bias, Othello has more recently been condemned as a militarist and patriarch, occasionally with necrophiliac tendencies.[4] Such negative judgements seem gratuitous, sometimes downright ethnocentric; but my purpose here is not to argue the case of character yet once more, as such, but to concentrate on details of the endplay, notably Desdemona's and Othello's last lines, their context, content, and reference. Evidently these were – are – important components of Shakespeare's design, whatever the qualities of Othello the (critic's) man. But if these terminal couplets taken together mean as they appear to mean, then a rereading of Shakespeare's tragedy in modified perspective necessarily follows: of a play in which the tragedy of a *sympathetic* Moor *must* be the action intended, and as such is subtly, potently, and movingly concluded. Recognizing intentional design does not compel concurrence, of course, but it reasonably invites reflection and might give pause.

III

In September 1610, when the King's Men performed *Othello* in Oxford, Henry Jackson of Corpus Christi College was affected as deeply by a motionless player as by the dialogue and kinetic action. In a letter, he wrote (in Latin) that 'assuredly that rare Desdemona, killed in front of us by her husband, although she consistently pleaded her cause eloquently, nevertheless was more moving dead, when, as she lay

still on her bed, her facial expression alone implored the pity of spectators'.[5] It *is* striking, as Julie Hankey has written of Jackson's account, that 'there is no mention of Othello's blackness. He is simply a "husband", and she (though a boy, "she" enough) his victim.'[6] It is also Shakespearian: Desdemona herself says that she 'saw Othello's visage in his mind' (1.3.252), where colour is as colour does. Only a spectator could respond to the eloquence of silence in quite this way, but even the terminal dialogue of the lovers waited upon time for critical attention. As late as 1957 it could be noted that, though 'the full import of the story is made clear in Othello's last speech', that speech 'is seldom given the attention it merits';[7] that is, the 'Soft you, a word or two' speech. By now, that 'last speech' has been much written on, usually with reference to Eliot's famous assessment of 1927: 'I have always felt that I have never read a more terrible exposure of human weakness – of universal human weakness – than *the last great speech* of Othello . . . What Othello seems to me to be doing in making this speech

---

[4] For the last, see Stanley Cavell, 'Epistemology and Tragedy: A Reading of *Othello*', *Daedalus* 108 (1979), repr. in *William Shakespeare's 'Othello': Modern Critical Interpretations*, ed. by Harold Bloom (New York, 1987), p. 16; Stephen Greenblatt, 'The Improvisation of Power', *Renaissance Self-Fashioning: From More to Shakespeare* (Chicago, 1980), p. 252; and Janet Stavropoulos, 'Love and Age in *Othello*', *Shakespeare Studies*, 19 (1987), 135, which is more emphatic ('a perverted *pietà*').

[5] 'At vero Desdemona illa apud nos a marito occisa, quanquam optimè semper causam egit, interfecta tamen magis movebat; cum in lecto decumbens spectantium misericordiam ipso vultu imploraret.' Corpus Library's Fulman Papers, vol. 10, ff. 83ᵛ–84ʳ, printed by Geoffrey Tillotson, together with detailed comments on 'Othello and *The Alchemist* at Oxford in 1610', in the *TLS*, 20 July 1933, p. 494, whence the Latin is quoted here.

[6] *Plays in Performance: 'Othello'* (Bristol, 1987), p. 18.

[7] Albert Gerard, ' "Egregiously an Ass": The Dark Side of the Moor. A View of Othello's Mind', *Shakespeare Survey* 10 (1957), repr. in *Aspects of 'Othello': Articles Reprinted from 'Shakespeare Survey'*, ed. by Kenneth Muir and Philip Edwards (Cambridge, 1977), p. 19.

is *cheering himself up* . . . I do not believe that any writer has ever exposed this *bovarysme*, the human will to see things as they are not, more clearly than Shakespeare.'[8]

'The last great speech' is where critics' contending Othellos rise or fall. In 1984 Norman Sanders wrote in his New Cambridge edition that 'the greatest disagreement' is between those for whom the '*last great speech* (5.2.334–52) re-elevates the hero to his former grandeur and nobility' and 'those who consider the Moor merely credulous and foolish', for whom 'T. S. Eliot may speak in his notorious condemnation of the death speech' (p. 24, italics mine). Discussion of Othello's 'last speech' has not seldom been bedevilled by ambiguity, though 'Othello's last *great* speech' is obviously enough 'Soft you, a word or two'. It is *not* his 'final lines', however, although at least one recent critic apparently believes they are, because that is what he called them in 1989.[9] Othello's entire *last utterance* is the heroic couplet, 'I kissed thee ere I killed thee. No way but this: / Killing myself, to die upon a kiss', followed in the New Cambridge edition by the stage direction, '*He [falls on the bed and] dies*' (5.2.354–5); and in the Oxford edition by '*He kisses Desdemona and dies*' (5.2.369). In both, only 'He dies' comes from a substantive text (Q; 'Dyes' F), but the couplet implies Oxford's stage direction, and the reference to 'the tragic loading [F; lodging Q] of this bed' justifies the New Cambridge expansion.[10]

The usually scant attention paid to *these* lines by critics who discuss them at all may be due not only to the lightning rod of the preceding 'great speech' but also to the history of performance and the received impression conveyed by earlier reviews and criticism. Writing recently on *Othello* 5.2 in performance,[11] James R. Siemon notes that during the years 1766–1900 'Othello appears almost never to have been allowed to die upon a kiss', because, in forty-five of fifty-two prompt-books of the period (86.5 per cent), 'the lines about having kissed Desdemona before he

killed her are missing, either through cutting or omission' (p. 49). Nearly half (23 of the 52, 44 per cent) 'end the play on some version of his suicide lines – "I took by the throat the circumcised dog, / And smote him thus" – adding sometimes an invented exclamation – "O Desdemona" – to this rather abrupt end.' Although this personal exclamation is an emaciated substitute, it is fair to note that it has at least the right focus, direction, and potential spirit.

Since the Procrustean practice of truncating the play thus is no longer common, *that* cannot account for critics' scant attention to Othello's last words, so the relative silence may well be due to a pervasive sense that the play is over, or ought to be, when he stabs himself at 'smote him thus' – because (it may be thought) whatever follows is redundant if not anticlimactic. Leslie Fiedler is partly of this turn of mind, writing that *Othello*'s

is a world whose central symbol is the sword, the phallic significance of which Shakespeare takes pains to make clear . . . [K]nowing himself his own dearest enemy, his potency was magically restored, though only long enough for him to die and, dying, kiss the cold lips of a corpse. 'To die upon a kiss', he says, . . . evoking the pun, which Shakespeare so much loved, on 'die' meaning 'come' as well as 'go'. What stays in our minds, however, is not Othello's closing erotic couplet, but the longer speech, . . . a speech whose central images come from politics and war.[12]

---

8 'Shakespeare and the Stoicism of Seneca', p. 111, italics mine.

9 See James L. Calderwood, 'Signs, Speech, and Self', *The Properties of 'Othello'* (Amherst, 1989), p. 109.

10 The 1793 (+ 1803, 1813) variorum edition of Shakespeare's *Works*, vol. 15, contains Steevens's acute citation of antecedent lines by Marlowe's dying Zenocrate that is not in Furness's New Variorum *Othello* (1886) or in many if any subsequent editions: 'So, in the Second Part of Marlowe's *Tamburlaine*, 1590: "Yet let me kiss my lord before I dye, / And let me dye with kissing of my lord"' (2.4.69–70).

11 '"Nay, that's not the text": *Othello*, v.ii in performance, 1766–1900', *Shakespeare Quarterly*, 37 (1986), 38–51.

Fiedler could be right, but 'our' minds suggests the confidently supposed unanimity of a collective *reader's* perspective, not the auditor–spectators' for whom the plays are especially designed; and in performance Othello's last moments *and lines* are often powerfully moving and *therefore* memorable, like Desdemona's mute and monumental eloquence for Henry Jackson in 1610; for some, at least as affecting and memorable as the longer speech preceding.

To the sympathetic, Othello's 'last great speech' is a reasoned, self-possessed, and earnestly purposeful as well as ineluctably 'rhetorical' appeal – by a frank and honest, honourable, and responsible man, even a hero, eloquent by custom or even nature – for just judgement of himself that is made no less to the outer audience *of* the play than to his immediate audience in Cyprus. It is thus doubly a public as well as personal speech, an extemporaneous and thoroughly natural 'oration' very like his first public speech, beginning 'Most potent, grave, and reverend signors', which led to his account of his courtship (1.3.76–94, 127–69). Having appealed for others' justice in 'Soft you', he concludes with his own by executing himself. Surviving the first cut like Antony in the later play, he turns forever from public speech and the world to the private vein of personal intimacy to address his last words, a heroic couplet, to the body of the wife he had loved not wisely but too well, had killed, and loves again. Jealousy is *not* a 'mature' emotion, but it is a painful fact of amatory life at one time or another for most who live and love.

M. C. Bradbrook has written that 'the ending must be felt as triumphal; the ritual of the kiss is spousal',[13] and the late Helen Gardner that 'the close of Othello should leave us at peace', and she quotes *The Phoenix and Turtle* (1601): 'Death is now the phoenix' nest, / And the turtle's loyal breast / To eternity doth rest' (lines 56–8).[14] These readings share a kind of 'dramatic optimism', which might well be

called for and I should not deplore, but it is a dire strait of mind from Brecht's agitprop-oriented perspective. There remains a tenable position neither alienated nor uplifted, dark, perhaps, but no less sympathetic. In tragedies of this kind a balance is characteristically struck between the irreversible loss and the glory of what might have been, which is known as such for what it has been. What was great and potentially greater, once lost, holds good for what it was and memorially remains.

IV

Donne and Shakespeare – in his extreme vein as metaphysical poet in *The Phoenix and Turtle* just quoted – afford access to what the playwright has provided formally and emotionally by way of endplay in *Othello*, where he has first wife, then husband, dying separately yet together not only by the force of thought and feeling for the other, but – beyond character – by form, the heroic couplet of terminal expression that Shakespeare makes them share. In answer to Emilia's 'O, who hath done this deed?' Desdemona's first-line-abbreviated couplet is of course 'Nobody, I myself. Farewell. / Commend me to my kind lord. O, farewell!' (5.2.133–4). Each speaks last of the other in his and her own way, the same way.

The terminal heroic couplets *are* bound together – by prosodic form, by the loving concentration of each speaker on the other, and by the implication of mutual affection not

12 Leslie Fiedler, 'The Moor as Stranger; or, "Almost Damned in a Fair Wife"', *The Stranger in Shakespeare* (New York, 1972), p. 194.

13 M. C. Bradbrook, 'Images of Love and War: *Othello, Coriolanus, Antony and Cleopatra*', *The Living Monument: Shakespeare and the Theatre of His Time* (Cambridge, 1976), p. 167. Also see her *Shakespeare: The Poet in His World* (New York, 1978), pp. 176–9.

14 Helen Gardner, 'The Noble Moor' (1955), *Interpretations of Shakespeare: British Academy Shakespeare Lectures*, ed. by Kenneth Muir (Oxford, 1985), p. 179.

physically reciprocated but restored finally in mortality by the force of like minds and hearts expressing something understood, not strictly comprehensible but *apprehensible* by the imagination shared by lovers, lunatics, poets, spectators suspending disbelief. If this design goes unnoticed, obviously there will be no such mortal and delicate convergence. Anything may be dismissed or smirked out of court, of course, but once seen in this light, the design will not easily be forgotten. It consists further and especially in the shared use of 'myself' to invoke an ancient, Judeo-Christian, and proverbial idea about the unity of friends and lovers that goes back through Cicero to Aristotle's *Nichomachean Ethics* (9.4.5/1166a.32), where 'the friend is another self', even to the *Iliad* in one tradition; and to the Old Testament, where husband and wife are supposed to become one flesh, in another.[15]

V

The sharing of 'my[]self' with the other is a key element in the complement of terminal couplets. Both lovers are made to use prominently and emphatically the personal pronoun 'myself' – or possessive pronoun 'my' with noun 'self' as it was in the Quarto of 1622 and the Folio of 1623. The identification of friend or lover as a second self, or of two as being a single, compound self, was a commonplace in Shakespeare's day. A dramatic use close in time to *Othello* is Henry Porter's in *Two Angry Women of Abingdon* acted by the Lord Admiral's Men in 1598, the year before Porter died: 'O my wife, you are my selfe' (sig. c4, 3.520 f.). And *very* close in time to the composition of *Othello*, John Florio's translation of Montaigne's essay 'Of Friendship' (1603) says that

In the amitie I speake of, they [friends] entermixe and confound themselves one in the other, with so universall a commixture, that they weare out, and can no more find the seame that hath conjoyned them together. If a man urged me to tell wherefore I loved him, I feel it cannot be expressed, but by

answering; 'Because it was he, because it was my selfe.'[16]

Mystical vision, philosophical conception, metaphysical conceit are almost as much a matter of degree and direction as of kind. Given these ranging variations on a theme common from antiquity, it is not surprising to find in *The Two Gentlemen of Verona* a sentiment and expression that, though expanded and explicit instead of condensed and allusive, is very like that in *Othello*. Valentine in soliloquy, banished on pain of death by Silvia's father, asks,

And why not death, rather than living torment?
To die is to be banished from myself,
And Silvia is my self. Banished from her
Is self from self, a deadly banishment . . .
She is my essence, and I leave to be
If I be not by her fair influence
Fostered, illumined, cherished, kept alive.
I fly not death to fly his deadly doom.
Tarry I here I but attend on death,
But fly I hence, I fly away from life.

(3.1.170–3, 182–7)

VI

The *plot* of *Othello* is captured well by its notorious arch-critic Thomas Rymer himself:

Othello, a Blackmoor [sic] Captain, by talking of his Prowess and Feats of War, makes Desdemona a Senators Daughter to be in love with him; and to be married to him without her Parents knowledge; and having preferred Cassio, to be his Lieutenant, (a place which his ensign Jago sued for) Jago in revenge, works the Moor into a Jealousy that Cassio Cuckolds him: which he effects by stealing and conveying a certain Handkerchief, which had, at the Wedding, been by the Moor presented to his Bride. Hereupon, Othello and Jago plot the Deaths of

---

15 *Iliad* 18.89–92 (Achilleus of the dead Patroklos, 'even as mine own self', '*ison eme kephale*'); Genesis 2.23–4 (Geneva translation).
16 Florio, *Montaigne's Essays*, 1632 edn, ed. by J. I. M. Stewart (London, 1931), vol. 1, pp. 190–1.

Desdemona and Cassio, Othello Murders her, and soon after is convinced of her Innocence. And as he is about to be carried to Prison, in order to be punish'd for the Murder, He kills himself.

What ever rubs or difficulty may stick on the Bark, the Moral, sure, of this Fable is very instructive.

First, This may be a caution to all Maidens of Quality how, without their Parents consent, they run away with Blackamoors....

Secondly, this may be a warning to all good Wives, that they look well to their Linnen.

Thirdly, This may be a lesson to Husbands, that before their Jealousie be Tragical, the proofs be Mathematical.[17]

The morals are heavily facetious, but *Othello is* in its way a casque-to-cushion domestic tragedy, and commonplaces of the kind are indeed present – though they are assumed and more or less marginal, hardly the heart of the matter. The art of the design is that on the one hand it achieves simultaneously the building of a strong foundation in a plausibly intuitive mutual understanding and deep affection both sexual and otherwise personal between an in-experienced but perceptive and forceful young woman, and an older, black military officer of North African royal 'siege' (1.2.22), of high station by both birth and achievement, and of wide experience of wars and diplomacy but not of domestic affairs of the heart. And, on the other hand, it enables their destruction by the agency of a relentlessly machinating malefactor of universally acknowledged 'honesty' who uses the trust he has earned in military service, his observation and understanding of human vulnerability, and the very virtues of his victims the lovers as the leverage to destroy them. Raised to the scale of tragedy, but otherwise just like 'real life': *How To Win Friends* ...

The inclusive tragedy is, then, that lovers extraordinarily well suited to each other and capable of the greatest mutual love, despite appearances to the contrary and obvious but superficial obstacles, are forced into separation – permanent or temporary but mortal – by death almost as soon as they begin to reap the marital harvest of their goodness and compatibility. Goodness revealed proclaims its vulnerability unawares and invites attack – in *Othello* by the redoubled force of its eternal opposite in a form, a person, least likely to be recognized as such. It is surely a fact not only that if Iago were the Moor, he would not be Iago; but that, if Iago were not Iago, there would be no *tragedy* of *Othello, the Moor of Venice.*

VII

The final moments of the endplay follow hard upon Desdemona's dying. Having cried out that she has been 'falsely, falsely murdered!' (5.2.126) and then assured Emilia who has come to her that 'a guiltless death I die' (132), she replies to Emilia's 'O, who hath done this deed?' in her terminal couplet extemporized immediately though in some confusion to exonerate Othello. His innocence of culpable design would seem to have been somehow on her mind, since in the Willow Song (in F, not in Q) she had sung '"Let nobody blame him, his scorn I approve" – ', then quickly reflecting, 'Nay, that's not next.' In her terminal couplet, 'Nobody' is an instinctive deflecting of Emilia's question and an impossible answer, though it obviously has a tacit, unintended application to an Othello not himself. Her second answer, 'I myself', is all but impossible, yet the only option open to her without naming Othello, making false accusation, or inventing a suspect even as she dies. It is supremely apt and ironical precisely because, insofar as she is wife, friend, lover, she *is* Othello as he her; she himself *did* kill herself, through his corporal agency. Her next 'move' can most reasonably be taken as a natural continuation of her thinking singlemindedly of Othello from the moment she has uttered 'Nobody'. Othello, the nobody for the nonce, presents his demobilized self as no longer the soldier that he was. Desdemona dies

---

17 *The Critical Works of Thomas Rymer*, ed. by Curt A. Zimansky (New Haven, 1956), p. 132.

true to her word, to herself, to Othello: as she had said, prophetically as is seen in retrospect, 'his unkindness may defeat my life, / But never taint my love' (4.2.164–5).

Othello at bay and near the end, 'Enter Lodovico' (5.2.288 +), who asks the generically and thematically epic and tragic as well as contextually practical question, 'Where is this rash and most unfortunate man?' (289). Othello's answer: 'That's he that was Othello. Here I am' (290), I, nobody. There are many ways of explicating this, but even a modest gloss would note that the diminished and isolated Othello feels himself unmanned and sees Desdemona as though bearing his sometime manhood into death, so much in consonance with the independent spirit she displayed in 1.3, the Court Scene, especially in the speech beginning, 'That I did love the Moor to live with him, / My downright violence and storm [F; scorne Q] of fortunes / May trumpet to the world' (1.3.248–50). Such public forthrightness, there, is of a piece with her earlier hinting privately to Othello of her feelings for him when she 'bade me, if I had a friend that loved her, / I should but teach him how to tell my story, / And that would woo her' (1.3.163–5). Thus there was aptness as well as affection in Othello's greeting her on his arrival in Cyprus as 'my fair warrior' (2.1.183), of which we see more when she promises Cassio to champion his cause: 'Assure thee, / If I do vow a friendship I'll perform it / To the last article' (3.3.20–2).

If Desdemona shows – an engagingly – youthful impetuousness in some ways, she shows maturity and even wisdom in others, here also epitomizing on behalf of the playwright, as it were, the tragedy of Othello himself:

> Something sure of state,
> Either from Venice or some unhatched practice
> Made demonstrable here in Cyprus to him,
> Hath puddled his clear spirit; and in such cases
> Men's natures wrangle with inferior things,
> Though great ones are their object. 'Tis even so;
> For let our finger ache and it indues

> Our other, healthful members even to a sense
> Of pain. Nay, we must think men are not gods,
> Nor of them look for such observancy
> As fits the bridal. Beshrew me much, Emilia,
> I was – unhandsome *warrior* as I am –
> Arraigning his unkindness with my soul;
> But now I find I had suborned the witness,
> And he's indicted falsely.[18]

(3.4.138–52 recalling 2.1.183, italics mine)

These lines look forward to Desdemona's first 'falsely murdered' and subsequent revision in defence of Othello; she did not know it, nor did 'we', but *in extremis* and in retrospect that is seen to be the case.

Disarmed and nearing his end, Othello continues to express his sense of lost manhood: 'I am not valiant neither, / But every puny whipster gets my sword. / But why should honour outlive honesty? / Let it go all' (5.2.250–3). For a moment, he would even have Iago 'live; / For in my sense 'tis happiness to die' (5.2.295–6). Desdemona dead, how could it be otherwise for him, especially to live in knowledge of his guilt? The earlier lines' suggesting a kind of transmigration of soul between lovers who share it informs Othello's last words and his agonized awareness of lovers' union violently sundered by him: 'I kissed thee ere I killed thee. No way but this [of kissing and killing]: / Killing myself [i.e., killing, now, my own self; having killed myself already, the self you were – that's she and he that was Othello – and (here) I am], to die upon a kiss' – as though, having killed the better part of himself in Desdemona, he now justly executes the worse part – Iago's – in himself, in his own way, himself the kisser and the kissed, honour following honesty in

---

[18] These lines and 3.3.193–6 strongly reflect (on) each other, and on the resort of each speaker to notions of justice, trial, and proof: 'No, Iago, / I'll see before I doubt; when I doubt, prove; / And on the proof, there is no more but this: / Away at once with love or jealousy.' Desdemona *is* more trusting than Othello, but it is also not she but he who is *driven* to disbelief and jealousy as 'abused by some most villainous knave, / Some base, notorious knave, some scurvy fellow' (4.2.143–4).

death, his life upon her faith. Othello rises by his falling, if his tragic movements are read aright. At least that is how Shakespeare seems to have intended them by their design.

VIII

If this reading of complementary terminal couplets in the endplay and the context of the whole is true to the overall dialogue and its significance, and to what may reasonably be taken to be the feelings of the principals as they would be performed by actors in an unforced reading, then on such accounts it may be taken to express in some measure the meanings intended by the play(wright). The design of the earlier part of the play will adjust itself in critical perspective to this conclusion accordingly. Unstrained productions tend to confirm this reading by presenting both Desdemona and Othello sympathetically – as they were presented with great success in Trevor Nunn's 1989 studio production first at The Other Place and then at the Young Vic, with the black opera singer Willard White as Othello, and Imogen Stubbs as a youthful and very forceful Desdemona; and as they were in an effective London fringe production, also with a black Othello (Gary Lawrence, with Louise Butcher as Desdemona), by the Court Theatre Company in mid August 1992.

One must agree with Fiedler that Othello's 'potency' *is* restored as he kills himself, and there is a sense in which his utterance and sentiment are undoubtedly 'erotic'. But it is doubtful whether his last couplet is fraught with the explicitly sexual sense of 'kill' and 'die' occasionally employed in Jacobethan usage, including Shakespeare's, though it may easily be argued thematically into place in several interpretative dialectics. Whatever the comprehensive particulars of meaning and significance of the terminal couplets, a finally *positive* resonance seems designed for each, and their correspondency 'unites' Desdemona and Othello – before an audience – in still life and by death forever and absolutely, in their own

way like Romeo and Juliet, and Antony and Cleopatra.

The question whether Othello achieves 'adequate' recognition of his guilt and some profound insight into the Meaning of Things – so well understood by post-Victorian critics requiring no less of tragic heroes – is in the play not so much answered unequivocally as benignly begged in the ineluctable irony and pathos of the endplay. The lovers are united in peace *only* at the violent end of a fleeting married life in which they were able to be together undisturbed virtually for moments only, from the beginning of the action to the end. The irony is made almost unbearable by the survival of the lovers' destroyer, whose shadow cast over the life of the play extends beyond the end of the action in the BBC-TV production (1981), where Bob Hoskins' mocking laughter continues to echo through the screen credits even after he has been led down a corridor and out of sight. The script, so far from translating the horror of the spectacle into terms even of solace, much less of transcendence, frames it before its maker-marrer, Iago, a tale tolled once and for all.

And yet, Desdemona and Othello are at last beyond the reach of envious malice, and theirs is implicitly some version of a peace that passeth all understanding, whether heavenly bliss secured or in prospect, or the nitrogen cycle not yet even dreamt of. So much for the irony. The play's plenitude of Christian reference – more in its own day than in ours – may shed prevenient grace upon the endplay and imply a hope of resurrection and reunion. But even if death is seen as final, there is the sweet oblivious antidote of nothingness, the pain of which is only in the spectacle, the eye of the beholder, the present the dead have passed beyond.

The pathos of the persons is simplicity itself. There can hardly be a greater human loss to death than that of spouse by loving, living spouse, a loss beyond enduring when the living spouse has brought about the death. That is the ultimate tragedy of Othello the Man. How indeed *could* Honour outlive Honesty?

'THE CATASTROPHE IS A NUPTIAL': THE SPACE OF MASCULINE DESIRE IN *OTHELLO*, *CYMBELINE*, AND *THE WINTER'S TALE*

LAWRENCE DANSON

I want in this essay to listen to some of Shakespeare's jealous husbands as they discover the pathos and panic of male sexuality within a marital economy of masculine possessiveness. Since my attention to the suffering of *men* may seem perverse, let me begin by acknowledging the infinitely greater impositions of that economy on women. Petruccio's boast – 'I will be master of what is mine own. / She is my goods, my chattels. She is my house, / My household-stuff, my field, my barn, / My horse, my ox, my ass, my anything' (3.3.101–4) – may conceal or reveal whatever lovable little ironies it wants, but still it registers the plain facts of the Elizabethan laws of coverture. Modern historians who disagree on other matters agree on this: thus Lawrence Stone writes that 'By marriage, the husband and wife became one person in law – and that person was the husband. He acquired absolute control of all his wife's personal property, which he could sell at will'; and Martin Ingram, who thinks that Stone exaggerates the iron claim of patriarchy and underestimates the role of affection in Elizabethan marriage, writes that 'married women had no property rights independent of their husbands; while the law prescribed that "the husband hath ... power and dominion over his wife, and may keep her by force within the bonds of duty, and may beat her" (albeit not in "a violent and cruel manner")'. Ann Jennalie Cook quotes a 1632 treatise called *The Lawes Resolutions of Womens Rights*: '"*That which the Husband hath is his owne*", while "*That which the Wife hath is the Husbands*"': 'At the end of the wedding day', Cook writes, 'the woman yielded up her body, her name, and her worldly goods.'[1]

So I start my discussion of men's problems with Othello, who was 'taken by the insolent foe / And sold to slavery' (1.3.136–7) and is therefore the only one of Shakespeare's jealous husbands who has himself been the property of another person and therefore been subjected to something comparable to the status of a married woman. We know tantalizingly little about Othello's life as a slave except that it was not the condition to which he was born; rather, he fetches his 'life and being / From men of royal siege' (1.2.21–2), a lineage that stresses the privileges both of patriarchy and royalty. But possibly because Othello has known both extremes of an economy in which human beings can be chattel, he articulates, in one of the most astonishing lines of psychic suffering torn from the self-tormentings of Shakespeare's jealous men, the terror that undermines the privilege of male possessiveness: 'O curse of marriage, / That we can call these delicate creatures ours / And not their appetites' (3.3.272–4). The line undoes itself, I suggest, in much the way that the ideology of marital possessiveness repeatedly undoes itself in Shake-

---

[1] Stone, *The Family, Sex and Marriage in England 1500–1800*, abridged edn (New York, 1979), p. 136; Ingram, *Church Courts, Sex and Marriage in England 1570–1640* (Cambridge, 1987), p. 143; Cook, *Making A Match: Courtship in Shakespeare and His Society* (Princeton, 1991), p. 166.

speare. The unconstrainable residue Othello calls 'appetite' – the always and inevitably unconstrainable residue: "Tis destiny unshunnable, like death. / Even then this forkèd plague is fated to us / When we do quicken' (3.3.279–81) – denies what the depersonalizing epithet 'creature' tries to affirm. In effect Othello's line puts a self-possessed human being, the owner of her own appetites, in exactly the space where it tries to posit the possessible product of masculine creation. In marriage, woman's 'appetite' ought to be under male control, but 'appetite', like 'honour', is 'an essence that's not seen' (4.1.16). Bloody sheets on the marriage morning betoken what a husband can take but say nothing about what a wife can withhold. Slaves know that something is always withheld from the master; married men, like Othello, fear it until they too believe they know it.

Othello's 'O curse of marriage, / That we can call these delicate creatures ours / And not their appetites' both defines and undoes a specific construction of marriage, one based on the unfulfillable imperative of masculine possessiveness.[2] Through a verbal quibble, the line also hints at a potentially tragic contradiction in the way the gendered human subject is defined within the possessive regime of marriage. It says that 'we' men cannot have a woman's appetites as 'ours': the status of the pronoun is in question – as, to take a comparable case, it is when Prospero says of Caliban, 'This thing of darkness I / Acknowledge mine' (*Tempest* 5.1.278–9); and also in question is the definition of *property* that the possessive pronoun draws with it, a definition which extends (as James Calderwood has reminded us) from 'the outward sense of "things owned"' to 'the inward sense of "a defining quality, characteristic, attribute"', in the sense of that which is proper to me.[3] So 'we' men cannot call these delicate creatures' appetites 'ours' not only because 'we' can never be sure 'we' fully own or control a property that can't be seen, but also because 'we' define a woman's

appetite as something always alien, the defining attribute or property of the other, the always not-ours.

In the generalized realm of Othello's 'we' and 'ours', men feel jealous of whatever in female appetite is beyond their sole possessing ('I had rather be a toad / And live upon the vapour of a dungeon / Than keep a corner in the thing I love / For others' uses' [3.3.274–7]), and jealous also because men are inevitably excluded from experiencing a woman's appetite as their proper own. That exclusion is caused in part by the biological facts of different sexualities but it is in part also a socially conditioned self-exclusion. In order to call these delicate creatures' appetites ours, 'we' men would have to know those appetites, experience them as proper to us rather than fear them as something alien; so that for a man to accomplish the proprietary imperative of marriage he would, in effect, have to become what he's made woman to be, and thus undo precisely the mastery of the accomplishment.

What we call Othello's jealousy, then, is, as Stanley Cavell has written, 'directed to the sheer existence of the other, its separateness from him'.[4] I'd add to Cavell's account that such jealousy is not only produced by difference but is itself productive of difference: it is an effect of Othello's desire to know that Desdemona is fully possessed by him at the same time that he estranges – constructs as foreign, unknowable to him – the female sexuality

[2] Cf. Katharine Eisaman Maus, 'Horns of Dilemma: Jealousy, Gender, and Spectatorship in English Renaissance Drama', *ELH*, 54 (1987), 561–83: '[Othello] laments an arrangement that grants men ownership of women but which cannot grant them the usual correlatives of possession, knowledge and control', p. 578.

[3] *The Properties of* 'Othello' (Amherst, Mass., 1989), p. 10.

[4] *Disowning Knowledge in Six Plays of Shakespeare* (Cambridge, 1987), p. 9. Cavell adds, 'The violence in masculine knowing, explicitly associated with jealousy, seems to interpret the ambition of knowledge as that of exclusive possession, call it private property', p. 10.

which he *will* not possess because it threatens his masculine sense of self. In the bafflement of his desire for possession the jealous husband creates an elusive, interiorized space within woman, a space he can open but can never fill, neither by phallic penetration nor by imaginative speculation into the metaphorical space of his wife's appetitive freedom. This is the space for erotic exploration which proprietary desire converts into the goal of colonial exploitation, a female interior to be claimed in the name of a patriarchal crown.[5]

The jealous husband's tropism towards his wife's elusive interior converts an economic and social imperative of possession into a powerful because always thwarted erotics. Donne's 'Elegy 19: To His Mistress Going to Bed' makes explicit the analogy between an individualized consciousness of masculine sexual proprietorship and its global political equivalent:

> License my roaving hands, and let them go
> Before, behind, between, above, below.
> O my America! my new-found-land,
> My kingdome, safeliest when with one man man'd,
> My Myne of precious stones, My Emperie,
> How blest am I in this discovering thee![6]

Later in this essay we'll hear how Donne's 'How blest am I' is answered by Leontes' 'How accurst in being so blest': America's a big country, and the imperializing claim to possess her singly, to man her with one man, is mocked by the vastness the roving hands discover. In Shakespeare, the eroticized discovery of the new found land of female interiority engenders an endless anxiety: the more open a woman is made by her husband's jealous speculation or erotic attention the more available she is to occupation by other men, 'the general camp, / Pioneers and all' (3.3.350–1). Even conception, which might be thought to fill a space literalized, now, as what Elizabethan obstetrics characterized as a mobile and greedy womb, only increases male anxiety about possessing that which is within.[7] Possessive desire for the

unseen essence shapes the space 'we' men want to fill with proprietary knowledge, but that space 'we' shape becomes the 'you' compounded precisely of the absence of knowledge.

Materialist critics have claimed that the 'unified subject of liberal humanism' (in Catherine Belsey's phrase) is a product of the late seventeenth-century bourgeois ascendancy; its supposedly self-possessed interiority 'is a chimera, an effect of language, not its origin'. Francis Barker looks into the heart of Shakespeare's most famously interiorized character and finds that 'At the centre of Hamlet, in the interior of his mystery, there is, in short, nothing. The promised essence remains beyond the scope of the text's signification; or rather, signals the limit of the signification of this world by marking out the site of an absence it cannot fill.'[8] I find these analyses of the interiorized character persuasive, only I want to claim that, here as elsewhere, Shakespeare anticipated both his critics and the historical event: Shakespeare's jealous husband is the precursor, in a sense the progenitor, of that bourgeois critic who in Barker's scheme empties his own fears and desire into the bottomless textual space. We

---

[5] On male efforts to control the female body, see Peter Stallybrass, 'Patriarchal Territories: The Body Enclosed' in Margaret W. Ferguson, Maureen Quilligan, Nancy J. Vickers, eds., *Rewriting the Renaissance: The Discourse of Sexual Difference in Early Modern Europe* (Chicago, 1986), pp. 123–42; Linda Woodbridge, 'Palisading the Elizabethan Body Politic', *Texas Studies in Literature and Language*, 33 (1991), 327–54; Georgianna Ziegler, 'My Lady's Chamber: Female Space, Female Chastity in Shakespeare', *Textual Practice*, 4 (1990), 73–90.

[6] *The Poems of John Donne*, ed. Sir Herbert Grierson (Oxford, 1933), lines 25–31.

[7] Audrey Eccles, *Obstetrics and Gynecology in Tudor and Stuart England* (Kent, Ohio, 1982), quotes a text by Guillemeau: 'In some Women the wombe is so greedy, and lickerish that it doth euen come down to meet nature, sucking, and (as it were) snatching the same, though it remaine only about the mouth and entrance of the outward orifice thereof' (p. 29).

[8] Belsey, *The Subject of Tragedy* (London, 1985), pp. 33, 54; Barker, *The Tremulous Private Body* (London, 1984), p. 37.

see something like that process at work in Othello's language when he turns Desdemona into an ambiguously fluid site and source:

> But there where I have garnered up my heart,
> Where either I must live or bear no life,
> The fountain from the which my current runs
> Or else dries up – to be discarded thence,
> Or keep it as a cistern for foul toads
> To knot and gender in! (4.2.59–64)

But with Desdemona's protest, 'Alas, what ignorant sin have I committed?', Othello's language recognizes that the source of Desdemona's ignorant sin – the fountain or cistern within her female body – is the product of his own readerly creation: 'Was this fair paper, this most goodly book, / Made to write "whore" upon?' (4.2.73–4). Unsure of his possession of what he cannot see or will not have as his proper own, Othello, in the torment of his self-exile, creates in the goodly book called 'Desdemona' the space of his own exclusion.

The alienness Othello creates in Desdemona with his discovery of her open yet unpossessible interior leads, of course, to his demand to 'see it' and thus 'prove' – not in his readerly imagination only but actually – 'prove [his] love a whore' (3.3.364). The emphasis throughout the 'temptation scene' is partly on the need to see a truth beyond demonstration, and partly on the need to define the female interior as a threatening or degraded realm to be excluded rather than entered or embraced. Iago himself says that Othello cannot be 'satisfied': 'Would you, the supervisor, grossly gape on, / Behold her topped?' (3.3.400–1); as Katharine Maus nicely puts it, Iago 'pretends that the practical difficulty of surprising an illicit couple in bed represents a real epistemological limitation ... [The] demand for ocular proof comes to represent an impossible aspiration to the absolute knowledge of another person.'[9] But Iago not only increases the insatiable hunger to know; he also helps create the idea that the elusive object of knowledge will inevitably be a horror too great to be endured.

Throughout the scene, Iago himself cunn-ingly plays – or perhaps better, foreplays – the woman's part, as that part is typically construed in the imagination of Shakespeare's anxiously desiring male characters. To Othello's demand, 'If thou dost love me, / Show me thy thought', comes Iago's coy response, 'My lord, you know I love you' – which Othello can only follow with his own 'I think thou dost' (3.3.119–22). Capitalizing both on Othello's experience as a former slave who knows that no one can own another's appetites, and as a husband who fears it, Iago baits Othello with a prospect that is not only unattainable but also 'vile and false':

> Though I am bound to every act of duty,
> I am not bound to that all slaves are free to.
> Utter my thoughts? Why, say they are vile and
>   false,
> As where's that palace whereinto foul things
> Sometimes intrude not? Who has that breast so
>   pure
> But some uncleanly apprehensions
> Keep leets and law-days, and in sessions sit
> With meditations lawful? (3.3.139–46)

Iago shapes within himself a masculine idea of feminine space. The interiors Iago figures – a palace, a law court, his breast – retain their secrets no matter how much they're forced: you cannot know his thoughts if his heart were in your hand (3.3.167). The space he creates is gendered female both because it seems to Othello to solicit a penetration it ultimately denies, and also because it contains those 'uncleanly apprehensions' which men project into the space created by their frustrated desire for possessive knowledge.

So far I've spoken only about one case of marital jealousy. I'll return to more particulars, but first – and with appropriate brevity – I want to generalize about what I'll grandly call the construction of male sexual desire. To desire is, of course, to be without: to lack gratification; equally, of course, it's a positive state,

---

[9] 'Proof and Consequences: Inwardness and its Exposure in the English Renaissance', *Representations*, 34 (1991), 29–52; p. 42.

the excitation which is the condition for gratification. You must lack in order to desire, and you must lose the desire in order to be gratified. It's not a perfect arrangement but it has its points. So it's worth asking why male sexual desire in Shakespeare so frequently figures not as a source of pleasure but of torment, or at best a heaven that leads to hell.

One reason for this – not inevitably but frequently – unhappy state of affairs is, I suggest, the masculine requirement for control both of the self and of the sexual other.[10] That requirement, which is by its nature unfulfillable, puts in play the corresponding fear of lack of control. The desire and the fear are mutually constitutive. Under the sway of that fear, male desire must either be endless – a yearning toward a consummation which must not be achieved – or it's a movement toward the achievement of its own defeat. Thus, in its most anxiously inflected form, male sexual desire becomes the unappeasable state of affairs sonnet 129 defines as 'Th'expense of spirit' that finds no rest whether 'had, having, or in quest to have'. It's what Giacomo calls 'That satiate yet unsatisfied desire, that tub / Both filled and running' (Cymbeline 1.6.50–1). Frequently, a man's inability to achieve a simultaneity of release and control is blamed on woman: the masculine fear of being in a motile state that defies possessive control is one source of the misogynistic trope of female insatiability. Adonis, who needs no one, confronts in Venus the very essence of perpetual need: 'Glutton-like she feeds yet never filleth' (Venus 548). Hamlet describes Gertrude hanging upon his father as if 'increase of appetite had grown / By what it fed on' (1.2.144–5). And Cleopatra is designated both cause and effect of this state of affairs where desire is precisely that which cannot be adequately ended: 'she makes hungry / Where most she satisfies' (Antony 2.2.243–4).

The most extensive and frightening anatomy of the idea of insatiable masculine desire is Troilus and Cressida, a play in which 'To have done is to hang / Quite out of fashion'

(3.3.145–6): there's no satisfaction, only detumescence (the death of desire) or an endlessness of ardour. What pertains on the world-stage of a battlefield where men struggle for possession of a woman pertains also in more localized sexual affairs. Troilus, unarmed or effeminized by his love, is still man enough to fear having what he most desires to have:

> What will it be
> When that the wat'ry palates taste indeed
> Love's thrice-repurèd nectar? Death, I fear me,
> Swooning destruction, or some joy too fine,
> Too subtle-potent, tuned too sharp in sweetness
> For the capacity of my ruder powers.
> I fear it much; and I do fear besides
> That I shall lose distinction in my joys,
> As doth a battle when they charge on heaps
> The enemy flying.   (3.2.18–27)

In the temporal world of masculine desire, where 'good deeds' immediately convert to 'alms for oblivion', Troilus either 'tarries' ('Have I not tarried', he asks Pandarus, 'still have I tarried' [1.1.19, 22]) or he 'dies': 'How my achievements mock me' (4.2.72) will be Troilus' consummatory cry.

Part of Troilus' problem is that he inhabits a generically unstable dramatic universe, not quite a tragedy or a comedy. Now it is a truth universally acknowledged – and why not, since it was propounded by Northrop Frye? – that Shakespearian comedy is typical of the larger class New Comedy in 'proceeding toward an act which, like death in Greek tragedy, takes place offstage, and is symbolized in the final embrace'.[11] There are adequate material reasons why the 'act' has to take place offstage: there's the problem of boy-actors and the problem of political and religious sensibilities, any of which will adequately explain why the representation of sexual intercourse is impossible on the

---

10 Cf. Edward A. Snow, 'Sexual Anxiety and the Male Order of Things in Othello', English Literary Renaissance, 10 (1980), 384–412.

11 'The Argument of Comedy', English Institute Essays 1948, ed. D. A. Robertson (New York, 1949), p. 60.

Shakespearian stage. But still I want to suggest, *pace* Frye, that the hymeneal end of comedy doesn't stand in for the real consummation but forestalls and avoids it – and given the masculine anxiety I'm describing, that's why we can call it a happy ending. In Shakespeare, unmarried sex threatens loss, destruction ('Th' expense of spirit', Troilus' swooning destruction), but sex within marriage presumes a controlling, possessive knowledge that can never be attained. Marriage is supposed to socialize sexuality, but those delicate female creatures' appetites can't be socialized, because they can't be put into the confines of male possession. Espousal, then – not technically marriage, which only comes into being at the moment of consummation[12] – is the perfect comic resolution because it puts a fiction of control – of ending, achievement, possession – in place of the experience of male sexuality as loss, defeat, exclusion.

Janet Adelman writes, from a more rigorously psychoanalytic perspective than mine, that 'the bed trick in *All's Well* [is] as much a part of a deep fantasy of escape from sexuality as it is an attempt to bring the married couple together'.[13] That fantasy of escape, as much as the promise of consummation, is generically gratified in Shakespearian comedy by the movement toward a conclusion in which nothing is concluded except a promise of something ever more about to be. The hymeneal end of Shakespearian comedy is prophylactic against the destructiveness Shakespeare's men fear in consummated sexual desire.

From this point of view, *Love's Labour's Lost*, which delays its resolution for 'a twelve month and a day', is less anomalous than it's usually taken to be. Its four noble young men begin the play vowing to eschew the world of sex and women. They want to achieve self-perpetuation by a sort of parthenogenesis which avoids the risks of the more common form of procreation: they aim to cheat 'cormorant devouring Time' of the good deeds it gobbles up in Troilus' disastrously sexualized world, and they

would become, without other aids, 'heirs of all eternity'. Neither the play's noble women nor its less noble characters of either sex share this austere regime; the sexual indulgence of Costard and Jaquenetta rebukes Biron and company's self-protective monasticism as surely as do the gibes of the French princess and her women. The Spanish fantasime Don Armado also embraces the more usual route. Boyet intercepts the love letter in which Armado, so learnedly as to be barely comprehensible, compares his wooing of Jaquenetta to King Cophetua's wooing of 'the penurious and indubitate beggar Zenelophon' (4.1.65). The course of that love ran as true love ought to do in comedy: the king overcame the beggar, and therefore, writes Don Armado, drawing now on the language of dramaturgical theory, 'the catastrophe is a nuptial' (4.1.75). Technically, Armado is right: as Ben Jonson writes in *Discoveries*, 'the parts of a Comedie are the same with a *Tragedie*' and at the end of both is the part called the catastrophe.[14] But beyond the comedy's fifth act – outside the park's pale, after a twelvemonth and a day – we may, on the evidence of other Shakespearian treatments of sex and marriage, suspect that the nuptial will be catastrophic in more than purely formal ways.

In comedy the catastrophe is a nuptial; in tragedy and romance, the nuptial is prologue. For Othello as well as for Posthumus in *Cymbeline* and Leontes in *The Winter's Tale* the marital prophylaxis fails. Marriage releases upon Othello, Posthumus and Leontes the torment of a sexuality which marriage was supposed rigorously to proscribe within the

---

12 Cook, *Making a Match*, p. 165.

13 'Bed Tricks: On Marriage as the End of Comedy in *All's Well that Ends Well* and *Measure for Measure*', in Norman Holland, Sidney Homan and Bernard J. Paris, eds., *Shakespeare's Personality* (Berkeley, 1989), pp. 151–74; pp. 158–9.

14 *Discoveries* line 2625, in C. H. Herford, Percy Simpson, and Evelyn Simpson, *Ben Jonson*, vol. 8 (Oxford, 1947), p. 643.

proprietary bounds of Christian and English legal doctrine, but which they find is 'slippery' (the word appears both in *Cymbeline* and *The Winter's Tale*), a sexuality which leaks and spills from the woman-as-other whose appetites men can never call their own.

My fluid metaphors are suggested by Othello's figuring Desdemona as either 'fountain from which [his] current runs' or 'cistern for foul toads to knot and gender in'. In *Cymbeline* the idea of the wife as a watery site is complexly joined with the idea of the wife as property – the one idea, as we would expect, confounding the other, since you can't *keep* things that flow like a fountain or breed like a cistern. A language of possessiveness is present from as early as the leavetaking of Posthumus and Innogen: conventionally enough, Posthumus gives, in exchange for Innogen's ring, his bracelet as 'a manacle of love' which he puts 'upon this fairest prisoner', her arm (1.1.123). Once entered into the realm of commodified value, Posthumus is easily susceptible to Giacomo's revaluations. Posthumus wants to claim that Innogen is absolutely the best of women, but good, better, and best, as Giacomo cunningly convinces Posthumus, have only relative meanings in an exchange economy. So Giacomo, playing on the idea of relativized value, agrees that 'If [Innogen] went before others I have seen – as that diamond of yours outlustres many I have beheld – I could not but believe she excelled many; but I have not seen the most precious diamond that is, nor you the lady' (1.4.70–4). Posthumus tries to put Innogen's value outside the realm of exchange: his diamond, he tells Giacomo, 'may be sold or given', but his lady 'is not a thing for sale, and only the gift of the gods' (80). Giacomo's devastating reply – which introduces the idea of fluidity (of woman as water) into the argument – insists that whatever a man can keep a man can lose:

You may wear her in title yours; but, you know, strange fowl light upon neighbouring ponds. Your ring may be stolen too; so your brace of unprizable estimations, the one is but frail, and the other casual.

A cunning thief or a that-way accomplished courtier would hazard the winning both of first and last.
(1.4.86–91)

The movement of metaphor from the apparent solidity of diamond-like virtue to the unpossessible fluidity of 'neighbouring ponds' horrifyingly suggests the instability of a love rated in terms of marital possessiveness.

For Posthumus, as for Othello, doubt about his ability to keep his wife from the realm of masculine exchange-value leads to – or is it caused by? – doubt about his ability to know the Innogen constituted and defined by her unseen unpossessible appetite. And once in doubt, Posthumus finds doubt everywhere; as Othello does with Desdemona, he even converts the evidence of Innogen's chastity into evidence of her slipperiness. 'Me of my lawful pleasure she restrained', he remembers – invoking, as Othello also does, a realistically implausible history of marriage in this drama of newly- or indeed barely-weds –

And prayed me oft forbearance; did it with
A pudency so rosy the sweet view on't
Might well have warmed old Saturn; that I
    thought her
As chaste as unsunned snow   (2.5.10–13)

To the jealous Posthumus, Innogen's oddly salacious-sounding 'pudency' now seems the deceitful delaying tactic of a 'that-way-accomplished' woman, a woman perhaps like Cressida, who knows that 'Women are angels, wooing; / things won are done. Joy's soul lies in the doing' (*Troilus* 1.2.282–3). Patricia Parker tells us that such sexually provocative delaying tactics can go by the name 'dilation': Parker cites Andreas Capellanus on this supposed female tactic in the art of love, and says that 'By the time of Eve's "sweet reluctant amorous delay" in Book IV of *Paradise Lost*, "dilation" in this sense was almost a *terminus technicus* for the erotics of prolongation'.[15] To the jealous Post-

---

[15] *Literary Fat Ladies: Rhetoric, Gender, Property* (London, 1987), pp. 16–17.

humus, the memory of Innogen's 'pudency' has an effect similar to the imputation of sexual appetitiveness. A wife's chaste refusal is as effective as her sexual compliance in exciting the doubt that becomes jealousy. It opens a space both between Innogen and Posthumus and within Innogen herself, a space filled now not with erotic tension but with the anxiety of Posthumus' inability to know her appetites and intentions.

(Several critics, invoking different evidence for different purposes, have questioned whether Innogen is merely chaste or in fact technically a virgin throughout the play.[16] If, as they plausibly argue, the marriage of Posthumus and Innogen was not consummated, *Cymbeline* would show an otherwise unlikely affinity to *The Taming of the Shrew*, where there is also a wide gap of time between the contract and the post-fifth act consummation. But in *Cymbeline* the evidence must remain inferential; and a degree of textual uncertainty seems to me appropriate: it mimics the legal status of marriage in the period, when church and state were trying to regulate more precisely the time and conditions when marriage comes into being – and thereby making visible the actual insubstantiality of 'marriage' as a natural fact. The custom of *de futuro* and *de praesenti* spousal contracts supposedly required, but did not always get, the further legitimation of a church ceremony, and only then could intercourse legally take place and a man thereby enter into possession of his wife's property. The multiplication of formalities as a woman dwindled into a wife suggests an anxiety in the legal realm corresponding to the individual anxiety I've been discussing, where a requirement of certitude creates the very conditions which baffle certitude.)

The scene of Giacomo's nocturnal invasion of Innogen's chamber (2.2) powerfully dramatizes the process by which male erotic longing creates (with ambiguous consequences) a masculine idea of the female space he can never fully occupy. As Giacomo emerges from the trunk into the bedroom, the sleeping Innogen, like Lucrece to Tarquin, becomes the object of his controlling male gaze. Critics have wondered why Giacomo doesn't in fact do what he will later claim to have done: David Bergeron, for instance, argues that Giacomo's abstinence means that he's literally impotent.[17] This misses, I think, the source of the scene's erotic power, which is the male voyeuristic fantasy of controlling a woman without risking the failure which consummated sexuality so often entails in Shakespeare. The sleeping Innogen lies open to Giacomo, but only by not taking sexual possession of her can the fantasy of possession be gratified.

Giacomo's inventory recreates Innogen as metonymy: she is her white skin, ruby lips, azure-laced eyelids – a conventional blazon, yet (I want to claim) one that is being converted into something dramatically and historically remarkable. She is also the 'movables' Giacomo itemizes to 'enrich [the] inventory'. And of course she is that bracelet with which Posthumus had made her arm his prisoner: only now the pledge of constancy is figured with the word that designates woman as unpossessible: 'Come off, come off; / As *slippery* as the Gordian knot was hard' (2.2.33–4). Finally, there's the most intimate of these metonymies, 'On her left breast / A mole, cinque-spotted' (2.2.37–8). Giacomo himself describes the process by which these externalities – the metonymies that inventory Innogen – will become the metaphor for her threatening womanly otherness: the bracelet, he says, 'will witness

---

16 David M. Bergeron, 'Sexuality in *Cymbeline*', *Essays in Literature*, 10 (1983), 159–68; p. 160. Bergeron cites Murray M. Schwartz, 'Between Fantasy and Imagination: A Psychological Exploration of *Cymbeline*', in *Psychoanalysis and the Literary Process*, ed. Frederick Crews (Cambridge, Mass., 1970), pp. 219–83; p. 232. The most recent version of the argument for non-consummation was made by Anne Barton in a paper delivered at the Twenty-fifth International Shakespeare Conference, Stratford-upon-Avon, August 1992.

17 'Sexuality in *Cymbeline*', p. 165.

outwardly, / As strongly as the conscience does within, / To th' madding of her lord' (35–7); and the 'secret' of her mole 'Will force him think I have picked the lock and ta'en / The treasure of her honour' (41–2). The locked treasury of a woman's honour is the most expectable of tropes; but in this room, under this man's gaze, in a context that explicitly recognizes a difference between outward witness and inward conscience, it not only recreates the idea of woman as economic possession but creates the contradictory idea that the tokens of exchange – the visible, knowable parts of woman – hide a more essential, ultimately unknowable, unpossessible woman within.

Throughout the scene, Giacomo writes down the objects of his scrutiny. At the end of his inventory his attention turns to the book Innogen 'hath been reading late, / The tale of Tereus. Here the leaf's turned down / Where Philomel gave up' (2.2.44–6). The association of Innogen with her book recalls Othello's question, 'Was this fair paper, this most goodly book, / Made to write "whore" upon?' The idea of woman-as-book recognizes the extent to which these wives have become objects of male fantasy, fictions of female otherness. The projection of male sexual anxiety creates the idea of a female subjectivity intractible to male possessiveness; by the same token, however, it locates in woman all that a man would reject in himself and essentializes the idea of 'the woman's part':

> for there's no motion
> That tends to vice in man but I affirm
> It is the woman's part; be it lying, note it,
> The woman's; flattering, hers; deceiving, hers;
> Lust and rank thoughts, hers, hers; revenges, hers.
> (2.5.20–4)

Of all Shakespeare's jealous husbands Leontes is perhaps the most febrile of fictionalizers, as the title of his play, *The Winter's Tale*, makes the process of imaginative creation most prominent. Like Othello, or like a Narcissus not of self-love but of loathing, Leontes is compelled to peer into those horrifying depths his own imagination creates:

> How blest am I
> In my just censure, in my true opinion!
> Alack, for lesser knowledge – how accursed
> In being so blest! There may be in the cup
> A spider steeped, and one may drink, depart,
> And yet partake no venom, for his knowledge
> Is not infected; but if one present
> Th'abhorred ingredient to his eye, make known
> How he hath drunk, he cracks his gorge, his
>   sides,
> With violent hefts. I have drunk and seen the
>   spider. (2.1.38–47)

Where is this cup and what is the poisonous knowledge it contains? For us, it's Leontes' own mind and his own jealous imaginings; but for Leontes it's Hermione, the vessel (to alter Othello's phrase) from which his current runs, which now contains in its depths the proof of her inward foulness. Like the other husbands I've been listening to, Leontes cannot fully articulate an idea of his wife as a subject possessing an inward essence: what we hear instead, in imagery like this of the cup and the spider, is his intimation of the inaccessible inwardness of her appetites confusedly expressed as a pollution of his own interior, like the pollution that turns Othello's 'fountain' to a 'cistern'.

Images of unconstrainable female fluidity run throughout Leontes' self-tormenting. Camillo must be blind if he can't see that 'My wife is slippery' (1.2.275). Leontes finds himself 'Inchthick, knee-deep, o'er head and ears a forked one!' (1.2.187): he's measuring the rising tide of his infamy, the troubled waters in which, as he's just previously said, 'I am angling now' (181); but he's also taking the measure of Hermione's treacherous depths. Like Othello, Leontes rushes to generalize his case, but with a metadramatic immediacy which seeks to infect the male members of the theatre audience – 'even at this present, / Now, while I speak this' – with his condition:

There have been,
Or I am much deceived, cuckolds ere now,
And many a man there is, even at this present,
Now, while I speak this, holds his wife by th' arm,
That little thinks she has been sluiced in's absence,
And his pond fished by his next neighbour, by
Sir Smile, his neighbour. Nay, there's comfort in't,
Whiles other men have gates, and those gates
    opened,
As mine, against their will.   (1.2.191–9)

Here the idea of female fluidity becomes literally the image of female genitalia. Giacomo, too, in *Cymbeline*, speaks of 'neighbouring ponds' on which 'strange fowl light' (1.4.87): no landowner can secure his sole fishing rights in these women. Not only the fish can be taken; in Leontes' imagining, the pond itself is subject to the law of sexual hydrodynamics and can be 'sluiced' away. As clearly, terribly, as self-defeatingly as anywhere in Shakespeare, Leontes follows the logic which makes his wife a property that he can never possess:

be it concluded,
No barricado for a belly. Know't,
It will let in and out the enemy
With bag and baggage.   (1.2.204–7)

That metonymic identification of Hermione as unbarricaded belly – of her body's concavity as the place of her never-to-be possessed identity – is graphically reinforced by her visible pregnancy. Polixenes has made her 'swell like this', Leontes believes; her swollen state and, indeed, the presence on stage of Mamillius, her body's previous issue, introduces into *The Winter's Tale* a poignant complication only latent in either *Othello* or *Cymbeline*. The ubiquitous, virtually obsessive Elizabethan fear of cuckoldry can in part be explained as a consequence of the laws of inheritance, that is, of the actual possibility that a man's estate will fall into the possession of another man's child. But in Leontes' speculation about paternity there's a characterological surplus-value: Shakespeare invests the fact of paternity with a psychological importance absent from previous (usually comic) treatments of the cuckold's fear that he may be raising another man's child. Not only Leontes' adjunctive estate but his own identity is in question as he looks upon the lines of his boy's face:

methoughts I did recoil
Twenty-three years, and saw myself unbreeched,
In my green velvet coat; my dagger muzzled,
Lest it should bite its master, and so prove,
As ornament oft does, too dangerous.
How like, methought, I then was to this kernel,
This squash, this gentleman.   (1.2.156–62)

For Leontes, Mamillius signifies doubly: as the fruit (or here, more exactly, the vegetable) of a woman's body, he's the sign of Leontes' entrance into a world where masculine self-possession depends on the ability to possess a woman's sexual appetite and reproductive capacity ('they say we are / Almost as like as eggs. Women say so, / That will say anything' [1.2.131–3]); at the same time the child embodies the men's fantasy of a world free from the danger of adult heterosexuality ('We were as twinned lambs that did frisk i'th'sun, / And bleat the one at th'other. What we changed / Was innocence for innocence' [1.2.69–71]). In the men's recollections of early childhood, the only transaction was easy and equal '[ex]change'; the phallic dagger of sexual possessiveness was as yet merely ornamental. But in the adult world where a man's self-definition depends on keeping 'mine' separate from 'thine', 'affection...stabs the centre' (140). Hermione's swollen belly figures the female space, both physiological and psychological, which a husband unbarricades only to discover that it contains a life of its own, and which he can close only by killing

Certainly there were cuckolds, real and imagined, ere Shakespeare began to dramatize their torments and tormentings. And certainly there has always been sexual jealousy, inside and outside of marriage and regardless of gender or sexual preference. In this essay I've only wanted to claim that the peculiar consciousness of self and other that we see in the jealous husbands of *Othello*, *Cymbeline*, and *The Winter's Tale* registers a turn from what had previously figured mainly as an economic and social phenomenon toward an interiorized correlative which yields the repertoire of the modern psychological subject. Shakespeare puts into play the full mystification of marriage as bulwark against an unappeasable sexuality which threatens male control both of the public realm and the realm of the individual.[18] His anxious husbands try desperately to know, in order to possess, the women they would keep as their wives. In the process these characters discover, within themselves and for us, a new range of psychological complexity. But that discovery, the opening out of *themselves* to us, depends on another, more troubling 'discovery' these male characters think they make about the threateningly foreign country of women.

I put the word 'discovery' in inverted commas to indicate its ambiguous status. What the jealous husband 'discovers' as his wife's irreducible difference from himself is also the myth he creates to protect his idea of masculinity and to explain his anguish within a regime of sexual possessiveness. As such the myth of female otherness is, no doubt, a very bad thing, the potent tool of patriarchy which first creates the idea that women are a threat and then creates the means to control that threat. Yet I find the situation not entirely without socially redeeming value. For one thing, it's its own (no doubt inadequate) punishment: male jealousy does kill women, but in Shakespeare, at least, it also tends not to make men happy. As Toril Moi observes in her essay about differences between male and female sexual jealousy, 'Killing the woman one loves would seem counterproductive'.[19] For another thing, and to take the situation at its most optimistic reading, we might say that the jealous sexuality that unsuccessfully strives to turn a person into a property creates, in the very failure Shakespeare

dramatizes, the possibility for a different economy where, to alter Locke's phrase, not only 'every Man' but every Woman too, 'has a *Property* in his [or her] own *Person*'.[20]

As a sad matter of fact, liberal individualism was – and continues to be – very slow to accept the case Emilia makes in *Othello* for equal opportunity based on equal appetites:

> Let husbands know
> Their wives have sense like them. They see, and smell,
> And have their palates both for sweet and sour,
> As husbands have. (4.3.92–5)

To return to the legal realm where this essay began: in England, married women were still subsumed within their husband's legal person, their properties literally not their own, until passage of the Married Women's Property Acts of 1870 and 1882. In the United States in 1992 the Supreme Court upheld the right of states to require a husband's consent to his wife's choice to have an abortion: a married woman with income of her own can file a single income tax return, but the space and contents of her body remain a joint possession. But in Shakespeare, in plays like *Othello*, *Cymbeline*, and *The Winter's Tale*, the tragic failure of male possessive desire implicitly but powerfully recognizes a realm of female self-possession; and that recognition (again, on the optimistic reading) is the precondition for a conceivable state where a man knows a woman's sexuality neither as threat to be expelled nor possession to be controlled.

---

18 Cf. Jonathan Dollimore, *Sexual Dissidence* (Oxford, 1991): 'Female constancy is the paradigm to which other kinds of stability, sexual and political, refer, and upon which they depend, dreadfully and of course impossibly', p. 162.

19 'Jealousy and Sexual Difference', in *Sexuality: A Reader*, ed. Feminist Review (London, 1987), pp. 134–56; p. 149.

20 John Locke, *The Second Treatise of Government*, para. 27, in *Two Treatises of Government*, ed. Peter Laslett (Cambridge 1960, rev. 1963): 'Though the Earth, and all inferior Creatures be common to all Men, yet every Man has a *Property* in his own *Person*. This no Body has any Right to but himself' (p. 328).

RECONSTRUCTING *THE WINTER'S TALE*

KENNETH C. BENNETT

Perhaps William Butler Yeats anticipated the arrival of the post-modernist movement called deconstruction in his splendid poem, 'Lapis Lazuli'. After all, the carved Chinese stone that he received from Harry Clifton contains not only a scene suggestive of the journey of life and the role of art amidst all the tragedy, but

> Every discoloration of the stone,
> Every accidental crack or dent,
> Seems a water-course or an avalanche ...

In other words, as in deconstructionist doctrine, the work of art contains the elements of its own undoing. A critic who patiently 'teases out' the contradictory aspects of any piece of literature, especially the way in which the rhetoric works against the overt statement, can show how the meaning is subverted, just as the crack in the lapis lazuli threatens to destroy the carving. In fact, no critic is needed. Eventually the work will deconstruct itself; even individual words are forever engaged in the process of their own subversion as new meanings develop, new texts are brought to bear on old ones, and the stream of language constantly shifts. Deconstruction may indeed be a very elaborate way of insisting on a Heraclitean view of life and language.

The great flux of decay and re-creation of meaning is nowhere more evident than in the stage history of Shakespearian drama since mid-century. Anyone who has sampled the vast variety of productions of Shakespeare in that period is intensely aware of the purposeful assaults on the old doublet-and-hose meanings

that go against all previous interpretations. Happily Shakespeare has been strong enough not only to withstand such reshaping but to return, like the mythological hero he has become, revitalized. I am reminded particularly of the Michael Bogdanov production of *The Taming of the Shrew* (1978, 1979) by the Royal Shakespeare Company with Jonathan Pryce and Paola Dionisotti, which turned the play into a feminist tract with exceptional skill and ingenuity. While I cannot with any precision call this production consciously deconstructive, it served something of the same purpose, showing how a text can be made to work against itself – or at least work against traditional meanings.

Like directors and producers, critics of Shakespeare have sought ever more for new 'approaches' and methodologies. Unlike the first three hundred years of commentary, which leaned heavily towards the moralistic,[1] the past half century has tended to stress variety of interpretation, focusing on the question of what the individual plays are 'about'. And if Stanley Fish is right, we are all doomed to more of this since 'Like it or not, interpretation is the only game in town.'[2] It is difficult to quarrel

---

[1] The play's first critic, Simon Forman, was apparently happy to find a moral, however limited, in the thievery of Autolycus, though he concluded nothing from Leontes' story.

[2] Stanley Fish, *Is There a Text in This Class?* (Cambridge, Mass., 1980), p. 355.

with this judgement. Surveying the enormous literature on any one play, for example, one is overwhelmed by how many different and conflicting attempts there are. (By the way, only a handful of these are specifically deconstructionist.) The major effort has been to find new 'readings' based on new, improved 'approaches'. Though eventually there may be an end to this spate of interpretation, it is – and has been for a long time – a thriving operation. It is almost as if in the face of the massive violence and destruction of the twentieth century, all the critics were attempting to behave like artists (and deconstructionists, following Oscar Wilde, assert that criticism is just as creative as literature itself and not merely an adjunct or subordinate operation); without knowing it they behave like the 'Chinamen' in 'Lapis Lazuli'. In the face of all the tragic scene on which they stare, they immerse themselves in art, and then 'Their eyes mid many wrinkles, their eyes, / Their ancient, glittering eyes, are gay'. Like the glittering eyes of the Ancient Mariner and the flashing eyes of the speaker in 'Kubla Khan', the Chinamen's eyes are those of the seer and betoken prophetic vision. The chief difference, as I see it, is that in the nineteenth century, the eyes of the poet were very special eyes indeed, the eyes of the hero; while in our own era the eyes have become those of everyman, each with his unique insight, attempting to be definitive yet doomed to subjectivity or temporality. Inevitably language itself interferes with consistent interpretation. As Howard Felperin puts it in his article on *The Winter's Tale*, 'If we cannot know except through the dark glass of language, we might as well accept what is a necessary limitation on our knowledge.'[3]

Perhaps, like many others, I have become at least partly convinced of Derridean assertions concerning the deconstructive nature of meaning, the superiority of poetic expression which acknowledges and 'foregrounds' the ambivalences of language, and insists on 'the ultimate subjectivity of all interpretation'.[4] One

is tempted, as a lover of Shakespeare, to follow Mr Felperin's lead and argue that Shakespeare's plays are great because they embody these paradoxical views of language. But just as almost all critical commentary and literary theory tends to be, directly or indirectly, an apologia in the long stream of replies to Plato,[5] so the vast majority of writers about Shakespeare tend to be his admirers and defenders. It is comforting to know that your favourite writer illustrates your favourite theory better than anyone else. And perhaps such things are no accidents.

Ultimately the key questions raised by deconstructionist criticism of Shakespearian texts (as opposed to deconstruction itself) are two: Can the general drift of the traditional meanings be totally and irrevocably reversed? Are the meanings of the plays condemned to the limbo of undecidability? To make the discussion as concrete as possible, I have selected two articles that deal with these issues in reading *The Winter's Tale*. The first of these is Howard Felperin's '"Tongue-tied our Queen?": The Deconstruction of Presence in *The Winter's Tale*', which contends that, contrary to tradition, Hermione may be guilty as charged and the Delphic oracle cannot be relied on to support her innocence. To be sure, Mr Felperin makes an opening disclaimer: ' ... my

---

[3] Howard Felperin, '"Tongue-tied our Queen": The Deconstruction of Presence in *The Winter's Tale*', in *Shakespeare and the Question of Theory*, ed. G. Hartman and P. Parker (London and New York, 1985), p. 16.

[4] Jacques Derrida, 'Letter to a Japanese Friend', in *Derrida & Differance*, ed. D. Wood and R. Bernasconi (Coventry, 1985), pp. 16–17.

[5] Not only have Aristotle and the Renaissance critics who followed in his wake made it their main business to defend poetry against charges of untruthfulness and lack of moral instruction, but the New Critics saw literature as attaining special insight not affordable by scientific discourse. Deconstructionists, too, despite their reactive departures from the New Critics, have found literature more truthful than other forms of discourse because it frankly acknowledges and exploits the rhetoricity of language.

purpose is *not* to contend that all commentators on the play until now have been wrong, and that Leontes is right in supposing his wife has betrayed him'.[6] But he goes on to say on the same page that he wants 'to question the definitiveness of the oracle's pronouncement and the basis for our happy consensus', and much of the subsequent argument hinges on reading Hermione's exchanges with Polixenes in a dark, incriminating fashion. After quoting extensively from Act 1, scene 2 (lines 83–6, 91–6, 106–89), he comments:

So much of what Hermione says may be construed either within or outside the bounds of royal hospitality and wifely decorum. Her emphasis on greater warmth in persuasion, that is, may signify flirtation; the indefinite antecedents of her royal pronouns, self-incrimination; her earthy wit, bawdry; and her rhetorical juxtapositions of 'husband' and 'friend,' a fatal identification of the two ... Once our suspicions are aroused – and there is at least some language in these scenes that cannot help but arouse them – they become, like Leontes' own suspicions, promiscuous and contagious, tainting with doubt and duplicity all that passes between Hermione and Polixenes.[7]

If our suspicions are tainted like Leontes', we are in poor shape indeed. Is it not possible that the dramatic ambiguities are there for strictly dramatic purposes? The audience needs to ask whether there can be any truth in Leontes' conjectures so that the suspense is maintained, and by a much-used, reliable convention, Shakespeare keeps the audience in some doubt but keeps it ahead of the protagonist. Crucial, too, is the fact that a visual element is involved; this is not just a 'problem of linguistic indeterminacy'.[8] Would that we knew how the stage action went in Shakespeare's day.[9] Did Hermione 'paddle' on Polixenes' palm? And if so, precisely with what emphasis? We are fated not to know. But this does not mean that the meaning was not determined in Shakespeare's day. If, however, this argument is not persuasive, I believe we have to consider what the consequences of Hermione's guilt would be. If she has overstepped the bounds of decency, then the supportive courtiers, especially Paulina, were sadly mistaken and remain so. And, especially difficult to swallow, if Hermione and Polixenes actually have been having an affair, then Perdita will be headed for incest at the end and Leontes will have done penance to no purpose but to be reunited with a sullied wife as a cuckold. The possibility of Hermione's guilt, in light of the ending – especially its tone – is unthinkable by Act 5.

The other issue raised by Professor Felperin is the reliability of the oracle of Apollo. Unlike the theophanies in *Pericles* and *Cymbeline*, the god does not actually appear in *The Winter's Tale*, and so his message becomes suspect.

Despite its extraordinary clarity and definitiveness, the pronouncement turns out ... to be disturbingly difficult to verify or validate. Since it is supposed to be itself a validation, there is nothing left to fall back on when its validity is questioned, other than Cleomenes' awe. The god's language without the god to back it up is a bit like paper currency without any gold behind it ... Once cut off from the presence of their divine speaker, with his univocality of meaning and intent, Apollo's words enter the realm of the human, the fallible, the ambiguous, in sum, the interpretable, where they can be contradicted or dismissed, for all we know, with impunity.[10]

What this argument fails to take into account is that even if the gods actually appear, as Diana and Jupiter do, their words – and actions – are part of the fiction and therefore just as subject

---

6 Felperin, '"Tongue-tied our queen"', p. 5.

7 Ibid. p. 9.

8 Ibid. p. 8.

9 If Hermione is innocently encouraging in her movements, the audience sees that Leontes is overreacting. What if she does otherwise? This may be a problem, but according to the actress Gemma Jones, who has tried it, acting a guilty Hermione 'is fun to play ... but observation on the exercise is that it is perverse and destructive to attempt to give Leontes a rational jealousy'. 'Hermione in *The Winter's Tale*', in *Players of Shakespeare*, ed. P. Brockbank (Cambridge, 1985), pp. 158–9.

10 Felperin, '"Tongue-tied our Queen"', p. 8.

to deconstruction as the Delphic oracle. The kind of 'presence' that the gods have is not the kind of presence that, say, the author would have if giving a live commentary. But neither sort is the philosophical sense used by Derrida and others. That kind of presence indicates true being – parousia – and would, presumably, require the real Apollo (not an actor as Apollo) to appear in order to validate his words. The clearest statement that I know on this subject is Geoffrey Hartman's: 'Now myth, ritual, and art are clearly mediations rather than media. They presuppose a discontinuity, a separation from the presence they seek. Theophany, epiphany, and parousia are formal concepts defining that presence.'[11] Perhaps the matter may be viewed this way: neither the gods, as characters, nor their words partake of real presence, but the audience believes that the gods and their words *represent* that presence as long as there is no reason to disbelieve.[12]

After all, we have suspended our various disbeliefs by entering into the drama voluntarily. There is no need to worry about the referentiality of Shakespeare's oracle; Shakespeare may not even have got the name right. Does 'Delphos' refer to 'Delphi' or 'Delos' or is it a handy portmanteau?[13] But, reading or seeing, the audience is not worrying about that; rather, it accepts the authority of the oracle *within the context of the play*. Even if the Elizabethan audience would most likely have been sceptical of oracles – and I dare say modern audiences are even more so – they could easily forgo their doubts for the sake of the fiction. There is no reason why we cannot, and indeed we must if the fiction is not to be destroyed. That we can suspend our disbelief is the result of Shakespeare's technical mastery of drama. Given the tyrannical, irrational behaviour of Leontes, who is going to believe him, as opposed to the oracle, in Act 3? Now, it may be perfectly true that we have no hard evidence of the oracle's authority – no ocular or aural proof – but we are dealing with a fiction and its conventions, not referentiality. If we have our

doubts, as Mr Felperin does, it is because we can, as scholars have done for a long time, find inconsistencies – if not large holes – in the texts from a logical or 'scientific' scrutiny of the plays. But plays work by their own methods, including convention and emotion.

It is the overall effect that counts for so much in performance, and the context for the oracle's pronouncements is set up very carefully in a scene that seems almost superfluous. Felperin speaks slightingly of 'Cleomenes' awe', but the first scene of Act 3, by its very tone, lends whatever credence is necessary to the oracle before its words are read. Shakespeare's evocative poetry creates a positive emotional effect that suggests the elevated benignity of the oracle. Furthermore, and perhaps most importantly, we have no reason to disbelieve Cleomenes and Dion. One of the fundamental conventions of all drama is that minor neutral characters – functionaries, if you will – can be used for expository purposes and the creation of predispositions. A number of parallels can be cited within the play itself; one or two will suffice. First, in Act 2, scene 1, a nameless lord protests the villainous treatment of Hermione, and asks Leontes to call back his queen rather than sending her off to prison. He then grows bolder in support of Antigonus' admonitions to the King:

> For her, my lord,
> I dare my life lay down, and will do't, sir,
> Please you t'accept it, that the Queen is spotless
> I'th' eyes of heaven, and to you – I mean
> In this which you accuse her. (2.1.131–5)

---

[11] Geoffrey Hartman, *Beyond Formalism: Literary Essays 1958–1970* (New Haven, 1970), p. 14.

[12] Paul de Man had no difficulty in accepting the divinity of Galathea in Rousseau's *Pygmalion*: '... Galathea's divine status is affirmed from the start and is constitutive for the text'. *Allegories of Reading; Figural Language in Rousseau, Nietzsche, Rilke, and Proust* (New Haven, 1979), p. 182.

[13] See J. H. P. Pafford's note to 3.1.2 in the Arden Shakespeare edition (London, 1963) for the most likely explanation.

The anonymity of this courageous man has the effect of saying to the audience, 'Look here, even the lesser lights are rising up in protest; isn't it likely that the King is wrong?' In one of the nicest touches of the play, Shakespeare has this same lord, after his fierce defence of Hermione, be the one to applaud Leontes' subsequent decision to consult the oracle at Delphos. He merely says, 'Well done, my lord' (2.1.190), but in the context, it shows that he is not simply a naysayer or malcontent, and that he has the sense to agree with what is obviously a right action. These four words, then, have the function of confirming Hermione's innocence by confirming the character of the lord. Incidentally, the audience has, almost without knowing it, absorbed the information that the lord in question is a minor character, one that may not appear again, yet one that is on the side of the right. All this information is subject to change later, but, in this case, our reading of the conventions goes on almost subconsciously and our conclusions are confirmed.

A different example appears in Act 2, scene 2, when the Jailer describes Paulina: when he enters, she asks him, 'Now good sir, / You know me, do you not?' and he replies, 'For a worthy lady, / And one who much I honour' (lines 4–6). This may be an idle compliment at this point, but then the integrity of the Jailer is established when he refuses to conduct her to the queen against the 'express commandment' (line 9) of the King. As in the first example, this action tends to reinforce the opinion of Paulina. To seal this impression, Shakespeare has Emilia, another neutral character, commend Paulina directly in a short passage ending, 'There is no lady living / So meet for this great errand' (lines 48–9). Thus the groundwork is laid for the confrontation between Paulina, the newly born Perdita in her arms, and the reluctant Leontes, and no one in the audience now can be against her, despite her stridencies.

Because none of these characters, nor indeed any in the whole play, has any referentiality, there is an absolute need to establish certainty within the fiction regarding various matters, and this can be handled, as it is commonly by all writers, simply by supplying information through characters whom we have no reason to disbelieve. Perhaps Antigonus was not really eaten alive by a bear, but we believe the extraordinary story because it is told to us by the Clown, not Autolycus. Thus, despite a variety of problems and ambiguities which create divergencies in interpretation, the broad outlines of the play remain intact, supported as they are by the conventions of belief that all readers participate in, even though they may be only barely aware of it. Unless we are very naïve, like the sailor who jumped on the stage to stop Othello from strangling Desdemona, we accept much when we read or see a play, including various ambiguities, inconsistencies, and implausibilities, and these can change during the course of the action. In Act 3, for instance, we believe what Paulina says about Hermione's death and what Leontes says about visiting the dead bodies of his wife and his son (3.2.233–35), but by the end of Act 5 we have discarded these statements in view of the new story that Paulina tells of Hermione's sixteen years' sequestration. The contradiction in the text is lost in the great sweep of the action. Of course we presumed Hermione dead, but in the *coup de théâtre* of the statue coming to life, the crucial impression is that of a woman-made miracle. Obviously, Shakespeare has manoeuvered his plot so well that only the most perversely discerning would insist on the explanation of events in Act 3, scene 2. That we accept the restoration of Hermione is again conventional; the new positive ending supersedes earlier 'events', now forgotten in the joy of the ending.

But is it happiness unalloyed? The question has been raised in the second of our articles, 'A Wife Lost and/or Found', by Joyce Wexler. The ending of *The Winter's Tale* for her may be as ironic as the ending of Michael Bogdanov's version of *The Taming of the Shrew*:

The reunion of Hermione and Leontes need not be staged as a reconciliation. Polixenes reports that Hermione embraces her husband, and Camillo adds that she 'hangs about his neck'. Since these two observations are the only textual evidence that Hermione forgives Leontes, the scene could also be performed to keep forgiveness in question. The embrace which two of the king's friends consider warm could be limited to a perfunctory, wifely response to Leontes' tardy and reluctant kiss. Then she would turn from him to her daughter. Love for Perdita, not Leontes, has sustained Hermione all these years.[14]

Without being facetious, one might suggest that Hermione could give a substantial embrace to Perdita before even acknowledging the existence of Leontes. But should she? As in the first act, much of the meaning is conveyed through tone and action, and a wide latitude of direction is possible. Such undecidabilities arise from lack of knowledge concerning the original productions, not a rhetorical subversion. But the descriptions of Polixenes and Camillo, like the judgements of the Lord and the Jailer previously discussed must be taken at face value, and their import is clear enough. One serves to reinforce the other. The length of the embrace between Hermione and Leontes is significant, especially when it is broken only by the purposeful intervention of Paulina, who asks Perdita to 'interpose' after eight lines of speech by Paulina, Polixenes, and Camillo, and after who knows how many pauses of admiration at the reunion.

Professor Wexler stresses the fact that Hermione speaks only to her daughter. (As a matter of fact, she starts her only speech at the end by addressing the gods.) But Professor Wexler comes down hardest on Leontes when she contends that Hermione does not forgive him. Her argument is based on what she considers the natural reaction any woman would have to a husband who behaves like Leontes:

How can a woman forgive her husband for causing the death of their son and ordering the murder of their daughter? The play expresses both the wish for forgiveness and the impossibility of receiving it. Leontes repents his errors, but he never recognizes they have permanent consequences. He never learns

that what is done cannot be undone. Only according to the Christian doctrine of forgiveness could Hermione be seen as an agent of divine grace capable of accepting imperfect penance. Indeed, only God could forgive Leontes – no wife could.[15]

The *only*s of the last two sentences are big words. The first suggests that the play cannot be interpreted as a Christian statement, despite a number of critical efforts to show just that. The second suggests that all wives would act the same way, and that therefore Hermione, as a wife, would do the same. The fallacy of this syllogism is patent. Hermione may well be the one wife in the world who would, and she may well be 'an agent of divine grace', Christian or not, as far as some readers are concerned. Is this a decidable matter? Perhaps not. But again I find it much more likely that Hermione forgives Leontes and that she is happy in so doing. That she really loves him – whether he deserves it or not – seems clear from all she has said, even when Leontes reviled her, and from her patient waiting. What does not seem appropriate to me about Professor Wexler's interpretation is her bringing a judgement from experience (no wife would forgive a man like that) and applying it to the play. Such a method assumes a kind of referentiality about the play that a deconstructionist would and should resist, and Professor Wexler invokes Derrida from the start of her argument.

Despite her avowed allegiance to 'the undecidability of texts',[16] Wexler decides against Leontes. She also decides at times, as I have earlier suggested one may, on the basis of inference and the reaction of the audience to stage convention. As an example of the first, she declares, 'The plot's emphatic denial of rational grounds for Leontes' suspicion leads to a search for the sources of his behavior in his unconscious.'[17] To say this implies a kind of

---

14 Joyce Wexler, 'A Wife Lost and/or Found', *The Upstart Crow*, 8 (1988), 106–17; p. 116.
15 Ibid.
16 Ibid., p. 106.
17 Ibid., p. 108.

foreknowledge on Shakespeare's part concerning the unconscious and an implied authorial intention that I, for one, cannot believe to be indubitably factual. A little further on in her argument, Professor Wexler asserts what seems to me, at any rate, undecidable. In the following passage in which Leontes tries to justify to Camillo his suspicions of Hermione and Polixenes, she accuses him of equating his fantasies with reality:

> Is whispering nothing?
> Is leaning cheek to cheek? Is meeting noses?
> Kissing with inside lip? . . .   (1.2.286–8)

How do we know this is falsehood? We may suspect – and do – but we also do not know for certain what he *has* seen. Felperin has asserted that this is undecidable, but Wexler sees it otherwise:

As desperate as Lear on the heath, Leontes asserts what he has not seen. As dependent as Othello on his idealized image of his wife to validate his life, Leontes dreads being deceived. Producing the facts he needs to justify his feelings, he lets his fears rather than his senses control his idea of reality. The more firmly he insists he is right, the more clearly the audience knows he is wrong.[18]

Now this sort of judgement is based on exactly the sort of convention that I described earlier in connection with Professor Felperin's article. As Shakespeare once wrote himself, 'The lady protests too much, methinks.' Clearly, Gertrude was capable of reading dramatic convention. So is Professor Wexler, so are we all. The problem is in supposing that the only grounds for conviction about meaning are rational and that the 'truth' about discourse is revealed solely by deconstruction.

We must always keep in mind that deconstruction depends on prior structure and that it is not, according to Derrida, a method of criticism; rather it is something that inevitably happens without conscious intent.[19] The disruption or dissemination of the text depends on a prior understanding of that text; the undecidability of meaning depends on the creation of meanings in the first place. We must not let the current emphasis on deconstruction overshadow the constant and inevitable attempts of the mind to produce a sensible structure. The mind in the act of reading tries to construct a unity, a meaning from the assemblage of words (and spaces) called a text. The reader, as we are now well aware, participates in the process of creating the text to a greater or lesser degree, depending on the radicality of reader-response theory one adopts. Using the author's verbal assemblage, the reader selects, enlarges and transforms the text, making it his or her own. In an effort to understand someone else's structure of words, she or he creates another structure, not necessarily purely verbal, since it may involve visual, aural, and other sensory images, as well as feelings and emotions, and quite likely some undefined, even non-conscious reaction. This process inevitably involves some putting together (after all, the words are all separate – a fact so obvious that we tend to forget it) and some reduction (a text of any length, even a short poem, is not all held simultaneously in the mind as, say, a picture is).

Unifying, as opposed to deconstructing, is a much more varied activity than is usually thought. In fact, unity as a concept is not nearly as unitary as its users – and we are all its users – tend to imply. There are various levels of unity – differing degrees of abstraction and varying strengths of coherence. There are perhaps more kinds of unity than can ever be anatomized, ranging from the grammatical to the archetypal. The deconstruction of all these unities, although it may always be in process, is, as long as there is life, a losing proposition. Deconstructing unity or any form of meaning is like cutting off the Hydra's head: more unities will spring into being to take its place. This is especially true in the realm of practical criticism, where new unifying principles like

---

[18] Ibid. p. 109.
[19] Derrida, 'Letter to a Japanese Friend', pp. 4–5.

feminism and the new historicism are making new connections within and among texts and thus creating new unities. Like deconstruction, reconstruction is going on all the time in a seemingly spontaneous generation of meanings.

The most common type of unity, that which most readers would think of first if called upon for an illustration, is thematic. The eternal question about any work is, what is it 'about'? what does it speak 'of'?[20] This kind of unity is an idea – or moral, even – that is inferred from the work and not ordinarily explicit within it. An example – perhaps extreme – of this kind of urge to unify occurs in an essay by Frank Kermode:

And in the end the play seems to say (I borrow the language of Yeats) that 'whatever is begotten, born and dies' is nobler than 'monuments of unageing intellect' – and also, when truly considered, more truly lasting.[21]

Aside from the fact that Kermode may be misinterpreting Yeats and that as he himself says his 'formula' for the play may be 'partial and moralizing', the point seems quite plausible – as one unifying theme. But there can be and have been such attempts to give and find a centre for the play; to summarize them would be as tedious as it is superfluous. To decide which is the best would be impossible. Instead, let us examine another approach to the problem of unified meaning:

... the world *The Winter's Tale* leaves us with is neither an object of knowledge nor of belief. It would be an object of belief, of course, or symbolize one, if we could feel that *The Winter's Tale* was an allegory. I have been assuming that it is not: that in Shakespeare the meaning of the play is the play, there being nothing to be abstracted from the total experience of the play.

Another minority opinion, this time from Northrop Frye's *A Natural Perspective*.[22] But this passage (from a book published in 1965) seems to presage deconstructive attempts to resist finding a centre. It also looks back to Cleanth Brooks, who expounded the 'heresy of

paraphrase' in an effort to stem the tide of reductionism. Again I would suggest that the use of the term or the concept of unity as a unitary notion is reductive in itself. The multitude of unities is what we must abide, willy-nilly, and Frye's has no less validity than Kermode's.

In addition to thematic unities (which, by the way, are products of mimetic criticism), we can sketch in some other broad categories, each admitting of virtually infinite variation. The next is formal or structural, the sort that was inaugurated by Aristotle and expanded by Renaissance critics. Again, *The Winter's Tale* presents us with extremes of critical views. For a long time the play was considered disunified (and therefore condemned), largely because it violated the 'classical' unities of time and place. Not all the action – the subplot and the sheep-shearing scene, for example – was considered pertinent, either. But at least as far back as 1958, when Nevill Coghill defended Shakespeare's construction, the various 'faults' began to be seen rather as tours de force. Such faults, Coghill said, 'may seem valid in the study, but have no force on the stage'.[23] Nowadays one hears few if any complaints about the play in these respects. Other types of formal unity can be cited: Charles Frey has made a convincing case for rhythmic unity in the scenes,[24] and even Northrop Frye, despite his comments on thematic unity, points out an ingenious textual

---

[20] It is of interest that according to their etymologies, both 'about' and 'of' originally had the meanings of 'outside of' or 'away from' (*OED*). In other words, the derivations suggest that the meaning is implied, even referential, and does not reside in the text per se.

[21] Frank Kermode, Introduction to *The Winter's Tale*, The Signet Classic Shakespeare (New York, 1963), p. xxxv.

[22] Northrop Frye, *A Natural Perspective: The Development of Shakespearean Comedy and Romance* (New York, 1965), p. 116.

[23] Nevill Coghill, 'Six Points of Stage-Craft in *The Winter's Tale*', *Shakespeare Survey* 11 (1958), p. 31.

[24] Charles Frey, *Shakespeare's Vast Romance: A Study* (Columbia, Mo., 1980).

parallel between Antigonus' and Autolycus' shoulders:

Some very curious echoes indicate the starting of a new action: part one ends with the clown hearing the cries of Antigonus as the bear tears out his shoulder bone; part two begins with that same clown hearing the cries of Autolycus pretending that his shoulder blade is out.[25]

Although not unity on a grand scale, this shrewd connection of details carries considerable cohesive force.

The larger unities tend to be intertextual, especially those that connect *The Winter's Tale* with other romances. This, too, has been a relatively recent phenomenon, but has gained widespread acceptance despite the fact that the category was not used in the First Folio, a fact which suggests the strength of the desire to seek new unities. The critics known as the Christian Humanists also find a larger unity, and see the archetypal pattern of sin and redemption as the backbone of the play. (Others see the same pattern but see it as secular allegory.) It is also possible to see the play as central to the oeuvre of Shakespeare, as the unifying climax to his career in studying the nature of human error, suffering, and restoration of the soul. In such a view, the unity of the play and the unity of the poet's work merge to form one of the largest syntheses of all. The idea is not without plausibility.

By now the reader is well aware of my rather obvious but convenient method of anatomizing unity. Let me simply say very briefly that, yes, there is affective unity, though little has been said about that. There is a strong empathy developed for Hermione (can *that*, too, be deconstructed?) that controls our feelings even and especially for Leontes, who achieves whatever sympathy he gets on her account. And given Shakespeare's talents this tragi-comedy succeeds in blending hornpipes and funerals, not to mention jealous fits and magical restorations, without violating my sense of unity of tone.

Much harder to establish is the nature of any genetic unity for *The Winter's Tale*, though it is easy enough to imagine originary impulses on Shakespeare's part, such as that suggested in the discussion of intertextual unity. Authorial intentions can be postulated, but in the case of Shakespeare never proved. But there are other originary unities to consider, such as the impetus provided by Greene, the major source. One *could* imagine that the play took its shape from Shakespeare's relationship with his early rival and that he purposely drew on a variety of works by Greene – *Pandosto*, *Menaphon*, the coney-catching pamphlets, and even possibly *Greene's Vision*, which contains accounts of jealousy[26] – with the idea of showing, as he often did, the true nature of the matters treated by his source. One *could* also imagine that the intense and groundless jealousy of Leontes was inspired by Greene's own jealousy of Shakespeare. All this is highly speculative, and not offered with any seriousness; rather it is an attempt to show yet another way the matter of unity can be considered and the way in which the mind (in this case mine) can attempt to pull things together while at the same time going against a natural inclination towards hard facts and strong logic.

What I can argue seriously is that the urge toward unifying the texts we know and linking them with the other parts of the world which are perceived as having a bearing is overwhelmingly strong – stronger than any urge to deconstruction, however inevitable that may be. I would also stress the need to treat 'unity' as a plural phenomenon. Critics who declare that there is no unity of one type often fall back on another (Frye is a notable example). Even the deconstructive articles of Wexler and Felperin contain strongly unified views, however subversive of more orthodox unities. Despite my

---

[25] Frye, *Natural Perspective*, p. 115.
[26] Pafford, Introduction to the Arden edition, pp. xxxiv–xxxv.

strictures, I do not believe, as do some, that deconstruction is the rough beast that slouched toward the Bethlehem of literature to be born. What seems to be true is that the deconstructive nature of language and utterance is countered by an inevitable tendency to construct and to reconstruct. The effort to attain a solidly unified interpretation may be like the efforts of Sisyphus to roll his rock uphill only to have it roll back to the bottom again, but that doesn't seem to stop our Sisyphean interpreters from trying. Sisyphus, you will remember (I looked it up), was reputed to be the most cunning of mankind. He actually bested that master of roguery, Autolycus.[27]

[27] I would like to acknowledge the efforts of Heather Adams, Kirsten Zook and Richard M. Eastman, who all contributed substantially to the making of this article.

LATE SHAKESPEARE: STYLE AND THE SEXES

RUSS McDONALD

Shakespeare's turn from tragedy to romance coincides with a similarly radical change in the style of his verse. This complicated and self-conscious poetry has attracted a wide variety of labels, from Baroque to incompetent to post-modern, but it has not been carefully described nor have its implications been adequately assessed. These metamorphoses of dramatic mode and verse style are partly attributable to Shakespeare's evolving and contradictory opinions about language itself, and the late tragedies, especially *Antony and Cleopatra* and *Coriolanus*, are a good place to start in studying these changes because together they constitute a kind of hinge or pivot on which Shakespeare turns from one kind of drama to another. For my purposes, their particular utility derives from their dependence upon similar conflicts of gender that not only help to forecast Shakespeare's narrative and thematic interests but also influence the kind of poetry he will devise for the final phase of his career.[1] Recent criticism has begun to establish that, historically speaking, certain expressive styles could be sexually coded, and I shall draw upon some of that work to assert that what we witness in the final phase of his career is the feminization of Shakespeare's dramatic and poetic style.[2]

The argument that follows, simply stated, is that the complex verse patterns of the late plays are intimately related to Shakespeare's imaginative recovery of the feminine, that the origins of these thematic and stylistic conflicts emerge clearly in the last classical tragedies, and

that the romances constitute a conditional resolution of these concerns. My method will be to notice certain poetic and rhetorical properties in a pair of crucial texts and to abstract from those notes some conclusions about the direction and significance of Shakespeare's subsequent work. This method assumes artistic agency, an author in whose dramatic productions we may observe both a distinctive style and distinct mutations within that style. In this respect it resists the claims of much recent discursive criticism, which behaves as if a play were author of itself and knew no other kin. The currently low repute of formalist criticism notwithstanding, I am persuaded by Patricia Parker's contention that 'to pay attention to the structural force of rhetorical figures' or characteristics of artistic technique is to 'suggest that the impasse of a now apparently outworn formalism and a new competing emphasis on politics and history might be breached by questions which fall in between and hence remain

---

[1] *Timon of Athens* is profitably considered in these terms and should probably be grouped with *Coriolanus* and *Antony and Cleopatra*, but problems of date and restrictions of space lead me to exclude it from this essay.

[2] See, for example, Patricia Parker, *Literary Fat Ladies: Rhetoric, Gender, Property* (London: Methuen, 1987), esp. pp. 8–35, and Howard R. Bloch, *Medieval Misogyny and the Invention of Western Romantic Love* (Chicago: University of Chicago Press, 1991), pp. 1–63, and Joel Fineman, *Shakespeare's Perjured Eye: The Invention of Poetic Subjectivity in the Sonnets* (Berkeley: University of California Press, 1986), pp. 125–9.

unasked by both'.[3] The application of rhetorical patterns to larger structures has contributed to significant advances in the narratological study of prose fiction, notably in the work of Peter Brooks and Tzvetan Todorov, but surprisingly little of such work has been attempted in the study of drama.[4] This essay represents an effort in that direction.

Everyone perceives the striking change in verse style at this period – *The Winter's Tale* is much harder to read or to hear than *Macbeth*, for example – and it is possible, of course, to identify certain stylistic predilections with the mode of tragedy and others with that of romance or tragicomedy, although relatively little specific work has been done in this line. But we may go further than this. As feminist and psychological critics explore the conflicts of gender and sexuality that animate Shakespeare's narratives, particularly those in the Jacobean phase of his career, it becomes increasingly clear that the passage from tragedy to romance is achieved partly by means of Shakespeare's reconception of the feminine. The major tragedies, particularly *Hamlet*, *King Lear*, and *Macbeth*, depend to a large extent upon Shakespeare's portrayal of female sexuality as degenerate, predatory, or even demonic. In the romances such malign forces, while not imaginatively banished, are accompanied and finally overwhelmed by the power of the creative and nurturant female.[5] To read the transition that occurred between 1606 and 1609 in this way is not necessarily to reinscribe upon Shakespeare's mind and art a Dowdenesque ascent from conflict to harmony; the sexual and political vicissitudes represented in the final plays strike me as too pervasive and intense to support such a reading. But it seems indisputable that the formal changes originate in the same process through which Shakespeare readjusts the dramatic balance between Lady Macbeth and Lady Macduff, for example, or between viragoes and virgins. I believe that Shakespeare's recovery of the feminine can be shown to manifest itself stylistically, even syntactically and metrically, as he exchanges what has been called the end-stopped form of tragedy for the more open form of romance.[6] He moves away from more regular and controlled forms of blank verse into a poetic style that is elliptical, syntactically involuted, and flagrantly extrametrical. The complex poetic rhythms of the late work provide an aural equivalent of re-imagined relations between men and women that, while not without conflict and pain, are grounded in mutual exchange and productive difference.

I

Coriolanus stages, in the clash between the hero and his mother, a contest between some of the opposing views of language and compositional style that the playwright inherited from his predecessors and shared with his contemporaries. Caius Martius' passionate solipsism and hubris express themselves in his contempt for flattery, his discomfort with spoken praise, and his unwillingness to state his desire for the consulship, each of these refusals being an

---

[3] *Literary Fat Ladies*, p. 96.

[4] Peter Brooks, *Reading for the Plot: Design and Intention in Narrative* (New York: Alfred A. Knopf, 1984), and Tzvetan Todorov, *The Poetics of Prose*, tr. Richard Howard (Ithaca: Cornell University Press, 1977), esp. pp. 143–77.

[5] A survey of Shakespeare's depiction of female sexuality in this late phase is found in Cyrus Hoy, 'Fathers and Daughters in Shakespeare's Romances', *Shakespeare's Romances Reconsidered*, ed. Carol McGinnis Kay and Henry E. Jacobs (Lincoln: University of Nebraska Press, 1978), pp. 77–90. Illuminating work in this line has been done by C. L. Barber and Richard P. Wheeler, *The Whole Journey: Shakespeare's Power of Development* (Berkeley and Los Angeles: University of California Press, 1986), and Coppélia Kahn, *Man's Estate: Masculine Identity in Shakespeare* (Berkeley: University of California Press, 1981). The most recent and detailed treatment of gender at this point in Shakespeare's career is that of Janet Adelman, *Suffocating Mothers: Fantasies of Maternal Origin in Shakespeare's Plays, 'Hamlet' to 'The Tempest'* (London: Methuen, 1991).

[6] See Adelman, *Suffocating Mothers*, pp. 73–4, 190.

expression of what might be called linguistic absolutism.[7] We recognize his kinship with Cordelia, that other purist, when he objects to the public account of his military victory as 'acclamations hyperbolical' and 'praises sauced with lies'. Love of fighting is accompanied by fear of language: 'yet oft / When blows have made me stay I fled from words' (2.2.71–2). This view of language derives from the discursive constraints of the hero's occupation, the military privileging of action over words, a reluctance to reveal too much, a belief in the self-evident rightness of a cause; and in announcing his suspicion of the word, Martius echoes Plutarch's frequent emphasis on the reticence or plain speech of the Spartan soldiers, a bias known alternatively as Lacadaemonian or Laconian or Laconick.[8]

The protagonist's drive for stylistic purity makes itself felt on his first entrance: his opening sentence is 'Thanks'. The laconic style is to a large extent a function of syntactic reticence. There are no superfluous words, few smooth transitions, little decoration. Grammatically, we can be even more specific than that: there are almost no conjunctions, Martius' speeches lack connectives, both within and between sentences, and such withholding creates a disjunctivity that sets every utterance apart from every other.[9] The pertinent rhetorical figure here is *asyndeton*, the omission of conjunctions between words, phrases, or clauses. Puttenham describes asyndeton as 'loose language', judging it 'defective because it wants good band or coupling'; it violates the rhetorician's sense of communicative decorum in that it is discontinuous, neither smooth nor effectively integrated into a natural-sounding whole. Puttenham identifies the military pertinence of such verbal patterns when he illustrates the figure with the famous Caesarean triplet 'I came, I saw, I overcame', in which the conqueror, 'shewing the celeritie of his conquest, wrate home to the Senate in this tenour of speach no lesse swift and speedy then his victorie'.[10] Although asyndeton normally describes the relation of clauses within sentences, Shakespeare has effectively magnified the grammatical figure by suppressing couplings between sentences so as to create a severely limited economy of verbal means.

Coriolanus contains numerous illustrations of

---

[7] Since language itself is so important an issue in *Coriolanus*, it is treated in some detail in general studies, especially those by G. Wilson Knight, *The Imperial Theme* (Oxford: Oxford University Press, 1931); Derek Traversi, *An Approach to Shakespeare*, 2nd edn (New York: Doubleday, 1966); Maurice Charney, *Shakespeare's Roman Plays: The Function of Imagery in the Drama* (Cambridge, Mass.: Harvard University Press, 1961); Norman Rabkin, *Shakespeare and the Common Understanding* (New York: The Free Press, 1966); Jonathan Goldberg, *James I and the Politics of Literature* (Baltimore: Johns Hopkins University Press, 1983); and Adelman, *Suffocating Mothers*, pp. 146–64. More specific studies of the problem of language include Lawrence Danson, *Tragic Alphabet: Shakespeare's Drama of Language* (New Haven: Yale University Press, 1974), pp. 142–62; James Calderwood, '*Coriolanus*: Wordless Meanings and Meaningless Words', *SEL*, 6 (1966), 185–202; Carol M. Sicherman, '*Coriolanus*: The Failure of Words', *ELH*, 39 (1972), 189–207; Page du Bois, 'A Disturbance of Syntax at the Gates of Rome', *Stanford Literature Review*, 2 (1985), 185–208; Leonard Tennenhouse, '*Coriolanus*: History and the Crisis of the Semantic Order', *Drama in the Renaissance: Comparative and Critical Essays*, ed. Clifford Davidson, C. J. Gianakaris, and John H. Stroupe (New York: AMS Press, 1986), pp. 217–35; and Lisa Lowe, '"Say I Play the Man I Am": Gender and Politics in *Coriolanus*', *Kenyon Review*, 8 (1986), 86–95. Indispensable are Kenneth Burke, '*Coriolanus* and the Delights of Faction', *Hudson Review*, 19 (1966), 211–24, and Stanley Cavell, '*Coriolanus* and the Interpretation of Politics ("Who does the wolf love?")', rpt. in *Disowning Knowledge in Six Plays of Shakespeare* (Cambridge: Cambridge University Press, 1987), pp. 143–77.

[8] See Philip Brockbank's Introduction to his Arden edition (London: Methuen, 1976), esp. pp. 68–71.

[9] Throughout this essay I depend heavily upon the excellent analysis found in John Porter Houston, *Shakespearean Sentences: A Study in Style and Syntax* (Baton Rouge: Louisiana State University Press, 1988), especially Chapter 7, 'Syndeton and Asyndeton in *Coriolanus*', pp. 159–78.

[10] *The Arte of English Poesie*, a facsimile reproduction with an Introduction by Baxter Hathaway (Kent State University Press, 1970), pp. 185–6.

this technique, notably the hero's fierce attack on the multitude in the opening scene, but a brief passage that captures Martius' grammatically sundered style is his request for merciful treatment of the Coriolan citizen who had befriended him: 'I sometime lay here in Corioles, / And at a poor man's house. He us'd me kindly. / He cried to me; I saw him prisoner' (1.10.81–3). The spare and ungenerous syntactic patterns – in an expression of generosity – attest to the protagonist's impatience with the niceties of rhetorical progression. Rarely is the movement from one sentence to the next made explicit, with the transition usually achieved by force. (It should be noted that 'And at' in line 82 is an emendation adopted from Hanmer; the Folio prints 'Corioles / At a poor man's house'.) The hero's language is not only grammatically asyndetic: in vocabulary and tone it also gives the impression of stinginess. His normal syntax is rather strictly paratactic and simplified, and he is especially given to 'enumeratory patterns', a form of expression implying simplicity, order, and lack of argumentative subtlety.[11]

It is not difficult to see how Shakespeare's most habitually isolated hero should speak a language in which the interdependence of sentences is suppressed, in which clauses do not touch, in which the prevalent tone is firm and unyielding. His speech constitutes the grammatical equivalent of his famous desire for freedom from familial or other kinds of relation, his desire to 'stand / As if a man were author of himself / And knew no other kin' (5.3.35–7). Such values and patterns are appropriate to tragedy, in which the movement is toward separation and extinction, which is usually given over to a solitary hero, and in which that hero is usually male.[12] The laconic, separated speech of Coriolanus is not only a military style; what is even more pertinent is that it is a historically masculine style.

Coriolanus' stylistic independence helps to extend grammatically and prosodically the critique of masculine self-sufficiency that Shakespeare inherited from his sources and developed with some care. 'Manlines' is a principal topic in Plutarch's introductory sketch of Martius' character, and Shakespeare depicts an early version of the masculine mode of behaviour in Volumnia's approving words about her grandson: 'He had rather see the swords and hear a drum than look upon his schoolmaster' (1.3.57–8). The separation of 'words' from 'swords' (in which it is contained) plays on a relation familiar to London audiences at least as early as *Tamburlaine*, and here the quibble helps to clarify what it means to say that boys will be boys: the child, attracted by the eloquence of military action, shuns the schoolmaster who teaches him language arts. The son exhibits 'a con*firm*'d countenance'; the father attacks the patriciate for being soft on the populace. Plutarch reports that Martius 'dyd so exercise his bodie to hardnes' that he always won at wrestling or games of strength, and those who lost to him 'would say when they were overcome: that all was by reason of his naturall strength, and hardnes of warde, that never yelded to any payne or toyle he tooke apon him'.[13]

---

[11] *Shakespearean Sentences*, pp. 160, 161–2. This spare grammatical base line causes eccentricity or deviation to stand out. G. Wilson Knight picks out a surprisingly large number of bizarre words, many of them polysyllables, that obtrude from a plainer style of diction, words such as 'conspectuities', 'empiricutic', 'directitude', 'factionary'. 'Many of these cause blank amazement among the rabble, or Volscian menials: and are thus related to the main idea of the aristocrat contrasted with commoners. So, in our line units, there is, as it were, an aristocrat among a crowd of plebeian words, and often that protagonist word falls with a hammer-blow that again reminds us of metal' (*The Imperial Theme*, p. 160).

[12] See Page du Bois' comments on the separating effect of the play's rhetoric: 'Anacolouthon is the appropriate rhetorical figure for this tragedy, which is about breaks in lines – not just breaks in lines of speech or thought, but breaks in descent, in lineage, breaks in city walls, breaks in bodies, wounds, breaks in the continuity of surface. *Coriolanus* is about the failure to follow ...' 'A Disturbance of Syntax', p. 187.

[13] 'The Life of Coriolanus', in Geoffrey Bullough, ed., *Narrative and Dramatic Sources of Shakespeare*, vol. 5 (New York: Columbia University Press, 1964), pp. 506–7.

This emphasis on physical 'hardnes' manifests itself repeatedly, perhaps most notably when Aufidius speaks of Coriolanus' 'body whereagainst / My grained ash an hundred times hath broke, / And scarr'd the moon with splinters' (4.5.108–10). His body, in other words, is as hard as his head, and the ideal of manly self-sufficiency and impenetrability is repeatedly thematized. Coriolanus fulminates that the competing claims of plebeians and patricians will allow 'confusion' to 'enter 'twixt the gap of both' (3.1.113–14), fearing that to yield to popular demands sets a precedent 'which will in time / Break ope the locks o'th' senate' (3.1.140–1). He asks leave to depart during Cominius' praise of him because he cannot stand to hear his 'nothings monstered', thus drawing upon the sexual implications of 'monster', in the sense of hermaphrodite. What is aurally striking is that Shakespeare has found a stylistic equivalent for integrity and manly impenetrability. Wilson Knight's discussion of the metallic quality of much of the play's imagery – fins of lead, lead roofs, iron walls, metal gates, stone barriers – suggests a harsh visual background that is sustained by what we might call the prosodic angularity of the work.[14] Shakespeare's stark arrangement of the hero's syntactic and grammatical forms creates an aural impression consistent with what has been identified as his 'phallic aggressive pose'.[15]

The habit of discursive withholding, of limitation and parsimony, makes Coriolanus particularly uncomfortable in the marketplace, where his most formidable challenges occur and where the discourse of commerce clashes with his reticence and ideal of self-sufficiency. In other words, the military hero can't make it in the business world. The marketplace depends upon the language of exchange, a flexible discursive economy in which the rhetorically rigid soldier cannot participate. He 'pays himself with being proud' (1.1.31–2), as one of the citizens puts it, and the narrative context of dearth, beggary, and unfair distribution supplies added point to the discursive emphasis on

Coriolanus' 'sufficiency' and refusal to negotiate, his unwillingness to show his wounds in public. The commercial dimension of this desire for independence is captured paronomastically in his attack on tradition as 'custom' in the rhymed soliloquy in Act 2: he will not become the people's customer. Ceremony, ritual, politics, all forms of exchange (except the speechless one of physical combat) are repellent to him. Volumnia seeks to overcome her son's class- and gender-based fear of the marketplace, and she comes close, in Act 3, scene 2, to teaching him the art of 'policy' or negotiation. Her urging of compromise and diplomacy is another way of asking her son to lower his moral price, but his absolutism forbids haggling. Although he makes an effort to get with the patrician programme, resolving to go 'to the market-place', 'mountebank their loves, / Cog their hearts from them, and come home beloved / Of all the trades in Rome' (3.2.132–4), when he gets there his intolerable consciousness of being bought appears in his sardonic promise to respond as calmly 'as an hostler that for th' poorest piece / Will bear the knave by th' volume' (3.3.33–4). The climax of this central public episode, the banishment, occurs after he is taunted with the word 'traitor', in which we may also hear the mercantile sense of 'trader'.[16] Coriolanus can accept neither denotation and so calls off the deal: 'I would not buy / Their mercy at the price of one fair word' (3.3.94–5).

In dramatizing such conflicts Shakespeare exploits the connotative interchangeability of

---

[14] *The Imperial Theme*, pp. 155–7.

[15] Janet Adelman, *Suffocating Mothers*, p. 151. The section on *Coriolanus* originally appeared as '"Anger's My Meat": Feeding, Dependency, and Aggression in *Coriolanus*', in *Representing Shakespeare: New Psychoanalytic Essays*, ed. Murray M. Schwartz and Coppélia Kahn (Baltimore: Johns Hopkins University Press, 1980). See also Robert J. Stoller, 'Shakespearean Tragedy: *Coriolanus*', *Psychoanalytic Quarterly*, 35 (1966), 263–74.

[16] I owe this observation to my former student Catherine Loomis of the University of Rochester.

economics and sexuality. Coriolanus' contemptuous wish to be possessed by 'Some harlot's spirit' in order to get through the performance in the marketplace partakes of both discourses, since 'harlot' comes from the Old French word for vagabond, and his inability to 'discharge' the part contains an economic metaphor embedded in his refusal to act. This mixture of the verbal, the economic, and the sexual is extended in the connection between discourse and discharge apparent in Volumnia's loquacity, her endless need to relieve herself verbally. We hear it also in the first scene in the marketplace: 'or if he show us his wounds and tell us his deeds, we are to put our tongues into those wounds and speak for them' (2.3.5–7). One need not be very adept at psychological criticism to feel the effect of this cluster of images: the political 'custom' of showing wounds and asking approval is an act of commercial exchange, the buying of the consulship, and this becomes a complicated verbal and sexual transaction, the taking of the tongue/phallus into the wound/hole which then becomes a mouth.[17] To Coriolanus, real men do not play the receiver in the sexual act, nor do they sully themselves in business. All intercourse – political, commercial, sexual, theatrical, or verbal – is debased, a form of prostitution. It becomes increasingly clear that Coriolanus' distrust of language is a fear of dependency, of vulnerability, and of the feminine.

II

Coriolanus' laconic style is a sceptical response to the instabilities of all language, and it is fair, if ironic, to say that Shakespeare poured a good deal of himself into the creation of his uncommunicative hero. This play restages the Shakespearian concern, familiar from the earlier tragedies, with the infidelity of verbal signs and the limits of representation. Here the emphasis falls on the faulty verbal foundations of politics. Much of the play's political vocabulary derives etymologically from words having

to do with speech, and their reiteration helps to establish the inevitability, in the political realm, of dialectic, uncertainty, and multivocality.[18] The most striking critique of the verbal foundations of political process appears in the elaboration of the words 'voice' and 'voices' in the central movement of the play. Shakespeare took the noun from North, who took it from '*voix*' in Amyot's translation of Plutarch. As D. J. Gordon pointed out, its appearance owes something not only to the classical source but also to contemporary Jacobean political procedures, specifically the elections for parliament.[19] In the tribunes' declaration that 'the people / Must have their voices' (2.2.139–40), the word is a synonym for 'vote', and this declaration begins to suggest other possible senses – 'opinion', 'will' (as in 'the voice of God'), 'desire', and 'choice'. But neither Plutarchan source nor narrative demand can account for Shakespeare's worrying of the word, culminating in the protagonist's bitter reiterations:

Here come moe Voyces.
Your Voyces? for your Voyces I have fought,
Watcht for your Voyces: for your Voyces, beare
Of Wounds, two dozen odde: Battailes thrice six
I have seene, and heard of: for your Voyces,
Have done many things, some lesse, some more:
Your Voyces! Indeed I would be consul.

(TL 1517–23)

I have departed here from the modern text to cite the Folio, where the insistent capitalization

---

17 Adelman is especially illuminating on this passage, since the oral imagery is an essential element in the dependency theme: see *Suffocating Mothers*, pp. 153–5.

18 On the uses and abuses of etymology in literary studies, see Derek Attridge's fascinating essay, 'Language as History / History as Language: Saussure and the Romance of Etymology', in *Poststructuralism and the Question of History*, ed. Attridge, Geoff Bennington, and Robert Young (Cambridge: Cambridge University Press, 1987), pp. 183–211.

19 'Name and Fame: Shakespeare's *Coriolanus*', in *The Renaissance Imagination*, ed. Stephen Orgel (Berkeley: University of California Press, 1975), pp. 203–19.

of 'Voyces' in this passage signals its importance.[20] The noun 'voices' is used fifty-four times in the Shakespeare canon, two-thirds of them (36) in this play, and twenty-seven times in this scene alone.[21] Its prominence has to do with its synecdochic function: it stands for the instability and contingency that Coriolanus deplores in human interaction, of which politics is the epitome and language the flawed medium.

It is one of the great ironies of *Coriolanus* that the hero's credo, his intolerance of ambiguity, should be expressed in a pun, the paronomastic toying with 'vice' and 'voice'. Kökeritz demonstrates the frequent levelling of the diphthong OI and the long I, and he offers a particularly relevant example from Act 2 of *Cymbeline* when he shows that the Folio spelling of *voyce* for *vice* in Cloten's discussion of music is not a misprint but rather a pun.[22] *Coriolanus* may be thought of as a study of the vice of voice, or the political complexities deriving from the weaknesses of the word. Several heads, many voices, 'The multitudinous tongue' – these are the conditions of politics that Coriolanus wishes to control or escape because they are incompatible with his need for unity and independence. Shared responsibility in political affairs, expressed in Coriolanus' fears about what happens 'when two authorities are up', corresponds to shared meaning of words: the protagonist's horror of polysemy is another form of his contempt for political representation. His idealism gives him the illusion of freedom, from the constraints of language or of any other such limits, and that illusion is the source of his destruction.

III

Shakespeare's self-consciousness about the perils and the possibilities of language coincides with the contemporary debate over the proper forms of prose style and the philosophical implications of those positions. A brief review of the dispute reminds us that the old-fashioned Ciceronian model, with its elaborate syntactical constructions, symmetrical patterns of words and clauses, and devotion to ornament, was in conflict with the self-consciously modern approach, modelled on Seneca, with its obviously broken periods and asymmetrical grouping of words, a severity of vocabulary and sound, and a Spartan disdain for decoration.[23] In the late Roman world, Ciceronian eloquence was thought of as Asiatic or exotic, Senecan directness as Attic or classical. The foundations of these two opposed attitudes are quickly discernible: the Ciceronians valued language for its own sake and considered stylistic extravagance a proper development of its value and possibility; their opponents, devoted as they were to clarity of expression and a more functional view of the word, considered such extravagance dangerous in that it increased one's vulnerability to the potential treachery of language. Roger Ascham defended his taste for Cicero and the elaborate style by accusing his detractors as follows: 'Ye know not, what hurt ye do to learning, that care not for wordes, but for matter, and so make a deuorse betwixt the tong and the hart.'[24] To concentrate entirely on

---

20 *The Norton Facsimile of The First Folio of Shakespeare*, prepared by Charlton Hinman (New York: W. W. Norton, 1968). Elsewhere in the play, 'voice' and 'voices' are sometimes capitalized, sometimes not. For this detail, I am grateful to Richard Proudfoot.

21 My source for the statistics of usage is Marvin Spevack, *A Complete and Systematic Concordance to the Works of Shakespeare* (Hildesheim: Olms, 1968), vol. 3, *The Tragedies*.

22 Helge Kökeritz, *Shakespeare's Pronunciation* (New Haven: Yale University Press, 1953), pp. 151–2.

23 The historical background is found in Morris W. Croll, *Style, Rhetoric, and Rhythm*, ed. J. Max Patrick, Robert O. Evans, *et al.* (Princeton: Princeton University Press, 1966), and George Williamson, *The Senecan Amble* (Chicago: University of Chicago Press, 1951). Jonas A. Barish's *Ben Jonson and the Language of Prose Comedy* (Cambridge, Mass.: Harvard University Press, 1960) offers a useful development and application of these principles.

24 *The Scholemaster*, ed. Edward Arber (Birmingham, 1870), p. 118.

meaning, thus overlooking the means by which that meaning is achieved, is to neglect such important factors as persuasion and instruction. At the other pole stood the formidable Francis Bacon, who considered the imitation of Cicero, 'the first distemper of learning, when men study words and not matter.' 'Then did Car of Cambridge and Ascham with their lectures and writings almost deify Cicero and Demosthenes, and allure all young men that were studious unto that delicate and polished kind of learning.'[25] Different values are at issue here: the elaborate versus the clear, the delicate versus the rough, the roundabout versus the pointed. Obviously the Tudor–Stuart debate over kinds of writing involved a good deal more than syntactical preferences. Is language a medium and nothing else? Or since language is necessary as an expressive tool, ought we to develop and relish its manifold properties?

Words: can't live with 'em, can't live without 'em. It will have become clear by now that this debate is grounded in conceptions of sexual difference and is related to the figuration of language as feminine and action as masculine in early-modern language theory.[26] The misogynist tradition inherited from the middle ages propagated the notion that language resembles women in being treacherous and unreliable, subject to extravagance, malleability, and error. It originated in the classical period and received virulent expression in the writings of the Church Fathers, particularly Tertullian, St John Chrysostom, and St Augustine. As Howard Bloch has demonstrated in some detail, this gendered conception is responsible for the series of identifications, which manifest themselves repeatedly in the humanist rhetoric of the sixteenth and seventeenth centuries, of the masculine with the primary, with essence, with form, with unity; and of the feminine with the secondary, the accidental, the material, the duplicitous or ambiguous.[27] In the most notorious anti-feminine passages in medieval literature, a familiar and loudly asserted complaint against women is the proclivity for loud complaint. Garrulousness, nagging, shrewishness, bickering, demanding – the most familiar laments from the *molestiae nuptiarum*, or the tradition of anti-marriage literature, have to do with the verbal miseries inevitably attendant upon the taking of a wife. In other words, the attack on women was often a simultaneous attack on language. Commentators reached as far back as Eden to connect the female with the decorative, the artificial, the inessential: in the Genesis account, Eve's verbal seduction of Adam into eating the fruit of the Forbidden Tree led to the need for covering, and from that time forward there existed a contest between the natural body and the dressings invented for it. As Tertullian put it, 'with the word the garment entered'. In a related treatment of the topic, St Augustine distinguished between numerical signs as masculine and verbal signs as feminine.[28] Numbers were identified with the virtues of constancy, order, and clarity, in short, with the spirit. Words connoted corruption and impermanence and were linked with the body, specifically with the female body and its traditional adornments – clothing, makeup, hairstyle, jewelry.

We might now return to Bacon's attack on Ciceronian style as 'that delicate and polished kind of learning' that 'allured' the boys from

[25] *The Advancement of Learning*, ed. Arthur Johnston (Oxford: Clarendon Press, 1974), p. 26.

[26] The most thorough discussion of this tradition is found in Bloch, *Medieval Misogyny*, pp. 13–35. For background on some of the patristic writers, particularly the Platonic roots of their gynophobic thinking, see also Jonas A. Barish, *The Antitheatrical Prejudice* (Berkeley: University of California Press, 1981), chapters 1 and 2.

[27] *Medieval Misogyny*, pp. 18–30.

[28] Tertullian's '*cum voce vestis intravit*' is from *De Pallio*. Augustine's remarks are found in *De Ordine*: 'From that time forth she [Reason] found it hard to believe that the splendor and purity [of numbers] was sullied by the corporeal matter of words. And just as what the spirit sees is always present and is held to be immortal and numbers appear such, while sound, being a sensible thing, is lost into the past.' Both are quoted in Bloch, *Medieval Misogyny*, pp. 46, 220.

Cambridge: *delicate* and *polished* are gendered adjectives, pejorative terms for a sissified style. Patricia Parker summarizes this debate by offering a major instance from the early Tudor period: 'Erasmus in his *Ciceronianus* (1528) speaks of seeking in vain in Ciceronian eloquence for something "masculine" and of his own desire for a "more masculine" style. Ciceronian copia in these discussions is both effeminate and the style of a more prodigal youth, to be outgrown once one had become a man: "I used to imitate Cicero", writes Lipsius; "but I have become a man, and my tastes have changed. Asiatic feasts have ceased to please me; I prefer the Attic." '[29] And this bias appears also in the Renaissance view of the femininity of verse and the Puritan attack on the effeminacy of the stage: we remember Sidney's *Defence*, written as a rejoinder to the attack on poetry as immoral, frivolous, and unmanly. Thomas Howell's *Devises*, published in 1581, contains a six-line poem entitled 'Women are wordes, Men are deedes',[30] and we should think of Hotspur, that quintessential man of action, who proclaims his contempt for 'mincing poetry' and who is infuriated when the King's effeminate ambassador addresses him on the battlefield in 'many holiday and lady terms'. The still-prevalent view that poetry or dramatics is for girls, while science or mathematics, real learning, is for boys descends from this derisory association of women and words.

IV

It is an easy leap from this historical identification of the ungoverned female tongue with speech in general to Shakespeare's depiction of the loquacious Volumnia as foil to her laconic son. She employs her limitless verbal energies to try to modify his absolutism, urging flexibility, compromise, and interpretation. Another way of putting it is to say that she attempts to open his closed text, to puncture his wall of impenetrability, to seduce him into performing a fiction of humility. After assert-

ing the value of 'gentle words' in taking in an enemy city and commending the need to 'dissemble' in the proper cause, Volumnia shifts her emphasis to the practical, telling him that if he cannot speak the proper words as he asks the citizens for the consulship, then at least he can appear to be accommodating. She sets forth in one extraordinary sentence the way he ought to look and the way he ought to sound:

> I prithee now, my son,
> [*She takes his bonnet*]
> Go to them with this bonnet in thy hand,
> And thus far having stretch'd it – here be with
>   them –
> Thy knee bussing the stones – for in such business
> Action is eloquence, and the eyes of th'ignorant
> More learned than the ears – waving thy head,
> With often, thus, correcting thy stout heart,
> Now humble as the ripest mulberry
> That will not hold the handling: or say to them,
> Thou art their soldier and, being bred in broils,
> Hast not the soft way which, thou dost confess,
> Were fit for thee to use as they to claim,
> In asking their good loves, but thou wilt frame
> Thyself, forsooth, hereafter theirs so far
> As thou hast power and person.   (3.2.72–86)

The immediate relevance of this passage is found in its grammatical structure, particularly the contrast with Coriolanus' masculine style. Even if we punctuate the passage so that it divides into two sentences, there is no break in thought. The length and the syntactical involutions suggest the association of women and copia. The paratactic, additive form of the plea, supported and extended as it is by the participles, connotes the endlessness of female speech, the ungoverned lingual quality inherent in the misogynist tradition; at the same time, the hypotactic intrusions and parentheses attest to the indirections and potential waywardness of women and their words. Rhythmically, the expectations established by the pentameter are

---

[29] *Literary Fat Ladies*, p. 14.
[30] *Howell's Devises 1581, With an Introduction by Walter Raleigh* (Oxford: Clarendon Press, 1906), p. 31.

at odds with the liberty and variety of the phrasing: the semantic and rhythmic drive introduces disruptions that poke holes in the order of the line and threaten a kind of aural chaos.[31] There are other kinds of gaps as well – the elision of words; the breaking in of parenthetical phrases; logical fissures, as words and ideas tumble out pell-mell. In this plea for duplicity we hear the complicated verbal patterns that Shakespeare will develop in the romances soon to come.

Coriolanus, then, presents a contest of styles, with each side sexually marked. The Baconian, phallic position informs the laconic speech of Coriolanus, who flees from words. Volumnia, on the other hand, represents Ciceronian loquacity and indirection. The 'tradition of the copia of discourse' described by Patricia Parker seems particularly relevant to this conflict between mother and son, feminine and masculine: as she puts it, 'Augustine in the *Confessions* has a whole chapter devoted to "increase and multiply" (XIII.xxiv) in the sense of the interpreter's opening and fruitful extension of a closed or hermetic scriptural text, what the rhetorical tradition would call 'dilating or enlarging of the matter by interpretation'. But this 'matter' and its enlarging also easily joined with '*mater*'.[32] The matter on which this mater enlarges in the great oration in 5.3 is a feminine plea for language as a sign of connection, and her speech begins with an effort to tempt her son away from his linguistic chastity. She has become, like the plebeians in the first scene, a beggar from whom Coriolanus deliberately withholds his 'good word': 'Speak to me, son'; 'Why dost not speak?'; 'Yet give us our dispatch.' Begging for mercy, suing for the word of reconciliation instead of the deed of destruction, playing the go-between from which the word *interpreter* etymologically derives, she unfolds the multiple senses of the texts of 'loyalty' or 'honour' or 'nobility' and thus saves the city by an act of interpretation. She is supported by two women and a child, and she presses a 'suit' or 'petition' that asks, sig-

nificantly, that Coriolanus 'reconcile' the two sides, that he 'Rather … show a noble grace to both parts / Than seek the end of one' (5.3.122–3). It is a demand for recognition of duality by her monomaniacal son, and her eloquent and extravagant defence of the city constitutes an appeal, if an unconscious one, for the values of exchange, community, communication, and multivocality. Coriolanus at first refuses to 'capitulate again with Rome's mechanics', and the word 'capitulate', deriving from the process of organizing an oration under headings, is characteristic of his obstinacy because it is a verbal metaphor: he will not come to terms. When he does give in, he surrenders not only to the claims of the female, but also to the inescapability and conditionality of language. Volumnia's victory is limited, however. Although she seems to persuade him of the need for human connection, his deed is accomplished ironically without language, as the famous stage direction indicates: '*He holds her by the hand, silent*'. I want to urge that we read this surrender of son to mother as an allegory of Shakespeare's professional uncertainties around 1607.

V

But allegories, as Mrs Malaprop knew, are found on the banks of the Nile, and the relevance of *Antony and Cleopatra* to this discussion of language and gender will be immediately clear. The contest between the masculine and feminine or the Senecan and Ciceronian is encoded in the several poetic and rhetorical patterns that the sophisticated but fundamentally binary structure of the play serves to promote. Some of these contrasts, most of them familiar, include the imagistic tension between a masculine Rome and a feminine

---

[31] See the excellent discussion in George T. Wright, *Shakespeare's Metrical Art* (Berkeley: University of California Press, 1988), pp. 207–48.
[32] *Literary Fat Ladies*, p. 15.

Egypt; the contest between the hyperbolic and deflationary and the tendency of the former to tip over into the latter but to recuperate itself nevertheless; the identification of Cleopatra with abundance, of Caesar with scarcity, and Antony's unstable relation to both; the opposition between the Attic and Asiatic discourses.[33] What is worth articulating here is, first, the way that Shakespeare appeals to the misogynist–linguistic tradition in his creation of the Egyptian queen, both invoking and rejecting the censure implicit in it, and second, the way that the characters produce and are produced by the stylistic effects of the play. As Rosalie Colie puts it in her brilliant analysis, '"Style" is – especially in the Attic–Asiatic polarity – a moral indicator, but here displayed as deeply thrust into the psychological and cultural roots of those ways of life. In this play, a given style is never merely an alternative way of expressing something: rather, styles arise from cultural sources beyond a character's choice or control.'[34]

The infinitely various Cleopatra is the embodiment of those values for which Volumnia so eloquently and lengthily pleads – multiplicity, equivocation, and even, in the sexual sense, compromise. Enshrined on the barge through the medium of Enobarbus' encomium, she is the ultimate floating signifier, the play's main figure (like her ancestor Falstaff) of verbal prowess and ambiguity, the focus for its concern with the transgression of limits, whether of nations or genders. The repeated attention to her clothing, most notably her appearing 'in the habiliments of the goddess Isis', associates her with the moon-deity, a figure of pagan mystery and mutability.[35] Moreover, that get-up locates her in the region of theatre and language, of coverings and tissues and mysterious femininity, and such associations give greater point to her unmanning Antony by dressing him in her tires and mantles.

Her changeability makes her poetic voice especially difficult to classify, as she mimics Roman seriousness, plays with words for the material pleasure they offer ('music – music, moody food / Of us that trade in love'), and assumes the language of tragic heroine at the end of the play. One of her familiar verbal tics is her penchant for *ecphonesis*, and in prominent places:

THIDIAS He knows that you embraced not
   Antony
As you did love, but as you feared him.
CLEOPATRA O.   (3.13.55–7)

The 'infinitely meaningful phoneme'[36] creates the sense of flexibility and openness that is coded as female and represents speech – the word – at its most fundamental. The frequency of 'O' is matched by a host of pleonasms, as in the repetitions of 'Come' (and 'welcome')

---

[33] *Antony and Cleopatra* has generated a large number of stylistic studies, of which David Bevington's Introduction to the New Cambridge Edition (1990) provides a useful survey. For my purposes, the most helpful studies include those of G. Wilson Knight, *The Imperial Theme*, pp. 199–262; Rosalie Colie, *Shakespeare's Living Art* (Princeton: Princeton University Press, 1974), pp. 168–207; Janet Adelman, *The Common Liar: An Essay on 'Antony and Cleopatra'* (New Haven: Yale University Press, 1973); Madeleine Doran, *Shakespeare's Dramatic Language* (Madison: University of Wisconsin Press, 1976); G. R. Hibbard, '*Feliciter audax: Antony and Cleopatra*, I', 1–24', in *Shakespeare's Styles: Essays in Honour of Kenneth Muir*, ed. Philip Edwards, G. K. Hunter, and Inga-Stina Ewbank (Cambridge: Cambridge University Press, 1980), pp. 95–109; and Charney, *Shakespeare's Roman Plays*. Also useful, although less specifically concerned with style, is Robert Ornstein's 'The Ethic of the Imagination: Love and Art in *Antony and Cleopatra*', in *Later Shakespeare*, ed. John Russell Brown and Bernard Harris (London: Edward Arnold, 1966), pp. 31–46.

[34] *Shakespeare's Living Art*, p. 179.

[35] See Adelman, *Suffocating Mothers*, pp. 183–4, and Colie, *Shakespeare's Living Art*, p. 195.

[36] The phrase is David Willbern's, from his suggestive essay 'Shakespeare's Nothing', in Schwartz and Kahn, *Representing Shakespeare*, pp. 244–63; the quotation appears on p. 249. On this point I have also profited from an unpublished paper by Edward Snow, 'Cleopatra's O', delivered in the plenary session at the 1989 meeting of the Shakespeare Association of America.

during the monument scene (4.16) and succeeding episodes: 'Where art thou, death? / Come hither, come. Come, come, and take a queen / Worth many babes and beggars' (5.2.45–7). As this excerpt indicates, Cleopatra's language at the last becomes not only more elevated but more 'poetically' marked, with a noticeable increase in alliteration, internal rhyme, and other echoing effects. The final speeches also exhibit a remarkable range of syntactical structures. The reverie addressed to her maids immediately after Antony's death ('No more but e'en a woman') is full of exclamations, questions, sentences of varying length, and stops and starts, not to mention the prominent images and their poetic presentation ('Our lamp is spent, it's out'). It is unnecessary to elaborate on such poetic properties: what is important is that they support the association of Cleopatra with language and its creative powers.

This female realm of language is disturbing to Caesar as inimical to Roman values. His view of amorous passion is figured in terms that carry a discursive charge, that are explicitly associated with the Asiatic style: slack, effeminate, inflated, voluptuous.[37] Sharing Coriolanus' viewpoint, he distrusts words as uncertain, dislikes conversation, associates language with liquor and other threats to manhood and duty. As he puts it in leaving Pompey's galley after the bacchanal,

> Strong Enobarb
> Is weaker than the wine, and mine own tongue
> Splits what it speaks. The wild disguise hath almost
> Anticked us all. What needs more words? Good
> night.   (2.7.119–22)

Earlier Caesar has lamented Antony's degeneration into 'an ebb'd man', and the diction of this passage brings together the causes of such a deformation: the splitting tongue, 'disguise' as a term for revelry, unruly behaviour, unnecessary words. Antony's conciliatory promise to Octavia before the wedding, 'Read not my blemishes in the world's report. / I have not kept my square, but that to come / Shall all be done by th' rule' (2.3.6–7), is offered, like the marriage itself, mainly for Caesar's benefit and expresses succinctly the fundamental Octavian values. 'Report' is fallible and untrustworthy, for words are roundabout and irregular. Or, to quote Caesar himself in the negotiations with Pompey, 'There's the point' (2.6.31). Caesar's masculine commitment to the point, the purpose, the job to be done, matches Coriolanus' impatience with circumlocution and inefficiency; it stands in contrast to Antony's dallying with Cleopatra, a digression which not only effeminizes but makes him the subject of talk.

If we are to read Shakespeare's professional development allegorically, as I have proposed, then Antony becomes the central figure for the dramatist poised stylistically between the masculine and the feminine, the Attic and the Asiatic. The hero's dissolute behaviour is censured by Octavius in language of dissolution ('the ebb'd man'), and Antony himself adopts such terms in the celebrated passage from the suicide scene (4.15.1–14) that begins with the image of the shifting cloud, continues with the liquid metaphor of lost difference ('as indistinct / As water is in water'), and ends with 'Here I am Antony, / Yet cannot hold this visible shape'. Stylistically, the distinction between masculine and feminine loses its outline in the union of Antony and Cleopatra, and thus its subtleties make the play even more clearly indicative than *Coriolanus* of the work to come. Our familiarity with the visual, imagistic stress on permeability, dissolution, and the loss of recognizable shape needs to be supplemented with an awareness of the aural equivalent. As the rhythms and syntax of *Antony and Cleopatra* indicate, the contours of Shakespeare's verse tend to melt in the heat of the Egyptian sun.

Metrically the play is uncommonly subtle, even for Shakespeare, even for this phase: it is

---

[37] See Colie, pp. 199–200.

marked by the increasing frequency of the short sentence, the brief outburst that acts to challenge the sovereignty of the pentameter line. Very frequently, as George T. Wright points out about the late style in general, 'The sense runs over ... into the next line, a tendency facilitated by Shakespeare's radically increased usage of weak and light line-endings', or what used to be called feminine endings.[38] If *Coriolanus* exhibits its hero's dedication to a disconnected, masculine style, much of *Antony and Cleopatra* displays the complementary form, a style that is irregular, digressive, and, according to the conceptions of the period, feminine. Rhythmically, the sense o'erflows the measure of the line. In its syntax, *Antony and Cleopatra* depends heavily on the figure known as *hyperbaton*, or, as Puttenham Englishes it, 'the trespasser'. Its description is found in Book III of the *Arte*, 'Of Ornament', the section prefaced by his elaborate comparison of writing with the sartorial splendour of 'Madames of Honour'. The most notable of these figures 'of tollerable disorder' is the parenthesis, or, in its English equivalent, 'the inserter'. After providing a particularly extended example, Puttenham comments that 'This insertion is very long and utterly impertinent to the principall matter, and makes a great gappe in the tale', and he cautions that 'you must not use such insertions often nor too thick, nor those that bee very long as this of ours, for it will breed great confusion to have the tale so much interrupted'.[39] Such an account of discontinuity pertains to both the grammatical and the scenic syntax of *Antony and Cleopatra*: not only is the incidence of inverted word orders and disrupted sentences uncommonly high, but the inserted episodes, digressive scenes, and disordered geography make for a notoriously choppy theatrical narrative, a feature that contributed to the neo-classical discomfort with the play. These characteristics, increasing metrical irregularity and syntactic disorder, combine with other grammatical and rhetorical propensities, such as frequent ellipsis and a reliance on verbless constructions, to create a verse-style that is closer to prose than in almost any of the earlier works. Formally speaking, it is copious, unruly, and demanding.

The final movement, from Antony's suicide to the end of the play, constitutes the bridge between the tragedies and the romances because it attests to Shakespeare's developing attitude toward fictional language. Cleopatra inserts herself into what might have been simply the tragedy of Antony, making a great gap in Plutarch's tale. She not only memorializes Antony in a virtuosic act of poetic construction but also stages her own spectacular denouement by the creative manipulation of clothing and jewelry and words. In the represented death of the historical female is the birth of the fictional Cleopatra, the exchange of mimesis for poesis. But this final episode depends upon an imaginative scrambling of gender, a recombination of the masculine and feminine. Cleopatra, a boy actor neither man nor woman, talks her way into the male role of tragic hero, using women's weapons and speaking much of the time about a man. Janet Adelman has argued that 'In the tragedies that follow from *Hamlet*, heroic masculinity has been constructed defensively, by a rigid separation from the dangerous female within and without', and that 'by locating Antony's heroic manhood within Cleopatra's vision of him, Shakespeare attempts in effect to imagine his way beyond this impasse'.[40] This imaginative union of the masculine and the feminine helps to account for Shakespeare's reconceived attitude towards words, verse style, dramatic mode, and the theatrical enterprise itself.

VI

The critical disagreement over the final effect of *Antony and Cleopatra* is itself testimony to the playwright's ambiguous attitude towards

---

[38] Wright, *Shakespeare's Metrical Art*, p. 222.
[39] *The Arte of English Poesie*, pp. 180–1.
[40] *Suffocating Mothers*, p. 177.

ambiguity at this crucial moment in his career. If there is something of the sceptical Coriolanus and the dubious Caesar in Shakespeare, there is something of the extravagant Volumnia and Cleopatra as well. On the one hand, all the plays of this phase exhibit a suspicion of language and its inadequacies; on the other, they also display an attraction to its material pleasures, creative ambiguity, and conciliatory power. The victories of Volumnia and Cleopatra, although predicated on defeat, clearly represent a triumph of the values of theatre and of voice, with all its vices. Accommodating his Baconian suspicions of language and its representational capacities, Shakespeare embraces the possibilities of ambiguity rather than seeking to control them. He commits himself to the vice of voice, accepting and making use of what has been called, in another context, 'the gift of gap'.[41] In other words, the space between the signifier and the signified, the territory that frightens both Coriolanus and the Renaissance Senecans, may indeed be treacherous. Gaps in tales may, in Puttenham's terms, 'breed great confusion'. But as his verb suggests, such a space is also generative, full of fanciful opportunity, and Shakespeare determines to exploit rather than suppress these possibilities. The romances give us a reconstituted conception of the theatre, an admission that while words may not adequately represent reality, they can provide an alternative version of it. There is continuing suspicion of the word in these dramas,[42] but such distrust is accompanied by a resignation to or acceptance of its limitations and a renewed pleasure in the possibilities of fictional language.

The end of the tragic sequence implies, in the rejection of Coriolanus' view, the triumph of a 'feminine' style. In other words, Shakespeare commits himself to poetry marked by his culture as female, returning to Ciceronian principles of ornament and verbal pleasure. The masculine, separated, univocal speech of Coriolanus gives way to a verse characterized by poetic extravagance and multiplicity. The late tragedies are exceptional in that properties of

language coded as masculine and feminine may be conveniently assigned to individual speakers of the appropriate gender, but even here, with these relatively schematic divisions, we must be wary of crude distinctions that the subtlety of these late texts forbids. The 'femininity' of Volumnia and Cleopatra is complicated by the masculine associations with which Shakespeare has tinged them (for example, Sicinius' contemptuous question to Volumnia after the banishment, 'Are you mankind?', and Cleopatra's remembrance of the 'sword Phillipan'). By asserting Shakespeare's devotion to a feminine style late in his career, I do not mean to suggest anything so blunt as that all the major dramatic voices, from Pericles' to Prospero's, be considered 'female'. What I do suggest is that the famous difficulties of the late verse are best understood in light of the historical affiliations of style and gender, and that what we hear connotes the discursive subtlety and complexity coded by Shakespeare's culture as feminine. The exploitation of the mid-line caesura, the juxtaposition of short and long sentences, the piling of clause upon clause, the frequency of ellipsis, the inversion of subject, verb, and object, the extremes of hyperbatonic syntax, the high incidence (almost one in three) of extrametrical lines and light endings – all these features constitute a reconfiguration of Shakespeare's poetic style that incorporates grammatically and metrically the conflicts of sexual difference explored in the dramatic narratives.[43] Aurally demanding and self-consciously artificial, the romantic style involves a

---

41 See R. A. Shoaf, 'The Play of Puns in Late Middle English Poetry: Concerning Juxtology', in *On Puns: The Foundation of Letters*, ed. Jonathan Culler (London: Blackwell, 1988), p. 53.

42 Anne Barton, 'Shakespeare and the Limits of Language', *Shakespeare Survey 24* (1971), pp. 19–30.

43 All these features have been given some attention by the few commentators who have written extensively on the later style. See especially J. M. Nosworthy's Introduction to the Arden edition of *Cymbeline* (London: Methuen, 1955); F. E. Halliday, *The Poetry of*

contest between sense and form, between the semantic energies of the sentence and the restrictions of the iambic pentameter. These stylistic tensions and resolutions grow directly from the sexual conflicts that Shakespeare examines in the late tragedies and develops, with new resolutions, in the romances. If there is a single property of the late style that distinguishes it from the earlier verse, it is the unusual freedom with which its various components, from clauses to words to lines, are joined together in an uneasy but finally successful equipoise. We might say the same for the various forms of sexual relations, healthy and unhealthy, in the romances. It is a short step from copula to copulation.

It is worth re-examining Lytton Strachey's pejorative suggestion that Shakespeare in his late years was bored and careless.[44] The late style does suggest carelessness, but it is what we should think of as a kind of insouciance, a playfulness consistent with the magical stories he chooses to tell and the hypertheatrical way in which he stages them. The difficulties of the late style amount to a form of play, a sporting with poetic effects that is a function of Shakespeare's newly developed recreative view of language and that suits the thematic emphasis on re-creation permeating the late work. His reconsideration of the feminine has ramifications that go beyond language to the kind of stories such language embodies. The discursive extravagance associated with Volumnia and Cleopatra is helpful in thinking about this formal shift, since the word 'extravagant' derives from the Latin for straying or errancy, and one of the principal characteristics of romance is its dependence upon wandering, doubling, and excess.[45] For the Elizabethans and Jacobeans, romance was already a notoriously feminine form: as John Lyly declared, romance 'had rather be shut up in a lady's casket than open in a scholar's study'.[46] And tragedy, with its historical authority, was evidently masculine. This prejudice survives in the familiar privileging of tragedy over comedy: love

stories are merely pleasurable tales, useless fictions for and about women; real men read tragedies. After the Roman spareness of *Coriolanus* and the Caesarean scenes of *Antony and Cleopatra*, Shakespeare offers his audience – with a vengeance – the staples of romantic fiction: stolen infants, wicked stepmothers, wronged wives, Italian villains, shipwrecks, tearful reunions, oracles, witches, magic potions, airy spirits, and, everybody's favourite, a voracious bear. And the style is romantic as well. In *Pericles*, *Cymbeline*, *The Winter's Tale*, and *The Tempest*, limitation is replaced with amplification, simplicity with extravagance, mimesis with poesis.

The assertion that these stylistic and formal revisions are implicated in a recovery of the feminine is given greater point when we remember that the theatrical platform from which this new verse was spoken was a target of attack as unmanly and threatening to sexual boundaries. One brief passage from William Prynne's *Histriomastix* will make the point, the famous serial rant against 'effeminate mixt Dancing, Dicing, Stage-playes, lascivious Pictures, wanton Fashions, Face-painting, Health-drinking, Long haire, Love-lockes, Periwigs, womens curling, pouldring and cutting of their haire, Bone-fires, New-yeares-gifts, May-games, amorous Pastoralls, lascivious effeminate Musicke, excessive laughter, luxurious dis-

---

Shakespeare's Plays (London: Gerald Duckworth & Co., 1954), esp. pp. 28–33, 49–52, 167–87; James Sutherland, 'The Language of the Last Plays', in *More Talking of Shakespeare*, ed. John Garrett (London: Longmans, 1959), pp. 144–8; N. F. Blake, *Shakespeare's Language: An Introduction* (London: Methuen, 1983); and Wright's *Shakespeare's Metrical Art*.

44 'Shakespeare's Final Period', *Books and Characters: French and English* (New York: Harcourt, Brace and Company, 1922), pp. 51–69.

45 See Harold Bloom, *A Map of Misreading* (New York: Oxford, 1971), p. 103, as well as Patricia Parker, *Inescapable Romance* (Princeton: Princeton University Press, 1979).

46 See Richard Helgerson, *The Elizabethan Prodigals* (Berkeley: University of California Press, 1976), p. 42.

orderly Christmas-keeping, Mummeries ...'.[47] Implicit in this list of crimes is a censure of fiction-making, a prejudice Prynne shares with the Church Fathers already cited. To indulge in story-telling is to show dissatisfaction with the divinely created world by attempting to remake it. Every play, of course, from the *Agamemnon* to *Angels in America*, represents a reordering of the material world, and *Coriolanus* and *Antony and Cleopatra*, although based on North's adaption of Amyot's translation of Plutarch's arrangement of earlier reports of historical event, are no less acts of imagination than *A Midsummer Night's Dream*. Nevertheless, we recognize in Shakespeare's move from tragedy to romance a new devotion to the principles of fabulation that make the theatre vulnerable to the attacks of its enemies because they make it what it is.

It is tantalizing to recall that the theatres were shut for most of 1607, presumably giving a dislocated Shakespeare more time than usual to read and write;[48] Beaumont and Fletcher were making themselves known at about this time and altering audiences' tastes; Queen Anne's promotion of the masque was changing the shape of theatre at court; the King's Men were about to expand in new directions, performing for different audiences at Blackfriars. Surely all these conditions had an effect on Shakespeare's alteration of his professional course. It may be relevant, moreover, that Shakespeare's mother died in 1608. I am reluctant to read Mary Shakespeare as Volumnia, but I have no hesitation in seeing the playwright as Antony caught stylistically between Rome and Alexandria and giving up the serious work of history and tragedy for the fatal Cleopatra of imagination and romance. For a time, at least: the alternative titles of *Henry VIII/All is True* attest to uncertainties of mode that reflect conflicts of gender. Even now we may need to be reminded that *The Tempest* is not the end of the story and that Shakespeare never entirely resolved these questions of stylistic difference.

---

[47] Quoted in Barish, *The Anti-Theatrical Prejudice*, p. 85.
[48] See J. Leeds Barroll, *Politics, Plague, and Shakespeare's Theater: The Stuart Years* (Ithaca: Cornell University Press, 1991). A cautionary rejoinder to some of Barroll's conclusions is found in E. A. J. Honigmann, 'Plague on the Globe?', *New York Review of Books*, 19 November 1992, pp. 40–2.

THE VIRGIN NOT: LANGUAGE AND
SEXUALITY IN SHAKESPEARE

WILLIAM C. CARROLL

'New plays and maidenheads', according to the Prologue of *The Two Noble Kinsmen*,

> are near akin:
> Much followed both, for both much money giv'n
> If they stand sound and well. And a good play,
> Whose modest scenes blush on his marriage day
> And shake to lose his honour, is like her
> That after holy tie and first night's stir
> Yet still is modesty, and still retains
> More of the maid to sight than husband's pains.
>
> (Prol. 1–8)

The endless renewal of the spoken word, the play whose every performance is almost but not quite the originary 'first night's stir', is comparable here to the virgin whose maidenhead is taken yet 'still is modesty', still *seems* 'more of the maid' than not. I want to take up here some of the ways in which plays and maidenheads are related, how Shakespeare's dramatic language represents sexuality. It will be necessary to narrow the focus considerably, of course – in terms of language and sexuality in Shakespeare, here, if anywhere, is God's plenty. My argument will therefore only concern female sexuality as a production of male discourse, and I mean to use the term 'sexuality' rather than 'gender' because I will examine the biological semantics at work in the plays. Some feminist theorists have argued that female sexuality is, in patriarchal discourse, unrepresentable – conceptually available only as lack, invisibility, or negation.[1] I will pursue that position through the different, sometimes contradictory ways in which the language of several early modern writers, par-

ticularly Shakespeare, represented female sexuality and biology. Ultimately, I will examine some of the mystifications of the Tudor–Stuart discourse of virginity, the *ne plus ultra*, so to speak, of female sexuality – looking particularly at how certain modes of discourse registered the presence or absence of virginity.

To begin with, female sexuality in Shakespeare's plays is invariably articulated as linguistic transgression – that is, a verbal replication of female obliquity. Often, the ordinary relation between signifier and signified has slipped, been dislocated or even reversed, the linguistic equivalent of the world turned upside down.[2] The chief rhetorical figure here is the pun. It's not surprising that Dr Johnson termed the pun Shakespeare's 'fatal Cleopatra', employing the supreme Shakespearian example of female sexuality to indicate how Shakespeare's masculine persuasive force, to borrow Donne's term, was weakened and deflected by the 'irresistible' fascinations of the feminized quibble. For the heroic, manly playwright, 'a quibble is the

---

[1] One of the best discussions of sexuality in the early modern period is Mary Beth Rose, *The Expense of Spirit: Love and Sexuality in English Renaissance Drama* (Ithaca, 1988).

[2] For a recent analysis of the crisis of the sign in this period generally, see Barry Taylor, *Vagrant Writing: Social and Semiotic Disorders in the English Renaissance* (Toronto, 1991). The 'world turned upside down' trope, in relation to women, is analysed in Natalie Zemon Davis's classic essay, 'Women on Top', in *Society and Culture in Early Modern France* (Stanford, 1975).

golden apple for which he will always turn aside from his career, or stoop from his elevation'.[3] In employing this terminology of swerve, fall, and decline, Johnson touches on something important about the sexualized energy of the pun, as a linguistic field of subversion and transgression.[4] Yet Johnson has also suggestively reversed the actual analogy by transforming the beautiful Atalanta, who abandoned her race with Hippomenes to pick up the golden apples, into the male playwright distracted by effeminizing verbal structures. This gender reversal is necessary for Johnson's understanding of unstable language as feminine and therefore seductive. Johnson thus suggests part of my argument here: that patriarchal discourse equates destabilizing verbal forms and female sexuality.

The pun and its inversion, the malapropism, permit the introduction into utterance of female sexuality without ever seeming to name or recognize it. The references may be comic – as in the Latin lesson in *The Merry Wives of Windsor*, and the English lesson in *Henry V*, with its mispronunciations of 'foot' and 'count' – or they may be sinister – as in the references to 'country matters' and 'country forms' in *Hamlet* and *Othello* – but such linguistic forms continually enact some type of subversion of the master discourse. When Bottom assures his fellows that they will meet in the woods, 'and there we may rehearse most obscenely' (*Dream* 1.2.100–1), we have little reason to doubt him.[5]

This kind of wordplay permits the eruption of female sexuality into ordinary utterance. In *Love's Labour's Lost*, for example, Costard has been put in Armado's custody as punishment for his transgression with Jaquenetta:

ARMADO
Sirrah Costard, I will enfranchise thee.
COSTARD
O, marry me to one Frances! I smell some *l'envoi*, some goose, in this.
ARMADO
By my sweet soul, I mean setting thee at liberty, enfreedoming thy person. Thou wert immured, restrained, captivated, bound.   (3.1.117–22)

In a complicated series of misunderstandings, Costard has come to equate '*l'envoi*' with 'goose', a common slang term for a prostitute. So his fear is that he will be forced to marry a prostitute named Frances. Her name, in turn, has come from the mishearing of 'enfranchise' as 'one Frances' – the word for liberation turns into its opposite, signifying a forced marriage. Costard's linguistic incapacities have created a phantom virago, a loose woman with designs on him. A similar betrayal of subconscious threats occurs in *The Merry Wives of Windsor*, when Quickly mishears the answer 'pulcher' as 'polecats' during the Latin lesson. The lesson continues:

EVANS
What is your genitive case plural, William?
WILLIAM
Genitive case?
EVANS
Ay.
WILLIAM
Genitivo: '*horum, harum, horum*'.
QUICKLY
Vengeance of Jenny's case! Fie on her! Never name her, child, if she be a whore.   (4.1.52–7)

Thus 'pulcher' becomes a slang word for 'whore', virtually the opposite of the original word. And in one of Quickly's most remarkable transformations, 'genitive case' becomes 'Jenny's case' – the prostitute by name and, considering her profession, her most valuable

---

[3] *Samuel Johnson: Rasselas, Poems, and Selected Prose*, ed. Bertrand H. Bronson (New York, 1958), p. 252.

[4] There is a substantial body of critical commentary on the Renaissance use of the pun; see in particular the luminous work of M. M. Mahood, *Shakespeare's Wordplay* (London, 1957), and Sigurd Burckhardt, *Shakespearean Meanings* (Princeton, 1968). See also William C. Carroll, *The Great Feast of Language in 'Love's Labour's Lost'* (Princeton, 1976).

[5] Freud remarks that the malaprop 'does not possess [any inner] inhibition as yet, so that he can produce nonsense and smut directly and without compromise' (Sigmund Freud, *Jokes and Their Relation to the Unconscious*, ed. James Strachey (New York, 1960), p. 185).

possessive as well; here a grammatical term itself generates the sexual chimera. 'Horum', of course, predictably mutates into a verb. Through a kind of acoustical genius, Costard and Quickly achieve a creation *ex nihilo*, the fabrication of comically and sexually aggressive females – two ladies of the night, Frances and Jenny – from the swerves and frictions of language.

If puns and malapropisms offer the sexual low road, the eruption of the carnivalesque sexual into high discourse, then their linguistic opposite is represented by a far more stylized form of verbal dislocation, the riddle. However riddles are categorized, one common structural feature is that 'the referent of the description' is withheld, to be guessed at by an audience – all signifiers and no signified, in short.[6] This 'temporary threat of discontinuity' Roger Abrahams aptly terms 'epistemological fore-play', leading to the riddler's clarifying and satisfying solution to the problem – providing the absent signified.[7] Shakespeare's plays encode female sexuality in riddles so as to mystify it in terms of obliqueness or absence. We may think immediately of such examples as the casket riddles in *The Merchant of Venice*, which double the mystification, with one riddle on the outside of each box and another on the inside, leading to another kind of inside/outside riddle, as the treasure chest that contains the woman leads to the woman that contains, and is, the sexual treasure. Bertram's riddle in *All's Well That Ends Well* also relies on synecdoches and verbal dislocations to encode Helen's aggressive (in his view) sexuality: 'When thou canst get the ring upon my finger, which never shall come off, and show me a child begotten of thy body that I am father to, then call me husband; but in such a "then" I write a "never"' (3.2.57–60). Bertram has sworn, in the phrase which suggests my paper's title, 'to make the "not" eternal' (3.2.22), to leave the riddle forever unresolved, epistemological foreplay with no climax.

In Shakespeare's first romance, however, the 'not' does and must remain eternal for Pericles. The riddle he reads encodes incest, the missing signified the daughter of Antiochus:

> I am no viper, yet I feed
> On mother's flesh which did me breed.
> I sought a husband, in which labour
> I found that kindness in a father.
> He's father, son, and husband mild;
> I mother, wife, and yet his child.
> How they may be and yet in two,
> As you will live resolve it you.
>
> (*Pericles* Sc.1.107–14)

It is worth recalling here that Shakespeare, as Goolden has noted, has altered his sources by making the missing signified of the 'I' in this riddle be, not the father, but the daughter.[8] This change not only 'sharpens the focus on the princess', as Gorfain notes,[9] but defines female sexuality as absence – and, if the riddle is answered, as transgression. In a final example, when Mariana appears before the Duke at the end of *Measure for Measure*, her riddling responses to his questions lead him to conclude, 'Why, you are nothing then; neither maid, widow, nor wife!' (5.1.176–7). But the Duke's 'nothing' is then re-presented in Mariana's riddling self-proclamation:

> My lord, I do confess I ne'er was married,
> And I confess besides, I am no maid.
> I have known my husband, yet my husband
> Knows not that ever he knew me. (5.1.183–6)

Once again, the power of negation, of the 'not',

---

6 Roger D. Abrahams, 'The Literary Study of the Riddle', *Texas Studies in Language and Literature*, 14 (1972), p. 187. On the distinction between 'oppositional' and 'non-oppositional' riddles, see Alan Dundes, 'Toward a Structural Definition of the Riddle', in *Analytic Essays in Folklore* (The Hague, 1975).

7 Abrahams, 'The Literary Study of the Riddle', p. 182.

8 P. Goolden, 'Antiochus's Riddle in Gower and Shakespeare', *Review of English Studies*, n.s. 6 (1955), 245–51.

9 Phyllis Gorfain, 'Puzzle and Artifice: The Riddle as Metapoetry in "Pericles"', *Shakespeare Survey 29*, (1976), p. 14. Ruth Nevo describes this riddle as 'dream work methodized', in *Shakespeare's Other Language* (London, 1987), pp. 39–41.

becomes the defining category of a woman's sexuality. Mariana's riddle that 'my husband / Knows not that ever he knew me' anticipates the paradox of the former virgin who 'still retains / More of the maid to sight', but also begins to lead us toward darker and more tragic moments in the plays, particularly to Othello, who kills the wife he knew not he knew.

If puns and riddles occlude female sexuality by displacing it from the plays' high discourse, we might expect a less oblique representational strategy in the names given to female sexuality, and to the female genitalia specifically, but the realm of the referential, as we will see, is no less one of mystification. Usually, the name given to the female sex organs in Shakespeare's plays is a variant of the patriarchal metaphors of absence or containment: the O, the pit, ring, case, box, casket, the subtle hole, her C's, U's, and T's, the lake, pond, swallowing tomb, the placket, chimney, the fault,[10] and so on. Here are the images, now familiar from psychoanalytic and philological scholarship, of absence, emptiness, darkness, fall, invisible depth. From the 'unhallowed and bloodstained hole' (2.3.210) and 'detested, dark, blood-drinking pit' (2.3.224) of Titus Andronicus, to the 'sulphurous pit' (Lear F 4.5.125) of Lear, Shakespeare produces one misogynistic representation after another; virtually all of them suggest that the female genitalia, in one way or another, locate 'hell ... darkness ... burning, scalding, stench, consumption' (Lear F 4.5.124-5).[11]

The most contested and paradoxical category of semantic description, however, is the category of the virgin, who is metonymically defined by the names given to her hymen. The religious and psychological value of virginity was of course under interrogation in early modern England. On the one hand, the cult of the Virgin Mary taught, as Marina Warner has noted, 'that the virginal life reduced the special penalties of the Fall in women and was therefore holy. Second, the image of the virgin body was the supreme image of wholeness, and wholeness was equated with holiness'. The

virgin body was believed to be perfectly sealed up, 'seamless, unbroken'. This belief was based in part on inaccurate medical knowledge – 'the hymen was thought to seal off the womb completely ... caulking the body like tar on a ship's timbers', as Warner notes, though Renaissance anatomists, as we will see, were not as certain as this formulation.[12] The virgin's body, to employ a vocabulary derived from Bakhtin, is 'classical', with its key orifice closed, rather than 'grotesque'. The hymen thus became the most important fetishized commodity possessed by a woman, a barrier both physical and spiritual, a sign from God marking the Second Eve. As Mary Douglas has shown, the 'body's boundaries can represent any boundaries which are threatened or precarious';[13] the hymen is an ultimate threshold, a

---

10 See John H. Astington, '"Fault" in Shakespeare', Shakespeare Quarterly, 36 (1985), 330–4. See also Janet Adelman's suggestive comments on this pun in Hamlet, in Suffocating Mothers (London, 1992), pp. 23–4, 252–3.

11 Shakespeare uses a few terms that appear in contemporary anatomies and midwifery books – the mother, the lap – but they are exceptions to the general pattern. The 'mother' was the uterus (cf. Lear's 'O, how this mother swells up toward my heart', Lear F 2.2.231). The 'Lap or Privities' was 'that part into which the necke of the wombe determineth, and is seated outwardly at the forepart of the share bone, and is as it were a skinny addition of the necke, as Galen speaketh ... aunswering to the prepuce or foreskin of a man' (Helkiah Crooke, Microcosmographia: A Description of the Body of Man (London, 1615), p. 237; subsequent textual references are to this edition). Hamlet's request of Ophelia – 'Lady, shall I lie in your lap?' (Hamlet 3.2.107) – is thus quite explicit, as the ensuing dialogue indicates. The best overview of English Renaissance gynaecological knowledge is Audrey Eccles, Obstetrics and Gynaecology in Tudor and Stuart England (Kent, Ohio, 1982).

12 Marina Warner, Alone of All Her Sex: The Myth and the Cult of the Virgin Mary (New York, 1976), pp. 72–4.

13 Mary Douglas, Purity and Danger: An Analysis of the Concepts of Pollution and Taboo (London, 1984), p. 115. For a discussion of the ways in which 'sexual states and functions are used as markers of social identity', using modern ethnographic evidence, see Kirsten Hastrup, 'The Semantics of Biology: Virginity', in Defining Females, ed. Shirley Ardener (New York, 1978).

barrier to men, marking the fall into sexuality, the transition from maiden to woman, the making of the virgin not. The hymen's liminal status gives it an enormous symbolic importance as a construct of patriarchal discourse.[14]

The cult of the Virgin, however, was under attack in Reformation England, and even Queen Elizabeth's appropriations of Catholic iconology as the Virgin Queen did not overcome the sceptics and iconoclasts.[15] Elizabeth's own dalliances were public gossip, even her monthly gynaecological status, and Ben Jonson could speculate to Drummond of Hawthornden that Elizabeth 'had a Membrana on her which made her uncapable of men, though for her delight she tryed many, at the comming over of Monsieur, ther was a French Chirurgion who took in hand to cut it, yett fear stayed her & his death'.[16] There was also a strong libertine tradition which demystified and subverted the value of virginity. Catullus, for one, furnished the Renaissance its standard comparison between the natural world and sexuality, preeminently through the unplucked flower that loses its bloom (LXII. 39–47). He also commodifies virginity, suggesting that the maidenhead can be precisely divided to reflect the economic stakes of those who have invested in it:

> Your maidenhead [*virginitas*] is not all yours but
>   in part your parents';
> Your father has a third, your mother is given a
>   third,
> Only a third is yours.   (LXII.62–4)[17]

This passage stands behind Chapman's continuation of 'Hero and Leander',[18] among other texts, and leads to paradoxical arguments that virginity is not a something, an intact hymen, but a nothing. Marlowe's witty argument, in 'Hero and Leander' Sestiad I, is typical. Virginity and marriage, the narrator argues, are completely different:

> This idol which you term virginity
> Is neither essence subject to the eye,
> No, nor to any one exterior sense,
> Nor hath it any place of residence,

> Nor is't of earth or mould celestial,
> Or capable of any form at all.
> Of that which hath no being, do not boast;
> Things that are not at all, are never lost.
>   (1.269–76)

---

14 Cf. the answer in *The Problemes of Aristotle, with other Philosophers and Phisitions* (London, 1597) to the Question, 'Why doth a woman love that man exceeding well, who had hir maidenhead?': 'Is it bicause that as the matter doth covet a forme of perfection, so doth a woman the male? or is it by reason of shamefastnes? for as that divine *Plato* saith, shamefastnes doth follow love. It is reason that the love and esteeme of him who loosed the bonds of hir credite and shame. Or is it bicause the beginning of great pleasure, doth bring a great alteration in the whole, bicause the powers of the minde are greatly delighted, and sticke and rest immoveably in the same? And therefore *Hesiodus* giveth counsell to marry a maide' (14ᵛ). In his essay on 'The Taboo of Virginity', Freud offers a more sophisticated but equally gender-biased explanation of the same alleged phenomenon: 'The maiden whose desire for love has for so long and with such difficulty been held in check, in whom the influences of environment and education have formed resistances, will take the man who gratifies her longing, and thereby overcomes her resistances, into a close and lasting relationship which will never again be available to any other man. This experience brings about a state of "thraldom" in the woman that assures the man lasting and undisturbed possession of her and makes her able to withstand new impressions and temptations from without' (Sigmund Freud, *Sexuality and the Psychology of Love*, ed. Philip Rieff (New York, 1963), p. 70).

15 On the Elizabethan appropriation of the cult of the Virgin, see Frances A. Yates, *Astraea: The Imperial Theme in the Sixteenth Century* (London, 1975), pp. 29–120; Roy Strong, *The Cult of Elizabeth* (Berkeley, 1977); Louis Adrian Montrose, '"Shaping Fantasies": Figurations of Gender and Power in Elizabethan Culture', *Representations*, 2 (1983), 61–94; and C. L. Barber and Richard P. Wheeler, *The Whole Journey: Shakespeare's Power of Development* (Berkeley, 1986), pp. 23–38.

16 Carole Levin, 'Power, Politics, and Sexuality: Images of Elizabeth I', in *The Politics of Gender in Early Modern Europe*, eds. Jean R. Brink, *et al.*, Sixteenth Century Essays and Studies, 12 (1989), 95–110; *Ben Jonson*, ed. C. H. Herford and Percy and Evelyn Simpson (Oxford, 1925–52), 1.142.

17 Guy Lee, ed., *The Poems of Catullus* (Oxford, 1990), p. 75.

18 Stephen Orgel, ed., *Christopher Marlowe: The Complete Poems and Translations* (Harmondsworth, 1971), 'Hero and Leander', Sestiad v.473–8. Textual quotations from Marlowe and Chapman are from this edition.

The libertine argument may be aimed at seduction, but it also turns on a definition of absence and negation that can lead in more disturbing directions. Iago taps into the vision of the 'not', the no-thing, when he tells Othello: 'Her honour is an essence that's not seen. / They have it very oft that have it not' (*Othello* 4.1.16–17). The handkerchief may be offered as a substitute membrane which can be seen, handled, and passed back and forth, but virginity itself is one of those 'things that are not at all', 'they have it very oft that have it not'. The thing itself can be known only through signs, thereby permitting a semiotic slippage which can be manipulated by an Iago for his own ends.

Paroles' dialogue on virginity with Helen in *All's Well That Ends Well* follows the same line of sophistic logic. His argument proceeds from the libertine assumption: 'It is not politic in the commonwealth of nature to preserve virginity', because 'loss of virginity is rational increase' (1.1.124–6).[19] Virginity is a paradoxically self-annihilating commodity: 'by being once lost [it] may be ten times found; by being ever kept it is ever lost ... 'Tis a commodity will lose the gloss with lying: the longer kept, the less worth' (129–30, 150–1). Time forbids the quotation of this entire dialogue, but it ends with an elaborate personification which inverts the gender and age of the virgin:

Virginity like an old courtier wears her cap out of fashion, richly suited but unsuitable, just like the brooch and the toothpick, which wear not now. Your date is better in your pie and your porridge than in your cheek, and your virginity, your old virginity, is like one of our French withered pears: it looks ill, it eats drily, marry, 'tis a withered pear – it was formerly better, marry, yet 'tis a withered pear.

(1.1.152–60)

Turning the young maiden into the old courtier, this passage moves toward an equation between the hymen and male impotence; for every intact virgin, it seems, another male has failed. Helen's response to Paroles – 'Not my virginity, yet ... ' (line 161)[20] – provides the first instance of the rhetoric of negation which

resurfaces later in the play in the central riddle, already quoted, in which Bertram says 'I have wedded her, not bedded her, and sworn to make the "not" eternal' (3.2.21–2), and in Diana's challenge to the King in the final scene, 'Good my lord, / Ask him [Bertram] upon his oath if he does think / He had not my virginity' (5.3.186–8).

The language which Shakespeare employs to signify virginity thus generally trades on various forms of paradoxical negation, but the names given to the hymen itself suggest both positive and negative categories. The name 'hymen', to begin with, signifies both the god of marriage, and marriage generally, as well as the physical membrane; the same word thus

---

[19] Erasmus makes this argument in *Proci et puellae* (1523); see *The Colloquies of Erasmus*, trans. Craig R. Thompson (Chicago, 1965, pp. 86–98). For a concise discussion of the Renaissance doctrine of Increase, with special attention to Shakespeare's sonnets, see J. W. Lever, *The Elizabethan Love Sonnet* (London, 1956), pp. 189–201. Donne (the attribution is in doubt) argues in Paradox XII, 'That Virginity is a Vertue', that 'surely nothing is more unprofitable in the Commonwealth of *Nature*, then they that dy old maids, because they refuse to be used to that end for which they were only made ... *Virginity* ever kept is ever lost' (John Donne, *Paradoxes and Problems*, ed. Helen Peters (Oxford, 1980), pp. 56–7). Cf. Comus' argument in Milton's 'Comus': 'List Lady, be not coy, and be not cozen'd / With that same vaunted name Virginity; / Beauty is nature's coin, must not be hoarded, / But must be current, and the good thereof / Consists in mutual and partak'n bliss, / Unsavory in th'enjoyment of itself. / If you let slip time, like a neglected rose / It withers on the stalk with languish'd head' (*John Milton: Complete Poems and Major Prose*, ed. Merritt Y. Hughes (New York, 1957), lines 737–744, p. 107). Even the anti-libertine argument employed the same rhetoric, as may be seen in the thirteenth-century homily, *Hali Meidenhad*: 'Maidenhood is a treasure that, if it be once lost, will never again be found. Maidenhood is the bloom that, if it be once foully plucked, never again sprouteth up' (*Hali Meidenhad*, ed. Oswald Cockayne (London, 1866), p. 10).

[20] Helen's line strikes me as not necessarily a textual crux, as some editors have thought – thus Bevington's *The Complete Works of Shakespeare*, 1.1.165n, as well as the Riverside edition – but as her serious musing on Paroles' comic paradoxes: '*Not* my virginity'.

figures the object which defines the virgin, and the ritual which demands the loss of that object.[21] The state of virginity thus exists only as a condition of potential loss. The god of marriage makes two formal appearances in Shakespeare: first, at the end of *As You Like It*, to 'join in Hymen's bands' (5.4.127) the four couples, and again in the opening scene of *The Two Noble Kinsmen*, accompanied by a traditionally dressed virgin, 'encompassed in her tresses, bearing a wheaten garland' (1.1.1s.d.). Neither play includes a description of the god himself.[22]

More metaphorically, the hymen is a 'maidenhead', a usage which the OED dates from the mid-thirteenth century. Shakespeare uses the term frequently, often in the sense of a commodity, a thing to be acquired or taken, or a trophy of male conquest and possession. Thus Jack Cade asserts in *The First Part of the Contention (2 Henry VI)*: 'There shall not a maid be married but she shall pay to me her maidenhead, ere they have it' (4.7.118–20). But Shakespeare also understands the symbolic inversion at work in this name, by which the head of a maiden becomes a maidenhead, resulting at times in fantasies of punishment and dismemberment.[23] In *Romeo and Juliet*, Samson promises to be civil with the maids:

> I will cut off their heads.
> GREGORY The heads of the maids?
> SAMSON Ay, the heads of the maids, or their maidenheads, take it in what sense thou wilt.
>
> (1.1.22–5)

This displacement figures in several of the plays, but particularly in *Measure for Measure*, where the plot lines converge in the figure of the executioner, Abhorson, and his new assistant, the bawd Pompey. As Ragozine's head is substituted for Claudio's head, so is Mariana's maidenhead substituted for Isabella's.[24]

The hymen is further objectified as a *valuable* object; thus Laertes warns Ophelia not to open 'your chaste treasure ... / To [Hamlet's] unmastered importunity' (*Hamlet* 1.3.31–2).

Virginity is a rare jewel but, as Marlowe puts it in 'Hero and Leander', 'Jewels being lost are found again, this never; / 'Tis lost but once, and once lost, lost for ever' (II.85–6). In *Pericles*, Boult threatens 'To take from you [Marina] the jewel you hold so dear' (*Pericles* Sc.19.180), following the Pander's (or Bawd's) command to him, 'Crack the ice of her virginity, and make the rest malleable' (Sc.19.167–8). Thus virginity is valuable, rigid, reflective, and fragile – an irresistible challenge to possess, not a spiritual state but merely a physical condition.

In perhaps the most common metaphoric name, virginity is an unplucked flower, usually a rose; to penetrate the hymen is to deflower. The metaphoric origins of this ancient comparison are easy enough to imagine, and the

---

21 So in Catullus' famous wedding song, the god is summoned by the singing of virgins: '"o Hymenaee Hymen, / o Hymen Hymenaee", / ut lubentius, audiens / se citarier ad suum / munus, huc aditum ferat / dux bonae Veneris, boni / coniugator amoris' (LXI.39–45). ['"O Hymeneal Hymen, / O Hymen Hymeneal", / So that the more gladly, hearing / Himself summoned to his proper / Duty, he may make approach here / As the bringer of good Venus / And good love's uniter': Lee, *Poems of Catullus*, pp. 58–9.]

22 Cartari, in *Le imagini de i'dei* (Lyons, 1581), offers an illustration of Hymen with the following commentary: 'Hymen was shown by the ancients in the form of a handsome young man crowned with a diversity of flowers, in his right hand a lighted torch and in his left hand a red veil (or it could be saffron) with which new brides covered their head to face the first time they went to their husbands. And the reason for this ... is that the wives of priests among the ancient Romans almost always wore a similar veil. Because they were not allowed to divorce, as others were, the covering of the bride with the veil came to mean the desire for the marriage never to be dissolved. This does not preclude also the symbolic meaning of the chaste modesty of the bride, which is the same as Pudor, respected by the ancients so much that it was worshipped like a god' (quoted in John Doebler, *Shakespeare's Speaking Pictures* (Albuquerque, 1974), p. 37).

23 Cf. Lear's vision of the simpering dame, 'Whose face between her forks presages snow' (*Lear* F 4.5.117).

24 In *Pericles*, Boult tells Marina, 'I must have your maidenhead taken off, or the common executioner shall do it' (Sc.19.153–4).

usage in Shakespeare, and certainly in all of Renaissance literature, is pervasive; I will mention here only the 'little western flower' struck by the 'bolt of Cupid', in *A Midsummer Night's Dream*, 'Before, milk-white; now, purple with love's wound' (2.1.165–7). Some contemporary scientific treatises, however, literalized the flower metaphor in their anatomical descriptions. In *The Anatomie of the Bodie of Man* (1548), for example, Thomas Vicary uses the metaphor of 'deflouring' but reserves the term 'flowres' as a specific name for the menses, a term which had become common usage among Renaissance anatomists, midwives, and physicians.[25] In his *Microcosmographia* (1615), however, Helkiah Crooke brings biology and metaphor more closely together. 'The Caruncles [small pieces of flesh and membrane] are foure', Crooke says in his description of the hymen, 'and are like the berries of the Mirtle, in every corner of the bosome one'. All these parts and others, taken 'together make the forme of the cup of a little rose halfe blowne when the bearded leaves are taken away. Or this production', he goes on, 'with the lappe or privity may be likened to the great Clove Gilly-flower when it is moderately blowne' (223 [sic: actually 235]). No wonder Perdita, just five years earlier, did not want 'streaked gillyvors, / Which some call nature's bastards' (*The Winter's Tale* 4.4.82–3) in her garden. Crooke's attempt to bring the semantic domains of metaphor and biology together was echoed in other anatomies, including the anonymous *Aristotle's Master Piece*, where the hymen

is like the bud of a rose half blown, and this is broken in the first act of copulation with man: and hence comes the word *Deflora* to deflower; whence the taking of virginity, is called deflowering a virgin: for when the rose bud is expanded, virginity is lost.[26]

The flower is thus both a metaphor and, through acts of transference and supposed observation, allegedly also a close description of the thing itself.

Crooke goes on to further definitions of the hymen: 'It is called *Hymen quasi Limen*, as it were the entrance, the piller, or locke, or flower of virginity' (223 [sic: 235]), and later, 'they call it *Claustrum virginitatis, the lock of virginity*: for which their opinion they bring testimonies out of the holy scriptures' (255) – namely, the custom of displaying the virginal blood on the

---

[25] Thomas Vicary, *The Anatomie of the Bodie of Man* (1548), eds. F. J. and Percy Furnivall (London, 1888), pp. 77–8. According to Ambrose Parey, the term 'flowers' is used 'because that as in plants the flower buddeth out before the fruits, so in women kinde this flux goeth before the issue, or the conception thereof' (*The Workes of that famous Chirurgion, Ambrose Parey*, trans. Thomas Johnson (London, 1634), Book 24, p. 945). Textual references are to this edition; I will refer to Parey by his Englished name rather than Pare. James Rueff, in *The Expert Midwife* (London, 1637), employs the same terminology of deflowering (also describing former virgins as 'robbed of their best Iewll' (Book 2, p. 59).

[26] *The Works of Aristotle, The Famous Philosopher* (New York, 1974), p. 18. This description is quoted again in *Aristotle's Experienced Midwife* (in *The Works*, pp. 80–1), and in *Aristotle's Last Legacy* (in *The Works*, p. 233). The textual history of these spurious works is obscure; Eccles locates copies of the *Master Piece* from 1694, the *Last Legacy* from 1690, and the *Midwife* from 1700, but all are 'certainly derived from much older works' (Eccles, p. 12). In the case of the *Problemes of Aristotle* – usually included with the other three works – printed copies exist from 1595. In Hoby's translation of Castiglione's *Courtier* (1561), however, Lord Gasper reports 'a great Philosopher in certaine Problemes of his, saith' that a woman always loves the man who 'hath been the first to receive of her amorous pleasures' (Baldassare Castiglione, *The Book of the Courtier*, trans. Sir Thomas Hoby (London, 1928), p. 199) – i.e. the passage from *The Problemes of Aristotle* quoted in note 14, above. The modern editor cites Aristotle's *Physics* as a source, but Thomas Laqueur (*Making Sex: Body and Gender from the Greeks to Freud* (Cambridge, Mass., 1990), p. 277, n. 23) reports that this idea cannot be found there. The reason is that it comes from the spurious *Problemes*, apparently from an edition much earlier than the earliest known version listed in the STC. By 1615, the idea has become completely conventional: 'Whence is the Proverb (as it hath been said) *Maydens love them that have their maydenhead*' (Richard Brathwaite, *A Strappado for the Divell* (London, 1615), M3ʳ).

wedding sheets. Some anatomies also offer as a name the term 'Cento', which translates as 'patchwork'. Thus the liminal threshold must be locked and contained, yet the membrane itself is almost indescribably fragile, mere threads.[27]

Shakespeare employs one name which puns on all the dislocations and mystifications that we have already examined – that is, the virgin knot (thus my title again). What was a virgin knot? It is equated with but apparently distinct from the so-called marriage knot and the true-lover's knot. The true-lover's knot is the iconographic image of the elaborately encoiled and overlapping thread, with no beginning or end, which unites true lovers via a 'knot formed of two loops intertwined' (OED) – a kind of early Möbius strip, used as an *impresa* or perhaps worn on the sleeve; the OED offers examples from the fourteenth century. Examples may be seen as well in portraits of the time – such as that of Sir Henry Lee (1568) in the National Portrait Gallery – in emblem books, and, in *The Two Gentlemen of Verona*, in Julia's proposal to 'knit' up her hair 'in silken strings / With twenty odd-conceited true-love knots' (2.7.45–6). The 'true-love' was also a kind of flower which was said to resemble the true-lovers knot – which leads us back to the flower of the hymen itself.[28]

The marriage knot, on the other hand, was the mystic union of two lovers through marriage, what Milton termed 'the inward knot of marriage, which is peace & love' and 'the holy knott of mariage'.[29] The marriage knot could not be dissolved by man, as Spenser noted: 'His owne two hands the holy knots did knit, / That none but death for ever can divide' (*Faerie Queene* 1.12.37.1–2); marriage is 'the knot, that ever shall remaine' (*Amoretti* 6.14).[30] Shakespeare's usage is straightforward: Warwick in *The True Tragedy of Richard Duke of York* (*3 Henry VI*) refers to the 'nuptial knot' (3.3.55), Capulet plans to 'have this knot knit up tomorrow morning' between Juliet and Paris (*Romeo* 4.2.24), and in *Cymbeline* those who marry are

said 'to knit their souls ... in self-figured knot' (2.3.114–16). The knot of love may also indissolubly link friends or family: Gloucester in *1 Henry VI* refers to the 'knot of amity' to be gained through the alliance with France (5.1.16), Malcolm describes 'those strong knots of love' which are Macduff's family (*Macbeth* 4.3.28), and Agrippa claims the marriage between Antony and Octavia will make Antony and Octavius 'brothers, and ... knit your hearts / With an unslipping knot' (*Antony* 2.2.132–3). Hippolyta in *The Two Noble Kinsmen* elaborates the metaphor in this

---

27 'Claustrum' was also used in *Aristotle's Master Piece*, pp. 10, 18. For 'Cento', see Rueff, *The Expert Midwife*, Book 2, p. 52.

28 For Sir Henry Lee's portrait, see Roy Strong, *Gloriana: The Portraits of Queen Elizabeth I* (New York, 1987), p. 141, plate 149. Cf. the title of Richard Brathwaite's excruciatingly long re-telling of the Pyramus and Thisby story: *Loves Labyrinth: Or the True-Lovers Knot* (London, 1615). The OED gives *Hamlet* 4.5.39 as a reference to the true-love flower, where Ophelia sings of 'sweet flowers, / Which bewept to the grave did – not – go / With true-love showers'. Cf. also Vaughan's remarkable poem, 'The Knot', where the heavenly Virgin is addressed: 'Thou art the true Loves-knot; by thee / God is made our Allie, / And mans inferior Essence he / With his did dignifie. / For Coalescent by that Band / We are his body grown, / Nourished with favors from his hand / Whom for our head we own. / And such a Knot, what arm dares loose, / What life, what death can sever? / Which us in him, and him in us / United keeps for ever'. (*The Complete Poetry of Henry Vaughan*, ed. French Fogle (New York, 1964), lines 5–16, p. 302). Phillip Stubbes complains of the fashion in 1583, noting the 'sleeves ... tyed with true-looves knottes (for so they call them)' (Phillip Stubbes, *Anatomy of the Abuses in England*, ed. F. J. Furnivall (London, 1877–9), I.74).

29 *The Complete Prose Works of John Milton*, ed. Ernest Sirluck (New Haven, 1959), D.D. 2.269.31, M.B. 2.467.30. The author of *Hali Meidenhad* notes: 'Look around, seely maiden, if the knot of wedlock be once knotted, let the man be a dump or a cripple, be he whatever he may be, thou must keep to him' (p. 32).

30 J. C. Smith, ed., *Spenser's Faerie Queene* (Oxford, 1909), 1.12.37.1–2; Ernest de Selincourt, ed., *Spenser's Minor Poems* (Oxford, 1910).

description of the friendship of Pirithous and Theseus:

> Their knot of love,
> Tied, weaved, entangled with so true, so long,
> And with a finger of so deep a cunning,
> May be outworn, never undone.   (1.3.41–4)

The marriage knot or true-lover's knot cannot be 'undone', 'untied', or 'dissolv'd', then. It is for ever.[31]

But the virgin knot is something else. In *Pericles*, Marina is determined to preserve her honour:

> If fires be hot, knives sharp, or waters deep,
> United I still my virgin knot will keep.
> Diana aid my purpose.   (Sc.16.142–4)

And Prospero warns Ferdinand not to be another Caliban with Miranda:

> If thou dost break her virgin-knot before
> All sanctimonious ceremonies may
> With full and holy rite be ministered …
>   (*Tempest* 4.1.15–17)

And so Bertram's riddle in *All's Well* turns on this pun – 'I have wedded her, not bedded her, and sworn to make the "not" eternal' (3.2.21–2) – on both the marriage knot and the virgin knot; he resists the eternal knot by refusing to untie the physical knot. Clearly, the virgin knot – an external figure for the hymen within – is meant to be 'untied' or broken in marriage. But what kind of a knot is it? a square knot? a double half-hitch? surely not a sailor's knot? For Othello, the word conveys everything ugly about what he thought had been his virgin wife: turning the fountain of his life into 'a cistern for foul toads / To knot and gender in' (*Othello* 4.2.63–4).

There were at least two contending mythological accounts of the virgin knot. In 'Hero and Leander' Sestiad v, Chapman refers to the general union of lovers in his long narrative of Hymen's own wedding. The god of marriage himself was eternally bound, when Juno's priest took

> the disparent silks, and tied
> The lovers by the waists, and side to side,
> In token that thereafter they must bind
> In one self sacred knot each other's mind.
>   (v.355–8)

But if the 'sacred knot' will never be dissolved, another ritual is also invoked:

> The custom was that every maid did wear,
> During her maidenhead, a silken sphere
> About her waist, above her inmost weed,
> Knit with Minerva's knot, and that was freed
> By the fair bridegroom on the marriage night,
> With many ceremonies of delight.   (v.389–94)

Minerva – said to be a perpetual virgin in some Renaissance accounts – seems a plausible choice here, yet Chapman's identification of the knot with Minerva is probably a mistake, as D. J. Gordon has suggested.[32]

A second mythological account – certainly the traditional one – is given by Ben Jonson in his masque *Hymenai*, where the eternal knot

---

31 Milton allows that 'the knot of marriage may in no case be dissolv'd but for adultery' (*Complete Prose Works*, D.D. 2.240.29), while Donne prays in erotic language for a separation from the knot in 'Holy Sonnet xiv': 'Yet dearly I love you, and would be loved fain, / But am betrothed unto your enemy, / Divorce me, untie, or break that knot again, / Take me to you, imprison me, for I / Except you enthral me, never shall be free, / Nor ever chaste, except you ravish me' (*John Donne: The Complete English Poems*, ed. A. J. Smith (London, 1976), p. 314). Cf. Leantio's dying words for Bianca in Thomas Middleton's *Women Beware Women*, ed. J. R. Mulryne (London, 1975): 'My heart-string and the marriage-knot that tied thee / Breaks both together' (4.2.44–5).

32 In 'Chapman's Use of Cartari in the Fifth Sestiad of "Hero and Leander"', *Modern Language Review*, 39 (1944), 280–5, D. J. Gordon suggests that Chapman inferred an allusion to Minerva in Cartari's phrase, 'In quo Deam Virginensem vir invocabat'; yet in other passages of Cartari which Chapman has obviously read, the identification with Hercules is quite clear: 'Cingulum id Herculano nodo vinctum'. Cartari, in turn, is simply paraphrasing (as he acknowledges) Sextus Pompeius Festus: 'Hunc Herculaneo nodo vinctum' (*Sexti Pompei Festi: De Verborum Significatu Quae Supersunt Cum Pauli Epitome*, ed. Wallace M. Lindsay (London,

and the knot to be dissolved seem to blend together. 'Reason' describes the dress of the bride, including

The zone of wool about her waist,
Which, in contrary circles cast,
Doth meet in one strong knot that binds,
Tells you, so should all married minds.

(lines 173–6)[33]

The description of the 'personated bride' in the stage directions offers a bit more information: 'her zone, or girdle about her waist, of white wool, fastened with the Herculean knot' (lines 51–2). Jonson's own footnote offers this explanation: 'That was *nodus Herculeanus* [Hercules' knot], which the husband at night untied in sign of good fortune, that he might be happy in propagation of issue, as Hercules was, who left seventy children' (p. 517). Jonson cites as his authority Sextus Pompeius Festus, who indeed specifies the number seventy, though the great majority of authorities suggested a more modest number: Rabelais, for instance, describes Hercules as one of the 'certain fabulous fornicators ... who made women of fifty virgins in a single night'. Even Christian critics of pagan eroticism, such as Clement of Alexandria, held the line at fifty, as Jonson himself did in *The Alchemist* (2.2.39).[34] The knot of Hercules, in turn, may be associated with the Amazonian belt, the 'golden belt of Thermodon', as Golding translated it (*Metamorphoses* IX.233). In one of his twelve labours, Hercules defeated the Amazon Hippolyta and seized the belt or girdle she wore, freeing the way, in effect, for Theseus' capture of Hippolyta. The figure of the Amazon, as several scholars have shown, represents an effeminizing, demonized female power, suppressed and contained within patriarchal discourse.[35] Queen Elizabeth, herself frequently compared both to Minerva and to an Amazon, is pictured in two of the Armada portraits with an elaborate knot on her dress precisely in front of her genitals; her virginity is thus signified as intact, just as the maidenhead of England is now safe from the Spanish attack.[36]

But whether the virgin knot derives from Hercules, from Minerva, or from biological semantics, it also remains a 'not', a negation. If it is understood as the '*Hymen quasi Limen*', it is a liminal no-thing, perhaps a knot or puzzle to be undone, a zero, a 'nothing'.[37] Some

1913), p. 55). Chapman may have made an association with Minerva's shield, with which the maiden warrior-goddess defended her virtue. On the iconography of Minerva's shield, see James Nohrnberg, *The Analogy of the Faerie Queene* (Princeton, 1976), pp. 456–7. For a broader study, see Rudolf Wittkower, 'Transformations of Minerva in Renaissance Imagery', *Journal of the Warburg Institute*, 2 (1938–9), 194–205.

33 Ben Jonson, *The Complete Masques*, ed. Stephen Orgel (New Haven, 1969). Textual references are to this edition. In *Aristotle's Master Piece*, 'the Zone, or girdle of chastity', is defined as the hole in the middle of the hymen, through which the menses flow (p. 18). The terminology of the 'Zone' may derive from Catullus' famous phrase, 'zonam soluere virgineam', 'to undo a virgin's girdle' (Lee, *Poems of Catullus*, LXVII.28, p. 112).

34 *The Five Books of Gargantua and Pantagruel*, trans. Jacques Le Clercq (New York, 1936), p. 390; *Clement of Alexandria*, trans. G. W. Butterworth (London, 1919), p. 69. Sextus Pompeius Festus seems to have been the first to escalate the number ('septuaginta'), which was also copied by Cartari. Natalis Comes (Chapter Seven of the *Mythologiae*) gives the number as fifty. At some point, moreover, a further escalation in Hercules' sexual power took place, as he is said not just to impregnate fifty (or seventy) virgins, but to do it in a single night (so Jonson at *Alchemist* 2.2.39).

35 See Celeste Turner Wright, 'The Amazons in Elizabethan Literature', *Studies in Philology*, 37 (1940), 433–56; Winfried Schleiner, '*Divina virago*: Queen Elizabeth as an Amazon', *Studies in Philology*, 75 (1978), 163–80; Gabriele Bernhard Jackson, 'Topical Ideology: Witches, Amazons, and Shakespeare's Joan of Arc', *English Literary Renaissance*, 18 (1988), 40–65; and Simon Shepherd, *Amazons and Warrior Women: Varieties of Feminism in Seventeenth-Century Drama* (New York, 1981).

36 See Strong, *Gloriana*, pp. 130 (pl. 138) and 132 (pl. 139). In other portraits, a pearl or other jewel holds the same symbolic place on her dress – pp. 127 (pl. 136), 129 (pl. 137), and 151 (pl. 168).

37 In a very suggestive essay, David Willbern traces 'Shakespeare's Nothing', in *Representing Shakespeare*, eds. Murray M. Schwartz and Coppélia Kahn (Baltimore, 1980). See also the brilliant commentary on the sexual economy of the 'O' in James L. Calderwood, *A Midsummer Night's Dream* (London, 1993).

contemporaries speculated that there was no such thing as the hymen as a matter of biological fact. In his long section on the female reproductive system in *De usu partium*, the premier reference work in the period, Galen never mentions the hymen, and indeed, there seemed to early modern writers no defined *use* for the hymen – except to mark by its absence the loss of virginity. Adherents of the so-called one-sex model of the human body, moreover, either do not mention the hymen or cannot relate it to anything equivalent in the male system.[38] In *Microcosmographia*, Crooke is consistently definitive in his comments, but turns exceedingly tentative in his description of the hymen, referring to what 'many will have to bee a slender membrane ... This they say is broken in the devirgination'. For the 'true History of the Hymen', though, Crooke refers to other texts rather than to any actual observation (233 [sic: 235]). In the 'Questions' at the end of this chapter, moreover, Crooke's answers raise more questions: 'Almost all Physitians thinke that there is a certain membrane ... which they call Hymen. This membrane they say is perforated in the middest' (255). In examining the claim that a virgin will bleed when the hymen is first deflowered – the sole function of the hymen from a male point of view – Crooke invokes textual precedent, but it is not clear: '*Falopius* yeeldeth to this opinion, *Columbus* writeth that he hath seene it, [but] *Laurentius* sayeth' that after many dissections of young maidens 'hee could never finde it though he searched curiously for it with a Probe; which (sayth he) might have beene felt to resist the Probe if there had beene any such thing, and therfore he thinketh that it is but a meere fable. Yet notwithstanding thus far he giveth credite to *Columbus* and *Falopius*, that hee thinketh there is sometimes such a membrane found', but it may be only an 'Organicall disease' or malformation. The letting of blood by the virgin, then, may not always occur, and is no sure sign of virginity. 'Wee must therefore', Crooke concludes, in a passage which must have unsettled many a man at the time, 'finde out some other locke of Virginitie' (256). Similarly, in *The Anatomy of Melancholy* (1621), Robert Burton takes up the argument about whether the sign of virginity is the hymeneal blood, quoting authorities from the Bible, the Greeks, the Egyptians, the Carthaginians, and so forth; revealing the instability of this sign of virginity, Burton concludes that as a test for virginity, hymeneal blood is 'no sufficient trial', according to some authorities, 'And yet others again defend it.'[39] A similar doubt is registered in *Aristotle's Master Piece*, where the anonymous author describes various ways in which the requisite signs of the hymen's presence may fail to appear. The conclusion registers a zone of uncertainty and potential anxiety:

> when a man is married and finds the tokens of his wife's virginity, upon the first act of copulation, he has all the reason in the world to believe her such, but if he finds them not, he has not reason to think her devirginated, if he finds her otherwise sober and modest: Seeing the Hymen may be broken so many other ways, and yet the woman both chaste, and virtuous. Only let me caution virgins to take all imaginable care to keep their virgin zone entire, that so when they marry, they may be such as the great Caesar wished his wife to be, not only without fault but without suspicion also.[40]

---

38 Thomas Laqueur's definitive study, *Making Sex: Body and Gender from the Greeks to Freud*, has no entry in its Index under 'hymen'; the subject is significantly absent throughout. Neither of the two most popular midwifery books available in England in this period – Eucharius Roesslin, *The byrth of mankynde* (London, 1540; 13 editions), and James Guillemeau, *Child-Birth or, The Happy Deliverie of Women* (London, 1612; 2 editions) – ever mentions the hymen, even in their descriptions of the female reproductive system. In *The Sicke Womans Private Looking-Glasse* (London, 1636), John Sadler makes a single, one-line reference to the hymen (Chapter 1, p. 5).

39 Robert Burton, *The Anatomy of Melancholy*, ed. Holbrook Jackson (London, 1932), 3.3.2 (p. 284).

40 *Aristotle's Master Piece*, in *The Works of Aristotle, The Famous Philosopher*, p. 20.

But no wife can be without a 'fault', in all the senses of that term; the 'tokens' of virginity are unstable, and if the husband 'finds them not, he has not reason to think' his wife is not a virgin. Ambrose Parey, on the other hand, is not tentative or qualifying at all:

it is worth observation, that in all this passage there is no such membrane found, as that they called *Hymen*, which they feigned to be broken at the first coition. Yet notwithstanding *Columbus*, *Fallopius*, *Wierus*, and many other learned men of our time think otherwise, and say, that in Virgins a litle above the passage of the urine, may be found and seene such a nervous membrane, placed overtwhart [sic] as it were in the middle way of this necke, and perforated for the passage of the courses [i.e. menses]. But you may finde this false by experience. (Book 3, p. 130)

Parey notes the contradictions among different authorities, including midwives, as to the supposed location of the membrane. Those who rely on the appearance of hymeneal blood as the sign of virginity are making a mistake, he argues, giving as one incredible example a story of prostitutes who have learned to *counterfeit* virginity, by putting into their vaginas 'the bladders of fishes, or galles of beasts filled full of blood, and so deceive the ignorant and young lecher, by the fraud and deceit of their evill arts, and in the time of copulation they mix sighes with groanes, and womanlike cryings, and the crocodiles teares, that they may seeme to be virgins, and never to have dealt with man before' (Book 24, p. 938). Virginity is here reduced to one of the performing 'arts', constituted by nothing more than a set of manipulable signs; but as we have seen, even the existence of virginity's physical manifestation, the hymen, was always constituted by secondary and tertiary signs and emblems. That these could be manipulated, or could not be relied upon to convey any truth about women, is the surprising discovery of much contemporary medical discourse, which questions the very existence of the hymen. If the virgin might actually be a harlot, then the 'lock' of virginity

is no sure thing. Maybe, maybe not. The evidence of the hymen's presence depends on the status of the sign, which can only (perhaps) point to its absence. As Parey mused on the contradictions of the hymen, 'But truly of a thing so rare, and which is contrary to nature, there cannot be any thing spoken for certainty' (Book 24, p. 938).

Thus the mystery of virginity that attracts, confuses, and bedevils many of the male characters in Shakespeare's plays, the fetishized commodity that is and is not. The plays circle round this mystification through an oblique language of indirection and negation. The not/knot pun slides further and further from its signified, unable to name it but unable to escape it. Flute tells us, 'A paramour is, God bless us, a thing of naught' (*Dream* 4.2.14), allowing sexual transgression and emptiness to mate in a pun. Ophelia takes up Hamlet's suggestive pun in similar language:

HAMLET Be not you ashamed to show, he'll not
   shame to tell you what it means.
OPHELIA You are naught, you are naught.

(3.2.137–40)

And Richard III confounds Clarence's guard,

Naught to do with Mrs Shore? I tell thee, fellow:
He that doth naught with her – excepting one –
Were best to do it secretly alone.

(*Richard III* 1.1.99–101)

We may even begin to hear more complex resonances in Viola's paradoxical self-declarations: 'I am not that I play' (*Twelfth Night* 1.5.177) and 'I am not what I am' (3.1.139).

In the Shakespearian language of sexuality, then, a woman is not a virgin whose knot is nought because she has been naught. Virginity is continually invoked, described, celebrated, occluded, denied, and denounced, and language can only obliquely represent it. It remains a kind of negation *ex creatio*. 'What I am and what I would', Viola tells the audience, 'are as secret as maidenhead' (*Twelfth Night* 1.5.206–7).

FLESHING HIS WILL IN THE SPOIL OF HER HONOUR: DESIRE, MISOGYNY, AND THE PERILS OF CHIVALRY

MICHAEL HATTAWAY

MEASURE FOR MEASURE

To begin with, a description of an excellent but disconcertingly politically correct production of *Measure for Measure* by Compass Theatre Company.[1] The group, directed by Neil Sissons, is a small one and, as with Peter Brook's *A Midsummer Night's Dream*, they generated a stunning new reading of the text by doubling members of the cast. Isabella and Mistress Overdone were played by the same actress; Angelo, Claudio, and Barnardine by one actor, and the authority figures of the Duke and Elbow by another. The revelation of the production came with the recognitions of the last scene. In that final sequence, the Friar is unmasked as the Duke: in this production, in a resonantly quoted gesture, Angelo was also stripped down – the cast wore modern dress – to the long-johns he had worn as Claudio in prison. At the Duke's question 'Which is that Barnardine?' (5.1.477), the actor simply adopted the half-crazed mannerisms he had deployed for Barnardine during the short sequence that follows.

David Westbrook had played Angelo as a compulsively smiling, bespectacled, and totally bald young man whose first act on acquiring power was to tidy the Duke's desk. He looked like the most dangerous sort of train-spotter who revealed his true day-dreams as he wrestled Isabella to the ground at the end of 2.4. Handy-dandy, which was which? The doubling of the actors led to an equation of the 'naturalness' of Claudio's 'tilth and husbandry'

with the depravity of Angelo the 'virgin violator': Claudio was merely Angelo in disguise, and, more horribly, Angelo was Claudio in disguise. The Duke's second question, 'What muffled fellow's that?' (5.1.485) acquired another, generalized, meaning – the production ended with the Duke, a comfortable, cherubic, humorous fellow, chortling to himself centre stage. He too, it turned out, was 'muffled': the director had highlighted the moment when he had 'pardoned' Isabella for refusing to lay down her chastity, and his plan to bring her 'heavenly comforts of despair / When it [was] least expected' (4.3.107–8) was thereby revealed as part of a long-hatched plan to get her into his bed. One might go further: the doubling of Isabella and Mistress Overdone suggested that both, in a patriarchal world, were transgressors. By proposing to Isabella, the Duke was at once exercising his power over a woman who had challenged his authority and seeking to turn into fact the fantasy of taking sexually an unattainable woman. Men without their little brief authority were indeed poor forked creatures: Angelo/Claudio had to be comforted and led off by a horrified Isabella (Helen Franklin) who looked back at the Duke her 'saviour' with an expression that would have been apt if Elbow had propositioned her.

---

[1] 12 February 1992 at the Opera House, Buxton.

This was undoubtedly brilliant and, equally undoubtedly, a post-feminist production. The insight of the production was of our time, and there is no evidence either in the text or even in my sense of what a performance would have meant to contemporaries that would enable me to dismiss it out of hand on critical or 'historical' grounds. Indeed I want to examine and try to explain, if not to condone, some of the appalling attitudes towards women within other plays that productions of this kind may expose. They lay bare a disconcerting degree of misogyny[2] – to such an extent that I am prepared in this context, to speak of 'Shakespeare's works' rather than 'Shakespearian texts'. Shakespeare's plays of love – in tragedy, comedy, and romance – often expose ploys of hatred. The tones of 'happy' romantic comedy are so continually displaced that we might concede that what Lactantius deemed to be the subjects of ancient comedy, 'the debauching of virgins and the amours of strumpets',[3] apply equally to Shakespeare in the Renaissance. I shall end by drawing attention to particular passages where it is obvious that misogyny is problematized.

These days, however, for a man 'reading as a woman' there is much discomfort, not only because one is invited to accept guilt on behalf of one's masculine forebears – and that's dangerous – but equally because, by endorsing the kind of statement the Compass production made, there is a danger of suppressing all that is erotic and enjoyable – in Renaissance terms, perhaps, what is 'wanton' or 'frolicsome' – and embittering all relationships between the sexes. For Shakespeare's plays explore not only the connections between sex and power but those between sex and pleasure. I do not want to launch here into another reading of Madonna as a cultural icon, but I do want to suggest that the Compass Company's reading suppresses what George Orwell called, in his wonderful essay on the art of Donald McGill (the artist who produced 'vulgar' seaside postcards), the Sancho Panza view of life, one of the 'two principles, noble folly and base wisdom [that]

exist side by side in nearly every human being'.[4] There is admittedly little cheerful relishing of sexual vulgarity of this sort in *Measure for Measure*. Lucio is relevant, but Lucio is hard to define. We might take his jibes at Angelo's sexuality as merely sniggering clubroom prattle, and feel that Shakespeare undercuts his role as a positive foil to sexual puritanism by having him abandon Kate Keepdown. Alternatively we may hear in his lines the sardonic tones and the verbal conceits of Pietro Aretino, the scourge of princes.

Concerning the wanton, we might consider the sort of values that are associated with, say, Costard in *Love's Labour's Lost* who seems simply 'happy' to consort with his wench. Again, however, I need to qualify as I am aware that there are dangers of attributing a happy and unconstrained sexuality to what were in those days called the base members of society. Freud may have been as guilty of this idealization when he wrote of the unproblematized sexuality of 'primitive man'[5] as Margaret Mead was when writing of the Samoans. Moreover, it is not just male clowns who celebrate sexual desire: Beatrice and Margaret in *Much Ado* (3.4), Rosaline and Maria in *Love's Labour's Lost* (4.1) speak 'greasily'. In cases like this, are the politically correct simply going to attribute this 'feminine bawdy' to the proclivities of a voyeuristic male author? Rather, to quote Orwell again, sexy talk represents 'a sort of saturnalia, a harmless rebellion against virtue'[6] –

---

[2] A prime Renaissance text, often reprinted, is the anonymous *Problems of Aristotle*; see also R. Howard Bloch, 'Medieval Misogyny', in R. Howard Bloch and Frances Fergusson (eds.), *Misogyny, Misandry, and Misanthropy* (Berkeley, 1989), pp. 1–24.

[3] *Divinae Institutiones*, 6.

[4] George Orwell, 'The Art of Donald McGill' [1942], in *Collected Essays* (London, 1961), p. 175.

[5] Sigmund Freud, *Civilization and its Discontents*, The Penguin Freud Library (Harmondsworth, 1985), p. 306.

[6] Orwell, p. 178; see Katharine Eiseman Maus, 'Transfer of Title in *Love's Labor's Lost*: Language, Individualism, Gender', in I. Kamps, ed., *Shakespeare Left and Right*, (1991), pp. 205–23.

for there are dangers under the present cultural regime that a neo-Bowdlerism may become prevalent.[7] Man may be a giddy thing, but male desire will not go away – nor need it be the driving force of a chauvinist or imperialist strategy. It may on occasion even be reciprocated.

Woven into what follows is a general analysis of misogyny in Shakespearian texts. I want, after some preliminary remarks about evidence and some account of contemporary debates, to think about possible psycho-analytical, social, and cultural explanations – perhaps descriptions is a better word – of Renaissance misogyny. I list these by order of convenience: it is impossible for me to prove *either* that the social is base and the others superstructure, *or* that the psychological is prior to either by virtue of being transhistorical. In particular texts we may come across the displacement of class hostilities onto gender but we can set this up as no over-arching explanation. My descriptions tend to the psycho-analytical[8] and ideological; they are less transparent than the terms in which the *querelle des femmes* was conducted in early modern England. 'Jane Anger's' *Protection for Women* (1589), and, a generation or so later, the texts associated with the play *Swetnam the Woman Hater* (1620), for example, are essentially rhetorical exercises.[9] The authors simply trade *idea* for *idea*, reversing the direction of masculine railing by looking out alternative *topoi* and *exempla* from the scriptures and the church fathers to confound Aristotle and expose how, as the mysterious 'Jane Anger' says, men 'confess we are necessary, but ... would have us likewise evil'.[10] Nor do I want to deal here with the 'humorous' type of the stage misogynist and his formal diatribes.[11]

I want to concentrate on three plays – *Love's Labour's Lost*, *All's Well that Ends Well*, and *The Winter's Tale* – in order to explore some of the particular connections made in the Renaissance between male sexuality and blood. Because blood is a metonym not only for a humour but also for social rank, I shall be invoking what I

said about Costard and implying that both Renaissance misogyny and our own 'anti-sexism' may well be products of élite cultures. Both may stem from what Orwell called 'high sentiments'[12] – and high sentiments can be dangerous.

EROS AND METAPHOR

To begin with language. It was well said of D. H. Lawrence that the representation of sex in his novels is a way of 'talking about something else', an area where 'Eros becomes metaphor'.[13] We are now equally aware of a hermeneutic circle, that 'something else' is often a way of talking about sex, and that consequently

---

[7] My awareness of these issues was sharpened by a paper given by Ann Thompson at a meeting of the Northern Renaissance Seminar.

[8] I concur with Stephen Orgel who writes, 'To take the psychoanalytic paradigm seriously, however, and treat the plays as case histories, is surely to treat them *not* as objective events but as collaborative fantasies and to acknowledge thereby that we, as analysts, are implicated in the fantasy. It is not only the patients who create the shape of their histories, and when Bruno Bettelheim observes that Freud's case histories "read as well as the best novels", he is probably telling more of the truth than he intends' ('Prospero's wife' in Margaret W. Ferguson, Maureen Quilligan and Nancy J. Vickers, eds., *Rewriting the Renaissance: The Discourse of Sexual Difference in Early Modern Europe* (Chicago, 1986), p. 52.

[9] The first recorded use of 'misogynist' in *OED* is in the anonymous play *Swetnam the Woman Hater* (1620); of 'misogyny' in 1656; a rehearsal of commonplaces concerning the imperfection of women is to be found in Book 3 of Castiglione's *Book of the Courtier*; see also Constance Jordan, 'Feminism and the Humanists: The Case of Sir Thomas Elyot's *Defence of Good Women*', in Margaret W. Ferguson, pp. 242–58.

[10] *Jane Anger her Protection for Women*, reprinted in Moira Ferguson, ed., *First Feminists* (Bloomington, N.Y., 1985), p. 66.

[11] See Linda Woodbridge, 'The Stage Misogynist' in *Women and the English Renaissance* (Brighton, 1984), pp. 275–99.

[12] Orwell, p. 177.

[13] Mark Kinkead-Weekes, 'Eros and Metaphor: Sexual Relationship in the Fiction of D. H. Lawrence', *Twentieth Century Studies*, 2 (1969), 3–20, p. 4.

gender and, possibly, desire itself, at the centre of our experience, is as conditioned by social forms and pressures as any other aspect of life. What we take to be the most intimate, the most authentic, the most unmediated is, because we can position it only within language, as much a social as a private phenomenon. The private is but an internalization of the social or, as Michel Foucault put it, 'there is no experience which is not a way of thinking'.[14] According to a 'hard' reading, sexuality is not just a biological drive but 'a way of fashioning the self "in the experience of the flesh", which itself is "constituted from and around certain forms of behaviour" ... Like the whole world for Nietzsche, ... sexuality is "a sort of artwork"'.[15]

Like woman, man is not born but made.[16] *Literary Love*, the title of a notable book by A. J. Smith, deconstructs itself – or turns out to be about far more than it proclaims. Because of this mediation in and by language, the authentic experience is endlessly deferred; desire is bound to be unfulfilled either because it fails to match the imaginary or, having matched it, reveals itself to be thereby inauthentic. (I do not think it is too far-fetched to claim that a consideration of the play of style in *As You Like It* leads to a profound questioning of whether the romantic is in fact authentic. Orlandos may be happier wooing their Ganymedes than wedding their Rosalinds.)

Donne's writings provide a convenient site for the investigation of the relationship between language and desire – if we can distinguish them. One need only invoke, from the second Satire, Coscus, once a poet and now a lawyer, who 'woos in language of the Pleas and Bench'.[17] Although Coscus is a fool, he, like all of us, can woo (and feel?) only in the language of another trade or practice. Eros is unattainable except through metaphor.

Donne's epigram 'On Manliness' gives us another example. The language game upon which it depends reveals that manliness is a construction:

Thou call'st me effeminate, for I love women's
    joys;
I call not thee manly, though thou follow boys.

The grammar of the poem serves to defamiliarize the word 'women's'. It can be a subjective or an objective genitive: the voice of the poem may be confessing that he enjoys what women enjoy or that he enjoys women. Experience in this world can be explained only by metaphor, and 'spiritual' or Platonic love rendered and experienced only by the language of this world. Biological division, sex, gives its name to 'sex' in the sense of desire – an unobvious case of metonymy (or is it synecdoche, the part for the whole?). In what might be the first use of the word 'sex' in its modern sense of carnal desire,[18] Donne seems to claim that desire is always driven by something else:

> This ecstasy doth unperplex,
>   (We said) and tell us what we love,
> We see by this, it was not sex,
>   We see, we saw not what doth move.

What, then, doth move?

BLOOD AND PARADISAL MARRIAGE

To the men of the Renaissance, the answer was simple, 'Blood' or 'Flesh and blood'. This is the reply churlish that the Duchess' Younger Son offers in *The Revenger's Tragedy* when he is asked what moved him to the rape of Antonio's wife.[19] Blood, of course, was one of the humours. To those with bad faith, like this

---

14 Paul Rabinow, ed., *The Foucault Reader* (Harmondsworth, 1986), p. 335.

15 Thomas Laqueur, *Making Sex: Body and Gender from the Greeks to Freud* (Cambridge, Mass., 1990), p. 13.

16 For Jacques Derrida on the way 'man' might be demarcated in terms of gender, see *Spurs: Nietzsche's Styles*, tr. Barbara Harlow, 1979, pp. 59–65, and 103–5.

17 'Satire 2', 48.

18 *OED*, sv. *sb3*, although the passage is not cited there.

19 Tourneur [or Middleton] *The Revenger's Tragedy*, ed. R. A. Foakes (London, 1966), 1.2.47; compare 'he hath fall'n by prompture of the blood' (*Measure*, 2.4.179).

Younger Son, it gave an excuse for transgressive behaviour; for Shakespeare's Angelo it is the centre of a tragic predicament: 'Blood, thou art blood' (2.4.15). It was a sign of a curse, ambiguously signifying lust and murder,[20] as we hear in De Flores' rebuke to Beatrice-Joanna in *The Changeling*: 'A woman dipped in blood, and talk of modesty'.[21] For sage Ben Jonson blood was part of a signifying system. He solved the brain/mind problem by arguing that a description of a physical condition could only be a metaphor for a mental condition.[22]

'Blood' therefore is what Empson called a complex word. Let us consider a moment in *All's Well* when the Countess is bidding farewell to her son:

Be thou blessed, Bertram, and succeed thy father
In manners as in shape. Thy blood and virtue
Contend for empire in thee, and thy goodness
Share with thy birthright.   (1.1.58–61)

'Blood' and 'virtue': the context suggests that these designate aspects of nature and nurture, inherited and acquired qualities. These words, however, are disconcertingly ambiguous: 'blood' can mean rank ('birthright') as well as 'good breeding',[23] 'virtue', manliness or mettle as well as goodness. This turns out not to be a simple binary opposition, but a quaternary one. When we deconstruct the passage we realize that there is an ideological agenda contained in it: rank gives licence to desire, and goodness depends on sexual valour.[24] The Countess is being proleptic, anticipating both Bertram's rejection of Helen and his (thwarted) attempt on Diana's virginity.

In another key we might notice how what we might have understood, before Foucault, as a biological imperative, desire, is described by the clown of the play, Lavatch, as something experienced by the 'other', in this case the body of the subject:

COUNTESS Tell me thy reason why thou wilt marry.
LAVATCH My poor body, madam, requires it. I am driven on by the flesh, and he must needs go that the devil drives.   (1.3.27–30)

The passage economically evokes a fierce Pauline Christianity that has generated, as the clown's plain speaking demonstrates, what Donne calls a 'serpent love',[25] an alienated sexuality. This ascription of desire to the blood and its demonization together constitute one part of what I would term a complex disorientation syndrome.

To analyse it, we might start with the physical. Anatomy was imperfectly understood, or rather what we take to be the empirical, something to be seen, was 'seen as' a version of the ideological. As Thomas Laqueur has claimed in his important analysis of the 'one-sex model' of Renaissance sexuality, most anatomists of the period sought to reveal similarities and not differences between cadavers of what we take to be the 'opposite' sexes, with a view of course to demonstrate that woman was but an imperfect version of the man.[26] It followed that they held both semen and the menses to be versions of blood. In the Hippocratic tradition,

---

[20] See Christopher Ricks, 'The Moral and Poetic Structure of *The Changeling*' EC 10 (1960), 290–306; compare Spenser, *The Faerie Queene*, 5.7.9–10 (on the priests of Isis), and Vittoria in Webster's *The White Devil*, ed. John Russell Brown (London, 1966), 'O my greatest sin lay in my blood. / Now my blood pays for't' (5.6.240–1).

[21] *Changeling*, 3.4.126.

[22] *Every Man Out of his Humour*, Induction, 103.

[23] Compare 'For Hamlet and the trifling of his favour, / Hold it a fashion and a toy in blood, / A violet in the youth of primy nature' (*Hamlet*, 1.3.5–7), and see David S. Berkeley and Donald Keesee, 'Bertram's Blood-Consciousness in *All's Well that Ends Well*', *Studies in English Literature*, 31 (1991), 247–58; for the way that bleeding was a disgrace for a man, see Gail Kern Paster, '"In the spirit of men there is no blood": blood as trope of gender in *Julius Caesar*', *SQ*, 40 (1989), 284–98.

[24] This is also registered in a line from 'A Lover's Complaint': 'O false blood, thou register of lies' (52).

[25] The phrase is from Donne's 'Twicknam Garden', a hymn of hatred for love.

[26] See *The Problemes of Aristotle* (London, 1597): 'Aristotle doth say that men have small breasts and women little stones' (Sig. C6^r); the same text also claims that milk is digested blood (Sig. C7^r).

'sperm, a foam much like the froth on the sea, was first refined out of the blood; it passed to the brain; from the brain it made its way back through the spinal marrow, the kidneys, the testicles, and into the penis. Menstrual blood, a phethora or leftover of nutrition is, as it were, a local variant in this generic corporeal economy of fluids and organs.'[27] Accordingly, we read in Thomas Vicary's *The Anatomy of the Body of Man*, 1577: 'And further it is to be noted that this sperm that cometh both of man and woman is made and gathered of the most best and purest drops of blood in all the body; and by the labour and chafing of the testicles or stones, this blood is turned into another kind, and is made sperm. And in man it is hot, white, and thick, wherefore it may not spread nor run abroad of itself, but runneth and taketh temperance of the woman's sperm, which hath contrary qualities, for the woman's sperm is thinner, colder, and feebler'.[28] This reinforces the over-valuation of the masculine and the devaluation of the feminine: we read in a misogynistic text of 1599, 'Woman ... [is] not framed for any respect or use than for a receptacle of some of our excremental humours':[29] woman is 'the pits'.

What we are meeting, in these patriarchal texts (which arguably served as documents of control rather than as descriptions of experience) is a deeply ambivalent attitude towards sexuality, both male and female. On the one hand it is a manifestation of manliness (*virtù*), on the other it is the enemy of goodness (virtue). Moreover because, in the Augustinian tradition, desire, since the fall, has not been voluntary, desire, like drink, makes and mars a man, causes him to lose control.[30] In a figure used in the 1615 translation of Varchi's *The Blazon of Jealousy*, *voluptas* supplants *voluntas*.[31] Or, to put it another way, misogyny may well imply misandry. The rules that were framed to control the behaviour of women served of course to control the behaviour of men. If a man 'fell' for a woman, it was easy to blame the *cause* of that fall, which was, paradoxically, the idealized object of his desire. In some cases this might be projected back onto the subject. So Othello, when he is vaunting of his success in winning Desdemona, sums it up in his half-proud, half-shamefaced line, 'I do confess the vices of my blood' (1.3.123).

We see this fear of women – or is it hatred? – registered in *Love's Labour's Lost*. The men of Navarre are young bloods, men of high degree in the prime of their youth. They proclaim that they are devotees of art (they are seeking fame), and that study, based on reason, is all too vulnerable to 'affections':

> Therefore, brave conquerors – for so you are,
> That war against your own affections
> And the huge army of the world's desires
>
> (1.1.8–10)

'Affections' means here both perturbations or diseases (*OED*, affection *sb* 10) and desires.[32] But in order to put down desire the men put down the cause of disease and desire – women. This 'happy' comedy is, we may come to feel, shot through with misogyny:

---

27 Laqueur, p. 35; for the implications in *Twelfth Night*, see pp. 114–15.
28 Thomas Vicary, *The Anatomie of the Bodie of Man*, 1577, *Early English Text Society*, Extra Series No 53 (London, 1888), p. 79; cf. *The Problems of Aristotle*: 'The seed ... is white in men by reason of his great heat, and because it is digested better ... The seed of a woman is red ... because the flowers is corrupt, undigested blood' (sig. E3ʳ).
29 E & T. Tasso, *Of Marriage and Wiving*, tr. R. Tofte (London 1599), sig C3ʳ; in *The Problems of Aristotle*, copulation is described as 'purging': 'it doth expell the fume of the seed from the brain, and it doth expell the matter of impostume' (sigs. E1ʳ⁻ᵛ and E2ʳ).
30 James Grantham Turner, *One Flesh: Paradisal Marriage and Sexual Relations in the Age of Milton* (Oxford, 1987), pp. 40 ff.
31 B. Varchi, *The Blazon of Jealousy*, tr. R. Tofte (London, 1615), p. 16; see Michel Foucault, *The Use of Pleasure*, vol. 2 of *The History of Sexuality*, tr. Robert Hurley, 1985, p. 6 for an exploration of the way men become 'the subject of desire'.
32 Compare Gal. 5.24: 'For they that are Christs, have crucified the flesh with the affections and the lusts'.

DUMAINE

    I would forget her, but a fever she
    Reigns in my blood and will remembered be.

                            (4.3.93–4)

In the subplot Armado, he who would combine the male roles of Mars and Mercury, explores the 'bitter-sweet' pun of *amare-amaro*:[33] 'Love is a familiar; love is a devil. There is no evil angel but love' (1.2.163–5).

Biron, who in the first set of wit in the play casts himself as the 'natural' man, unwilling to repress his desires, has a set speech later where his satirical wit serves only to reveal a comic unease that well may rest upon a degree of residual misogyny:

What? I love, I sue, I seek a wife? –
A woman, that is like a German clock,
Still a-repairing, ever out of frame,
And never going aright, being a watch,
But being watched that it may still go right . . .

And I to sigh for her, to watch for her,
To pray for her – go to, it is a plague
That Cupid will impose for my neglect
Of his almighty dreadful little might.

                            (3.1.184–98)

This is the sort of jocularity we find in misogynist texts like *Les quinze joyes de mariage*, translated anonymously in 1509 as *The fyftene Joyes of maryage* and again in 1603 as *The Batchelar's Banquet*,[34] probably by Robert Tofte who seems to have specialized in this sort of work.[35] If we read the text in this 'hard' manner we may conclude that Biron's great set speech in praise of love later in the play ('Have at you, then, affection's men at arms'[36]) is mere opportunistic rhetoric.

The way in which social form empowers feeling is manifest in Biron's lines

For every man with his affects is born,
Not by might mastered, but by special grace.[37]

                            (1.1.149–50)

This second line needs unpacking. 'Affects' is a pun: it means both 'affections' and 'affectations', has to do with both humours and

manners. In this comedy, as it happens, the 'affects' *are*, we might conclude, mastered, not, as is usual in comedy, by will or change but by 'grace'. The Princess and her ladies come upon the scene as, to pick up Biron's phrase, 'special graces'. The phrase has a specific meaning – it derives from Calvin who distinguishes 'special graces' from 'gifts of nature'. 'Special graces', he writes, 'God . . . diversely and to a certain measure dealeth among men that are otherwise ungodly'.[38] The ladies are, moreover, related to the classical tradition, to figures of Venus and the three Graces.[39] Artists customarily depicted the Graces with two figures facing and one with her back to the viewer[40] – which may explain the joke where all turn their backs on the masquers (5.2.160). The play ends with a set

---

[33] Edgar Wind, *Pagan Mysteries in the Renaissance* (Harmondsworth, 1967), p. 92.

[34] F. P. Wilson, ed., *The Batchelars Banquet* (Oxford, 1929).

[35] He wrote a poem about his unhappy adventures at a performance of the play; see G. R. Hibbard, ed., *Love's Labour's Lost* (Oxford, 1990), pp. 1–2.

[36] 4.3.288 ff.

[37] 'Special grace' is glossed by a commentator on Calvin as 'a special endowment of capacity, virtue, or heroism by which a man is fitted to serve the divine purpose in the world, while he himself may remain in the common state of human depravity'. Jean Calvin, *Institutes of the Christian Religion*, tr. F. L. Battles, 2 vols. (London, 1961), I, 276n; compare Pierre de la Primaudaye, 'Of Marriage', *The French Academie*, tr. T. B. (London, 1586): '[marriage is necessary] by reason of sin, which came in afterward, except in those to whom God hath granted the special grace of continency, which is as rare a thing as any whatsoever' (pp. 480–1).

[38] *Institutes*, 2.3.4, tr. T. Norton (London, 1562).

[39] See Boyet's compliment on the grace of the Princess (2.1.9–12); for the Graces, see Spenser, *The Faerie Queene*, 6.8.24, and the Gloss to April in *The Shepheardes Calender*. The Graces, Aglaia, Thalia, and Euphrosyne, were associated with brightness (*splendor*), freshness (*viriditas*), and happiness (*laetitia*) respectively (Wind, p. 269), and it could be that these determine the subjects of the poems to Maria ('. . . fair sun, which on my earth dost shine . . .' [4.3.57 ff.]), Catherine ('. . . Love . . . Spied a blossom passing fair' [4.3.99 ff.]), and Rosaline's cheerful witty personality.

[40] Wind, pp. 26 ff.

of deferred betrothals: Venus eventually tames Mars.[41] From that union, that *discordia concors*, would be born, according to Plutarch, 'the child Harmony'.[42] Shakespeare inscribes the idea in the musical *débat* between Owl and Cuckoo, Winter and Spring at the end of the play. That is a positive strand: equally, however, Amor is a god of death.[43]

ROSALINE [Cupid] hath been five thousand year a
  boy.
CATHERINE Ay, and a shrewd unhappy gallows,
  too.
ROSALINE You'll n'er be friends with him, a
  killed your sister.
CATHERINE He made her melancholy, sad, and
  heavy,
  And so she died.   (5.2.11–15)

The betrothals are contracted under the shadow of death, the death of the King of France. Cupid's labour may have been lost, and a 'hard reading' of the play might hint that no marriages are in fact going to ensue.

The ambivalence of this Renaissance attitude to sex informed attitudes not just to courtship but to marriage. There is pertinent material in *The Winter's Tale*. We start by thinking of Leontes and Polixenes looking back to a state of innocence when they were 'boy eternal' (1.2.66). Imprinted on this metaphor is, as Hermione makes plain, a dream of Eden from which men were expelled – because of the feminine:

We were as twinned lambs that did frisk i' th'
  sun,
And bleat the one at th'other. What we
  changed
Was innocence for innocence. We knew not
The doctrine of ill-doing, nor dreamed
That any did. Had we pursued that life,
And our weak spirits ne'er been higher reared
With stronger *blood*, we should have answered
  heaven
Boldly, 'Not guilty', the imposition cleared
Hereditary ours.
HERMIONE   By this we gather
You have tripped since.

POLIXENES   O my most sacred lady,
Temptations have since then been born to's; for
In those unfledged days was my wife a girl.
Your precious self had then not crossed the eyes
Of my young playfellow.
HERMIONE   *Grace* to boot!
Of this make no conclusion, lest you say
Your queen and I are devils.
      (*The Winter's Tale*, 1.2.69–84, emphases added)

Here we notice an allusion not only to the fall but to the question of pre-lapsarian marriage. Paradise, for these two men, was a world of masculine friendship, and there woman takes the role not of a Grace but of a serpent. They seem to be explicitly rejecting the largely Protestant notion of paradisal marriage,[44] a notion that had been at the centre of a controversy that had raged a year or so before the play was written between the academic dramatist William Gager[45] and the Revd William Heale who set out his case in *An Apology for Women* (1609). Heale constructs his vindication of women and exposure of the double standard with a goodly number of *sententiae* and *exempla* drawn from a wide range of authors. It ends with a commentary on 'the Eden of felicity',[46] the story of Paradise, in which Heale argues that woman exceeds man because of being made not out of dust but out of man's rib:

And parallel also unto the purity of this golden age was the perfection of man's and woman's soul. For when their bodies were first framed as a picture of wrought wax or an image of hewn stone, God breathed thereunto a lively soul, which he styled the breath of life. And that spirit, being of an aëreal substance and (as it were) angelical essence, defused itself into each part, giving motion, sense, and reason unto the whole.[47]

---

41 For the iconology of this figure, see Wind, pp. 89 ff.
42 Plutarch, 'Isis and Osiris', *Moralia*, v, 370.
43 Wind, pp. 152 ff.
44 See Mary Beth Rose, *The Expense of Spirit* (Ithaca, N.Y. 1988).
45 See Turner, pp. 1–2.
46 Heale, p. 10.
47 Heale, p. 60.

This suggests a resonance for the statue scene, but I wonder whether Paulina's 're-creation' of Hermione[48] *has* purged Leontes' misogyny. Like everyone I had noticed that Hermione does not speak to Leontes. However, I think I had failed to notice how the implied stage directions suggest that the scene could be played to show Leontes not in the throes of a redemptive joy, but as appalled, even disgusted. He was eager to kiss the 'statue' (5.3.80) but not the living woman. Paulina has to urge Leontes forward:

> Do not shun her
> Until you see her die again, for then
> You kill her double. Nay, present your hand.
> When she was young, you wooed her. Now, in age,
> Is she become the suitor? (5.3.105–9)

Leontes stays tongue-tied, possibly refusing the implied offer of a hand-fasting or new marriage contract,[49] as his wife seeks to reconjure old emotions:

> POLIXENES She embraces him.
> CAMILLO She hangs about his neck.
> (5.3.111–12)

The two do not exchange any dialogue, and most of what Leontes says has to do with procuring a marriage between Camillo and Paulina, as well as asking pardon from his wife and Polixenes.

FREUD

These are some of the Renaissance contexts, anatomical and theological, of misogyny. I now want to turn to various contemporary models. We are thoroughly familiar with the construction of the feminine in Shakespearian texts: 'Sacred and sweet was all I saw in her' says Lucentio of Bianca in *The Taming of the Shrew* (1.1.174). This suggests a strong process of suppression. What was suppressed was below the waist:

> The fitchew nor the soilèd horse goes to't
> With a more riotous appetite. Down from the waist

They're centaurs, though women all above.
But to the girdle do the gods inherit;
Beneath is all the fiend's. There's hell, there's darkness, there is the sulphurous pit, burning, scalding, stench, consumption. Fie, fie, fie; pah, pah!

(*Lear*, F 4.5.120–6).

This excess of Lear is obviously pathological, but the equation of hell with the vagina was a common trope,[50] a Renaissance equivalent to the identification of the Medusa's head with the female genitals made by Freud and others.[51] How might we explain? In *Much Ado* Claudio wants women to be sexually inert, to reaffirm their powerlessness in all that they do:

> CLAUDIO You seem to me as Dian in her orb,
> As chaste as is the bud ere it be blown.
> But you are more intemperate in your blood
> Than Venus or those pampered animals
> That rage in savage sensuality.
> (4.1.57–61)

Claudio's emotion seems to be in excess of the facts, telling us more about himself than about Hero. Her nature not her action is the butt of his pathological indictment of what he takes to be the excessive and transgressive. The invocation of animals aligns itself with Freud's

---

48 Freud, in 'Mourning and Melancholia', speaks of the way in which 'the loss of a love-object is an excellent opportunity for the ambivalence in love-relationships to make itself effective and come into the open'. *On Metapsychology* (Harmondsworth, 1984), p. 260.

49 This may quote the gesture of Hermione and Polixenes 'paddling palms' in the second scene of the play (1.2.117).

50 See Stephen Booth, ed., *Shakespeare's Sonnets* (New Haven, 1977), pp. 499–500, who cites among other texts Rowland's 15th Epigram from his *The Letting of Humour's Blood in the Head-Vaine* (London, 1600); consider also the designation 'hell' in the game of barley-break (see *The Changeling*, 3.3.165n).

51 Freud, *On Sexuality* (Harmondsworth, 1981), p. 311n.; for an essay that links the image to *Macbeth*, see Marjorie Garber, *Shakespeare's Ghost Writers: Literature as Uncanny Causality* (London, 1987), pp. 97 ff.

account of the way children may displace images of copulating animals into their fantasies concerning their parents' sexual intercourse. 'They adopt what may be called *a sadistic view of coition.*'[52] Stories in which humans copulate with animals may also be reworkings of this 'primal scene' narrative: Oberon's desire to humiliate Titania by having her fall for an ass is obviously relevant here.

Such bestial or sadistic images seem to emerge in Shakespeare as an index of immature or displaced sexuality. So Iago, who, as Lynda Boose has demonstrated,[53] is usefully thought of as an Aretinian pornographer rather than a Machiavellian devil, the 'shadow-side'[54] of the men in the play, kindles Brabanzio's fury not just by his racist taunts but by reminding him of how woman brings out the beast in man:

> Even now, now, very now, an old black ram
> Is tupping your white ewe.   (1.1.88–9).

Notice how he calls Desdemona a ewe and not a lamb, suggesting that she is out to wound Brabanzio's manhood and not just his family honour. And again:

> ... you'll have your daughter covered with a Barbary horse, you'll have your nephews neigh to you, you'll have coursers for cousins and jennets for germans ... your daughter and the Moor are now making the beast with two backs.[55]   (1.1.113–19)

For Othello he conjures images of bestiality, cunningly getting the Moor to see himself in Cassio's place and so raising 'spirits' that Othello had seemingly methodically suppressed:

> It is impossible you should see this,
> Were they as prime as goats, as hot as monkeys,
> As salt as wolves in pride, and fools as gross
> As ignorance made drunk. But yet I say,
> If imputation, and strong circumstances
> Which lead directly to the door of truth,
> Will give you satisfaction, you might ha't.[56]
>   (3.3.407–13)

Along with bestial fantasies we find a disconcerting sadism in the mental make-up of several of Shakespeare's heroes. It emerges in the 'manliness' of Tullus Aufidius, who eroticizes his enemy Coriolanus:

> Thou hast beat me out
> Twelve several times, and I have nightly since
> Dreamt of encounters 'twixt thyself and me –
> We have been down together in my sleep,
> Unbuckling helms, fisting each other's throat –
> And waked half dead with nothing.   (4.5.122–7)

This man's love is not for the 'Other' or woman but for his alter ego, both detested and admired. In *Timon* the hero's command to the whores Phrynia and Timandra, 'Hold up, you sluts, | Your aprons mountant' (4.3.135–6) suggests a metaphorical rape by the gold he pours into their laps, a grotesque parody of what Jove did to Danaë. My point is that misogyny of a particularly sexual kind seems to be apparent in an extraordinarily large number of Shakespearian texts.

THE CONDITION OF WOMEN AND MASCULINE CRISIS

If Freud is right, misogyny may be a function of a well-nigh universal function of childhood fantasies of the primal scene, and I don't know whether I can demonstrate that this sort of thing is what Foucault calls 'a historically singular form of experience'.[57] However, I do not

---

[52] 'On the Sexual Theories of Children', *On Sexuality*, p. 198.

[53] Lynda E. Boose, '"Let it be Hid": Renaissance Pornography, Iago, and Audience Response', *Autour d'Othello*, ed. Richard Marienstras and Dominique Goy-Blanquet (Amiens 1987), 135–43.

[54] Edward A. Snow, 'Sexual anxiety and the male order of things in *Othello*', *ELR*, 10 (1980), 384–412, p. 409.

[55] The figure appears in Rabelais, *Gargantua*, chap. 7, and see M. P. Tilley, *A Dictionary of the Proverbs in England in the Sixteenth and Seventeenth Centuries* (Ann Arbor, 1950), B151.

[56] Snow writes, 'In Freudian terms, Iago is alienating Othello from the sexual act by making him participate in it from the place of the superego' (p. 396).

[57] Foucault, *Pleasure*, p. 4.

think that it is difficult to demonstrate that there was a condition of woman question in the culture of the English Renaissance. Martin Ingram's work on church courts[58] shows an intense preoccupation with what Natalie Zemon Davis earlier called 'women on top',[59] those whom men considered a threat to the social system, who weren't 'sacred and sweet'.[60]

Perhaps one of the reasons that we have not perceived as clearly that there may have been a 'condition of men' problem is that 'literary' texts, written by men, tend to concern themselves with individual moral and emotional problems, to see women as simply a group that comprises the 'other'. However, whenever there has been any sort of movement for female emancipation we have tended to find group male sexual disorientation.[61] The plethora of cuckolding jokes in comedy may well manifest a fear of female emancipation.[62]

When we turn to a manifestation of this in Shakespeare, I want to start with Othello:

OTHELLO I had been happy if the general camp,
    Pioneers and all, had tasted her sweet
      body,
    So I had nothing known. I, now for
      ever
    Farewell the tranquil mind, farewell
      content,
    Farewell the plumèd troops and the big
      wars
    That makes ambition virtue!
    ...
    Farewell! Othello's occupation's gone.
                (3.3.350–62)

The lines are familiar, but that crucial triple sexual pun on 'occupation'[63] – it means role or vocation, as well as designating Desdemona as mere object – remains unglossed in the new Arden (1958) and even the New Cambridge (1984) editions. Othello's social identity entails his sexual identity. He perceives Desdemona's seeming violation of his *ethical* position, his marital honour, mainly as a violation of his *social* reputation, the kind of 'honour' of which Iago speaks. Desdemona had begun by 'deceiving'

her father (1.3.293): maybe Othello has begun to believe Brabanzio, and his only reaction to this 'unruliness' may be a more strenuous assertion of what he takes to be his essential maleness, what the text reveals to be simply masculine behaviour.

Another familiar moment, which shows that Othello saw not what doth move:

OTHELLO It is the cause, it is the cause, my soul.
    Let me not name it to you, you chaste
      stars.
    It is the cause. Yet I'll not shed her
      blood,
    Nor scar that whiter skin of hers than
      snow,
    And smooth as monumental alabaster.
    Yet she must die, else she'll betray
      more men.
    ...

---

58 Martin Ingram, *Church Courts, Sex and Marriage in England, 1570–1640*, Past and Present Publications (Cambridge, 1987).

59 Natalie Zemon Davis, 'Women on Top: Symbolic Sexual Inversion and Political Disorder in Early Modern Europe', in *The Reversible World*, ed. Barbara A. Babcock (Ithaca, N.Y., 1978).

60 See also D. E. Underdown, 'The Taming of the Scold' in A. Fletcher and J. Stevenson, eds., *Order and Disorder in Early Modern England* (Cambridge, 1985), pp. 116–36. This may have been itself a symptom of general economic decline as well as of the increasing power of the craft guilds (see Merry E. Wiesner's study of particular German cities, 'Spinsters and Seamstresses: Women in Cloth and Clothing Production', in Ferguson, pp. 191–205.) Doubtless aspects of witch-hunting can be attributed to analogous factors. We might also consider the rule of Elizabeth, the virgin queen (see Peter Stallybrass, 'Patriarchal Territories: The Body Enclosed', in Ferguson, pp. 123–42).

61 See two poems by Lady Mary Wroth, niece to Sir Philip Sidney, 'Love a child is ever crying' and 'Late in the forest I did Cupid see' (in Germaine Greer, *et al.* eds., *Kissing the Rod* (London, 1988), pp. 66–7). These we read, I think, rather differently if we know that they were written by a woman; compare also Lionel Trilling's preface to Henry James's *The Bostonians* (London, 1952).

62 Keith Thomas, 'The Place of Laughter in Tudor and Stuart England', *TLS* (21 January, 1977), 77–81.

63 Eric Partridge, *Shakespeare's Bawdy* (London, 1968), p. 155.

> When I have
> plucked thy rose
> I cannot give it vital growth again.
> It needs must wither. I'll smell thee on
> the tree.
> [*He kisses her*]   (5.2.1–15)

Yet again the masculinity lies in language. Writers have often noted Othello's idealization, not so his bad faith:[64] the Moor refuses to define the cause of his jealousy, he (wilfully?) confuses the final cause *for* which he will kill his wife with the efficient cause *by* which he is driven to kill his wife. Few would now agree with Bradley: 'The deed he is bound to do is no murder, but a sacrifice'.[65] The speech does far more than generate pathos, it makes us acutely uncomfortable. 'When I have plucked thy rose' means, of course, 'when I have taken your maidenhead'.[66] (It is not so glossed in the old or New Cambridge or new Arden editions.) The suggestion is that only by killing Desdemona can Othello meet with Desdemona's sexuality. 'Thy bed, lust-stained, shall with lust's blood be spotted' (5.1.37): this act, moreover, seems to him to be a way of exterminating female sexuality – and his own sexuality. Of Iago he exclaims:

> Ay, 'twas he that told me on her first.
> An honest man he is, and hates the slime
> That sticks on filthy deeds   (5.2.154–6)

The misogyny, based on a pathological aversion to the physical nature of marital copulation, could not be more apparent.

As Eliot made us aware years ago, one of the great questions of the play is whether Othello achieves recognition, sees some shame in motives late revealed, or whether he merely cheers himself up. Othello's 'O blood, blood, blood!' (3.4.455) may indicate some beginnings of awareness: it is a cry of vengeance, a piece of invective against his wife's sexuality, and maybe contains the beginning of recognition that he shares blood with Cassio, that passion will destroy order. At the end he is conspicuously silent about his love. Perhaps this silence betokens a recognition that at last – but too late – he has understood not only the moral innocence but the sexual nature of himself and his wife.

So Lavatch's 'blood', Hamlet's blood-curdled ghost,[67] Othello's 'O, blood, blood, blood!': they all partake of the devil, all generate echoes of the primal scene. They generate the overheated pornographic imagination of Hamlet brooding on reechy kisses and the underheated pornographic imagination of Iago.

VERDICTS

Our so-called patriarchal bard, in a fine frenzy of even-handedness, offers some fierce verdicts on transgressive or excessive masculine sexuality. Men are, as searchers after reputation rather than virtue, perverters of the parable of the talents:

> PAROLES He wears his honour in a box unseen
> That hugs his kicky-wicky here at
> home,
> Spending his manly marrow in her arms
> . . .   (2.3.276–8)

The taking of maidenheads is an index of virtue, but woman, the owner of maidenhead, causes man to spend, use up, his precious marrow,[68] his semen, his manliness.[69] And, from another sequence in *All's Well*, we hear the disconcerting line that gives this essay its title:

> SECOND LORD DUMAINE
> [Bertram] hath perverted a young gentlewoman here in Florence of a most chaste renown, and this night he fleshes his will in the spoil of her honour.
>   (4.3.15–17)

---

64 A notable exception is provided by Edward A. Snow (see n. 54) above).
65 A. C. Bradley, *Shakespearean Tragedy* (London, 1957 edn), p. 161.
66 Partridge, p. 176.
67 See *Hamlet*, 1.5.69–70.
68 Compare 'Venus and Adonis' where Venus proclaims 'My flesh is soft and plump, my marrow burning' (142).
69 For the economy of semen, see de la Primaudaye, p. 238, Laqueur, p. 101.

'Fleshes' means to give a first taste of flesh, as to a hawk: here losing virginity is an act of sadism and martial pillage.

Men are in short misogynists, seeking a sexual satisfaction that is endlessly deferred, and, if achieved, achieved only through fantasising:

HELEN [to the Widow]   O, strange men,
          That can such sweet use make of what
                    they hate,
          When saucy trusting of the cozened
                    thoughts
          Defiles the pitchy night; so lust doth play
          With what it loathes, for that which is
                    away.   (4.4.21–5)

This is a gaming metaphor – although it is not glossed as such in New Cambridge – but the pun on 'play' suggests both faking in bed and sexual molestation. It is a marvellous metaphor for what Freud terms the 'tendency to debasement in love'.[70] (There may also be an echo of an Aristotelian problem: a woman, he averred, 'always loveth the man that hath been the first to receive of her amorous pleasures ... and contrariwise the man hateth the woman that hath been the first to couple in that wise with him'.[71])

It is all too easy to pluck word crisis out of air, but I do want to suggest that the literary and possibly actual construction of sexuality was at odds with reality.

If we want to construct a historically singular model to account for this deformation we might look to chivalry. It was both a *residual* ideology as it is registered in the archaizing of Spenser, the conspicuously false consciousness of Beaumont and Fletcher,[72] and a *dominant* one as registered in the way Queen Elizabeth turned her chastity to power.[73] Originally chivalry was an ethic for legitimating war: 'as men are valiant, so are they virtuous'[74] – this comes from the sardonic 'Jane Anger'. When mediated through the chivalric epics, the code defines and supports an essentially individualistic ethic. It is a code for knights doing battle against enemies equal to them in rank in the feudal order or against 'paynims', evil others.

As part of a set of residual myths, it imports a set of rituals or metaphors into personal relationships. Manhood was not just a matter of biological age and sex, but became a category of achievement that is acquired only through rites of passage. Youths were invested as squires, then dubbed knights: these central rites of passage from boyhood to manhood, physiological process measured by sexual development, are figured around patterns of war. Margaret Tyler, translator of Ortuñez de Calahorra's *The First Part of the Mirror of ... Knighthood* (1578), tersely hints at this:

The chief matter therein contained is of exploits of wars, and the parties therein named are especially renowned for their magnanimity and courage. The author's purpose appeareth to be this, to animate thereby and set on fire the lusty courages of young gentlemen to the advancement of their line by ensuing such like steps.[75]

My hypothesis is that we can show, by a reading of Shakespeare, that chivalry, residual chivalry, affected male sexuality disastrously. Chivalry purports to relate to ethics but in reality it relates to politics. Warlike aims are disguised as service to the female – as we see the idealization of Helen in *Troilus and Cressida* – and turn the consorting of men and women to a hunt for prizes and maidenheads. Chivalry constructs women as passive, as ornaments, and imposes chastity (something that can be owned or taken by a man) as a means of legitimating male power. The condition of women becomes

---

70 See 'On the Universal Tendency to Debasement in the Sphere of Love' in Freud, *Sexuality*, pp. 247–60.
71 Aristotle, I Physics, xviii, cited by Castiglione, *The Book of the Courtier*, tr. Sir Thomas Hoby, Everyman edn, p. 199.
72 See Jonson, *The New Inn*, ed. Michael Hattaway (Manchester, 1984), p. 35.
73 See it mocked in Nashe's *Unfortunate Traveller* (in Salzman, pp. 262 ff.)
74 'Jane Anger', in Moira Ferguson, p. 70.
75 Reprinted in Moira Ferguson, p. 54.

a question of value, women become thereby tokens of exchange, and value is focused on their sexuality, on honesty rather than honour. Men idealize in order to suppress. Courtship is generally courtiership: women's desire is channelled towards their 'servants' or their lords as a way of sustaining dynasty. If the metaphors are not courtly they are martial: power is generated not through courtly negotiation but through 'the vocabulary of gentlemanly combat'.[76] Armed knights are conquered by ladies[77] – that sort of thing.

When, however, a man turns from chivalric warrior to chivalric 'servant' he is in danger of being 'unmanned', made effeminate,[78] and driven to mortal sin by feminine will. Listen to Lear's catechizing of the disguised Edgar:

LEAR   What hast thou been?
EDGAR   A servingman, proud in heart and mind,
    that curled my hair, wore gloves in my cap,
    served the lust of my mistress' heart, and did
    the act of darkness with her;

                    (Folio text, 3.4.78–82)

'Servingman' seems to me to be a pun here, both the *cavaliere servente* and a servant, the former reduced to the latter. As a loving warrior, Tomalin in Nashe's 'Choice of Valentines' is subject to the power of 'Priapus' who, against the power of his mistress Frances' dildo, is nothing:

Poor Priapus, [she exalts] whose triumph now
    must fall,
Except thou thrust this weakling to the wall;
Behold how he usurps in bed and bower,
And undermines thy kingdom every hour.

                          (247–50)

Book 5 of *The Faerie Queene* begins with a linking of chivalry with justice, and the main quest of the hero is to free Eirena – an idealized feminized figure of Ireland – from the giant Grantorto (the papacy). Proper rule is obviously not only Protestant but masculine. However, one of the most notable victories won by Artegall is that over the Amazon Radigund (5.4.33).[79] Artegall is accompanied by Talus the iron man whose attacks on Radigund are not only violent but wantonly tyrannical:

And euery while that mighty yron man,
With his stange weapon, neuer wont in warre,
Them sorely vext, and courst, and ouerran,
And broke their bowes, and did their shooting
    marre.   (V. 4.43)

Artegall is later rescued from the clutches of Radigund by his love Britomart, the incarnation of chastity who, having been granted a vision in the Temple of Isis or Equity,[80] becomes even more powerful. This all seems to contain much interest for the cultural historian. For the moment I should define it as an example of what Freud called 'negation':[81] 'woman is brought to the surface of social consciousness only to be repudiated'.[82] Or, as Foucault argued, codes of sexual conduct represent 'an elaboration of masculine conduct carried out from the viewpoint of men in order to give form to *their* behaviour'.[83] Men come to hate the very paragons of virtue they have created to save themselves from themselves. Which may be why a Hamlet, conscious of being like Claudius, prey to desire, so hates Ophelia.

This investigation is infinitely extendible. I

---

[76] See Nancy Vickers, '"The Blazon of Sweet Beauty's Best": Shakespeare's *Lucrece*', in Patricia Parker and Geoffrey Hartman, eds., *Shakespeare and the Question of Theory* (London, 1985), pp. 105–6.

[77] Compare *Pericles*, scene 6, 26.

[78] Cf. *Romeo*, 3.1.113–15; on the 'feminizing' of subjects by their princes see Joan Kelly-Gadol, 'Did Women Have a Renaissance?', in Renate Bridenthal and Claudia Koontz, eds., *Becoming Visible: Women in European History* (Boston, 1987), p. 159.

[79] See Thomas Healy, *New Latitudes: Theory and English Renaissance Literature* (London, 1992), pp. 94–5.

[80] *Faerie Queene*, v.7.

[81] 'The outcome ... is a sort of intellectual acceptance of the repressed, while at the same time what is essential to the repression persists'. 'Negation', in *Metapsychology*, p. 438.

[82] Dympna Callaghan, *Women and Gender in Renaissance Tragedy* (London, 1989), p. 12.

[83] *Use of Pleasure*, pp. 22–3.

have described four sites, anatomical, psycho-analytical, social, and ideological, but would be loath to claim that my descriptions have provided adequate *explanations* for the misogyny that seems to a modern reader to be a feature of these texts. Misogyny in most of these contexts seems to be a function of patriarchy, but the terms in which it is understood form part of a whole series of signifying systems, not all of which can be attached to historically specific cultural agendas. I have added some evidence to suggest that the centres of these texts are inhabited by a number of subjects who see *all* sexuality, all 'acts of darkness', as shameful and 'adulterous'.[84] Nashe tells in 'The Choice of Valentines' how Justice Dudgeon-Haft and Crabtree Face have driven his love Frances from rustic dancing on the town green into a brothel (21–4). He also writes in the dedicatory sonnet:

> Complaints and praises everyone can write,
> And passion out their pangs in stately rhymes,
> But of love's pleasures none did ever write
> That hath succeeded in these latter times.

True then and, unfortunately, perhaps true now.

---

[84] See Stephen Greenblatt, *Renaissance Self-Fashioning* (Chicago, 1980), pp. 248 ff.; compare Snow's conclusion that 'Shakespeare locates the principle of evil and malice at the level of the superego, the agency that enforces civilization on the ego'.

BOWDLER AND BRITANNIA: SHAKESPEARE AND THE NATIONAL LIBIDO

MICHAEL DOBSON

The inception of the 'Shakespeare industry' during the eighteenth century, with which I shall be largely concerned in this paper, has not always been considered an especially sexy topic, I admit, and it is probably still true that for most historians of Shakespeare criticism the period which gave us the first 'scholarly' edition (Rowe's, 1709), the first public squabble over textual editing (between Alexander Pope and Lewis Theobald, 1725–6), and the first solemn pilgrimage to Stratford (Garrick's Jubilee, 1769) isn't one with any very obvious erotic overtones. Nonetheless, it is precisely the sexual dimension of the Enlightenment's processing of Shakespeare that I mean to sketch here, and especially its inextricable connection with the development of English nationalism. I shall be suggesting that the definition of Shakespeare as an object of nostalgic veneration during the eighteenth century is inseparably bound up with both the construction of modern sexuality and the construction of English national identity; so bound up, in fact, that it would be possible to regard the Enlightenment Shakespeare we still largely inherit as not just the ally but the offspring of Bowdler and Britannia, propriety and nationalism. In the course of this argument I shall be illustrating how in the eighteenth century Shakespeare came to embody the national libido – albeit, paradoxically, at the expense of his own.

Thomas and Henrietta Bowdler, of course, did not publish the Family Shakespeare until 1807 (and it remained anonymous until the second edition of 1814, the title page of which credits Thomas with the entire project so as to preserve the reputation of his unmarried sister), but the name 'Bowdler' provides a convenient shorthand for that normative policing of sexuality which actually begins far earlier, gathering momentum in English culture throughout the eighteenth century. George Mosse, indeed, cites the Bowdlers' Shakespeare as the perfect exemplar of this movement (which he terms 'respectability') as early as the third page of his deservedly influential *Nationalism and Sexuality* (1985). Although Mosse's study otherwise neglects Shakespeare, and seems to me to date the full emergence of 'respectability' rather late, his argument that nationalism successfully co-opted earlier cultural forms while remaining unshakeably allied to a new model of propriety is one with considerable resonance for the Enlightenment's revaluation and re-use of Shakespeare:

Nationalism is perhaps the most powerful and effective ideology of modern times, and its alliance with bourgeois morality forged an engine difficult to stop. In its long career, it attempted to co-opt most of the important movements of the age, to

Parts of this paper derive from research towards *Imagining Gloriana: British Nationalism and the Representation of Elizabeth I, 1603–1990*, a study co-authored with Dr Nicola Watson (Northwestern University), and I am happy to acknowledge the assistance of my illustrious collaborator at every stage of its conception and development.

absorb all that men thought meaningful and held dear even while holding fast to certain unchanging myths and symbols ... But however flexible, nationalism hardly wavered in its advocacy of respectability.[1]

The Shakespeare who had survived into the bookstalls and theatres of the early eighteenth century offered these interlinked emerging ideologies of nationalism and respectability both opportunities and challenges. As a relic of the already thoroughly idealized days of Good Queen Bess, his authentic Englishness was not in question; indeed one of the reasons his plays now attracted more attention than those of Jonson or Fletcher was their interest in the national past – paradoxically, the more frequently his histories were rewritten to support different viewpoints during the constitutional crises of the 1680s and 1710s, the more transcendentally valuable they appeared to be. But he certainly wasn't respectable: his texts and his biography alike, as Margreta de Grazia has pointed out in *Shakespeare Verbatim*, were riddled with lowness, 'extravagance', 'licentiousness' and 'irregularity'.[2] De Grazia has brilliantly demonstrated the extent to which the whole enterprise of textual editing, from Rowe through Malone (and indeed the Bowdlers), was established specifically to deal with this embarrassing verbal wantonness: but what she does not point out is the extent to which this policing of Shakespeare's texts often goes hand in hand with the co-opting of their author as himself a policing figure. Jeremy Collier was already displaying this combined strategy of monitoring Shakespeare and then invoking him as a monitor in 1698, in his famous *Short View of the Immorality and Prophaneness of the English Stage*, which at first berates Shakespeare for smuttiness but subsequently congratulates him for making a properly improving example of Falstaff – 'He is thrown out of Favour as being a *Rake*', Collier notes smugly,

and dies like a Rat behind the Hangings. The Pleasure he had given, would not excuse him. The *Poet* was not so partial, as to let his Humour compound for his Lewdness.[3]

But this double move of at once redeeming Shakespeare for sexual propriety and invoking him as a potential redeemer of the contemporary public is displayed most fully by the cleaned-up version of *The Merchant of Venice* produced by George Granville, Lord Lansdowne in 1701, *The Jew of Venice*. The prologue to this adaptation, contributed by Granville's cousin Bevill Higgons, marks one of Shakespeare's first appearances in person – if that is the word – on the Augustan stage, and he is appropriately ushered onto it by one of his most distinguished polishers; as the curtain goes up, 'The Ghosts of *Shakespear* and *Dryden* arise Crown'd with Lawrel.'[4] The dialogue which ensues is almost obsessively concerned with sexual normality, here equated with both literary and national purity. Dryden reports to his elder colleague on the dismaying state of modern audiences, who, abandoning sterling British drama for foreign ephemera, have concomitantly abandoned heterosexuality:

[Dryd.] *Their sickly Judgments, what is just, refuse,*
And French Grimace, Buffoons, and Mimicks choose;
Our Scenes desert, some wretched Farce to see;
They know not Nature, for they tast not Thee ...
Thro' Perspectives revers'd they Nature view,
Which give the Passions Images, not true.

---

1 George L. Mosse, *Nationalism and Sexuality: Middle-Class Morality and Sexual Norms in Modern Europe* (Madison, Wisc., 1985), p. 9.

2 '"Extravagance" characterized accounts of Shakespeare's life just as "irregularity" distinguished his works, during the Restoration and beyond.' Margreta de Grazia, *Shakespeare Verbatim: The Reproduction of Authenticity and the 1790 Apparatus* (Oxford, 1991), pp. 75–7.

3 Jeremy Collier, *A Short View of the Immorality and Prophaneness of the English Stage* (London, 1698), p. 154.

4 George Granville, Lord Lansdowne, *The Jew of Venice* (1701), in Christopher Spencer, *Five Restoration Adaptations of Shakespeare* (Urbana, Ill., 1965), pp. 345–402; 'Prologue', pp. 348–9. 'The Profits of this *Play* were design'd for Mr *Dryden;* but, upon his Death, given to his Son', explains a footnote.

Strephon *for* Strephon *sighs; and* Sapho *dies,*
Shot to the soul by brighter Sapho's *Eyes:*
No Wonder then their wand'ring Passions roam,
And feel not Nature, whom th'have overcome.
For shame let genial Love prevail agen,
You Beaux Love Ladies, and you Ladies Men.

The creator of the Sonnets, wholly innocent of the homoerotic, is suitably despairing at this news – '*These Crimes, unknown, in our less polisht Age, / Now seem beyond correction of the Stage*' – but he promises to do what he can to remedy the situation, offering his play (now properly '*Adorn'd and rescu'd by a faultless hand*') as a contribution to the internal discipline which is the proper and unique function of literature:

> *The Law's Defect, the juster Muse supplies,*
> *Tis only we, can make you Good or Wise,*
> *Whom Heav'n spares, the Poet will Chastise.*

Granville's adaptation itself faithfully continues Higgons' crusade against 'foreign' sexual deviancy: while the attachment of Antonio to Bassanio is toned down, the attachment of Shylock to his ducats is spiced up into the realms of sexual perversion. In Granville's hands the Jew becomes a fetishistic precursor of Auric Goldfinger who, for once accepting Antonio's invitation to dinner, offers an explicit toast to the sole object of his desires –

'I have a Mistress, that out-shines 'em all –
'Commanding yours – and yours tho' the whole Sex:
'My Money is my Mistress! Here's to
'Interest upon Interest.   [*Drinks*
                                          (364)[5]

Processing Shakespeare's text for Augustan consumption (notably by quietly excising anything resembling 'French Grimace, Buffoons, and Mimicks', such as the Gobbos), Granville identifies its author as an unswervingly native foe to foreign dramatic genres and unnatural reproductive practices alike.

Given the interconnection already visible in this adaptation between the securing of Shakespeare as a native foe to foreign importations

and his promotion as a respectable champion of sexual normality, it is perhaps inevitable that as the level of investment in Shakespeare as a national hero increases over the ensuing decades – notably during the 1730s – the insistence on both his morality and his virility should increase likewise. Between his appearance in effigy in Lord Cobham's Temple of British Worthies at Stowe in 1735 and the unveiling of his monument in Westminster Abbey in 1741, a growing body of panegyric on Shakespeare presents him not just as a patriotic moral exemplar but as a tonic for national potency, in every sense.[6] To the playwright George Lillo, praising the advocacy of Shakespeare's plays carried out from 1737 onwards by the Shakespeare Ladies' Club, the Bard's drama serves as the snake-charming music by which the Ladies are arousing Britain's dormant masculinity: according to Lillo the Ladies' Club '*strove to wake, by* Shakespeare's *nervous lays, / The manly genius of* Eliza's *days*'.[7] This note is sounded more stridently at the close of the catchpenny

---

[5] I am indebted here to Laura Rosenthal's unpublished paper 'Disembodied Shakespeare: The Author as Ghost' (given at the conference 'Literary Property and the Construction of Authorship', Cleveland, Ohio, April 1990): on Granville's Shylock, see also J. H. Wilson, 'Granville's "Stock-Jobbing Jew"', *Philological Quarterly*, 13 (1934), pp. 1–15.

[6] For a (much!) more detailed account of the development of nationalist Bardolatry during this crucial period, see Michael Dobson, *The Making of the National Poet: Shakespeare, Adaptation and Authorship, 1660–1769* (Oxford, 1992), pp. 134–64.

[7] George Lillo, *Marina*, 'Epilogue'. In *The Plays of George Lillo*, ed. Trudy Drucker, 2 vols. (New York and London, 1979), vol. 2, p. 127. Even the Ladies' Club's own poet Mary Cowper sees their crusade as primarily engaged in the improvement of British manhood: see her poem 'On the Revival of Shakespear's Plays by the Ladies in 1738', which concludes by promising the Ladies' Club a bright future in which their activities on behalf of the Bard will have rescued Britain's young men from the pernicious influence of Continental culture, thereby securing themselves better lovers. BM Add. MSS 28101, 93v–94v: printed in Dobson, *Making of the National Poet*, pp. 150–1.

playlet *Harlequin Student*, produced at Henry Giffard's unlicensed Goodman's Fields theatre to cash in on the public interest aroused by the unveiling of Shakespeare's monument in the Abbey three years later. The conclusion of what has been for three-quarters of its duration a perfectly orthodox and hedonistic harlequinade is interrupted by a posse of angry gods, who proceed to lecture the audience for having tolerated the show so far. Jupiter, producing a full-size copy of the Abbey statue, suggests that instead they should

For ever thus th'unequall'd Bard adore,
Let Mimes and Eunuchs lull the Sense no more,
But with his Muse, your own lost Fame restore.[8]

In the duet between Minerva and Mars which ensues, Minerva exhorts the audience to

> Banish Foreign Songsters hence,
> Doat on *Shakespear's* manly Sense.
> Send th'Invading Triflers home,
> To lull the Fools of *France* and *Rome!* (p. 24)

Mars, even more anxious about the enervating consequences of Italian opera than Jupiter, warns the audience that 'Eunuchs taint the soundest [heart] / Weaken Man in every Part,' but promises that

> SHAKESPEAR's Soul-exalting Muse
> Will raise your Thoughts to nobler Views,
> Read but o'er his matchless Verse,
> Soon you'll prove the sons of *Mars*. (Ibid.)[9]

In an unidentified contemporary poem, preserved in manuscript in the Bodleian Library, this duet is extended to suggest that the power of Shakespearian drama has global as well as physical implications:

> While Britons bow at Shakespear's shrine
> Britannia's sons are sons of mine.
> Like him shou'd Britons scorn the Art
> That binds in chains the human heart
> Like him shou'd still be unconfin'd
> And rule the World as he the mind.[10]

It is worth remembering here that the claim that Britannia rules the waves was first made at exactly the same time as the claim that Shakespeare rules world literature; the latter, as this poem makes exceptionally clear, may indeed simply be a sub-clause of the former. By 1741 the world-beating power of Shakespearian drama is already figuring not just national but imperial potency.

In all these examples of texts in which the disciplining and promotion of Shakespeare seeks to discipline and promote British manhood, it is notable that the figure of Shakespeare, however salutary a force for virility, is represented as himself angelically free from flesh and blood – presented either as a ghost (his dangerous, erring corporeality bowdlerized away) or as a marble statue. The Shakespeare imagined by emergent nationalism, it seems, is the cause that sex is in others, but is not sexy in himself. This seems to be very significant, and I would like in the remainder of this paper to suggest why it might be the case, and with what consequences.

The most obvious reason for this neutering of the Bard is a continuing anxiety about the apparently unexemplary nature of the historical Shakespeare's sex life, as unacceptable, according to most of the traditions and even some of the documentary evidence, as the low puns excised from his texts by the likes of Granville,

---

8 [Henry Giffard], *Harlequin Student, or the Fall of Pantomime; With the Restoration of the Drama* (London, 1741), p. 22.

9 Theophilus Cibber, appropriately, had defended Giffard's theatre against closure two years earlier in very similar terms, expressing his horror that

> a Freeman of *London*, a Native of *England*, our Fellow-Subject, and our Brother in a Social Tye, shall be denied the Liberty that is allowed *French* Dancers, and Harlequins – to effeminate Eunuchs, and Sod-[omitica]l *Italians*; yet such shall be encouraged, and *Englishmen* despised!

Theophilus Cibber, 'An Address to the H—ble Sir J—B—' [1739], in *Two Dissertations on Theatrical Subjects* (London, 1755), p. 74.

10 *Ode to Shakespeare*, in Bodleian Library MS Mus d 14. The poem is set to music, attributed to William Boyce.

Pope and Bowdler. In the field of biography proper these moral qualms about the Bard's private life have been amply documented by Samuel Schoenbaum in *Shakespeare's Lives*, but a feeling that Shakespeare is much more convincing as a national icon if his body is left out of the picture entirely pervades a significant proportion of all Enlightenment writing about Shakespeare, in whatever medium. It is very striking, for example, that even when Shakespeare makes his first personal appearance in the novel – a form in which one would expect both intimacy and physical detail – he is still carefully denied a body, and is indeed specifically engaged in monitoring the sexual transgressions of others as a punishment for his own past licentiousness. In *Memoirs of the Shakespear's-Head in Covent-Garden* (1755), Shakespeare's ghost appears to one chosen client of the disreputable pub of the title, and explains miserably that he is undergoing purgatory: for a certain term his soul has been 'fix'd the Guardian of this *Bacchanalian Temple*, a Post alloted to punish me for the Errors of my youthful Conduct'.[11] An Old Hamlet posthumously recruited to the Vice Squad, Shakespeare proceeds temporarily to render his hapless auditor as invisible and ethereal as himself, and spends the rest of the narrative providing a guided tour of the seamy goings-on in progress in the tavern's various private rooms, offering a disgusted, moralistic commentary throughout. Once more, Shakespeare can only function as an adequately respectable figure at the expense of his own historical specificity, his own physicality.

This novel, presenting Shakespeare as the monitory ghost of a more sexually innocent past, is in precisely the tradition of Higgons' prologue to *The Jew of Venice*, a text which initiated other durable traditions too – notably that of Shakespearian homophobia. As Schoenbaum points out, for example, the first sustained biographical reading of the *Sonnets* – offered by George Chalmers in 1797 – insists that the Young Man sonnets are all definitely

addressed to a woman. Chalmers confidently identifies the woman in question, too – as Queen Elizabeth I – and it was here that for some writers one alternative to the representation of the National Poet's own sexuality, or perhaps one nationalized sublimation of it, might be found.[12] As early as 1702, John Dennis had explained away the unclassical imperfections of *The Merry Wives of Windsor* by claiming it was written in haste at the request of Elizabeth,[13] and this exculpatory rumour of a personal relationship between Shakespeare and his illustrious sovereign is one which snowballed as Shakespeare's status as a national hero rose. In 1739, Theophilus Cibber could claim that Shakespeare, although a mere player, was 'beloved by the Queen';[14] by 1763 the *Biographia Britannica* was insisting that Eliza had personally forgiven one of Shakespeare's notorious youthful misdemeanours, intervening to

---

[11] *Memoirs of the Shakespear's-Head in Covent-Garden. By the Ghost of Shakespear*, 2 vols. (London, 1755), vol. 1, pp. 5–6.

[12] George Chalmers, *An Apology for the Believers in the Shakespeare-Papers* (London, 1797), pp. 51–2, 55: see Samuel Schoenbaum, *Shakespeare's Lives* (Oxford, 1970), pp. 233–5. Despite his acknowledgement that they are fakes, Chalmers retains this idea from the Ireland forgeries, which include a letter from Elizabeth thanking 'goode Masterre William' for some 'prettye Verses': see Schoenbaum, pp. 207–8.

[13] See his introduction to his adaptation *The Comical Gallant; or the true amours of Sir John Falstaff* (London, 1702). Dennis went on to claim that the libertarian ideals expressed by Shakespeare's Brutus and Cassius provided the principal inspiration for Elizabeth's defiance of Spain: see his 'Prologue to the Subscribers for *Julius Caesar*' (1707) in *A Collection and Selection of English Prologues and Epilogues*, 4 vols. (London, 1779), vol. 3, pp. 1–2.

[14] Cibber makes this claim in the course of an argument that the British theatre has always been patriotically Anglican, reaching its apogee with Shakespeare: 'the first Traces of it were in *Henry* the VIIIth's time; it sunk with the PROTESTANT RELIGION beneath Queen *Mary*'s Persecution: In Queen *Elizabeth*'s time it flourished again, – and *Shakespear* was a Player, beloved by the Queen.' (Cibber, 'An Address to the *H—ble* Sir *J— B—*', p. 78).

prevent his punishment for poaching Sir Thomas Lucy's deer.[15] This particular story, repeated in several subsequent biographies, would be most fully and revealingly developed in two popular texts of the early nineteenth century. Sir Walter Scott – a writer always acutely aware of precisely what is at stake in the national legends he retails – puts it to especially good effect in *Kenilworth* (1821). Conflating Shakespeare's deer-poaching with more erotic trespasses, Scott, like Chalmers, has Shakespeare's sexual innocence certified by Elizabeth, in the course of a dialogue otherwise designed to assure the reader that the Bard was already recognized by the Crown as his nation's chief writer even in his own lifetime. Petitioned by Puritans to close the theatres, Elizabeth solicits the opinions of her entire assembled court on the subject of contemporary drama, and especially requests their views about 'one Will Shakespeare (whom I think, my lords, we have all heard something of)'.[16] Elizabeth herself declares, with the special prescience displayed by so many of Scott's more sympathetic characters, that Shakespeare's history plays will form a permanent part of Britain's literary heritage; but more striking than this orthodox opinion of the Bard's professional output is her corresponding insistence on correcting certain details of his biography. When Sussex offers some personal reminiscences, Elizabeth is quick to delete one particular detail of the familiar hearsay from the quasi-historical record:

'... [Shakespeare] stood, they say, a tough fight with the rangers of old Sir Thomas Lucy of Charlecot, when he broke his deerpark and kissed his keeper's daughter.'

'I cry you mercy, my Lord of Sussex,' said Queen Elizabeth, interrupting him; 'that matter was heard in council, and we will not have this fellow's offence exaggerated – there was no kissing in the matter, and the defendant hath put the denial on record.'

(p. 223)

Usefully guaranteeing Shakespeare's national status and his chastity at once, this imagined relationship between Shakespeare and the Virgin Queen forms the substance of the first English play to feature him as protagonist, Charles Somerset's *Shakespeare's Early Days* (1829), a play even more striking than the Scott novel on which it draws in its bowdlerization of Shakespeare's life. Fleeing Stratford after stealing a deer only in the cause of virtue – for the succour of a starving peasant – Somerset's Shakespeare arrives in London, pursued by Sir Thomas Lucy, where he is not only pardoned by Elizabeth but invested as Poet Laureate immediately after the defeat of the Armada. The tableau with which Somerset closes the play celebrates, in effect, the platonic betrothal of the National Poet to Britannia. Centre stage, Shakespeare kneels while Elizabeth hangs a miniature of herself, framed with diamonds, around his neck, to the accompaniment of a rousing chorus:

> Shakspeare! Shakspeare! none beside!
> Shakspeare is his nation's pride![17]

Although Shakespeare is here represented for once in the flesh, this popular play, remarkably, utterly suppresses his relationship with Anne Hathaway, not to mention any conjectural intrigues with young men or dark ladies. In Somerset's play the youth who leaves Warwickshire for London is not married, still less the father of three children. Once again, the representation of Shakespeare as 'his nation's pride', worthy to be placed at the right hand of Gloriana herself, seems to require the suppression of any actual historical details of his physical life.[18] The ghostly Shakespeare abstracted from his plays – themselves morally pruned for

15 *Biographica Britannica*, 6 vols. in 7 (London, 1763), 'Shakespeare'.
16 Sir Walter Scott, *Kenilworth* (1821: ed. H. J. C. Grierson, London, 1952), p. 222.
17 Charles A. Somerset, *Shakespeare's Early Days* (London, 1829), p. 48.
18 Cf. Anna Jameson's remarks 'On the Love of Shakespear' in *Memoirs of the Loves of the Poets*, published in the same year: '[T]he workings of his wondrous and all-embracing mind were directed by a higher influence

eighteenth-century performance, as Bell's acting edition (1773–4) shows most fully – might be worthy of national veneration, as might the blameless servant of the Virgin Queen imagined by Scott and Somerset – but the Shakespeare of the unexpurgated plays and uncensored biography simply didn't fit the role in which eighteenth-century England nonetheless needed to cast him.[19]

Above and beyond this simple bowdlerization of Shakespeare's life as a motive for these curiously sexless representations of a writer nonetheless charged with embodying his country's libido is the very nature of the nationalist project they serve, as it replaces local and specific allegiances with an internalized loyalty to a generalized national ideal. In resurrecting the Bard as an idealized British ancestor the writers I have quoted find themselves engaged in distilling the virtuous spirit of Shakespeare, independent of the actual details of his work or life, to stand for the virtuous spirit of British national identity, independent of regional, social and historical differences. Alongside a desire to establish the connection between Shakespeare's plays and Shakespeare's body – to demonstrate, to use Margreta de Grazia's term, Shakespeare's 'entitlement' in his own works (*Shakespeare Verbatim*, pp. 177 ff.) – there exists an equally strong current in nascent Bardolatry which seeks to deny that connection, to assert that the national poet's genius transcends mere Shakespeare just as the idea of Britain transcends the contingent British Isles. A bodily, specific Shakespeare would for this purpose be a distracting irrelevance anyway, quite apart from his recorded lapses from manly propriety; a bathetic Mr Shakespeare of sixteenth-century Stratford as opposed to the timeless national father invoked by Higgons and co. in the likeness of Old Hamlet. It is notable in this respect that the very investiture of Shakespeare as National Poet, the Stratford Jubilee of 1769, although at first glance a reverent return to Shakespeare's provincial origins, had as its central event Garrick's presentation to

the town of an 'official' likeness of Shakespeare-as-National-Poet – a copy of the idealized, metropolitan Abbey statue – to supplement or perhaps supplant the bathetic, archaic bust in Holy Trinity Church of the corpulent local burgher buried there.[20] This separation of the unbounded creative genius of 'Shakespeare' from the merely licentious body of William Shakespeare of course survives today in the form of the Authorship Controversy, the first major contribution to which, Colonel Joseph Hart's now famous digression on the Bard in *The Romance of Yachting* (1848), is motivated by precisely such a refusal to accept that the immoral Shakespeare of the biographies could have contributed anything to the immortal 'Shakespeare' of the Complete Works other than just the pieces which the Bowdlers cut out:

> The plays [William Shakespeare] purchased or obtained surreptitiously, which became his 'property', and which are now called his, were never set upon the stage in their original state. They were first spiced with obscenity, blackguardism and impurities, before they were produced; and this business he voluntarily assumed . . .[21]

The strain of sexually normative nationalism in

---

than ever was exercised by a woman, even in the plenitude of her power and her charms. Shakespear's genius waited not on Love and Beauty, but Love and Beauty ministered to *him*; he perceived like a spirit . . . ' (Anna Jameson, *Memoirs of the Loves of the Poets: Biographical sketches of women celebrated in ancient and modern poetry* (1829: Boston, Mass., 1857), p. 182).

19 Cf. the debate over Shakespeare's sexuality carried out in Walter Scott's *Woodstock; or, the Cavalier* (1826), in which the tradition that Sir William Davenant may have been Shakespeare's illegitimate son is anxiously countered in a bid to guarantee the morally uplifting status of the Complete Works: see Nicola Watson, 'Kemble, Scott and the Mantle of the Bard', in Jean Marsden, ed., *The Appropriation of Shakespeare: Post-Renaissance Reconstructions of the Works and the Myth* (Hemel Hempstead, 1991), pp. 73–92.

20 On the Jubilee, see especially Christian Deelman, *The Great Shakespeare Jubilee* (London, 1964); Dobson, *Making of the National Poet*, pp. 214–26.

21 Joseph C. Hart, *The Romance of Yachting* (New York, 1848), pp. 211–12.

eighteenth-century bardolatry has thus bequeathed us both the national institution of the Shakespeare industry and the heresy which is its most perennially bitter enemy.

I would like to conclude simply by pointing to a text which goes even further in suggesting how far the Enlightenment's deification of Shakespeare occurs at precisely the intersection of the allied imperatives of modern nationalism and modern sexuality, and it too is connected with the Stratford Jubilee. By 1769 Shakespeare was apparently on the point of transcending not only his own body but his own corpus: the celebration of the Jubilee, famously, did not seem to require the performance or even the quotation of any of Shakespeare's plays – just as for the majority of tourists today a reverent visit to Shakespeare's Stratford does not necessarily imply the remotest interest in visiting the Royal Shakespeare Theatre. In fact the Jubilee's invocation of the national spirit of the Bard was so vague that one contemporary wag suggested that Shakespeare was serving primarily as the pretext for a far more useful patriotic exercise. I quote from the *Middlesex Journal* of 10 August 1769:

It has been generally believed, that the institution of the Stratford jubilee was only a matter of taste and amusement; but the more sagacious see a great political view carried on at the bottom of it: this is the population of that manufacturing part of the country, which will be effected by drawing great numbers of people from the neighbouring towns, to repose together on the verdant banks of the Avon. The season seems peculiarly favourable to this important view by its heat, should the same continue.[22]

Shakespeare's Jubilee is here revealed, like the earlier panegyrics I have quoted, as above all a celebration of British productivity. However his involvement with Britannia and Bowdler alike may have mandated the lopping away of his particular textual and sexual lapses, for this commentator Shakespeare is nonetheless helping to populate the Midlands in the cause of England's industrial future. Whatever else the Jubilee did or did not celebrate, it surely marked the climax of the process I have been describing, Shakespeare's triumphant installation as Britain's national Willy.

---

22 This account of Shakespeare's Jubilee as a nationalized utilitarian love-in chimes well with Henry Abelove's account of a 'change in late eighteenth-century English conceptions of what sex is, what it is for', 'Some Speculations on the History of "Sexual Intercourse" During the "Long Eighteenth Century" in England', in Andrew Parker, Mary Russo, Doris Sommer and Patricia Yaeger, eds., *Nationalisms and Sexualities* (New York, 1992), pp. 335–42.

SHAKESPEARE AND THE TEN MODES OF SCEPTICISM

ROBERT B. PIERCE

Shakespeare as a thinker is notoriously hard to pin down. One can use the critical pronouncements of Ben Jonson or John Milton to interpret their works with some confidence, but for Shakespeare such pronouncements are hard to come by, and equivalent ideas within the plays and poems are veiled in dramatic irony or else tantalizingly incomplete. One could argue, as Bernard Shaw does, that Shakespeare's ideas are conventional and trivial, not worth recovering, even that he is hopelessly confused about the abstractions of philosophical thought and perhaps not very much interested in them.[1] However, that is not a position to be taken without at least considering alternatives.

One school of thought that was in part rediscovered in Shakespeare's day shares this ironic elusiveness and taint of anti-intellectualism in the eyes of its opponents: the radical scepticism associated with the name Pyrrho of Elis.[2] This philosophy as set forth in the manuscripts of Sextus Empiricus inspired Montaigne and others to take very seriously the teachings of Pyrrhonism as a means of living through an age of doubt and controversy about basic issues of philosophy and religion.[3] Irony comes naturally to the Pyrrhonist, who uses the tools of rational analysis to undermine the claims of reason. My aim is to demonstrate some striking parallels with Pyrrhonist thought in Shakespeare's plays and poems and then to speculate (with more boldness than sceptical restraint) on the significance of those parallels. This is to associate Shakespeare with scepticism as many critics have done, but in a more specific way, aiming at what is distinctively Pyrrhonist.

I shall apply to Shakespeare the Ten Modes that Sextus Empiricus offers as exercises to produce a sceptical way of thinking, which he says results by a happy accident in *ataraxia*, a state of contented nescience that is itself the human happiness which other philosophers seek in vain elsewhere. It is important to realize that the Ten Modes are not exactly arguments held to entail a philosophical system called

---

[1] Shaw expresses his views with characteristic vigour in 'Better Than Shakespear?', his preface to *Caesar and Cleopatra*.

[2] My discussion of the Ten Modes of Pyrrhonist thought is based on the arrangement and analysis in Julia Annas and Jonathan Barnes, *The Modes of Scepticism* (Cambridge, 1985). A full collection of the texts is in A. A. Long and D. N. Sedley, *The Hellenistic Philosophers* (Cambridge, 1987). Other helpful discussions are in A. A. Long, *Hellenistic Philosophy: Stoics, Epicureans, Sceptics*, 2nd edn (London, 1986); and Malcolm Schofield, Myles Burnyeat, and Jonathan Barnes, eds., *Doubt and Dogmatism: Studies in Hellenistic Epistemology* (Oxford, 1980).

[3] On scepticism in the Renaissance the standard text is Richard H. Popkin, *The History of Scepticism from Erasmus to Spinoza*, rev. edn (Berkeley, 1979); see also D. C. Allen, *Doubt's Boundless Sea* (Baltimore, 1964). Among many discussions of scepticism in Shakespeare see Graham Bradshaw, *Shakespeare's Scepticism* (Brighton, 1987); D. G. James, *Scepticism and Poetry: An Essay on the Poetic Imagination* (London, 1937); and Rolf Soellner, *Shakespeare's Patterns of Self-Knowledge* (Columbus, 1972), all of whom use a less specific, in the first two cases less defined, version of scepticism.

scepticism. Rather they are therapy, inhabiting others' ways of thinking in order to wean them from a false confidence in the truth of their beliefs. The sceptic repeatedly leads his or her pupil – Peripatetic, Stoic, Marxist, Lacanian, or whatever – from a familiar premise to the conclusion that for any one cherished belief there is another equally likely belief (indeed many); therefore suspension of judgement, *epoche*, is the wisest response. Anyone who thinks through the Ten Modes will be likely to abandon belief and so find the contentment of *ataraxia*.[4]

This mode of philosophizing is well adapted to drama and especially to Shakespeare. After all, plays are not a very good way of making assertions. Their words are largely spoken by characters, and it is not clear which of their assertions are endorsed by the author. When a reader turns for help to Shakespeare's pro-logues, epilogues, and choruses, which might be expected to voice his considered opinions, they turn out to be frustratingly devious. But drama, including Shakespearian drama, is well suited to take its audience through therapeutic experiences like the Ten Modes. I shall try to reveal such exercises in sceptical perception in Shakespeare, drawing freely from the whole canon. Certainly my examples are far from exhaustive; a reader might undergo a form of the Pyrrhonist therapy by searching out other places, perhaps with the result of attaining sceptical contentment, an unusual reward for reading a piece of literary criticism. I shall in turn briefly explain each mode in Sextus' formulation, give a short, straightforward example or two from Shakespeare, and then look at a more complex example.

The Ten Modes are ten categories of justi-fication for scepticism. They characteristically take the form of contending that something appears in some way under one condition and in another under a different condition, but that there is no reason to accept one appearance as real rather than the other. Thus the investigator is compelled to *epoche*. For example, water in a swimming pool might appear warm to someone coming from a cold shower and cool to someone coming from sunbathing. But there is no reason to prefer one appearance to the other. The rational position is not to choose between the two equally likely verdicts about the real condition of the water.

One should distinguish the sceptical position from relativism. In the swimming-pool example the sceptic believes that there is a real condition of the water – hot, cold, or whatever – but no way to determine what it is. (Tem-perature, as measured by a thermometer, is presumably a mechanical phenomenon that bears some undeterminable relation to hotness.) The relativist, on the other hand, believes that the water simply *is* hot to one person and cold to another; that is the only truth, and it need not be difficult to know. The ancient sceptics did not separate what we call value judgements from other perceptions as uniquely subject to error. My liking for an apple and my seeing it as red are both matters of its appearance to me, and both are untrustworthy guides to the real nature of the apple: in itself it may or may not have the property of likableness, just as it may or may not have the property of redness.

The First Mode of Sextus' sceptical therapy contrasts the sensory powers of human beings and other animals. There is good reason to think that other animals perceive many things differently from human beings, but there is no reason to give preference to human perception, and indeed we can infer that at times animal perception is superior, as with a dog's sense of smell. We humans have to experience this therapeutic mode by inference, since we do not directly experience other animals' senses and they do not give direct testimony about their

---

4 Cf. Ludwig Wittgenstein, *Philosophical Investigations*, trans. G. E. M. Anscombe (New York, 1953), part I, sec. 255: 'The philosopher's treatment of a question is like the treatment of an illness.' Annas and Barnes, *The Modes of Scepticism*, pp. 44–50, describe Pyrrhonism as a mode of therapy.

perceptions. The sceptic would of course be doubtful about such inferences, but the sceptic is trying to affect someone who believes in the power of rational inference, not to set forth positive dogmas of scepticism, which would after all be a contradiction in terms.

One might see as a Shakespearian example of this mode Hamlet's exclamation of disgust at his mother's hasty wedding: 'O God, a beast that wants discourse of reason /Would have mourned longer!' (1.2.150–1). To put the matter in Sextus' terms, a hypothetical animal would find the loss of its mate more upsetting than the queen did the loss of her husband. Surely, however, Hamlet's point is that Gertrude's reaction is clearly wrong; given though he is to sceptical reflections, the Hamlet who bitterly looks on at the wedding celebration in Act 1, scene 2, has no doubt about his judgements of Gertrude and Claudius; they are inferior to the hypothetical beast. Sextus actually argues that animals are capable of reason, by way of justifying his contention that their perceptions should not be assumed to be inferior to humans'. At any rate, Hamlet's reflection can stir sceptical thoughts in the reader/viewer beyond what the Prince himself intends: do beasts grieve in the way that humans do? are they in fact incapable of reason? At least this and other passages in Shakespeare impel us to question our anthropocentric confidence. Watching Hamlet's tormented judging can be an exercise in not judging for us. One thinks also of that other moralist Jaques, who speculates that to the deer of the forest Duke Senior's men look like usurping invaders, and Jaques is inclined to share their view.

Drama doesn't usually give much opportunity to show the perceptions of non-human characters; Lance's dog never voices his case against his master's accusations. However, Shakespeare creates several non-human characters who have human language, and he uses them to raise questions about human perception. Oberon and Robin Goodfellow see human beings who don't see them, and their comments show their confidence in their superior understanding as well as in their sensory powers. These 'shadows', as Robin calls himself and his fellows, may be more real as well as more comprehending than the human characters who don't see them – and the human audience who do.

In *The Tempest*, a play influenced by Montaigne, Caliban and Ariel are vividly contrasted with the wholly human characters in how and what they see. The fine garments that distract Stefano and Trinculo from their plot against Prospero are 'but trash' to Caliban. At this point one is tempted to side with the servant-monster's estimate, but the play as a whole is equivocal in its estimate of clothing. Prospero is grateful that Gonzalo provided him with those same garments for his and Miranda's exile, though the food, water, and books that Gonzalo also provided have been more tangibly important. At the end of the play Prospero is careful to change into other similar garments from Gonzalo's supply, thus resuming his identity as Duke of Milan. There is much bemused attention throughout the play to what characters' clothes look like. And what about these garments in particular? In the eyes of the audience are they splendid or tawdry? We know that the acting companies made a point of getting spectacular costumes, apparently even taking over courtiers' castoffs. But every theatregoer also knows that stage splendours are often factitious. Gilt and spangles make do for gold and jewels. Thus we are left in doubt what to make of the clothes that we see.

The opening of *The Tempest* presents another paradox of perception when we watch a shipwreck and then hear different characters' remarkably diverse accounts of what they experienced. The last of these accounts is Ariel's bright, icily cool description, in which Ferdinand's terror sounds the same register as the safety of the crew and passengers:

> Not a soul
> But felt a fever of the mad, and played
> Some tricks of desperation. All but mariners

Plunged in the foaming brine and quit the vessel,
Then all afire with me. The King's son Ferdinand,
With hair upstarting – then like reeds, not hair –
Was the first man that leaped; cried 'Hell is empty,
And all the devils are here'.   (I.2.209–16)

Ariel's language is both eerily inhuman and imaginatively compelling. But how are we to imagine 'Then all afire with me'? And how to reconcile it with what we ourselves saw during the first scene? There is no stage direction to indicate that Ariel is present to our eyes in the shipwreck scene itself, though some directors choose to have him there. And Prospero later raises the issue of whether the non-human Ariel can feel pity for the suffering party of Alonso (5.1.21–4). Thus the opening and other parts of Shakespeare's most philosophical comedy can be seen as a perceptual exercise pointing toward Sextus Empiricus' conclusion:

So, if the irrational animals ['so-called irrational animals,' Sextus calls them] are not less credible than we are when it comes to judging appearances, and if different appearances are produced depending on the variations among animals, then I shall be able to say how each existing object appears to me, but for the above reasons I shall be forced to suspend judgement on how it is by nature.

(Annas and Barnes, pp. 37–8)

Sextus' Second Mode argues from variations among human beings. Because people vary physically and psychologically, one cannot rely on their perceptions and judgements as guides to the truth. Not only does the same wine appear fine to one palate and sour to another, but philosophical issues appear one way to Platonists and another to Epicureans. There is no basis for choosing among these variant perceptions. It is not even rational to prefer one's own opinions to those of others, since choosing between opinion A and opinion B (one's own) is judging in a case in which one is among the parties.

This is perhaps the most common argument for scepticism, though it can also be used to defend relativism. It is not clear which stance is the basis when Hamlet torments Polonius about

'yonder cloud that's almost in shape of a camel' (3.2.364–5). And does Hamlet succeed in making Polonius see the different animals in the cloud, or is Polonius just humouring the supposed madman, as Hamlet suggests: 'They fool me to the top of my bent' (372)? One might choose scepticism rather than relativism as the implication of the episode, since presumably the cloud at any one moment has a shape, however indefinable that shape may be; it is the human tendency to project familiar forms on unfamiliar that allows us to see a camel or a weasel, the cloud acting like a Rorschach blot. We can't help imposing a pattern on confusing sense data. And of course we as audience see Hamlet and Polonius, but do not see the cloud. Since it exists for us only in their verbal references, we are not tempted to participate in this game of seeing shapes and so can grasp its arbitrariness all the more clearly. Their perceptual tangle parallels the tangle of evaluations of Claudius, and, as with the cloud, we cannot even be sure, for example, what Polonius' real judgement of the king is.

Shakespeare delights in staging the variations of human perception as different characters interpret an event or another character. In *Julius Caesar* he even shows how different philosophical schools respond to the same events. Cicero, the single most important source for Renaissance understanding of the issues of classical philosophy, plays a brief role in *Julius Caesar*. His response to the supernatural omens the night before Caesar's death measures the responses of the two characters specifically tied to philosophical schools, Cassius the Epicurean and Brutus the Stoic.

As an Epicurean Cassius should dismiss omens even more emphatically than Cicero does, the latter suggesting only that they are commonly misinterpreted, not that they are false or meaningless. But Cassius is so lacking in Epicurean calm that with a kind of hysterical bravado he defies the elements on the basis that they will punish only the guilty (1.3). And he explicitly abandons his Epicureanism when he takes seriously the omens of defeat that precede the Battle at Philippi (5.1). It is symbolically appropriate that Cassius' 'thick' sight (5.3.21) leads him to commit suicide on the basis of a mistake, thinking that his friend Titinius has been captured. Neither his Epicureanism nor his native shrewdness allows him to see reality clearly.

Brutus the Stoic responds very differently to the omens of the night before Caesar's death, placidly using the meteors as light by which to read a letter. There is something attractive in his calm demeanour, but its wisdom is not so clear. After all the omens truly foreshadow Caesar's death and the plunge of Rome into civil war. And their treacherous light enables Brutus to read a forged letter that plays a part in Cassius' deception of him. Cicero's warning to Casca can be seen as a sceptical commentary on all the Romans' attempts to read the prodigies that their senses present to them:

Indeed it is a strange-disposèd time;
But men may construe things after their fashion,
Clean from the purpose of the things themselves.

(1.3.33–5)

Things in themselves have a meaning, but human perceivers are likely to fashion some other meaning, seeing a camel in the cloud.

One of the more chilling doctrines of the Stoicism that Brutus professes concerns the propriety of grief. In the words of Epictetus:

When any disturbing news is brought you, bear this in mind, that news cannot affect anything within the region of the will. Can anyone bring news to you that you are wrong in your thought or wrong in your will? Surely not: but only that someone is dead; what does that concern you?[5]

There is a textual puzzle in Act 4, scene 2, of *Julius Caesar* concerning the passage in which Brutus responds twice to news of Portia's death. When Cassius chides him for his angry mood, suggesting that a Stoic should have more self-control, Brutus replies with Roman directness, 'No man bears sorrow better. Portia is dead.' Cassius is stunned by the news and

with his quick intuition grasps Brutus' pain, thereby opening it to the audience. We can hear the heroic effort in Brutus' words dismissing the subject:

Speak no more of her. Give me a bowl of wine.
In this I bury all unkindness, Cassius.

The second representation comes a few lines later when Brutus hears of Portia's death from Messala as if for the first time. This time he reacts according to Epictetus' model:

BRUTUS Why, farewell, Portia. We must die, Messala.
With meditating that she must die once,
I have the patience to endure it now.
MESSALA Even so great men great losses should endure.
CASSIUS I have as much of this in art as you,
But yet my nature could not bear it so.
BRUTUS Well, to our work alive.

If the text as it stands represents Shakespeare's intention, Brutus seems to put on an act for Messala's benefit, pretending not to know of Portia's death so that he can display Stoical fortitude. More likely, one of the two passages represents Shakespeare's second thoughts about Brutus, and many scholars consider the first version above as intended to replace the second.[6]

At any rate, the Messala version makes Brutus' Stoicism quite unpleasant. His little lecture on Stoic meditation and especially the wordplay on 'our work alive' – vs. Portia dead – are not very effective commercials for Stoicism. The other version presents a less rigorously Stoic Brutus, like the man who is tenderly concerned with Lucilius' health and who out of affection and respect tells Portia of

---

5 'Arrian's Discourses of Epictetus', trans. P. E. Matheson, *The Stoic and Epicurean Philosophers*, ed. Whitney J. Oates (New York, 1940), p. 371.
6 See the discussion in T. S. Dorsch, ed., *Julius Caesar*, new Arden Edition (London, 1955), note at 4.3.180–94. See also Grace Ioppolo, *Revising Shakespeare* (Cambridge, Mass., 1991), pp. 114–17.

the conspiracy. How should a Stoic react to his wife's death? The official answer of the ancient Stoa and its more rigorous followers is in Brutus' response to Messala; but it is hard not to prefer the other Brutus, who has powerful feelings to control. Thus the two Brutuses see Portia's death through different eyes. Which Brutus sees reality more clearly? The play doesn't say, and the sceptical view is that we can't know. One (apparent) certainty is that Cicero, Cassius, Caesar, and Brutus show vividly how human perception is altered by human variation.

The Third Mode argues from difference among the senses in a single individual. Part of this argument is that one sense may contradict another: a painting done in perspective may look as though it has recesses, but it feels flat to the touch. The implication is that roundness, flatness, and some other sensory experiences can be shared by different senses: something can both look and feel round or square. A second part of the argument is that we dare not assume that what is apprehensible to our five senses constitutes the reality of what we perceive. There may be attributes of an object for which we have no relevant sense, just as a person totally blind from birth cannot perceive or even imagine the redness of an apple. To assume that our senses give us an accurate picture of reality is an unwarranted act of faith, especially given the deceptions we know of, like optical illusions.

This mode lends itself to dramatization less than the others, but Duke Humphrey of Gloucester, in *2 Henry VI*, uses the idea that a blind man cannot make sense of colour references when he exposes Simpcox, who pretends that he has suddenly and miraculously regained his sight. Simpcox is able to identify colours, knowing that a cloak he is shown is red like blood and a gown black like jet. But he must have seen the colours before in order to recognize the similar redness in the cloak he now sees and in blood, which he claims he has never seen. Ingeniously, Gloucester uses human inadequacy

– neither the other senses nor reason can compensate for the absence of sight in this way – to arrive at a piece of knowledge: Simpcox is a fake.

Another commoner who blunders among his betters is Bottom. He alone among the mortals of *A Midsummer Night's Dream* actually sees and hears the fairies, but, looking back on the recalled experience, he cannot make sense of it, and he tangles up the senses while paraphrasing St Paul to express his puzzlement and awe: 'The eye of man hath not heard, the ear of man hath not seen, man's hand is not able to taste, his tongue to conceive, nor his heart to report what my dream was' (4.1.208–11). Human senses and powers collapse under the effort to report the experience that he recalls. Perhaps we all live in Bottom's dream and share his incapacity to find the truth in it.

The Fourth Mode finds evidence for scepticism within individual senses because circumstances affect perception. 'Circumstances' are especially inner states like being hungry or full, tired or refreshed, angry or calm, but also 'anterior conditions': the taste of wine is affected by what one has just eaten. Non-sceptical philosophers sometimes appeal to normal or natural conditions as a standard: something is truly red when it is seen as red under ordinary light. But 'normal' and 'natural' are impossible to determine: why should we consider a waking state normative rather than dreaming?

In *A Midsummer Night's Dream* Theseus and Hippolyta debate the reality of what the four lovers claim to have experienced in the night forest. Theseus' speech points out how internal conditions can distort perception:

> I never may believe
> These antique fables, nor these fairy toys.
> Lovers and madmen have such seething brains,
> Such shaping fantasies, that apprehend
> More than cool reason ever comprehends.
>
> (5.1.2–6)

Though to Theseus 'cool reason' is a safe measure for judging and dismissing the lovers' tale, Hippolyta finds plausibility in the consistency of their separate accounts. If Theseus offers a moderate sceptic's disbelief, Hippolyta expresses a Pyrrhonist's scepticism about even his scepticism.

Shakespeare is fond of dramatizing a character who watches some person or event which has to be interpreted: several times a male lover watching the woman he loves. Claudio in *Much Ado About Nothing* and Leontes in *The Winter's Tale* are deceived into misinterpreting. Fooled by Don John, Claudio twice thinks he sees Hero receiving another man as her lover, and Leontes is misled by mad jealousy into seeing harmless chat between his wife and Polixenes as lewd flirtation. In each case we as audience feel some confidence about our grasp of the truth, that Hero and Hermione are innocent. (In the former case Claudio even misperceives another woman as Hero.) However, the total misapprehension of the two men suggests how vulnerable to being undermined a powerful love is because its very power distorts the lover's perception.

Truth and misperception are harder to sort out when another young man looks on at the woman he loves: Troilus watching Cressida as she seems to flirt with Diomedes in the Greek camp in *Troilus and Cressida*. Looking on at Troilus looking on, Thersites provides one unambiguous reading of Cressida:

A proof of strength she could not publish more
Unless she said, 'My mind is now turned whore'.

(5.2.115–16)

But two intense emotions of love and jealousy battle in Troilus, with the result that he sees two different Cressidas:

This, she? No, this is Diomed's Cressida.
If beauty have a soul, this is not she.
If souls guide vows, if vows be sanctimonies,
If sanctimony be the gods' delight,
If there be rule in unity itself,
This is not she. O madness of discourse,
That cause sets up with and against thyself!
Bifold authority, where reason can revolt

Without perdition, and loss assume all reason
Without revolt! This is and is not Cressid.

(140–9)

Cressida's own self-image as shown in her brief soliloquy (109–14) is close to Thersites' view of her, and Ulysses has categorized her with comparable harshness at her arrival in the Greek camp. But Troilus cannot simply abandon his loved image of her tenderness and devotion to him.

Is Troilus the lover just wrong, a youthful enthusiast who must be educated to Cressida's worthlessness? There are three reasons for doubting that inference. First, the Cressida of the love scenes with Troilus does not look simply like an experienced strumpet playing on her lover's feelings. Sophisticated in the ways of love though she is, she seems startled and awed at the power of her feelings for Troilus. A full account of her nature ought to account for that as well as her desertion to Diomedes. Second, there is some discomfort for the audience in being pushed into the same point of view as Thersites: do we really want to see the world as he does? Finally, we may be swayed by feminist readings of the play that have included varying apologias for Cressida. Such readings either find motives for Cressida more attractive than shifting sexual desire, see the character as being or becoming a projection of male fantasies about women, or simply defend her behaviour as justifiable for a woman in a rigidly patriarchal society.[7]

Is there a truth about Cressida's motivation and a true valuation of her? There could be an unambiguous Cressida, motivated by shifting lust, by felt helplessness, or whatever. Alternatively, the part may be so constructed that

---

[7] For examples of such readings see Irene G. Dash, *Wooing, Wedding, and Power: Women in Shakespeare's Plays* (New York, 1981); Ann Thompson, *Shakespeare's Chaucer* (New York, 1978); and the essays by Janet Adelman, Carol Cook, and Lorraine Helms in Sue-Ellen Chase, ed., *Performing Feminisms: Feminist Critical Theory and Theatre* (Baltimore, 1990).

the actress is given the freedom to create either a strumpet or a canny, self-possessed woman caught in a trap. Perhaps the actress can deliberately leave the audience hesitating among different Cressidas. Responding as a sceptic, one is not surprised to find oneself in the dark with Troilus, Ulysses, and Thersites, studying an enigmatic drama of apparent flirtation and possible betrayal. In this play of thwarted expectations, it would be appropriate to leave the audience's quest for truth unsatisfied.

The Fifth Mode argues from positions, intervals, and places. 'Positions' refers to an object's orientation, so that the shape of a table looks different depending on whether one sees it from the bottom or the side. 'Intervals' refers to distance from the observer: not only do distant objects look smaller, but their colours are affected by the intervening atmosphere, and their details blur. 'Places' refers to an object's setting: thus bright sunlight affects the appearance of an object, and an oar looks straight in the air but bent when it is partly in water. Again there is no basis for choosing certain positions, intervals, and places as normative.

In the *Tragedy of King Lear* Edgar uses the paradoxes of size and distance to place his blind father in an imaginary landscape, the very edge of the Cliffs of Dover:

The crows and choughs that wing the midway air
Show scarce so gross as beetles. Halfway down
Hangs one that gathers samphire, dreadful trade!
Methinks he seems no bigger than his head.
The fishermen that walk upon the beach
Appear like mice, and yon tall anchoring barque
Diminished to her cock, her cock a buoy
Almost too small for sight.   (4.5.13–20)

The vividness compels us like the blind Gloucester to see things that aren't there (imaginary both as theatrical pretence and as not actually present even within the fictive world of the play; in both ways Gloucester is not on the edge of a cliff). We are captivated by the vividness of what Edgar creates and Gloucester sees in the mind's eye even while we realize its unreality.[8]

Portia in *The Merchant of Venice* is a connoisseur of the paradoxes of interval and position.[9] As she returns to Belmont, she sees a candle burning in her hall and chats with Nerissa:

PORTIA That light we see is burning in my hall.
  How far that little candle throws his beams –
  So shines a good deed in a naughty world.
NERISSA When the moon shone we did not see
    the candle.
PORTIA So doth the greater glory dim the less.
  A substitute shines brightly as a king
  Until a king be by, and then his state
  Empties itself as doth an inland brook
  Into the main of waters. Music, hark.
NERISSA It is your music, madam, of the house.
PORTIA Nothing is good, I see, without respect.
  Methinks it sounds much sweeter than by day.
NERISSA Silence bestows that virtue on it,
    madam.
PORTIA The crow doth sing as sweetly as the lark
  When neither is attended, and I think
  The nightingale, if she should sing by day,
  When every goose is cackling, would be thought
  No better a musician than the wren.
  How many things by season seasoned are
  To their right praise and true perfection!
                              (5.1.89–108)

Perceptions of light, virtue, rank, and music are all affected by interval and place. This passage, like the Pyrrhonists' sceptical arguments, moves easily between physical perception and judgements of value: the physical brightness of the candle reminds Portia of the glory of rank, and then her mind darts off to the beauty of both artificial and natural music.

Portia's last speech suggests an answer to scepticism: things can be properly estimated in the right time and place. The nightingale's song is beautiful at night. But when is the fitting time for Portia's consort of musicians? Is the ecstasy to which they move Lorenzo and Jessica

8 On the games with theatrical illusion and reality in the trick Edgar plays on his father, see Stephen Greenblatt, *Shakespearean Negotiations* (Berkeley, 1988), pp. 118–19.
9 Cf. the discussion of this passage in Bradshaw, *Shakespeare's Scepticism*, pp. 82–3.

caused by the real power of their music, or is their reality the commonplaceness of wrens by day? Nerissa suggests that 'silence bestows' this unique sweetness on the music, so she at least thinks it is not an attribute of the music itself. Is the glory that shines in a substitute his own and thus a gift from him that will be added to the king, or does the glory find its true owner when the king returns? The lovely image of the 'inland brook' is cryptic on that issue. Portia's glancing wit and Nerissa's less fanciful comments play over the tangle of paradoxes that characterize human perception.

Indeed the whole play is built on the inadequacy of outward perceptions to express inner reality. 'So may the outward shows be least themselves. / The world is still deceived with ornament', exclaims Bassanio as he confronts the three caskets, the least likely of which contains the image of Portia that will award her to him in marriage (3.2.73–4). Is it some virtue in Bassanio that allows him to locate her portrait, or is he just fortunate (or perhaps even given unfair help by Portia)? Likewise Shylock's 'merry bond' constantly changes its meaning and effect as people look at it from different angles, and only a woman in disguise can see the resolution of its paradoxes, a resolution freeing to Antonio and Bassanio, but cruel enough to the owner of the bond. Are Shylock and Antonio opposites or versions of the same social role seen from different perspectives? Neither Belmont nor Venice encourages confidence in our power to see the truth in a world of appearances.

The Sixth Mode argues from admixtures. No object is perceived by itself; instead the perception is mixed in two ways. First, other sensory impressions are mixed with it, so that for example incense comes to the observer confused with church music, mustiness, marijuana, or whatever. Second, the observer perceives and thinks by means of a physical medium. The eye sees using the aqueous and vitreous humours, and thought involves synapses and electrochemical processes in the brain.

Since all media distort what they transmit, perceptions and thoughts are distorted in ways we can only dimly comprehend. It is impossible for the intellect to compensate for all these mixtures and arrive at a clear idea of the object or to think clearly about it.

Both Antony and the audience have trouble arriving at a proper estimate of Cleopatra's love, in part because in her behaviour it is mixed with other emotions: her fear of physical harm and loss of power, her royal pride, her pleasure in dominating and tormenting men, etc. Antony is driven to frenzy trying to decide whether she intends to betray him to Caesar when he sees her flirting with Thidias (3.13). Antony's view of her is coloured by his mood: despair at the disgrace of Actium, a renewal of spirit after the victory near Alexandria, fatalistic calm as he nears death. Whether such admixtures are confusing to the eyes and minds of Shakespeare critics as they contemplate Cleopatra I leave to the reader.

One might think that the intellect could compensate for both external and internal admixtures, a view that thinkers as varied as Aristotle and Hume have held. But it is hard to find among Shakespeare's characters a rationalist so steady as to be implicitly trusted. Horatio is calmer than Hamlet, but too conventional in his thinking to be wiser; Ulysses' rationality mixes with a cunning that overreaches itself. *King Lear* can be seen as a study in the delicacy of the mind's balance. There is no more moving piece of psychology in Shakespeare than Lear's desperate attempt to hold down the madness that he feels rising in him like a physical presence:

O, how this mother swells up toward my heart!
Histerica passio down, thou climbing sorrow;
Thy element's below.   (2.2.231–3)

Yet this madness whose coming on he fears distorts his vision no more than the rage that has led him to disown and banish Cordelia; if anything, he judges better when mad. As Gloucester says by way of accepting his blindness, the analogue to Lear's madness: 'I stumbled when I saw' (4.1.19). The play's assault on reason and control climaxes when, confronted by the figure of Edgar as Poor Tom, Lear has one of his flashes of insight:

Is man no more than this? Consider him well. Thou owest the worm no silk, the beast no hide, the sheep no wool, the cat no perfume. Ha, here's three on 's are sophisticated; thou art the thing itself. Unaccommodated man is no more but such a poor, bare, forked animal as thou art.   (3.4.96–102)

Seeing clothes as a disguise hiding human reality is plausible, but Lear swerves into the madness of plucking off his own garments. And the ironies go deeper yet, since the naked figure in front of him is disguised, not Poor Tom but Lear's godson, the hunted fugitive Edgar. If nakedness itself is as much a distorting admixture as clothing, how is one to see 'the thing itself'?

The Seventh Mode argues from quantities and preparations. A substance like silver or quartz appears different in different amounts and forms: thus silver chips are black, while silver lumps are white. A food may be beneficial in small quantities and harmful in large. 'Preparations' seems to refer to mixing ingredients together, as for a medicine. Thus a compound in the wrong proportions may not have the proper medicinal effect. Annas and Barnes suggest that this mode is something of a catch-all, and they doubt its efficacy as an argument for scepticism as opposed to relativism: it is not that silver has some one colour that is undetectable, but rather that it is in fact black in chips, white in lumps. Still one might argue that the true colour of silver is that which most sharply distinguishes it from other metals; chips and filings are less distinctive of different metals than polished lumps. At any rate, arguments in this pattern are one way of inspiring distrust of information the senses give us.

Henry IV uses an argument from quantity when he blames Hal's fondness for low company as like King Richard's vulgarity rather than Henry's own caution:

By being seldom seen, I could not stir
But, like a comet, I was wondered at,
That men would tell their children 'This is he.'
               (1 Henry IV 3.2.46–8)

Infrequent public appearances create the Garbo effect, fascinating a gullible public. In Romeo and Juliet Friar Laurence uses the traditional example of medicinal plants to suggest the ambiguities of appearance:

Within the infant rind of this weak flower
Poison hath residence, and medicine power,
For this, being smelt, with that part cheers each
     part;
Being tasted, slays all senses with the heart.
Two such opposèd kings encamp them still
In man as well as herbs – grace and rude will;
And where the worser is predominant,
Full soon the canker death eats up that plant.
               (2.2.23–30)

Presumably he derives an orthodox Christian moral from the ambiguities he points to: human beings choose between their real nature, which lives in God's grace, and their potentiality for sin, which destroys the real self. Though some critics take this dichotomy as the moral, it is not so clear that Romeo and Juliet are malefactors of 'rude will' whose deaths are punishment for their sins; indeed the catastrophe may be the sad triumph of their purity. An audience may draw a more sceptical conclusion than Friar Laurence's from the admixture of 'grace and rude will' in human beings in general and the two young lovers in particular.

The Eighth Mode argues from relativity. The point is a complex and controversial one. It can be based on the principle that the nature of something is inherent in it. If we can know a thing only relative to other things, then we cannot know its nature. If my friend Fred is married, I must know him as a husband, but since he is a husband in relation to his wife, that is not part of his nature, and I cannot know that nature: I know only Fred the husband, not Fred in himself.

Another version of the argument from relativity notes that an object has certain properties in one relation but others in another relation. Fred is tall compared to Jane but short compared to Henrietta. Thus we cannot know whether Fred is absolutely tall or short. The relativist conclusion may seem more plausible here: there is no 'tall' independent of comparison to something else, so that 'Fred is tall' means nothing more than 'Fred is tall in comparison to X.' However, that is not so obviously true of 'Fred is intelligent', and surely at least some properties have a meaning independent of comparison even though we grasp them by comparison: Fred does or does not have the ability to solve difficult problems, though we find it convenient to measure his intelligence comparatively. But both relativist and sceptic can appeal to the omnipresence of relativity in human perception.

In *King Lear* Goneril's reaction to the news of Cornwall's death illustrates the problem of relativity:

> One way I like this well;
> But being widow, and my Gloucester with her,
> May all the building in my fancy pluck
> Upon my hateful life. Another way
> The news is not so tart.   (4.2.51–5)

Presumably the news is objectively good or bad for Goneril's benefit in doing either more harm or good to her plans. It eliminates one strong rival for power (and Cornwall is a more formidable obstacle than Regan herself). On the other hand, it frees Regan to marry Edmund. Goneril is unable to weigh the relative importance of these two consequences. Indeed her words suggest that her life is equally vulnerable to relativity: it will shift from pleasant to 'hateful' because her dreams of future contentment will be ended if she loses Edmund to her sister.

Ulysses mystifies Achilles in *Troilus and Cressida* by an account of the dependence of human excellence on others' opinion: is he claiming that such worth is objectively real, but that no one, not even the worthy individual, can know it apart from others' perception, or is he claiming that the worth exists only in their opinion?

> [the author] in his circumstance expressly proves
> That no man is the lord of anything,
> Though in and of him there be much consisting,
> Till he communicate his parts to others.
> Nor doth he of himself know them for aught
> Till he behold them formèd in th'applause
> Where they're extended – who, like an arch,
>   reverb'rate
> The voice again; or, like a gate of steel
> Fronting the sun, receives and renders back
> His figure and his heat.   (3.3.109–18)

At least before this speech Achilles is firm in a sceptical interpretation of Ulysses' 'strange fellow': the worthy qualities are real even if they are not known. Ulysses' language is elliptic and tantalizing: does 'lord of anything' question the man's control or the existence of the 'anything'? what exactly does the next line assert (or half-assert, given its 'though' and subjunctive 'be')? Ulysses abruptly shifts to his purpose of setting Ajax up as a rival after closing his philosophizing with two similes that render the 'parts' as evanescent things, the sound of a voice and an image of the sun with its heat, while public opinion is given the solidity of an arch or steel gate.

When the disguised Rosalind leads Orlando through a discussion of time in *As You Like It*, she plays on the relativity of experienced time (as opposed to clock measurement): maids about to be married, Latinless priests, rich men who lack gout, thieves, and lawyers experience time very differently from one another. She later chides Orlando for a failure to keep lovers' time when he is late for an appointment with her (4.1). It is fitting that characters find the leisure to discuss the paradoxes of experienced time in the clockless green world of the Forest of Arden.[10] The conclusion to such paradoxes

---

[10] Jay L. Halio, '"No Clock in the Forest": Time in *As You Like It*', *Studies in English Literature*, 2 (1962), 197–207, explores time in the Forest of Arden.

might be either sceptical or relativist: is there a clock back in Duke Frederick's palace that measures an objective time, the reality behind the various experienced times? Or is clock time just one more kind of experienced time, relative to clockmakers, compulsives, and scientists?

One possible answer to this question comes in *The Winter's Tale*, when Time himself as a chorus takes charge of the plot at the beginning of Act 4:

> Impute it not a crime
> To me or my swift passage that I slide
> O'er sixteen years and leave the growth untried
> Of that wide gap, since it is in my power
> To o'erthrow law, and in one self-born hour
> To plant and o'erwhelm custom. Let me pass
> The same I am ere ancient'st order was
> Or what is now received. I witness to
> The times that brought them in; so shall I do
> To th' freshest things now reigning, and make stale
> The glistering of this present as my tale
> Now seems to it.   (4.1.4–15)

Time speaks as a supernatural power who can untie the knot of error and wickedness that he has created, a being with the Christian God's presence to all eternity. He wields a symbolic marker of measured time, not a clock but an hourglass, whose turning coincides with the play's turning from tragic to comic-pastoral mode.

Yet in a curious way Time's proclamation of Providential control modulates into an artist's apology for violating the unity of time and for telling an old-fashioned tale: Time's chorus is one of Shakespeare's playful expressions of regret for not writing just like Ben Jonson. Of course none of the characters see either the divine or the apologetic Time as the audience does: they live out their story in a world where time seems to be just the colourless medium of their lives. Is Time the reality behind such experiences of time, unknowable but as solidly there as the actor who portrays him? – That would be the sceptical position. Or is the only reality the different experiences of time of the different characters (and the audience)? Is Time

a conventional device – an allegorical chorus – by which playwright and actor point to elements of the time that we experience? That would be the relativist position. If one answers that one cannot tell which position – the sceptical or the relativist – is right, one has by a sort of metasceptical exercise arrived at *epoche* and so taken one more step toward the Pyrrhonist's *ataraxia*. Thus Sextus Empiricus: 'As far as appearances go, time seems to be something, but when we come to the arguments for it, it appears unreal' (p. 124).

The Ninth Mode argues from the common and the rare. We perceive things as striking, beautiful, valuable when there are few of them or when we first experience them. The sun is by nature more impressive than a comet, but the rarity of seeing comets makes them awe-inspiring, especially the first time we see one. Annas and Barnes largely dismiss this argument as supporting relativism instead of scepticism: value and impressiveness are in fact relative to conditions like scarcity. The painting of the *Mona Lisa* is much more valuable than reproductions of it, not only because of superior artistic power, but because there is only one painting while there are many reproductions. However, there are surely aspects of beauty and value that are independent of rarity. If a reproduction of the *Mona Lisa* can give deeper pleasure than an original minor nineteenth-century landscape, is it not in one respect more valuable, even though the landscape would sell at a higher price? One might contend that such capacity to give pleasure is more real than the cash price, even though it is harder or even impossible to ascertain. We cannot really look at the *Mona Lisa* without the aura of its fame and rarity, but perhaps we ought to be able to if we are to seek pleasure wisely.

At any rate, the argument that rarity produces notability and value is common in Shakespeare, as it is elsewhere. Prince Hal justifies his slumming because it will make his reformation more striking: 'nothing pleaseth but rare accidents' (*1 Henry IV* 1.2.204). Benvolio expects

Romeo to shake off his infatuation with Rosaline when he sees 'all the admirèd beauties of Verona' (1.2.86). In a sense both predictions turn out to be true, which might suggest that rarity is a good guide to accurate judgement (Hal's view), or that experience, which allows Romeo to see Juliet's superiority, is more trustworthy. Miranda sees Ferdinand as splendid, having seen only one other young male, Caliban, while Ferdinand reacts in the same way to her after having studied 'full many a lady' (*The Tempest*, 3.1.39). It would seem difficult to find a stance of either small or abundant experience that would ensure accuracy in judgements of value. As human beings we will react strongly to rarity and novelty, and we will be strangely inconsistent in our judgements of value.

The Tenth Mode argues from customs and persuasions: to be more precise, from lifestyles, laws, customs, myths, and dogmatic suppositions. The argument is that these elements of a culture incorporate all sorts of contradictions from society to society, even from individual to individual. Some societies practise incest and some find it abhorrent; some believe the gods to be involved in human affairs and some don't. Again one might draw a relativistic conclusion from such examples rather than a sceptical one. The cultural relativist says that burial customs and bans on incest are matters not of objective right and wrong but of local custom. The sceptic would of course ask the relativist how he or she arrived at such confident knowledge that there are no objective standards. But even if the standards really exist, the variability of our behaviour and beliefs suggests that they are hard to locate. Sextus notes the special connection of this mode with value judgements, though whether the gods intervene in human affairs and what are the origins of the universe and human beings are also examples of variability.

Henry V and Catherine have a disagreement about the propriety of his kissing her before they are married (5.2). Though the sympathies of the audience may prefer British custom to French, and royal impetuosity to maidenly reserve, the truth is that Henry gets his kiss by power of will and rhetoric and by his authority as male and king, not by the evident superiority of the custom he espouses. Petruchio gives a similar defence of a less plausible social reform: wearing old clothes for weddings and formal visits (3.2). Here the audience may be pulled between the exhilaration of seeing his independence and our conventional sense that Katherine's splendid formal gown expresses a better frame of mind for a wedding ceremony.

Surely the heart of Shakespearian drama is conflicts of value in general and moral value in particular. Even before he learns of the murder, Hamlet despises Claudius for such vices as drinking too much and making a ceremony out of his vice. There is something in Claudius that shares Hamlet's values (just as there is something in Hamlet that at times impels him to act on Claudius' principles), but Claudius' moral scruples never acquire enough force to affect his behaviour; he even plans Hamlet's death immediately after trying to pray for forgiveness. Angelo in *Measure for Measure* is torn between a Puritanical code and a perverted sexual desire, while Isabella and Duke Vincentio are pulled between justice and mercy as they see them. There are times in Shakespeare when the issues seem clear: only the most paradoxical critics have difficulty choosing between Macbeth's values and Malcolm's. But certainly there are plays in which most of us experience difficulty finding a moral footing. Is Falconbridge right in his steady support for King John? What people and what values are deserving of sympathy in *Troilus and Cressida*? Is the price of integrity and compassion too high in the savage world of *King Lear*? Often enough it seems more plausible to see a dramatic episode or even a whole play as a sort of exercise in moral thinking with no answer book provided rather than as the espousal of a given set of principles.

Can one argue then that the Shakespeare

canon incorporates a consistent, conscious exercise in Pyrrhonism? Can one go further to find the key to Shakespeare's mystery, the heart of his dramatic enterprise, in Sextus' therapy? The first difficulty is transmission. It is on the face of it unlikely that Shakespeare could have known the substance of Sextus' argument before reading Montaigne, and though it does seem clear that he read and assimilated Montaigne, one cannot find an upheaval in mid-career suggesting that his plays suddenly embody a new philosophy of life. Nevertheless, sceptical ideas floated around freely before the rediscovery of Sextus Empiricus, readily available in Cicero and elsewhere. If it is unlikely that Shakespeare knew and accepted a fully articulated Pyrrhonist view of the world, he could have picked up pieces of it here and there.

What seems to me most likely is a temperamental affinity that pushed Shakespeare toward sceptical views of the world, an affinity sharpened and encouraged by encounters with bits and pieces of scepticism. (One would like to hypothesize especially forceful contacts not long before *Hamlet* and *The Tempest*.[11]) And a dramatist who likes to play with ideas could find stimulation in the idea of theatre as a form of philosophical therapy, leading people from their preconceptions toward experiences of *epoche* and thence toward *ataraxia*, quiet contentment with living in a world of appearances.

This temperamental affinity with Pyrrhonism, if I am right to find it in Shakespeare, is what Keats intuited as 'Negative Capability' in Shakespeare: 'when man is capable of being in uncertainties, Mysteries, doubts, without any irritable reaching after fact & reason'.[12] 'Irritable' is a splendid word for the disruption of *ataraxia* that hungering too much for truth can produce. But one side of this picture of contented temperamental Pyrrhonism does not quite match the man I infer from the writing. The

Pyrrhonist does not escape the normal human pains of disease, hunger, hope thwarted, friends and family who suffer; but he or she does avoid the anxiety created by knowing that these are bad things. Thought adds no torment to the Pyrrhonist's woes. But I think I detect in Shakespeare a compassion that troubles any anaesthetic clarity of spirit. The man who gave Othello the words 'But yet the pity of it, Iago. O, Iago, the pity of it, Iago!' (4.1.191–2) allowed himself to feel too much of the world's sorrows to attain philosophical calm. And after all, he knew enough practical psychology to write Leonato's dismissal of his brother's philosophical consolations in *Much Ado About Nothing*:

> I will be flesh and blood,
> For there was never yet philosopher
> That could endure the toothache patiently.
>
> (5.1.34–46)

It would be rash to dogmatize in an essay about scepticism, but in this human world of appearances, when I look at Shakespeare's art I sense shadows of Pyrrhonism flitting across the moments of human encounter with all the pains, joys, and puzzles of life in the little world of his plays. That man who played the elder Hamlet's ghost and Old Adam (if such legends contain enough truth for a world of appearances and doubts) might look on with gentle irony at our struggles to comprehend his dramatic exercises in multiple seeing. And behind the countless voices of his characters there may be just one whisper of advice after all: 'If you think you understand, watch, and listen, and think again.'

---

[11] Soellner, *Shakespeare's Patterns of Self-Knowledge*, p. 141, suggests such contact before the composition of *Hamlet* and *Troilus and Cressida*.

[12] John Keats, *Selected Poems and Letters*, ed. Douglas Bush (Boston, 1959), p. 261.

SHAKESPEARE PERFORMANCES IN ENGLAND, 1992

PETER HOLLAND

There seems to be a peculiar difficulty these days in fitting Shakespeare productions to the available theatre spaces. At one end of the range, small theatres and theatre-spaces do not necessarily either only deserve or only receive small-scale productions. The necessary aim of aptness and appropriateness of scale can often result in productions being oversized or, equally common at the other end of the spectrum, undersized for their stages. Some productions take on the scale assumed to be required by a particular space only to find that assumptions about that scale have carried with them, parasitically, assumptions about an appropriate style that are constricting and stultifying. As directors confront the often bewildering variety of spaces in which Shakespeare plays are now performed, their sense of scale often seems to go seriously awry. In the Royal Shakespeare Company the problems are exacerbated both by the tempting availability in Stratford of that most desirable of theatres, the Swan, a theatre into which many Shakespeare plays seem so naturally to fit, and by the awkwardnesses of the main house, a theatre into which the talents of the cast and crew seem now all too rarely to fit.

I take it that there are, along this particular faultline, two modes of production which ensure that the tectonic plates of production and theatre do not grind together, split apart or awkwardly overlay each other: the productions which manage the perfect and comfortable fit, small-scale in, say, the Other Place or medium in the Swan, and productions which make the space appear exhilaratingly barely able to contain them, the strain at the seams being a controlled part of the effect. Directors and companies are still attempting to come to terms with Buzz Goodbody's revolution of the 1970s[1] with its discovery that *Hamlet* will fit and will benefit from being fitted into a small tin hut; but they also confront the changing organization of theatre in Britain at the end of the century, allowing and encouraging touring companies to explore new possibilities of Shakespeare production. Contemplating this problem, I have divided this year's review into the sizes used for t-shirts: small, medium, large and XXXL.

SMALL

Through much of 1992 and in almost every conceivable corner of the United Kingdom (from Skye to Guernsey), the Medieval Players, a small professional company, could be found performing *Hamlet* Q1. With only seven actors in the company, their resources were even more straitened than the 1603 quarto requires but there was very little pruning. Assuming for their purposes that the text represents the play 'adapted to the practical exigencies of touring, tailored to the tastes of an audience unused to the plentiful theatrical fare that London enjoyed',[2]

---

[1] The best account is still Colin Chambers, *Other Spaces: New Theatre and the RSC* (1980).

[2] This and subsequent quotations are taken from the anonymous programme-note.

the company sought a style that connected performance with a medieval and renaissance tradition of travelling troupes. Whatever the scholarly opinion of such an assumption about the text, their decision led them to a mode of staging 'with fewer props and costumes, and with a far more direct story-line'. The company use a simple booth and trestle stage of the kind familiar to us from countless European illustrations; when I saw it, set up in Old Court of Corpus Christi College, Cambridge, during the July Cambridge Festival, within sight of the memorial to Marlowe and Fletcher, the stage's familiarity suggested a yearned-for continuity of performing tradition but also an entire appropriateness to their version of the text.

But the company also sought disjunction, trying to defamiliarize the play for an audience so that they would 'rediscover Hamlet – both Shakespeare's and the story itself – by having it placed before you anew'. While some members of the audience could be seen frantically checking through New Penguin texts in the fading light, others more readily left this text to have its own values, values which the production excellently represented. At no point did the company seem to evince the slightest apology or embarrassment for the oddities of language or action; the text, even when it is making less than sense, was spoken with a confident acceptance of its own logic, not as some shadow of a far greater other, Q2 or F. There was no difficulty in accepting Corambis and I became used to Rosincraft, Guilderstone and Leartes (pronounced tri-syllabically). Ben Benison's direction ensured a merciless pace that reconnected the audience to the pleasures of narrative rather than the different virtues of introspection. Patrick Knox's Hamlet, the only actor not to be doubling or quintupling roles, became an actively melancholic man in a fast-moving world. If his black hose and white shirt summoned up comforting shades of nineteenth-century tradition, the effect of his performance – as often throughout the production – was of something alien and distanced, not a refreshed

nearness. Both Hamlet and *Hamlet* were, for the most part, oddly uninvolving without my wishing to suggest by that any hint of a dissatisfying distance.

On the barest of platforms, gestural effects became simple and powerful: Leartes embraced warmly by Hamlet as he left the court, providing a neat bridge to Claudius' turning to his 'princely Sonne'[3] (and Hamlet's flinching from his step-father's touch) and a yawning chasm to their duel at the play's end, or Ofelia (Susannah Rickards) not playing her lute in the mad scene (though the original direction requires her entrance 'playing on a Lute, and her haire downe singing' G4[b]) but using it as a threatening weapon or to represent, most movingly, Corambis' head.

It was shocking, more shocking than in any other production I recall, to see Ofelia become coarse and vulgar and crude, as if the veneer of nobility had been stripped away to reveal a stereotyped East End barmaid beneath. Similarly Roy Weskin's Ghost, walking on stilts with a billowing cloak, making him tower over the others onstage, screamed in pain both from the murder itself and from the 'flaming fire' in which he was now 'Confinde' (sig. C3[b]). Such effects underlined a readiness for emotion that burst through the speed and thrills of melodrama.

Other scenes were allowed an unexpected prominence: Fortinbras' first scene, at only six lines even shorter than in Folio, was intensified in importance by its alienness, by Hamlet's absence and by its pointed brevity. Even the exigencies of doubling seemed not to obstruct: Corambis was forced to die unseen (though not unheard) because the actor would need to appear in the middle of the scene as the Ghost after a quick but not impossible costume change. Played with such conviction and

---

[3] All quotations are from a facsimile of Q1 (here sig. B3[b]) but see also the aggressively packaged version edited by Graham Holderness and Bryan Loughrey in their series *Shakespearean Originals* (Brighton, 1992).

1   *Hamlet* Q1, 1.1, The Medieval Players: Ghost (Roy Weskin) towers over Horatio (Will Lawrance),
Marcellus (Nicholas Collett) and Barnardo (Susannah Rickards)

energy before an appreciative audience, the Medieval Players' *Hamlet* Q1 never pretended to be more than a small play for small spaces, fitting neatly onto the tiny platform of their stage. Such unpretentiousness of scale deserves approval.

The opposite to 'unpretentiousness' ought to be 'pretentiousness', a word which Irving Wardle places on his critic's black-list, in his brilliant and sane account of the activity of a theatre critic.[4] It is not the term I would wish to apply to Sam Mendes's *Richard III*, premiered at The Other Place before heading out on tour. It was a production with clear pretensions, aims, and ambitions outstandingly realized. Above all it sought to make the play coherent, to find for it a structural shapeliness that its form as chronicle history often appears to be evading in performance. This may be a form of directorial imposition but the gains in clarity and architecture seemed ample compensation.

In Act 5 this was no more than a little rearrangement, intercutting chopped-up segments of successive scenes (5.3 to 5.6), the scenes of Richard and Richmond producing a remarkable balancing of the two opposing powers. For the first time Richmond seemed a worthy opponent, rather than a shallow nice guy and Mark Lewis Jones's slow calm delivery of the long final speech of the play released the tensions of the evening, establishing a new dramatic rhythm opposite to Richard's, a peacefulness and rest from, implicitly, the whole long history of civil strife. The audience has been waiting for this moment, for the necessary male antagonist to Richard. It was prepared for by this earlier splicing. In the juxtaposition of the two tent scenes and the circling of the ghosts, or the paralleling of the two speeches to the armies, Shakespeare was already aiming at the same effect. Mendes's cinematic switching, the orations to the armies counterpointed in chunks of lines with Richmond and Richard side by side on stage, simply intensified the effect already there in embryo. Some might have quibbled with the way the ghosts, obviously taking part in a late-night ghosts' drinking party, first all spoke to Richard and then all to Richmond; but no one could quibble with the thrilling splicing of the two orations, with the drumbeats, so strongly thematized in the production as the accompaniment of Margaret's curse, now reaching a tumultuous climax. There was, at a moment like this, a remarkable awareness of dramatic effect achieved with simple means and a sure-footed underlining of the play's rhythm, its natural architecture.

Mendes shares with great directors that ability to uncover a play's rhythm and make an audience feel its rightness. His approach to the larger shape was more extreme but no less convincing. Realizing that Margaret's prophetic curses punctuate the play and that their fulfilment defines the play's progress, he allowed Margaret (Cherry Morris) to reappear hauntingly, often framed by a doorway in the set's upper level, repeating part of her earlier speech as each character in turn fulfils her prediction and invokes her name in the course of realizing their own part in this line of death. Her curses in 1.3 and 4.4 became two strongly ritualized moments, as Margaret sprinkled a circle with chalk dust and then chalked her face. In Act 5 Margaret's presence was marked as a kind of ticking clock, tapping on a pole from her upper vantage point, brooding over the final stages of her oracular truth. This exceptional prominence for Margaret elicited a performance from Cherry Morris worthy to set beside my memories of Peggy Ashcroft in *The Wars of the Roses* in 1964, a mad woman, of course, but also a woman of strange and true power.

But then all the women in this production were good. Kate Duchêne's Elizabeth, in particular, made the audience understand that this is the greatest of all English plays of female grief, the one play to be set beside Euripides' *Trojan Women*. With her eyes red-rimmed and

---

[4] I. Wardle, *Theatre Criticism* (1992), p. 41.

staring, her hair unkempt and more like Margaret's than before, her confrontation with Richard in 4.4, too often on stage a pale recapitulation of the wooing of Lady Anne, became a pivotal moment. The scene ended because she had found a way of leaving the stage; Richard's comment as he slumped in his chair, harshly triumphant, 'Relenting fool, and shallow, changing woman' (4.4.362), only showed how completely he had failed to understand what she meant. It was the first moment at which this Richard was found to be devastatingly imperceptive, caught out by the inflexibility of grief. But the maturity of playing in the scene emphasized the horror of Richard's threat or rather the calm promise of 'Death, desolation, ruin, and decay' (340) if the marriage does not take place. Simon Russell Beale's delivery of the following lines, 'It cannot be avoided but by this; / It will not be avoided but by this', was quietly apocalyptic, not showy but absolutely confident.

A small-scale RSC tour, even with a company twice the size of the Medieval Players, necessitated doubling. The impossibility of touring with children had Kate Duchêne doubling both Queen Elizabeth and her son, Prince Edward. But the small size of the company often paid dividends, comic and structural, like turning Catesby and Ratcliff into the two bishops who accompany Richard's charade for the Mayor (3.7), a comic double-act echoing the remarkable discovery in the production of the comic duo of Northern executioners in 1.4, a routine of music-hall artists. Other effects were unequivocally architectural: Simon Dormandy's Ratcliff, for instance, became a multitude of linked executioners, an eerie presence, teetering on the edge of caricature Gestapo with his wire-rimmed spectacles and thin hands, but saved by the sheer viciousness of the action as he did no more than delicately close each victim's eyes to mark the moment of death.

This simple effect was terrifyingly brutal. Indeed the production found throughout a remarkable mode of theatrical brutality. I have never seen anything as brutal and callous as Richard's statement to Catesby, 'Rumour it abroad / That Anne, my wife, is very grievous sick' (4.2.52–3), spoken so calmly over Anne seated next to him and his casual explanation, not in an aside but directly to her, as if to a child, 'I must be married to my brother's daughter / Or else my kingdom stands on brittle glass' (62–3). Her exit, turning to him dignified but weeping, was greeted by the equally stony matter-of-fact rejection, 'Tear-falling pity dwells not in *this* eye' (67, my emphasis). The sheer simplicity of the staging, the proximity of the actors in The Other Place, the open glasnost politics in which he can announce to the victim herself her own imminent death belong to a terrifying normality and rationality of evil.

Simon Russell Beale's Richard veered alarmingly from style to style but always with tremendous control, a mature actor knowing how to manage his effects, from the comic opening in which offstage dogs really did 'bark at me as I halt by them' (1.1.23) to the frightening pause after York has climbed onto his back until he forced a squeaking laugh in the face of the dreadful humiliation. If Touchstone found 'Your "if" is the only peacemaker' (5.4.100), Richard demonstrated the opposite, Hastings' 'If they have done this deed, my noble lord' (3.4.73) inducing in him a bellow of rage suddenly exploding beyond the cunning of Richard's handling of the scene, '"If"?' (74). This was the rage of a man unable to be crossed or doubted, a man for whom the world has been constructed into his model. But it could modulate so quickly as Richard took one of the Bishop's strawberries and crushed it on his own shaven head as a wound to mock the Lord Mayor (3.5) or as Hastings' head, brought on stage wrapped up as a neat brown-paper parcel, was first cuddled by Richard and then transfixed with his stick. I wondered, too, whether the camper moments in Beale's performance hinted at a suppressed homoeroticism, aligned, in traditional RSC style, with the leather coat he

2 *Richard III*, 4.2, RSC, The Other Place, 1992: 'Why, Buckingham, I say I would be king': Richard III (Simon Russell Beale), Queen Anne (Annabelle Apsion) and Buckingham (Stephen Boxer)

wore in the second half, a hint, perhaps, of a man whose interest in women was never sexual but purely political.

From the sweet younger brother of 1.1, head clasped to Clarence's belly as Clarence kissed the top of his head, this Richard grew in confidence and mania, a man alone because he refused help. His coronation entry in 4.2 to the sound of crashing cymbals led to his stumbling and falling, his bad leg caught up in his kingly robes; the fall automatically made the others on stage (except the already enthroned and numbed Anne) move to help him – for who would not help a fallen cripple? – and eliciting

again that rage, 'Stand all apart' (4.2.1), and the request for help from the one man he would always turn to, 'Cousin of Buckingham'. In the United States it is becoming increasingly common to label people who are disabled or handicapped with the sobriquet 'differently abled', a term that to my ears is unbearably patronizing. Beale's Richard *was* differently abled, his intellect and self-sufficiency at odds with his body. This bunched-back toad fed off power, culminating in the drums of his army. The play began with a blackout and the sound of the tap of his stick and modulated his power into the drum-taps of another differently abled person, Margaret, his nemesis. I did not need the underlining that brought her on to make Richard despair in the final duel with Richmond, a fierce fight in a pit of dry peat revealed under the boards of the stage, but I saw the point.

This was, at its premiere, not yet quite a great production, let alone a 'definitive' one (another word Wardle damns[5]) – a better Buckingham might have helped – but it was an extraordinarily good one. It had the virtues of the RSC's traditions of work in small spaces, particularly at The Other Place: freshness, energy, drive, clarity. Above all it used the potential of the space for simple and strong effects. Quickly unrolling a map across the stage-floor at 4.4.363, for instance, left Richard and Richmond standing on the kingdom they were struggling for, an exemplary piece of Tim Hatley's design. As an image it was powerful but unfussy, a grand effect in a small theatre, an apt description of the production as a whole.

MEDIUM

Sir Peter Hall has, in recent years, set himself the task of making Shakespeare clear, the most challenging version of 'doing Shakespeare straight'. His recent style of Shakespeare production, unfussy, well-spoken, working extraordinarily hard to leave the text to do its own work, the art concealing art, is an ambition I would not quarrel with for an instant. It is an ambition exactly suited to the potentials of the Swan Theatre, the RSC's medium-sized theatre, and alongside the pleasures of welcoming Hall back to Stratford in 1992 came the pleasures of seeing him tackle the Swan stage for the first time in a production of *All's Well That Ends Well*. It was also the first time John Gunter had designed for the Swan but his response to it was disappointing. He offered a white picture-frame towards the back of the stage draped with heavy swags of blue curtain framing a mirrored back wall out of which popped little models of buildings to indicate the play's shifting locales like a scene direction in an old-fashioned edition. But the set added nothing to the work on the open stage-space.

All's Well That Ends Well is a precisely social play, deeply concerned with rank and status. Gunter's set seemed in marked contrast to the rest of the production, lacking, above all, the coherence of a world, the creation of a social context for the action. But his costumes, from the first scene onwards, clearly defined social difference: Bertram's huge ruff and extravagant shoe roses, Helen's[6] servant-like restraint, echoed later in the uniform of the Countess's steward in 1.3, here played, in relation to Lavatch, as an after-echo of Malvolio and Feste. Indeed, the movement of the play was precisely charted by Helen's costume changes, to the white aristocratic dress she wore to dance with the King, back to her Rossillion black modesty, the cloak and kit-bag of the pilgrim and finally a version of a wedding-dress for the last scene.

Hall's commitment to clarity is far from being a commitment to neutrality. When Helen outlines to the King her contract of cure, offering a guarantee for her treatment, 'The great'st grace lending grace' (2.1.160ff.), her invocation of God was accompanied by heavenly music and she spoke with divine inspiration, as if in a trance-like state her statement had been dictated to her, spoken through her, intensified by the sudden introduction, for the first time in the production, of an echo to surround her small voice: 'What is infirm from your sound parts shall fly, / Health shall live free, and sickness freely die.' (167–8). This was a beautiful recognition of the strange new diction

---

[5] 'If a classic could be defined once and for all it would immediately cease to be a classic: impaled on a definitive production like a moth in a display cabinet', Wardle, p. 41.

[6] Since references are to the Oxford *Complete Works*, I use its preferred form, 'Helen', rather than the production's preferred form, 'Helena'. Most Shakespeare productions are, incidentally, oddly uncaring about the forms of characters' names: as Stanley Wells has suggested, the common pronunciation 'Petrookio' is simply illiterate.

3 *All's Well That Ends Well*, 1.3, RSC, Swan Theatre, 1992: Lavatch (Anthony O'Donnell) lectures the Countess (Barbara Jefford)

of the speech, its new and elaborate image of the 'horses of the sun', its single massive, complex sentence stretching over more than eight lines. The understanding of the text informed the production decision, showing the audience what it had found. The moment had been prepared for by Helen's claim to the Countess that her father's 'good receipt / Shall for my legacy be *sanctified*' (1.3.243) and by the remarkable little catechism of faith that followed that claim: 'Dost thou believe't?' 'Ay, madam, knowingly.' (248–9), lines that, in their disruption of the rhythm of whole verse lines warned of their weighty significance.

Hall's work on the text was characterized by a strong attention to such detail. Helen's interview with the Countess disturbed me: where, in Barbara Jefford's fierce confrontation with Helen in 1.3, was the warm acknowledgement to Helen, her approval of Helen's right to love Bertram that I have so often seen? But it is not there in the Countess's language; instead Helen's long speech of love (187–213), spoken so helplessly, kneeling in the corner of the stage, is answered only by 'Had you not lately an intent – speak truly – / To go to Paris?' (1.3.214–15). Jefford, magnificent throughout, left the audience in no doubt that this grande dame had the measure of her son from the start, with her heavy emphasis on his need for manners: 'succeed thy father / In manners as in shape' (1.1.58–9). Her sense of shame late in the play was entirely a product of that grand style; Bertram's behaviour had shamed his family and the Countess by Act 5 was left in tears, unable to control herself in public, humiliated by her son's actions.

Touchstone pronounces 'much virtue in "if"' (5.4.100–1). Hall's *All's Well* will go down as the production that found much virtue in 'et cetera' (5.3.315). Helen's refusal to read the rest of that dreadful letter, tearing it in pieces before she announces 'This is done' marked the possibility of change, the possibility of forgiveness. Paul Taylor, writing in *The Independent*, saw the tearing as

a wonderfully double-edged gesture. On the one hand, it seems to be saying that all this can now be put behind them; but the thickened intensity of the action suggests that damage has been done that cannot be so easily forgotten and forgiven.

That full awareness that the past cannot be dismissed by saying 'This is done' (5.3.315) was followed through into the triangle of Countess, Helen and Bertram that formed on the side of the stage, a tentative, nervous grouping with Bertram still unable to look at Helen, as centre-stage, to warm audience laughter, the King began the play's action replay, announcing to Diana (the excellent Rebecca Saire), 'Choose thou thy husband' (5.3.329).

I have been suggesting that Helen's belief in the divine and blessed nature of her ability to cure was shown to be true by the music. I was less clear why the King's fistula took on overtones of the stigmata; a fistula is unequivocally an internal disease, a suppurating ulcer, not a running sore. It is precisely the invisibility of the disease that makes it so disturbing; the king sickens without outward manifestation. This is *All's Well That Ends Well*, not *Parsifal*.

But the production's real running sore was Anthony O'Donnell's brilliantly foul Lavatch, the clown as Mr Punch, even more embittered than his Touchstone (see below), with shaven head, sunken eyes and facial sores that anticipated the ones that may lie under Bertram's patch (4.5.93–7). The phallus he carried was an offensive weapon, the fool's bauble drained of all humour and now a threat of violence not of comedy. It was difficult to see why the Countess kept on such a vicious, angry figure, a representation of everything that seethed under the play. Demonic, deeply troubling, this Lavatch was untameable, menacingly non-human.

As such, Lavatch counterpointed the sheer humanity of Michael Siberry's Paroles. Loud, both through the uncontrollable strength of Siberry's acting style but also because this Paroles was so dominant, Paroles' extravagance, from his first entry with piles of luggage including a case of hat-feathers, was only a cover. This Paroles was consistently more intelligent, wittier, more fun than any other I have seen. His intelligence led him to adopt a role as a means of surviving. His humiliation at the hands of the others in 4.3, his genuine fear of torture and death, was, as a result, more painful and extreme. It was his pain, even more than Helen's, that made the production veer from comedy to tragedy, his humanity that made us shift uncomfortably in our seats. At the end of his ordeal, his speech of resilience, 'Simply the thing I am / Shall make me live' (4.3.335–6), was spoken from anger as much as hurt. His desperate pleas to Lafeu, his humiliating public appearance at court in the last scene were of a man trying to salvage dignity in the full consciousness of what he has lost.

If Paroles' plight was unequivocal, around Helen's there hovered a shade of something very disturbing indeed, the sense that Bertram, snobbish and foolish, arrogant and bumptious though we know him to be from his first moments onstage, does not deserve what happens to him. As the dance of the suitors was whittled down to a *pas de deux* and Bertram realized with mounting horror what was about to happen, the audience could share that horror with some sympathy. Sophie Thompson's Helen induced fear in Toby Stephens's Bertram here just as surely as her divine power had induced fear in Richard Johnson's King. But in addition the actress's physical appearance transformed the play. When Bertram's nemesis is played by someone like Harriet Walter (as in Nunn's famous production), the audience cannot begin to understand why he should reject someone so intelligent and attractive. But Sophie Thompson's Helen, short, dour and very weepy, was a figure one could well appreciate Bertram trying to avoid. The play rebalanced itself, not in Bertram's favour but with understanding of his position.

Humane and tentative, vulnerable and hurt, the characters of Hall's *All's Well* stumbled towards the end, with only Diana exuding the confidence of innocence triumphant and inviolate. Hall's method paid rich dividends, demonstrating as clearly as possible its comprehension of the complexities of this nervy play.

In Wardle's glossary of damnable terms figures the word 'eclectic': 'a word suggesting that the artist has not found his own voice, and is parroting other voices which the reviewer finds himself unable to specify'.[7] Alexandru Darie, director of a brilliant production of *A Midsummer Night's Dream* for the Comedy Theatre of Bucharest in 1991, directed the Oxford Stage Company's touring production of *Much Ado About Nothing*. Darie's eclecticism was of a different type, a bewildering bricolage of materials; as Paul Taylor commented, in *The Independent*, of this 'ethnic and cultural hodgepodge', 'if, to the strains of a sitar, an eskimo had suddenly wandered on shaking a shillelagh, it would not have seemed unduly eccentric'. A wedding ritual from Transylvania was juxtaposed with an opening Yoruba chant from West Africa; this is eclecticism with a vengeance, supposedly justified by the director's perception of *Much Ado* as a play peopled 'with characters from a variety of civilisations' (programme-note).

The production opened with a card game between Don John and a character dubbed 'Angel', who then played out their rivalry across the play's action, and with an extravagantly stylized[8] representation of war. The war between Don John and Don Pedro is disposed of at the opening of Shakespeare's text with almost perfunctory abruptness. Darie not only built it up into a full-scale battle on stage but altered the ending, in the year's oddest piece of rewriting, to turn the whole action of the play into a period of brief truce: the messenger's speech at the very end, 'My lord, your brother John is ta'en in flight, / And brought with

---

7 Wardle, p. 43.

8 'Stylized: The reviewer cannot name the style and probably does not understand what is going on', Wardle, p. 42.

4   *The Winter's Tale*, Theatre de Complicite, 1992: Leontes (Simon McBurney) and Paulina (Kathryn Hunter)

armèd men back to Messina' (5.4.124–5) had been rewritten to say 'My lord, your brother John is *turned* in flight, / And comes with armèd men back to Messina', threatening a renewal of the war that had ended as the play began and providing a new gloom to hover conveniently over the end. The director may have wanted to 'evoke an unstable world precariously caught between two wars where the time for happiness is brief but lived to the full' (programme-note) but the play does not. The ending of *Much Ado About Nothing* is quite difficult enough without such assistance. Darie's revision made the action into a trivial interlude in the serious (male) business of war where, one might argue, the play is a serious outcome of the trivial business of war. After the refreshing excitements of his *A Midsummer Night's Dream*, this was a dull rag-bag of expectations unfulfilled.[9]

'Eclecticism' need not be a pejorative term. Theatre de Complicite are a collective company whose members are somehow able to make their different backgrounds converge on a style of physical theatre that is distinctly alien to the English tradition. Many of the company were trained at the Jacques Lecoq school in Paris and the company's early work was devised rather than text-based. *The Winter's Tale* was their first attempt at Shakespeare. The resultant production, by Annabel Arden with Annie Castledine, had some misses, notably that perennial problem of representing rural festival in the sheep-shearing, but many more startling hits. The cumulative effect was exhilarating in its

---

9   'Complaints about "unfulfilled expectations" come from people who want always to be told the same old story', Wardle, p. 43.

refusal to take anything for granted, excitingly disorientating in its rapidly switching moods. To describe each style in turn would make the term 'eclectic' take on its pejorative overtones; cumulatively the effect was of a production style in which anything was possible to match a play perceived as narrating the joys of possibility.

For Complicite's *Winter's Tale* found the ending joyous, not unequivocally so, as the pain so sharply created in the first half was deliberately recalled in a series of gestures (a handshaking ritual with Camillo, Leontes' stroking Hermione's belly) and in one extraordinary reversal by which Paulina's earlier cradling of Leontes in a form of *pietà* in 3.2 now became his cradling her, fixing her marriage to Camillo with tender love and concern. But the achievement of joy out of pain and in the fullness of memory still allowed the production to end with a running swirling parade of the characters round the stage and up a ladder to the sounds of the polonaise from Tchaikovsky's *Eugene Onegin* overlaid with the noise of crackling flames. Again and again the cast took the full measure of the play's rhetorical moments: Simon McBurney's Leontes was almost hysterical at the statue's movement, twitching back then moving tentatively towards her, hardly daring to touch before releasing the pent-up tension with a massive, deep, full-throated cry of 'O, she's warm!' (5.3.109), as magnificent as the descriptions of Macready at such a moment.[10] The whole statue scene was marked by candles and ceremony with Hermione, veiled as a grieving figure, perched half-way up the ladder, giving her imposing height and making her walk down the ladder immediately powerful.

Such grandeur, achieved with simple means but a full acceptance of the actor's physical and vocal power, contrasted with the opening sequences. McBurney's Leontes was more neurotic and simply funnier than usual. In his dialogue with Leontes (1.2.212ff.), Camillo became little more than a comic stooge, not

following the argument, as Leontes made the images graphic and so made them comically exaggerated: 'slippery' (275), 'hobby-horse' (278), even 'inside lip' (288) were literalized as explanation, held up for Camillo's – and the audience's – regard but by being acted they became oddly trivialized. The jealousy was allowed a full quota of overtones of the comedy of cuckoldry. If this suggests Leontes as a comic figure, for all that jealousy can appear comic, yet, in a single line, 'Why then the world and all that's in't is nothing' (295) for instance, the tone could become visionary in its perversion.

The risk, treating Leontes as a trivially comic butt, was also offset by a violence predicated on his power as King, a power suggested in the robes of Polixenes and Leontes, strange coats made by stitching together half-a-dozen jackets so that the monarchs seemed to be trailing their subjects behind them. Where in 2.1 he slapped the lord and Antigonus on the face in a gesture that seemed oddly emasculated, by 2.3, pouring sweat in a t-shirt and track-suit bottoms and dousing himself liberally with bottled water, Leontes attacked his lords with hideous ferocity, clawing and scratching at them, close to gouging out their eyes or chopping off an ear, in his hysterical rage. Antigonus, made to 'Swear by this sword' (2.3.168), was forced to hold the blade and, the oath made, Leontes deliberately drew the sword through Antigonus' hands, cutting his palms. But all the time the violence could be offset by ridiculous comedy, a fey camp gesture for 'I am a feather for each wind that blows' (154) or the successive shouts of 'bastard' (140, 155, 161) turned into 'brat' (163) with a pause after the initial 'b' to tease us with 'bastard' again before coyly

---

[10] 'What a cry came with, "O, she's warm!" It is impossible to describe Mr Macready here. He was Leontes' very self! His passionate joy at finding Hermione really alive seemed beyond control'. Helena Faucit, Macready's Hermione, in *On Some of Shakespeare's Female Characters* (1893) quoted by Leigh Woods, *On Playing Shakespeare* (Westport, 1991), p. 157.

retreating from the word into the tamer form. Brilliant and unnerving, McBurney's performance was impossible for the audience comfortably to control and pigeon-hole. Unquestionably a tyrant, this Leontes could be turned by the deaths of son and queen into a twitching heap with staring eyes, demanding Paulina's tenderness as well as her ferocity, exiting to great shouts of 'sorrows' (3.2.242), the word taken up and shouted by the rest of the cast.

Unashamedly theatrical in its resources and achievements, McBurney's Leontes was supported by the simpler dignity of Gabrielle Reidy's Hermione, exhausted and barely post-natal in the trial scene, wearing a shabby army greatcoat but with the strength of voice to encompass the huge periods of her speeches. He also established a remarkable relationship with Kathryn Hunter's Paulina. Hunter, surely the first person ever to play Mamillius, Paulina, Time and the Old Shepherd in the same production, displayed extraordinary virtuosity, allowing the roles to move between the pain of the innocent child, the love of the woman and the comedy of the old man, each with its own value, none simply grist to her own brilliance. Adults playing children usually draw attention to their discrepancy; Hunter as Mamillius was straightforwardly credible and very moving in his/her innocence. Her sudden entry as Old Shepherd, after the appearance of a huge, vampiric bear from under the floor-cloth, switched tones with all the theatricality the moment needs, to the accompaniment of the rest of the cast baa-ing away as lost sheep, pursued by a human sheepdog.

This easy restoration of normality through the comic normality of human animals prepared the way for Marcello Magni's Autolycus, an Italian clown quite capable of ignoring his lines as he elaborated them in Italian or English (the two indistinguishable in his accent) – I particularly liked the way 'three-pile' (4.3.14) became 'an Armani suit'. Picking lecherously on women in the audience, Magni tapped straight into a full tradition of *commedia* styles,

playing out the timeless *lazzi* of trickery. An Autolycus so effortlessly engaging undercuts the nastiness of the con-man but defied being resisted.

An attempt at Mediterranean ethnicity for the sheep-shearing (full of peasants whose voices had wailed in accompaniment to Hermione's trial) was predictably awkward, the style not offering the cast enough to authenticate the rusticity. But the transition from 4.4 to 5.1, from Bohemia back to Sicilia, was accomplished by a remarkable procession, creating the journey by the cast's parade around the stage as they slowly transformed their costumes from one world's to the other's and took again the characters they had abandoned in the play's earlier shift of time and space, revealing Leontes crawling on his knees as if he really has spent the intervening years doing nothing else (and hence recalling Paulina on 'A thousand knees' at 3.2.209). Its move from pleasant comedy to myth, Leontes suggesting Grotowski's *Le Prince Constant*, provided the firm foundations for the rich profundity of the production's view of the play's ending.

Complicite's *Winter's Tale* may have had rough edges but its virtuosity and passion spoke of a dangerous play, a play it would be trivializing to trap generically by flattening its sharply clashing tones into a normative expectation. If only medium-scale touring through the country's theatres could always be as consistently intelligent and exhilarating as this.

LARGE

Such a production belongs in medium-sized theatres. Its ambitions and its individualism would never have survived the unyielding scrutiny to which a large house, like the main house at Stratford, subjects all work. Boldness and imagination that at times narrowly misses can convince in the Arts Theatre, Cambridge, while leaving the audience in Stratford only irritated as experimentation starts to take on the hues of cheap trickery. It would simply be

5   *The Winter's Tale*, 4.3, RSC, 1992: Autolycus (Richard McCabe)

unfair of me to allow Annabel Arden's *Winter's Tale* to be compared and contrasted too directly with Adrian Noble's production for the RSC, a production designed to respond to the awful threat the huge spaces and odd structures of Stratford pose.

My five 'large' productions are all from Stratford's main stage and add up, on balance, to a disappointing season. David Thacker, director of both *As You Like It* and *The Merry Wives of Windsor*, demonstrated how difficult the transition from the Swan to the main stage is. Bill Alexander's *The Taming of the Shrew* was a production whose intriguing argument got lost in a theatre this size. Only John Caird's *Antony and Cleopatra* seemed comfortably able to accept the scale both of play and theatre and ensure that the two harmonized. The RSC, like any other company, is allowed its less good years and in every production there was much to admire. But cumulatively the sort of riches Stratford has accustomed us to was missing.

Even Adrian Noble's *Winter's Tale*, a production much praised by the critics, left me unmoved (which might be thought allowable) and unconcerned (which is not). The production's unquestioned triumph was the sheep-shearing; I have never seen it done better. Noble created an exuberance that was unforced. It was partly the setting, partly the energy Richard McCabe's Autolycus imparted to every scene he was in. I could almost forgive him the fact that he is tone-deaf – and an Autolycus who cannot sing a single note does seem slightly odd casting, especially when Shaun Davey's music did not make allowances for his difficulties. He was always in inventive control whether gulling Graham Turner's Young Shepherd of item after item (including his watch and a condom and ending with his bicycle) in 4.3 or in the terrible realization that the change of clothes with Florizel (4.4.635–48) meant that he would lose every penny he had stolen at the sheep-shearing (neatly offsetting the harsh efficiency with which he went through wallet after wallet, purse after purse at

4.4.611, never letting the audience simply be amused at his theft). I could not quite believe in an Autolycus who reformed at the end of 5.2, stealing the Young Shepherd's watch again and then, overcome with remorse, dropping it back into the Young Shepherd's carrier-bag, but McCabe made it coherent. A lecherous, down-at-heel spiv in a loud suit, arriving on stage from the flies lowered on an enormous clutch of green balloons, 'out of service' (4.3.14) because, as the headline of the copy of *The Bohemian Gazette* that he held up made clear, 'Servant Guilty', he had been caught with his hand in the princely till, McCabe milked his performance for all it was worth like any music-hall comic, a Bohemian Max Miller. McCabe was endearing in his knavery and yet the sheer scale of the performance, overbearing and extreme, was troubling.

But the success of Bohemia was due as much to the familiarity and fine detail of the characters at the feast. There was in this very English, Edwardian village fete something comfortably and nostalgically recognizable, a myth of England past, jellies and trifles, small boys in short-trousered suits and the town band. Paul Taylor, in *The Independent*, suggested resonances of Stanley Spencer's Cookham paintings. Like them, it was a world that is oddly familiar and yet completely fictional. These villagers belonged in this uncomplicated world, a golden age of a recent past, living, stripped of the real rigours and poverty of a village community, in an idyll of paradisal innocence. Their humanity was the product of the careful detailing of the people, each a comic creation but each solidly there. I could almost forgive the theatrical cheapness of the dance of satyrs (4.4.340), performed by men each holding two red balloons as testicles of various sizes and an erect mop.

The problems were not in Bohemia. They were acute in Sicilia. Here Noble allowed himself one piece of excess in a hugely extravagant storm to accompany Apollo's anger (3.2.145), thunder and high winds flattening the courtiers, umbrellas skidding across the stage, leaving the language lost in the theatrical tempest. Otherwise, Noble created a clear space for actors to work in, marked only by Anthony Ward's gauze box. The box seemed to function, if I read it aright, as a division of space, a representation of another world, a different perception co-existing with the rest of the stage and always offering to burst onto it. Sometimes the box's world seemed conjured into existence, as Mamillius' shaking of a snow-storm toy brought the rest of the court, frozen in tableau in the box, into the play at the very start or his whispering of the sad tale of sprites and goblins made Leontes suddenly appear in an echoing world within the box, the real terror far more effective than his son's attempts to 'fright' Hermione. The box's threats or promises, the dreams of Leontes or the peaceful awe of the oracle, spilled over onto the other spaces of the court but in the first half the play only allowed them to produce further disharmonies. Only in the statue scene, as the mass of the court was crammed into the box facing downstage gazing at the single figure outside it, Hermione, isolated at the front of the stage, and then tumbled out towards her, were the two worlds finally integrated into the resolved union of forgiveness of the play's end. The cast and the audience, divided physically by the enigma of her silent presence (so powerful when she is placed with her back to the audience), are unified by our gaze at her, unified, too, emotionally by her re-animation; we too have needed the miracle of her return.

Noble has always had this remarkable ability to tie a play together through a visual language. Here it was the balloons. They functioned in three ways: marking the green world of Autolycus (ambiguously balloon or tree), divine intervention (Time) and parties. Mamillius' birthday party opened the play, the balloons' colours here oddly discordant with the plush velvet world of the stylish court but the colours were echoed by the balloons brought on for Mamillius' sister's party, the sheep-shearing over which Perdita presides. Significantly rain, the dominant weather of Sicilia, reappeared at the end of the sheep-shearing, prompting the clearing of the trestles and beginning the play's journey back to Sicilia.

But, balloons and box apart, Noble's Sicilia was a place for actors. Leontes may well be Shakespeare's most difficult role; the language, clotted and incomprehensible, reveals only the density of his imaginings. Leontes for all his attempts at communication is strangely non-communicative. Noble trimmed the role of some of its difficulty, cutting the 'Affection' passage (1.2.140–8), for instance, to barely two lines. But trimming the text of the first scenes is a mistake if it tries to make things clearer. Even with this directorial help, John Nettles, back with the RSC after a long break, showed his lack of technique for such a task. From the first guttural sounds of 'Too hot, too hot', he tried every trick but they stayed as tricks, his voice strangely dissociated from his body, the lines chopped meaninglessly into fragments (an old RSC device to suggest emotional extremes). Try as Nettles might, Leontes steadfastly refused to appear on stage.

And if Leontes is not there the drive and dynamic of the first half of the play goes for nothing. Samantha Bond's calm, warm, loving dignity as Hermione was unavailing. As she tried to patch this terribly public matrimonial squabble, going close to him even in the trial scene, trying to calm him and silence him, her hand over his mouth, she seemed more than usually isolated because the two actors seemed unable to connect their performances. As much as I admired what she was attempting here, the winning warmth of her affection for Polixenes or the deep sadness of her announcement of her parentage, 'The Emperor of Russia was my father' (3.2.118), here as aside to her gaoler, she was hamstrung by the limitations of her own voice, short of the deeper chest resonances that a Hermione needs.

On the two occasions I saw the production, Gemma Jones's Paulina reduced the audience to laughter. This Paulina, a county lady who obviously runs every charity committee with a rod of iron and is forever doing good works and opening bazaars, was far from the moral power the text can reveal. Leontes' irritation with her early in the play or the lords' later, when she has been torturing Leontes for sixteen years, seemed entirely justified. Paulina's accurate sense of how the true values are distorted by Leontes' imaginings was submerged behind social nuisance. I came to realize, precisely because the performance did not generate it, how completely the play is in her hands, how much we must admire her sheer determination, her truth and her love if we are to reach the end of the play's long journey.

In all these three cases the actors diminished the scale and complexity of the play to a pleasing but undisturbing story. Two devices in the play's transition marked the scale of Noble's difficulty: the appearance of Hermione's ghost to preserve her daughter, encouraging the bear to miss out on its hors d'oeuvre and go straight to the main course, and the arrival of Time's speech as a scroll attached to a balloon which floated down for Camillo, asleep in a wicker chair, to find and read. Bringing on a ghostly Hermione, floating inside the box, to protect Perdita, who at her mother's appearance cries for the first time, only muddles things – it is one of those moments where I want to sound very pedantic and to say that if Shakespeare had intended Hermione's ghost to appear he would have written the scene that way. The solution to the problem of Time's speech acknowledged the difficulty of finding a style by producing such a lack-lustre invention. I cannot recall seeing a successful *Winter's Tale* on the Stratford stage and Noble, disappointingly, could not alter my perception of the tradition.

I had always thought that *The Taming of the Shrew* was a play about gender-conflict. Bill Alexander's production nearly managed to convince me that the play is instead about class and that male subjugation of women is only an example of masters' oppression of servants. The

play's punning on 'gentlewoman', Kate as aristocrat and Kate as gentled by her treatment, tied the two firmly together. Anton Lesser's Petruccio found delight in calling Amanda Harris's Kate, after the sun/moon scene, 'my wife, this gentlewoman' (4.6.63), splitting the socially accurate last word into two, now true through her transformation, 'gentle woman'.

Alexander's production was clearly one dominated by ideas. The radical rewriting of the Induction was not only about updating to the 1990s; it was also an attempt to see the frame as an exercise in class mockery. As 'Lady Sarah Ormsby' warned 'Lord Simon Llewellyn' (alias a Huntsman and the Lord) at the sight of Sly, 'Leave him alone, Simon. Don't touch him. He's disgusting; probably working-class', her contempt seemed to drive the play forward. But for 'Simon', in addition, 'The drunk needs teaching a lesson so we'll mess around with his mind for a bit.' Language like this is not exactly Shakespeare and it is a little disingenuous to call it 'adapted from the 1594 Quarto text' as Alexander's programme-note suggested. But at least it makes clear what the production had in mind. Anything designed to humiliate Sly of course fails. Maxwell Hutcheon's Sly was too kindly, too little affected by the inhibitions of the class-assumptions of the young Sloanes, too normal compared with the neurotic anger and power-games of the Lord, a man brutally coercing his brother (not his page in this production) to play Sly's Lady. As Sly intervened to try to break up the fight in 5.1 with a broken bottle (the Petruccio-actor's response, 'it's all right; it's only a play' was at the same dismal level of invention as the Induction) or as he offered the starving Katherine food, Sly reacted with a natural good will that was alien to the noble world of his hosts.

The players at Llewellyn's house, servants of their aristocratic patrons, were as humiliated as, say, Grumio in the play. But revenge is sweet: the actors cast the aristos as extra servants at Petruccio's house, giving the troupe the pretext

6   *The Taming of the Shrew*, 5.1, RSC, 1992: 'It's all right; it's only a play.' Sly (Maxwell Hutcheon), clutching a broken bottle, is reassured by Petruccio (Anton Lesser)

both to humiliate and embarrass their masters, as their reluctant amateur actors were left helpless when Grumio walked offstage and joined the audience with 'Tell thou the tale' (4.1.64). The interval placed mid-way through a scene, before Petruccio's 'Thus have I politicly begun my reign' (4.1.164), underlined the point, closing the first half on the humiliation of the unwilling extras ordered around by Petruccio with the same arrogant right as the Lord had exercised in his vicious mind-game with Sly.

Such Pirandellian devices were balanced within the play by Petruccio's fury with Grumio and by Richard McCabe's Tranio, the first time Tranio has seemed much of a part to me, a servant outwitting his master and humiliating him as he sustained the disguise far longer than Lucentio wished. The play cohered but it did so at the expense of its own dramatic

energy. Humiliating the onstage audience may be a justifiable design but it stopped the forward movement of the play stone-dead. An amateur stumbling over his or her script may be an object of ridicule but it suspends the action while the awkwardness is played out. I found myself liking the idea but dismayed at its execution.

By the final scenes of the play, inner and outer mixed in a wholly new way. Kate and Petruccio's rapt and prolonged kiss at 5.1.139 caused not only a change in lighting but an outbreak of kissing among the onstage audience, with Sly shyly taking his 'lady's' hand. Kate's pleasure at the lesson she has learned from Petruccio, the sheer delight in game-playing, was also now shared by the Sloane playing the Widow in 5.2 who could confidently discard her script and improvise. The disaster of Bianca's marriage to Lucentio, with Bianca now making eyes at Tranio and Lucentio embittered in melancholic gloom on the side of the stage, was mirrored by the Lord's being rejected by his girlfriend as they finally left the stage. The solution of *The Shrew* became a rather visible lesson for the young aristocrats who had watched it. Game, its pleasures and perils, now ruled the stage. It was just as well that the frame's presence paid off by the end, for through much of the evening it was an intrusive presence, immuring seven actors upstage to provide only a distraction as they wandered around to refill their glasses at suitable gaps in the action.

I suggested before that this Katherine had learned from Petruccio the pleasures of game-playing but she had also come to appreciate that agreeing with someone was not always submissive. Her apology to Vincentio for her 'mistaking eyes' (4.6.46) became an apology to Petruccio; in this new world in which compliance seemed a positive possibility rather than an aspect of her sustained humiliation, 'everything' she now looked on 'seemeth green', fresh and new. Her 'mad mistaking' had been an error of perception, an assumption that everyone had only her worst interests at heart. Amanda Harris had clearly been to the same school as Lewis Carroll's Mock Turtle where she too had learned Uglification and Derision. The jutting jaw and dishevelled hair, the screwed-up eyes and furrowed brow softened by the end of the play as the rage went. But it took courage for an actress to spend so long distorting her features into such twisted shapes, using it as the means to feed and express her derision of the sweet prettiness of Rebecca Saire's Bianca, as well as tying her up and threatening her with a pair of scissors. Characteristically this Bianca was perfectly content – indeed positively keen – to hear Gremio's recital of his wealth and Tranio's capping of it (3.1). Kate, I assume, would find money only another aspect of her subjugation.

By contrast with the endless pacing of Harris's Kate, Lesser's Petruccio exuded calm confidence, seated while she flails around him in 2.1 before using his chair like a lion-tamer dealing with a large and recalcitrant cat. His witty assumption of agreement (2.1.298ff.) reduced her to foot-stamping fury, shocked and speechless as he circumscribed the space in which she could express her will. At the same time this Kate clearly fancied Petruccio like mad from the first time she clapped eyes on him (a trifle obviously pointed this) and her tears before the wedding were as much at the thought of not getting him as the public humiliation she was undergoing.

The Taming of the Shrew is in so many ways a paradox, our assumption that this is nothing more than the Katherine–Petruccio play belied by the play's dogged and prolonged pursuit of other actions. It was good to see a production trying to find a new balance in its materials, even if the potential of this Katherine and Petruccio deserved more than to be so effectively marginalized by the other focuses of attention. The resultant blur and lurching rhythm only served to underline the play's difficult architecture while trying too hard to find an interesting theatrical solution to it.

David Thacker's productions of *As You Like It* and *The Merry Wives of Windsor* had not the slightest interest in anything so revisionary. After his fine productions of *Pericles* and *The Two Gentlemen of Verona* I was expecting much and got little. *As You Like It* seemed bedevilled by the wish to give the audience the kind of traditional production Stratford theatre-goers are assumed to prefer. This desire to see the play done traditionally means, I assume, seeing a grand nineteenth-century style production, opulent in its costuming in renaissance dress, massive in its sets, undemanding in its performance. Thacker's *As You Like It* was the RSC's most sustained example of such work for some time.

I found myself sharing with Anthony O'Donnell's marvellous Touchstone – a man memorably described by Michael Billington in

The Guardian as 'a stubby little Napoleon end-lessly confined to St Helena' – the sense that life in this Arden was 'tedious' (3.2.18), inducing in me something of the same impotent, frustrated anger. There was a dull inevitability in Arden, in the way that sooner or later someone (Touchstone pushed by William in 5.1 as it happens) had to fall into the onstage pond – for there is no point having a pond onstage, it seems, unless someone falls in it – or in the way that 'It was a lover and his lass' (5.3) seemed to encourage everyone in the forest, assorted lords and previously unseen shepherdesses, to wander in and join in the chorus, posing in picturesque groups across the stage, reinforcing a mundane sense of the song, set here to remarkably senti-mental music by Gary Yershon. This was the same sort of soupy sentimentalism that made the music swell just before the interval as Duke Senior embraced Orlando as his substitute father at the end of 2.7 and we knew that Orlando was among friends. No wonder Michael Siberry's Jaques found melancholy an angry emotion, not least when the harsh bitter-ness of Arden, where the duke's picnic in 2.5 was a camp-fire and unenticing cooking-pot, turned, after the interval, into the glibness of a green world, uncomplicated and unde-manding.

More disturbing, because it suggested a lack of engagement with the potentials of the play, was the sad case of Celia. In 3.2, for instance, after Rosalind's comment to Celia that she will speak to Orlando 'like a saucy lackey, and under that habit play the knave with him' (3.2.289–90), Celia does not have a word to say throughout the remaining 130 lines of the scene. But Shakespeare surely leaves her onstage for a reason, for Rosalind as Ganymede needs no chaperone. This is a play full of onstage spectators; the very next scene has Jaques watching Touchstone and Audrey and only coming forward to give the bride away, 'or the marriage is not lawful' (3.3.63–4). But Phyllida Hancock as Celia was left with nothing what-soever to do; her presence was an encumbrance,

a diversion from the production's concentra-tion on Rosalind. Even Orlando seemed only a makeweight in the scene, Peter de Jersey perhaps a bit overparted but certainly given little help to turn the dialogue into a duologue; Orlando must be more than a dull feed to Rosalind's wit or else we cannot see why she should have fallen for him.

In any case Samantha Bond's Rosalind rarely seemed to be enjoying her own language. The journey Rosalind takes was summed up by her consulting the map to announce 'Well, this is the forest of Ardenne' (2.4.13), a physical not an emotional trajectory. I cannot sum her per-formance up better than the description offered by Lindsay Duguid: 'Samantha Bond's Rosa-lind is wholesome and pert with her slightly husky actress's voice and her gamine gestures (legs apart, arms akimbo, hands in pockets, and so on). The English actress playing Rosalind is a gender all her own.' (*TLS* 8 May 1992). If this was Rosalind in a limbo of gender, it was also Rosalind without sexuality. For in a play so full of sexual desire the production saw only clichéd romance, epitomized by the long hard look between Celia and Oliver at the end of 4.3 or their rapt attention to each other as they too were drawn onstage by the magnetic music in 5.3.

Shakespeare does not articulate the play as a straightforward sequence of court followed by forest. The oscillations between the two, flash-ing back to the court after the first sight of Duke Senior for 2.2 and 2.3 and again, even more viciously, for 3.1, counterpoint the gradual outlining of Arden. But if the court and forest sets are both as massive as those of Johan Engels then the intercutting of location becomes exceedingly tricky. So the text's sequence was changed and Shakespeare's version of simul-taneity or split-screen image became a simple and unthreatening succession, intensified by the cosy definition of Andrew Jarvis's Duke Frederick as a bald *and* bearded dictator from Ruritania, accompanied by torches and red light and a court of bowing grotesques.

7　*As You Like It*, RSC, 1992: The English actress playing Rosalind (Samantha Bond)

Yet Thacker's *As You Like It* had one interpretative achievement that I admired unreser-
vedly, beautifully exploring the melancholy of
love. As Rosalind demanded of Silvius, 'Wilt
thou love such a woman?' (4.3.68), the audience
was left with the overwhelming sense of
Silvius' helplessness to do anything else and
when he defined love at Phoebe's prompting
(5.3.78ff.) on a darkening stage, it became an
emotion of great pain and sadness. It was this
feeling that left the four, Rosalind, Orlando,
Phoebe and Silvius, sprawled in gloomy iso-
lation from each other across the stage as it
filled up during 'It was a lover and his lass'.
There was in this Arden no joy in love, no
pleasure, no happiness unless, as for Jaques, the
happiness was in the melancholy, the joy in the
annoyance. And the effect of this melancholic
sadness was to tie Jaques and Touchstone into
the play more firmly than usual. Jaques' anger,
so powerful and neurotic in Michael Siberry's
performance, was just another form of this
isolating desperation and I was left wishing that
this grief had been allowed free rein to undercut
and trouble further the pervasive blandness of
this version of traditional Shakespeare.

As You Like It had some redeeming features;
The Merry Wives of Windsor had none. The
play, so often a glittering success for the RSC,
became an inglorious catastrophe, devoid of
charm or interest, its excellent cast reduced to
performing dull gags at breakneck speed as if
desperate to get to the end before anyone
noticed that nothing was happening. The play's
language was ignored in favour of ancient pieces
of business and a great deal of burbling, mum-
bling and laughing at one's own jokes. No one
had the courage to suggest that the play's prose
is an extraordinary comic achievement. The
only line that raised a laugh was, with dreadful
predictability, Dr Caius' 'If there be one or
two, I shall make-a the turd' (3.3.225).

The play's plotting disappeared in the chaos
and the action became oddly surreal in its
incomprehensibility. Anton Lesser's Ford,
bowler-hatted and briefcased like a suburban
commuter in Elizabethan dress, suffered the
required extreme paroxysms of agony but was
also reduced to gnawing his handkerchief, pun-
ching holes in the furniture, stepping in bowls
of dirty water, pulling his hat so far down over
his eyes that he bumped into a bench and
tearing off his false moustache with a delayed
yelp of pain. That he was made to do the last
twice was only too indicative of the poverty of
comic invention; as Paul Taylor commented,
'To see that gag once might have been considered nostalgic, to see it twice ...' (his dots).
Only in the sudden scream of 'I beseech you'
(3.2.72), was there a glimpse of a pathology of
jealousy, a man desperately trying to keep
control and failing. Ron Cook as Dr Caius,
practising his fencing in 2.3, produced the one
splendid move of the whole production as,
trying out different rapiers from Rugby's bag,
he pulled out one that proved to be extremely
heavy and had to follow its momentum as it
arched over his body throwing him to the
ground. But he then spoiled the effect by lying
wriggling on the ground too long. His vertigo
as he negotiated one of the galleries across the
stage in Ford's house was another gag repeated
and thereby blunted.

Benjamin Whitrow's ancient bearded and
balding Falstaff was a dull old fool who clearly
did not believe in his own lecherousness, let
alone his ability to convince the wives of his
desire. He became marginal to the play, never
its dominant and dominating character. His
accent, which kept sliding to something much
less aristocratic, suggested a man come up
through the ranks, though nothing else did.
Cheryl Campbell and Gemma Jones as the
wives, in costumes of ludicrous excess, seemed
more than usual to have deserved their silly
husbands (John Nettles dully competent as
Page, carrying a birding-rifle throughout the
production for some reason). Only Anne Page
(Catherine Mears) survived by being disarm-
ingly normal in this gallery of cheap cari-
catures.

Windsor's population was initially glimpsed

8   *The Merry Wives of Windsor*, 3.3, RSC, 1992: 'Let me creep in here': Falstaff (Benjamin Whitrow) and the buck-basket, with Mistress Page (Gemma Jones) and Mistress Ford (Cheryl Campbell)

coming out of church but then vanished save for a wench (there is no other word) stolidly mopping the floor throughout 3.5. The exactness of the play's interest in a provincial town, something the RSC has in the past found and recreated, here disappeared into the ravening maw of poor farce, the play's particular virtues and pleasures obscured by the sight of actors mugging away in a vain attempt to keep the play going.

Such productions would look bad in any theatre and at their very worst on the pitiless main stage in Stratford. John Caird's *Antony and Cleopatra* which ended the season, whatever its problems, exuded a real confidence about the scale of play and stage, the necessity to represent the large scale grandly. If the opening and closing images of Antony and Cleopatra standing side by side at the back of the stage contemplating the Nile smacked of a rather strenuously romantic cliché, at least it made abundantly clear the full-blown emotion the play was seen as embodying.

This unequivocal view of the lovers was supported by some firm cutting. It is one thing to cut, say, the Parthian scene (3.1) in favour of a more single-minded concentration on the central action (for all that it shrinks the play's geography). But cutting Seleucus and Cleopatra's games over her wealth in 5.2 disambiguates the movement of the scene, making it easier, almost too easy, for Cleopatra to achieve a formal tragic emotion for her death. Clare Higgins did not seem to need such help but the refusal of complexity was strongly characteristic of the production style.

It can be aligned with the Clown scene soon after. Determined to find a determinism in the play, the production built up the Soothsayer (Jasper Britton) in 1.2 into a strange black-clothed figure daubed with white dust whose telling of Iras' and Charmian's fortunes involved sending them off into a genuine trance. In 2.3 his make-up now included eyes painted onto the palms of his hands. When Octavius' description of Antony and Cleopatra and their children in the marketplace (3.6.1–19) was played out onstage as the last action before the interval (taken in mid-scene), as Octavius spoke straight out to the audience, the soothsayer was revealed behind them as the family group processed downstage and exited. He was to be found on stage again watching Enobarbus' death in 4.10. Antony's invective at 4.13.30, 'Ah, thou spell!' was taken literally: Cleopatra appeared as a vision dressed as Isis brought on by the Soothsayer and protected from Antony's fury by his eye-hands. That he should appear yet again as the Clown in 5.2 was inevitable, carrying the basket that, then enigmatically, he had balanced on his head on his exit in 1.2,[11] but the choice of such patterning also neatly excised the scene's comedy in favour of an eerie supernatural control, with his forcing Cleopatra to look into the basket and, without harm to himself, holding up one of the asps.

There was, throughout the last scenes, a sense of cavernous desolation in the monument, here played out on the stage-floor since the raising of Antony by ropes attached to his stretcher had the surprising effect of lowering Cleopatra's group in the monument down to stage level. When Octavius' troops abseiled in like a Roman SAS brigade they left Charmian and Iras huddled scared in the corner and Cleopatra, now in a black wig rather than her earlier red one, also huddled on the ground. Mournful despair, intensified by the frequent recurrence of the music that defined Hercules leaving Antony in 4.3, was unremittingly accomplished, typified by the queen's shuddering wails through her realization that 'there is nothing left remarkable / Beneath the visiting moon' (4.16.69–70).

Such directness and emotional monochrome did not do justice to Clare Higgins's earlier achievements, moody anger giving way so quickly to laughter that it almost justified Paul Jesson's Enobarbus in his description of her 'infinite variety'. Cleopatra's skills as performer became also the pleasures of play-acting so that the bored waiting of 1.5 found Cleopatra dressed as Isis with flail and sceptre, anticipating the performance in 3.6. Tossing the Roman messenger's papers in the air in 1.1 or throwing Antony to the ground and kicking him hard in the ribs as 'the greatest liar' (1.3.38) typified her restless activity. It also produced a quite brilliant playing of the two-part scene with her own messenger (2.5 and 3.3), aided by Alan Cox's marvellous performance as the terrified servant, desperately trying to work out what could possibly placate this unpredictable tormentor and unerringly putting his foot in it with his eagerness to report 'I do think she's thirty' (3.3.28). Higgins was ably supported by her maids (Claire Benedict as an extrovert Charmian, Susie Lee Hayward as a quiet Iras sneaking a bite from the asp while robing her mistress), the production's definition of Cleopatra's enigma cumulatively striking.

Caird's skills could not, though, solve the problems of Richard Johnson's Antony. Returning to the role which he had played at

---

[11] This is a good example of the common problem of a director reading the play back to front. Audiences were likely to be bemused by the basket in 1.2, having no reason to know that the Soothsayer would be the clown and hence that, in effect, Cleopatra had the asps ready from the beginning of the play. Viewed from the perspective of the end of the play, the basket in 1.2 made perfect sense, provided one remembered it by that late stage.

9   *Antony and Cleopatra*, 1.1, RSC, 1992: Cleopatra (Clare Higgins) and Antony (Richard Johnson)

Stratford in 1972 (opposite Janet Suzman), Johnson was quite simply too old and wearied. While a production might reasonably have wanted to explore an age-gap between the lovers, it cannot dispense with a sexual charisma around Antony. If Antony is not attractive, even in an elderly grizzled way, the production's argument will tilt unbalanced and Johnson could do nothing to project a reason for Cleopatra's fascination with him to match his justifiable obsession with her. When Antony's callous laughter at announcing Fulvia's death (1.3.59) was met by this Cleopatra's serious and anxious comparison with her

own future ('Now I see, I see, / In Fulvia's death how mine received shall be' 1.3.64–5), Johnson was left weakly throwing his hands up in the air in mock-desperation at the difficulty of dealing with women, failing to take on the powerful question Higgins had thrown him.

What Johnson lacked in grandeur Sue Blane's set amply provided, its four pairs of massive shutters like sections of walls and monuments, rough stone on audience left, rendered brick on its right, drawn back for the Egyptian scenes and closing in for the Roman scenes to push their action right downstage.

Simple and small-scale devices spoke as eloquently as the grand tableaux: Lepidus and Octavius (John Nettles finely authoritative) conversing in 1.4 at a table designed for three triumvirs but with one seat conspicuously empty; Antony's courteous concern for Lepidus at 2.2.175–7 while Octavius pointedly ignores the old man; Antony, wishing Octavia (Phyllida Hancock) goodnight (2.3.7) by trying to kiss her lips as she formally turned her cheek to him, though she left the stage laughing easily with her brother; Thidias' whipped back being anointed while Octavius read Antony's letter in 4.1; Octavius quietly directing his explanation of the war (5.1.73–7) confidentially to Decretas, needing to explain himself to Antony's man. But the set could rise to the play's heights; with drummers on the two corners of the forestage for Ilona Sekacz's thunderous battle music, the production looked and sounded properly operatic.

Its directness was also reflected in the willingness to have characters unequivocally address speeches to the audience. Philo, at the very start of the play, had no Demetrius to speak to and instead offered his angry comments straight to us, describing something massively discrepant from the image of the lovers we could see; it was for the audience to 'Look where they come' (1.1.10) as they entered hopping ('forty paces through the public street' (2.2.236) perhaps). The play's argument was presented, imaged, and described, its gaps and discrepancies left for the audience to mark. In spite of its weak Antony the production unquestionably had the measure of the play.

XXXL

If Caird's *Antony and Cleopatra* was 'large' then 'XXXL' is the only possible label for something the size of Tim Supple's production of *Coriolanus* at the Chichester Festival Theatre, a co-production with the Renaissance Theatre Company. This, the third major *Coriolanus* in

my three years of reviewing for *Survey*, was without any doubt the biggest; indeed it had the largest cast I have ever seen in any professional Shakespeare production. Given permission by Equity to recruit local amateur actors as the crowd, something he had previously done for his production of *Oh What a Lovely War* at the Haymarket in Leicester, Supple marshalled a crowd of over fifty onto the vast expanses of the Chichester stage.

For the first time in my experience the crowd looked like a crowd, not the little huddle of most productions nor the sheepish group of members of the audience in Hall's *Coriolanus* at the National Theatre. Superbly drilled, this embodiment of the Roman and Volscian people was not strongly individualized. There was nothing here of the sort of detail that characterized Granville-Barker's crowd of over three hundred in a scene from *Julius Caesar* in 1911 ('"X 186 groans heavily and moves up stage, where he joins a doleful group consisting of Ys 48–54 and Zs 201–10", or something of that sort'[12]). Men, women and children moved quickly and comfortably across the stage or scrambled onto the set's upper levels, filling the spaces or clearing them to leave, for example, a large area for Menenius (Richard Briers) to exert his aristocratic control in the fable of the belly in 1.1 or hurtling off the stage completely into the edge of the stalls at the first appearance of Coriolanus (Kenneth Branagh). Anonymous and amorphous they may have been but the crowd was unremittingly human, a mass of humanity that could be despised by Coriolanus but called forth our humanity in sympathy. There was an exciting tension here between the sense of the operatic chorus under directorial control and the realism of these people, their lack of professional skills producing an unactorish normality onstage; as soldiers, the men

---

12 Hesketh Pearson, quoted in Ralph Berry, *The Methuen Book of Shakespeare Anecdotes* (1992), p. 123.

looked like a conscript army, tall and short, overweight and thin. But their sheer weight of numbers had its own exhilaration. Defending Coriolanus from the onslaught of the people in 3.1, the patricians became a tiny group, surrounded and hopelessly outnumbered, albeit better armed. The Volscian army, brought onstage in 1.2, was a solid wall of massive shields with strong overtones of modern riot police. The sounds of war were made by the crowd rhythmically striking their metal shields with poles or swords, creating deafening, clangorous noise.

Above everything else, the production revealed why Shakespeare might have used the speech-prefix '*All*', a mark that usually produces a rather embarrassing effect. Incited by Sicinius, 'What is the city but the people?' (3.1.199), fifty voices thundered back in unison 'True, / The people are the city' (199–200), a memorable sound in its volume and precision. Coriolanus whirled his sword back in response but it was no longer a threat, only a memory of the battle-field; the plebeian sound was far more threatening and powerful. This quantitative effect was not some after-echo of nineteenth-century production styles. For *Coriolanus* above any other Shakespeare play, the numbers matter; the play's argument, its structure of oppositions, its central balance depends on producing a balance at all. Supple's device simply worked.

Of course, colossal effects are not only achieved by numbers. Volumnia announces, hearing the trumpets of Coriolanus' victorious return to Rome, 'These are the ushers of Martius. Before him he carries noise, and behind him he leaves tears' (2.1.155–6). Nothing had prepared me for the sound of Judi Dench's voice at this point, ice-cold and mysterious, devastating in its confidence, totally uncompromising in its pitiless approval of her son's effect on the world. Dench was the Volumnia I have always hoped to see, one of the great performances of recent years. Almost normal in her first scene (1.3) as she played

games with Young Martius, teaching him to fight and arming him through the scene, Dench's Volumnia was perhaps little more than a rather objectionable mother-in-law, marking her triumph over Virgilia by taking her grandson with her 'out of doors'.

But the portrait built carefully thereafter. Her statement to Menenius after Coriolanus' banishment, 'Anger's my meat, I sup upon myself' (4.3.53), was terrifying because of its matter-of-factness, its simple, accurate truth for this driven character. By the climax of 5.3, cleverly blocked with Coriolanus seated at the down-stage point of the stage facing up so that Volumnia could play the entire scene out to the audience as well as to her son, Dench was crushed and humiliated, a woman who has never knelt before now kneeling to her son, a woman who has never had to plead for anything in her life now humbled before the figure she had moulded. As he tried to leave, 'I have sat too long' (132), her attempt at authority, 'Nay, go not from us thus', made it possible for him to move to strike her, something unimaginable in their relationship before. Now slowly she started to find again her anger and control; nothing else mattered to her but regaining her control over him, exerting her will single-mindedly. And the result was that she had never envisaged the consequence: Coriolanus' perception that 'Most dangerously you have with him prevailed, / If not most mortal to him' was a complete shock. For the first time he had proved wiser than she and that in the prediction of his death. Her face pulled suddenly into a mask of grief by her recognition of the truth of his statement and her re-appearance in the 'triumphal' entry of 5.5 was as a mourning statue of horror, a ghost, herself destroyed by her destruction of her son, the mother as filicide through the absolute belief in the necessity of proving her own power.

It would be good to be able to report that such great acting was matched by Branagh but I cannot. His 'O' in reply to her final speech (5.3.183), slumped as a crying mummy's boy,

10 *Coriolanus*, 3.1, The Renaissance Theatre Company at Chichester Festival Theatre: Coriolanus (Kenneth Branagh) turns his back on the plebeians and their tribunes

was drawn out for ever, not because the pressure of the emotion forced an unending wail but because the actor wanted to demonstrate the size of his lungs. A vocal trick, put firmly in its place by Aufidius' mocking mimicry of it to the Volscians ('He whined and roared away your victory' 5.6.100), it indicated Branagh's difficulty with the character as hero, offering not a representation of the play's paradoxes over the meaning of the word but a straightforward attempt to represent by device something his skill did not allow him to create.

Branagh was at his most comfortable in finding the part's comedy, the embarrassed laughter at 'I will go wash' (1.10.67) or shuffling out on his knees at 'Look, I am going' (3.2.134), the naughty little boy mocking his

mother though doing what she wants. It makes little sense to have a Coriolanus so socially at ease, adept and diplomatic in his greetings in 2.1 as Branagh managed. By the end, entering perched on a single ladder carried by soldiers (a deliberate echo of his entry in 1.4), waving a piece of paper like some Roman Neville Chamberlain and clearly ripe for a fall from his vulnerable perch, Branagh had proved to have lacked the vocal range and depth, the imagination and power of Dench.

Among a fairly weak supporting cast, Briers's Menenius was an honourable exception, particularly in his argument with the Volscian guards in 5.2 where the mask of geniality slipped and the underlying cold patrician contempt was sharply revealed. But elsewhere the old bluffer of tradition became a man of considerable political nous, a match for Jimmy Yuill and Gerard Horan as decent tribunes, men conspicuously out of place in the circle of cushions on which the patricians lolled for meetings. To be sure, the production was hardly notable for its sophisticated political reading of the play but, for all its limitations, Supple's *Coriolanus*, with Dench and a crowd like that, burst the bounds of normal Shakespeare production.

Nothing in the past year has burst those bounds quite as completely as the National Theatre's *A Midsummer Night's Dream*. Robert Lepage, the French-Canadian director, had only been known in England for his work in experimental theatre (*The Dragons' Trilogy*, *Tectonic Plates* and his brutal one-man show, *Needles and Opium*), though he had often directed Shakespeare, including *A Midsummer Night's Dream*, in Quebec. Inviting him to direct on the huge expanses of the Olivier stage was deliberately to propose something radically different. Different is not better and the result, visually magnificent, vocally catastrophic, was a production in which the play-text was not even a pretext, only a curious encumbrance to the theatrical poetics of the director's imagination. Take for instance the moment at which the lovers made their way along a line of five chairs, with, as Hermia reached the front one, Philostrate taking the rear one, now empty, and running to the front of the line with it over and over again as they made their slow progress across the back of the stage. As a stage image (of the repetitive type familiar from much performance art) the move was mesmerising and beautiful. But at the front of the stage Allan Mitchell's Theseus (who seemed for some reason to be blind) was trying to speak of lunatics, lovers and poets, a speech which neither had any perceptible link to the upstage action nor could compete with the hypnotic power of the visual image. It would be perfectly possible to argue that the importance of Theseus' speech has been grossly over-rated but Mitchell's delivery suggested portentousness

while the image denied it. The result was confusion rather than cohesion, the elements of the theatrical performance breaking apart into their fragmented constituent parts.

At least in the case of Mitchell's Theseus the language was potentially comprehensible. Lepage cast as Robin a French-Canadian actress-contortionist, Angela Laurier. Wearing tight red leggings and with one breast bare (as if she, not Hippolyta, were the play's amazon) she made her first entrance, at the opening of the performance, crab-like, walking on her hands with her legs outside her arms. Laurier proceeded in the course of the evening to reveal that the human body is capable of remarkable distortions, ending the epilogue by lying on her front, raising her legs slowly behind her and bringing her feet forward over her head to tuck them under her armpits. This is, of course, an astonishing feat, a physical metamorphosis of the body that might be argued aptly to represent Robin's transforming powers. Other tricks, particularly a dizzying high-speed spin on a cable for what seemed many minutes to represent Robin's travels round the world (from 2.1.176), were similarly extreme and dazzling.

But the glare of physical malleability shone sharply on vocal constriction. Wardle quotes critics' attempts to represent the phonetics of Eugenie Leontovich's notorious Cleopatra for Komisarjevsky in 1936 ('O weeerdee degarlano devar')[13] but my skills do not include trying to transcribe Ms Laurier's pronunciation. Even if I could, her voice was so underprojected that I doubt whether anyone beyond the first few rows realized that there was anything vaguely comprehensible being spoken. Like the problems of Linda Kerr Scott's Fool in Hytner's *King Lear* for the RSC in 1991, but magnified twenty times, the director's imaginative choice of a performer capable of extraordinary physical feats foundered on the

---

13 Wardle, p. 53.

complete failure to offer anything even barely adequate vocally. It only served to throw into unmitigated relief how crucial Robin's language is to making even the most basic narrative sense of the play.

In any case circus tricks, especially ones far beyond anything in Brook's vocabulary in his *A Midsummer Night's Dream*, are guaranteed to be distracting. Sally Dexter as Titania was hung up by her ankles for her sleep like some large bat (an image intensified by her black costume). For some of the time she was hidden but the audience could not know whether she was still hanging upside down; in effect from 2.2.30 to 3.1.122, a long period of stage time, the audience could think of nothing else but the blood rushing to Dexter's head – not the best way to ensure attention to the intervening action.

Michael Levine's set complemented the extreme nature of Lepage's view of the play. The stage was covered with an enormous shallow pond surrounded by grey earth that muddied throughout the course of the evening as the characters slithered and splashed their way across the central expanse of water. Not for nothing were the front rows of the audience provided with plastic macs to protect their clothes from the flying mud. Occasionally the light reflected off the water threw beautiful images onto the back walls, accompanying, for instance, Oberon's image of the 'mermaid on a dolphin's back' (2.1.150). But with the wood scenes played in pervasive gloom (the only lighting appeared often to be the single massive light-bulb dangling on its cord in mid-stage), the action accompanied almost constantly by strange, often Eastern music with a strong gamelan component, this has to be the darkest, bleakest view of the play ever taken.

If Brook's production used Kott to underline a certain degree of terror in the experiences of the night, Lepage's removed any vestige of pleasure in favour of fear and panic. Bottom's 'most rare vision' was one of the purest animality, a sustained, terrified awareness of his transformation (like Pinocchio on the way to becoming a donkey), marked by the sheer difficulty of enunciating, his tongue transformed with his head. His hands turned to hooves, Bottom had to carry Robin on his back, Laurier's feet serving as expressive ass's ears. Titania's erotic interest in him was particularly bestial, her normal humanity making the ass even more grotesque and horrible, frightening and unpleasant. In 4.1 Bottom's having sex with Titania was like the rutting of wild beasts (nasty, brutish and short). This is unremittingly coarse as a view of the play: Titania's desire to 'wind thee in my arms' (4.1.39), does not mean 'have sex with you' (a reading which sits oddly alongside the first part of the line, 'Sleep thou') and noisy humping rather distracted from the image of the ivy and the elm; 'O how I love thee' (44) became, inevitably, a deep post-orgasmic sigh.

In any case, Titania had had to order off the bed her attendant fairies, blue-faced and near-naked like Congolese Kota undergoing puberty rites (an identification I take from the programme). They had obviously wanted to turn the event into a group orgy. Rarely standing upright, the fairies slid malevolently through the pool like evil children beyond parental control, their monarchs dark deities who have clearly 'Come from the farthest step of India' (2.1.69). This dark world increasingly muddied the very young lovers whose scenes raced by until, with the dawn in 4.1, the huge black back walls of the stage lifted to reveal exquisite morning light, accompanied by the cast chanting, and the lovers left the stage through showers, washing away the experience and reappearing cleansed and freshly dressed for Act 5.

But the damp night-world seemed to have got to the workers, here inhabitants of cardboard city with Bottom (Timothy Spall) as a would-be medallion man with platform shoes and flared trousers far too short for him. What comedy there was in their rehearsal and performance was in tension with the dank, degraded world they inhabited, grimy figures,

11 *A Midsummer Night's Dream*, 2.1, Royal National Theatre, 1992: Oberon (Jeffery Kissoon) and muddy fairies

more miners than tradesmen, sitting hunched up brewing tea in a dirty billy-can, crouched in the frame of the hospital bed that, as in so many experimental productions I have watched, was the play's single major prop.

Throughout, the production offered strong overtones of dream. The opening, with Theseus and Hippolyta perched on one end of the bed as Philostrate poled it in circles, had the lovers slumped in a heap asleep on the bed, half-waking as the action called for them, as if the dream had begun long before the play left Athens. My dreams and my view of *A Mid-summer Night's Dream*, though, are certainly not as sustainedly melancholic as this one. But the play had become a drama of directorial imagination and caprice, the text disdained for the most part, though Sally Dexter is too fine an actress not to make something tremendous of 'the forgeries of jealousy' speech. Lepage's theatrical imagination is a rich and exciting one but it was simply not interested in the material of the play it was ostensibly illuminating, as opposed to the one Lepage would like to have been devising. Directors' work of this type is XXXL theatre. With Lepage's *A Midsummer Night's Dream*, I have seen the future and it is muddy.

PROFESSIONAL SHAKESPEARE PRODUCTIONS IN THE BRITISH ISLES, JANUARY–DECEMBER 1991

compiled by

NIKY RATHBONE

Most of the productions listed are by professional companies, but some amateur productions and adaptations are included. Information is taken from programmes, supplemented by reviews, held in the Birmingham Shakespeare Library. Details have been verified wherever possible, but the nature of the material prevents corroboration in every case.

ANTONY AND CLEOPATRA

Commonweal Theatre Company, the Shaw Theatre, London and tour of South West England: 9 April 1991
Director: Tony Hegarty
Music/Enobarbus: Max Hafler
Antony: Andrew McDonald
Cleopatra: Susan Curnow
The set used Egyptian lettering to symbolize Egypt and Roman to symbolize Rome. The Romans, in black, recalled Mussolini's Fascists.

Talawa Theatre Company, the Everyman Theatre, Liverpool and tour: 24 April 1991
Director: Yvonne Brewster
Designer: Helen Turner
Antony: Jeffery Kissoon
Cleopatra: Dona Croll
An all-black cast.

Birmingham Repertory Theatre: 6 April–4 May 1991
Director: John Adams

Designer: Roger Butlin
Antony: Malcolm Tierney
Cleopatra: Sylvia Syms
A traditional production.

Adaptation

All for Love by John Dryden
The Almeida Theatre, Islington, London: 25 April 1991
Director: Jonathan Kent
Designers: Peter J. Davison and Sue Willmington
Music: Jonathan Dove
Antony: James Laurenson
Cleopatra: Diana Rigg

AS YOU LIKE IT

Broken Seal at the Shakespeare Globe Museum, London: 17–19 July 1991

Cheek by Jowl at the Opera House, Buxton and tour: 3 September 1991–
Director: Declan Donnellan
Designer: Nick Ormerod
Music: Paddy Cunneen
Rosalind: Adrian Lester
An all-male cast. The production received some excellent reviews.

The Crucible Theatre, Sheffield: 15 November–7 December 1991. Director: Mark Brickman

Designer: Johan Engels
Music: Howard Goodall
Rosalind: Suzan Sylvester
A traditional production, with a good contrast between the court and forest scenes.

Adaptation

Wicked Bastard of Venus
The Custard Factory, Birmingham at the Edinburgh Fringe and touring: August 1991–
A re-working of *As You Like It* incorporating speeches from *Twelfth Night* in an exploration of sexual relationships.

THE COMEDY OF ERRORS

The RSC, Newcastle and the Barbican, London. Transfer from Stratford. See *Shakespeare Survey 45*

The Acting Company, Jeanetta Cochran Theatre, London, and tour with *Romeo and Juliet*: 12 March 1991–

The Mercury Theatre, Colchester: September–October 1991
Director: Michael Winter
Designer: India Smith

The Drum Theatre, Plymouth Theatre Royal: 6–16 November 1991
Director: Amanda Knott
Designer: Jo Hughes
The Drum Theatre was transformed into a Shakespearian playhouse, modelled on the Globe. The production was acted by an all-male cast, in period costume.

The Comedie of Errors
The Mermaid Theatre, London: 12 December 1991
A single improvised performance, supposedly re-creating the un-rehearsed conditions of the Elizabethan theatre. The First Folio Text was used.

Adaptations

Odd Socks Clown Theatre, Netley Abbey: 12 May and 11 August 1991
An adaptation for three actors.

Livespace Theatre Company, Norfolk at Aberdeen Arts Centre and tour: September 1991–
Director: Mike Jones
A re-working of the original, set in *Our Man in Havana*, Graham Greene land.

CORIOLANUS

The English Shakespeare Company, 1990 tour continues. See *Shakespeare Survey 45*.

CYMBELINE

Wales Actors Company, open air production touring Welsh castles: August 1991–
Director: Ruth Garnault
Imogen: Nickie Rainsford
A cast of seven. The production also played at the Edinburgh Necropolis.

HAMLET

Brunton Theatre Company, Musselburgh: January 1991
Director/Fortinbras: Charlie Nowosielski
Designer: Nick Sargent
Hamlet: Andrew Price
Fortinbras was brought on stage at the beginning of the action, and remained to watch events unfold. This Hamlet actively enjoyed the game of wits.

Bristol Old Vic: 21 March–27 April 1991
Director: Paul Unwin
Designer: Bunny Christie
Hamlet: Iain Glen
Excellent reviews. Iain Glen also played Hamlet in the film version of *Rosencrantz and Guildenstern are Dead*.

Moving Being; St Stephen's Theatre Space, Cardiff: 14 May–8 June 1991
In repertory with Heiner Müller's *Hamlet-machine*.

Theatre Clwyd, Mold and tour: 27 November 1991–
Director: Toby Robertson
Designer: Alana Guinn
Music: Donald Fraser
Hamlet: Geraint Wyn Davies
Gertrude: Martin McKellan
Casting a man as Gertrude gave Claudius' court an atmosphere of degeneracy, since the gender of the actor was unmistakable. The costumes and set were mainly red, with Hamlet in black. Fortinbras was portrayed as another degenerate usurper.

Film version

Hamlet, directed by Franco Zeffirelli, UK première: April 1991
Carolco Films
Designer: Dante Ferretti
Music: Ennio Morricone
Hamlet: Mel Gibson
Gertrude: Glenn Close
Claudius: Alan Bates
The Ghost: Paul Scofield
Polonius: Ian Holm
Ophelia: Helena Bonham-Carter
Generally well reviewed. The sensual portrayal of Gertrude was central to this production.

Adaptations

Hamlet/Hamlet by Antony Peters
The Performance Theatre Company at the Oval House, London: March 1991

Hameretto Yamato Nishikei (Hamlet, a Woodblock Print of Japan, or, a Yamato Brocade Print of *Hamlet*) by Robun Kanagaki
The Tokyo Globe Company at the Mermaid Theatre, London: 19–28 September 1991.

Also seen in Newcastle and Dublin
Director: Kohji Orita
Designer: Arata Isozaki
Hamlet/Ophelia: Somegoro Ichikawa
Written in 1886 and, according to the *Observer* review, not performed until now. Premièred in Tokyo during the World Shakespeare Congress, 1991. A Kabuki adaptation set in the Meiji period. The male star played both Hamlet and Ophelia in a slow, stylized production which emphasized the soliloquies.

HENRY IV Part I

The RSC at the Royal Shakespeare Theatre, Stratford: 25 March 1991–
Director: Adrian Noble
Designer: Bob Crowley
Music: Edward Gregson
Henry, Prince of Wales: Michael Maloney
King Henry IV: Julian Glover
Falstaff: Robert Stephens

HENRY IV Part II

The RSC at the Royal Shakespeare Theatre, Stratford, 23 May 1991–

HENRY V

Stafford Shakespeare Company, Stafford Castle: 8 August 1991–
Director: Geoffrey Davies
Costume designer: Richard Scollins
Music: Alastair Farrant and Annabel Blakeney
Henry V: Andrew Barrow
The Stafford Shakespeare Company was formed for this production by a mixed amateur and professional cast.

Chaos Theatre and the Brewery Players at the Nicol Centre, Cirencester and tour: August 1991–
Director: Phil Morle
Henry V: Damian Brent

HENRY VIII (*All is True*)

Chichester Festival Theatre: 22 May 1991–
Director: Ian Judge
Designer: Russell Craig
Music: Nigel Hess
Henry VIII: Keith Michell
Catherine: Dorothy Tutin
The set juxtaposed a modern office block with a mural of sixteenth-century London.

JULIUS CAESAR

Arts Threshold, London: November 1991
Director: Siddiq El Fadil
Designer: Thomasina Smith
The production was set in a modern Eastern bloc state.

The RSC at the Royal Shakespeare Theatre, Stratford: 24 October 1991–
Director: Steven Pimlott
Designer: Tobias Hoheisel
Music: Peter Salem
Julius Caesar: Robert Stephens
Brutus: Jonathan Hyde
Antony: Owen Teale

KING LEAR

The RSC, Newcastle and the Barbican, London. Transfer from Stratford. See *Shakespeare Survey 45*.

The National Theatre, British and world tour, with *Richard III*. See *Shakespeare Survey 45* for this 1990 production.

Sharers and Hirelings at the Duke's Theatre Club, Richmond: 29 October–23 November, 1991
Director: Dermot O'Brien
Lear: Kenneth McClellen
A new theatre company which intends to produce classical plays without compromising the text.

The Rose Theatre Company, London and tour: November 1991–
A workshop production which used minimal props and emphasized the primacy of the language.

Adaptations

Lear, an operatic version
The London Coliseum: 6–26 March 1991
Music: Aribert Reimann
Designer: Eberhard Matthies
Lear: Monte Jaffe
First performed: Munich 1978

The Banyu Inryoku Company, the Mermaid Theatre, London, Stratford, and Cardiff: 22 October 1991–
Director: J. A. Seazer
Lear: Keitoku Takata
This Japanese company combines acrobatic dance techniques, Western percussion, with the stylized theatrical make-up of the Japanese theatre in a unique blend of dance/drama pioneered by Shuji Terayama. Produced in the UK as part of the 1991 Japan Festival.

LOVE'S LABOUR'S LOST

The RSC, Newcastle and the Barbican, London. Transfer from Stratford. See *Shakespeare Survey 45*.

MACBETH

Traffic of the Stage, Windsor Arts Centre and national tour: 9 February 1991–
Director/designer: Tom Leatherbarrow
Macbeth: James Reynard
A traditional production.

Zip Theatre, Lichfield Arts Centre and tour: May 1991–
Director: Jon Lingard-Lane
Designer: Alison Ashton
Music: Tim Hubball and Alison Ashton

Macbeth: Tony Neilson
A very bloody production which had excellent reviews. The Porter, played by Cathy Pemberton, the serving woman and Seyton appeared as the Witches. The set was composed of tubular steel poles.

Regent's Park Open Air Theatre, London: 12 June 1991–
Director: William Gaunt
Designer: Bruno Santani
Music: Julie Cooper and Hugh Wooldridge
Macbeth: Peter Woodward

Ludlow Castle: 20 June–7 July 1991–
Director: Alan Cohen
Designer: Claire Lyth
Music: Michael Gregory
Macbeth: David Rintoul
A production which fully utilized the natural setting of Ludlow Castle, and had excellent reviews.

Third I productions, Man in the Moon Theatre Club, London: 3–18 September 1991
Directors: Mike Burgess and Troy Webb
A cast of five, using a cut text in a production described by reviewers as compelling. Considerable use was made of masks and mime. The set was dungeon-like.

The Northcott Theatre, Exeter: 24 September–12 October 1991
Director: John Durnin
Designer: Jessica Tyrwhitt
Lighting: Chris Ward
Macbeth: Colin Haigh
Set in a wooden circle surrounded by a trough of water. Beyond the circle the actors sat waiting for their cues. The lighting was the main feature of this set, and was used to suggest a smoking cauldron, the bars of a cage, and other effects.

The Schiller Theatre of Berlin at the Tivoli Theatre, Dublin: October 1991–
Director/Hecate/Porter: Katherina Thalbach

Macbeth: Markus Völlenklee
Produced as part of the Irish Life Dublin Theatre Festival. A very bloody production which portrayed Duncan as senile and vicious, and Malcolm as an effeminate wastrel. Excellent reviews.

Nottingham Playhouse: October 1991
Director: Pip Broughton
Designer: Jackie Gunn
Music: John McGlynn
A modern-dress production.

Adaptations

Solo Macbeth Rob Inglis solo performance at the Rose Theatre, London and schools: January 1991–
Five masks represented Lady Macbeth and the witches in a performance which focused on Macbeth's mental deterioration and was intended for schools audiences.

The Scottish Play, or, The Macbeth of the Football Pitch by Ian Brown
Perth Theatre and Scottish schools: 18 February 1991–
Director: Ken Alexander
Designer: Phili Josephs
A Theatre in Education project, performed with a shortened version of *Macbeth* adapted by John Clifford. Played in modern Scots accents with some key speeches from the original in Scots dialect.

Akogun by Rufus Orisayomi
Ritual Theatre Arts, London: 3–6 June 1991

Macbeth
Odd Socks Clown Theatre at Netley Abbey: 14 July and 13 October 1991
An adaptation for three actors.

Ubu-Roi with scenes from *Macbeth*
The National Theatre of Craiova, Romania at the Empire Theatre, Edinburgh: 16, 18–20 August 1991

Direction, adaptation, design and costumes: Silviu Purcarete
Music: Nicu Alifantis
Macbeth: Tudor Gheorghe
Jarry's *Ubu-roi* was intercut with scenes from *Macbeth* conveying the themes of political corruption and inhumanity. First performed 29 December 1990.

Macbeth
Antony Glen one-man show: Edinburgh Fringe and tour: September 1991–
A text cut to less than an hour and intended for schools performance.

MEASURE FOR MEASURE

Compass Theatre (Sheffield) touring production: June 1991–
Director: Neil Sissons
Isabella: Helen Franklin
Performed by a cast of six using minimal props and set. The production opened at the Tokyo Globe.

Theatre Set Up, tour of open air sites: June 1991–
Director: Wendy McPhee
Isabella/Juliet: Lucy Curtin
Set in the Victorian period.

The RSC at the Other Place, Stratford and tour: 18 September 1991–
Director: Trevor Nunn
Designer: Maria Björnson
Lighting: Chris Parry
Isabella: Claire Skinner
Angelo: David Haig
The RSC/BT tour, with *The Blue Angel*.

Plymouth Shakespeare Project at the Barbican, Plymouth: September 1991–
Director: Jojo Moreschi
Designer: Alison Watters
Isabella: Jane Richards

A community theatre project intended to make Shakespeare accessible to young people. Good reviews.

Rainbow Theatre, The Cockpit, London and tour: 23 October 1991–
Director: Nicolas Young
Designers: Alison Buckhurst and Matthew Kinley

Adaptation

Dear Isabel
The Custard Factory, Birmingham, Edinburgh Fringe and tour with *The Wicked Bastard of Venus*: 12 August 1991–
Directors: Clayton Buffoni and Julie-Anne Robinson
Isabel: Rachel Gartside
Angelo: Nick Segalle
Claudio: Jacqui O'Hanlon
A free adaptation for three actors which leaves Angelo triumphant.

THE MERCHANT OF VENICE

Compass Theatre Company, 1990 tour continues. See *Shakespeare Survey 45*.

The English Shakespeare Company, 1990 tour continues. See *Shakespeare Survey 45*.

Simply Shakespeare at Camden Lock: November 1991
Simply Shakespeare is a new professional company which hopes to perform Shakespeare once or twice a year.

THE MERRY WIVES OF WINDSOR

Kent Repertory Company at Hever Castle: August 1991
Director: Richard Palmer
Falstaff: Michael Powell
An open-air production.

Adaptation

Falstaff
The Mansaku Company at the Mermaid Theatre, London: 12–16 November 1991, also performed in Cardiff, and Stratford.
A Kyogen comic adaptation presented as part of the Japan Festival. Falstaff became a classic Kyogen character, a braggart Samurai. Played in traditional fourteenth-century style Kyogen costumes.

A MIDSUMMER NIGHT'S DREAM

Orchard Theatre Company, The Plough Theatre, Torrington and tour of the West of England: 15 February 1991–
Director: Bill Buffery
Designer: Meg Surrey
Music: Tom Nordon
A modern-dress production.

Regent's Park Open Air Theatre: 28 May 1991–
Director: Ian Talbot
Designer: Paul Farnsworth
Music: Mark Emney
Bottom: Roy Hudd
Very good reviews

Theatre Worx, The Plantation Gardens, Norwich and tour of Norfolk and Suffolk: 20 June 1991–
Director: Michelle Beavis

Footsbarn Travelling Theatre, Highbury Fields, London: 20–30 June 1991 and world tour.
World première, The Playhouse, Adelaide Festival Centre, Australia Festival Centre, Australia, 9 June 1990.
The text was adapted and modernized, Puck's part entirely reduced to bird-like whistling calls. Masks, dance and mime were used in an innovative and exciting production. Footsbarn create their work as an ensemble.

The Comedy Theatre of Bucharest at the Lyric Theatre, Hammersmith and tour: 6 July 1991–
Director: Alex Darie
Oberon/Theseus/Quince: Serban Ionescu
Performed in Romanian in a circus setting, with Oberon/Quince acting as director. The production emphasized the sexual elements of the play.

Cleveland Theatre Company, the Valley Gardens, Saltburn: 17 July–10 August 1991
Director: Alasdair Ramsay
Designer: Francis O'Connor
Music: Stuart Johnson
A promenade production set in the Victorian period, with mechanicals doubling as elves.

Dream Makers Ltd with Attic Theatre, Cannizaro Park, Wimbledon: 26–31 August 1991
Director: Leo Dolan
Designer: Roger Frith
A cast of amateurs, professionals and drama students.

A-One Theatre Company, Jackson's Lane Community Centre, London: September 1991
A mixed amateur and professional cast.

Magnificent Theatre Company, The Guildhall Arts Centre, Grantham and tour: 1 October 1991–
Director: Mark Brewer
Designer: Kit Line
Set in the Commonwealth with Theseus and Egeus costumed in Puritan black and Puck as a baby-faced satyr.

Adaptations

The Pocket Dream by Sandy Toksvig and Ellie Brewer
Nottingham Playhouse: 31 January–19 February and 25 April–18 May 1991
Director: Pip Broughton
Designer: Jacqueline Gunn
A successful farce. The cast of *A Midsummer Night's Dream* having failed to appear, the

theatre management stage an impromptu version. Mike McShane resplendent as Oberon in a cloak of artificial grass, Sandi Toksvig on wires as an air-sick Puck.

Bottom's Dream
Movingstage Marionette Company on their barge, London: October 1991
First performed 1983

MUCH ADO ABOUT NOTHING

The RSC, Newcastle and the Barbican, London. Transfer from Stratford. See *Shakespeare Survey 45*.

The Nuffield Theatre, Southampton: 11 April–4 May 1991
Director: Patrick Sandford
Designer: Robin Don

OTHELLO

The Swan Theatre, Worcester: 14–30 November 1991
Director: Pat Trueman
Designer: Sally Howard
Othello: David Harewood
Set in the 1930s.

PERICLES

Galleon at the Shakespeare Globe Museum, London: November 1991

RICHARD II

The RSC, Newcastle and the Barbican, London. Transfer from Stratford. See *Shakespeare Survey 45*.

The Redgrave Theatre, Farnham: 3 October–2 November 1991
Director: Graham Watkins
Designer: Colin Winslow
Richard: Christopher Cazenove

RICHARD III

The Royal National Theatre, British and world tour, with *King Lear*. See *Shakespeare Survey 45*.

Adaptation

Cambridge Experimental Theatre: 23 January 1991–
An adaptation for three actors.

ROMEO AND JULIET

The Acting Company, the Jeanetta Cochran Theatre, London: 12–16 March 1991, and tour, with *The Comedy of Errors*.

Factotum Theatre Company, the New Hereford Theatre, Hereford and tour: March 1991–
Director: Alastair Palmer
Designer: Judy Reaves
Romeo: Iain Baker
Juliet: Karen Gisbourne

The RSC at the Royal Shakespeare Theatre, Stratford: 22 August 1991–
Director: David Leveaux
Designer: Alison Chitty
Music: Ilona Sekacz
Romeo: Michael Maloney
Juliet: Clare Holman

The Gate Theatre, Dublin: 9 April 1991–
Director: Alan Stanford
Designer: Robert Ballagh
Romeo: Darragh Kelly
Juliet: Hilary Reynolds
Set in southern Italy in the late 1920s. Excellent reviews.

Re-action Theatre, Queen's Park, Brighton: 14–18 May 1991
Director: Robin Mannell
Music: Steven Wrigley

Plymouth Shakespeare Project, the Drum Theatre, Plymouth Royal: 5–8 June 1991
Director: Jojo Moreschi
Music: Alan Kennedy
Romeo: David Bell
Juliet: Shaney Murphy
A community theatre production with a cast of local actors

The Royal Lyceum Theatre, Edinburgh and Scottish tour: 25 October 1991–
Director: Ian Wooldridge
Designer: Paul Edwards
Romeo: Oliver Hayden
Juliet: Indra Ove
Two scenes and some dialogue were cut in this modern-dress production which had a minimal, monochrome set.

Harrogate Theatre: 30 October–16 November 1991
Director: Andrew Manley
Designer: Paul Edwards
Romeo: Nick Waring
Juliet: Beth Goddard

Adaptations

Julia
An opera by Rudolf Kelterborn. The Queen Elizabeth Hall, London and tour: 3 August 1991–
Director: David Freeman
Designer: David Rodger
Three inter-woven stories: *Romeo and Juliet*, Gottfried Keller's novel *A Village Romeo and Juliet* and the story of a contemporary Julia, set in West Bank Jordan. First performed at the Operafactory, Zurich, 23 April 1991, with subsequent tour of Eastern Europe.

Romeo and Juliet, a new ballet version to Prokofiev's music.
Northern Ballet Company, Blackpool Grand Theatre and tour: 12 February 1991–
Choreography: Massino Moricone

Director: Christopher Gable
Designer: Les Brotherston

Odd Socks Clown Theatre at Netley Abbey: 9 June and 8 September 1991
An adaptation for three actors.

Imule, Edinburgh Festival Fringe: 19–31 August 1991 and tour
A company of four from Exeter in an adaptation inspired by Yoruba tribal art. The tour continued into 1992.

THE TAMING OF THE SHREW

The RSC/BT 1990 tour continues. See *Shakespeare Survey 45*. The RSC production at Stratford, 1992, was based on this touring production.

The Rose Theatre Club, London: 19 May 1991–
Director: David Beaton
A modern-dress production with four male servants played as women in, according to reviews, a rather forced feminist reading.

The New End Theatre, Hampstead: 28 October 1991–
Director: Dee Hart
Designer: Sarah Deane
Petruchio: John Hay
Katherine: Debbie Radcliffe
Set in a 1930s riding school, with Petruchio 'breaking in' Katherine.

Adaptation

Pushkala Gopal and Unnikrishnan, tour continues. See *Shakespeare Survey 45*.
The production was radically re-worked in 1991.

THE TEMPEST

Buttonhole Theatre Company at the Rose Theatre Club, London: 1–25 May 1991
Director: Christopher Geelan

Designer: Bridget Kimak
Music: Matthew White
Prospero: David Verrey
A modern-dress production set on a white floor with a simple scaffold. The masque was based on Punch and Judy.

Phoebus Cart with Daylight Theatre at the Rollright Stones, Corfe Castle and the Shakespeare Globe site, London: 1 June 1991–
Director/Prospero: Mark Rylance
Designer: Jenny Tiramani
Music: Claire Van Kampen
Played in the round with four stages around the edge of the circle representing Earth, Air, Fire and Water. The play was seen as an encoded representation of the cyclic pattern of natural law. Production consultant, Peter Dawkins.

Pendley Theatre Company at the Limelight, Aylesbury and tour: June 1991–
Director: Andrew Bolton

The Oxford Stage Company, the Lawn, Lincoln and tour: 19 July 1991–
Director: John Retallack
Music: Howard Goodall
Prospero: Richard Durden
Set in the 1930s. The production also toured to the Tokyo Globe Theatre. Ariel was played by a woman, Diane Parish.

Daylight Theatre at the Edinburgh Fringe: 5–10 August 1991
Director: Susan Colverd
Prospero: Hugh Young
Played with *Prospero's Magic Book*, an adaptation for children. The company is involved in Shakespeare study weekends run by Sir George Trevelyan and Peter Dawkins, and also took part in Mark Rylance's production of *The Tempest*.

Prospero at the Gates of Dawn by Camden McDonald

Roar Material at the Harlequin's Theatre, Northwich and tour: 7 September 1991–

Thorndike Young People's Theatre, the Thorndike Theatre, Leatherhead and tour of local schools: December 1991
Director: Beth Wood
Four actors in a workshop production which used the pupils and taped voices in minor roles.

TIMON OF ATHENS

The Young Vic Company at the Young Vic, London: 28 February–10 April 1991
Adapted and directed by Trevor Nunn.
Designer: John Gunter
Timon: David Suchet
Apemantus: Barry Foster
For the first half the abstract set resembled the skyscrapers of a modern city. For the second half the stage became a refuse tip. The action was preceded by a bandit hold-up in which the victim was shot. This appeared to give added dramatic significance to Alcibiades' plea for mercy for the soldier who has killed a man, and also provided the buried treasure found by Timon. The confrontation between Timon and Apemantus in the second half was a particularly effective passage in a compelling production which received excellent reviews.

Adaptation

Timon of Athens, an opera by Stephen Oliver
The English National Opera at the London Coliseum: 17 May 1991–
World première
Director: Chris Dyer
Timon: Monte Jaffe
Scored for male voices only and set in an austere grey concrete box.

TITUS ANDRONICUS

The RSC, Newcastle and the Barbican, London. Transfer from Stratford. See *Shakespeare Survey 45*.

Adaptation

Titus Anatomy, Fall of Rome by Heiner Müller
Index Theatre, Manchester: 23 October
1991–
First produced Germany, 1985 under the title
Anatomie Titus, Fall of Rome, ein Shakespear-kommentar

TWELFTH NIGHT

Dundee Repertory Theatre: 7 February–2
March 1991
Director: Cliff Burnett
Designer: Monika Nisbet
Music: Iain Johnstone
Viola: Clare Marchionne
Set in India, with a largely Asian cast.

The Peter Hall Company, Sheffield Lyceum,
the Playhouse, London and tour; 12 February
1991–
Director: Peter Hall
Designer: Timothy O'Brien
Music: Stephen Edwards
Viola: Maria Miles
Malvolio: Eric Porter
A traditional period production with an
autumnal set in rich reds and golds.

The New Victoria Theatre, Stoke on Trent: 27
February–30 March 1991
Director: Bob Eaton
Designer: Lis Evans
Music: Bob Eaton
Viola: Andriana Carroll
Set in the 1960s to rock music. The androgyny
of Viola and Sebastian was emphasized.

The RSC at the Royal Shakespeare Theatre,
Stratford: 6 April 1991–
Director: Griff Rhys Jones
Designer: Ultz
Music: Ilona Sekacz
Viola: Sylvestre Le Touzel

D.P. Productions at the Tyne Theatre and Opera
House, Newcastle and tour: 9 April 1991–
Director/Sebastian: Ian Dickens
Designer: Mike Byrne
Viola: Lisa Marks
Set in Regency Bath.

The Cambridge Theatre Company, the Play-
house, Newcastle and tour: 4 June 1991–
Director: Nancy Diuguid
Designer: Bettina Munzer
Music: Orlando Gough
Viola/Sebastian: Pamela Nomvete
Orsino/Olivia: Vernon Gudgeon
A gender-bending production which received
mixed reviews.

The Duke's Playhouse, promenade production
in Williamson Park, Lancaster: 6 June 1991–
Director: Jon Pope
Designer: Julian Crouch
Viola: Bea Comins

London Bubble, performing in their tent in
London parks: 3 June–31 August 1991
Director: Jonathan Petherbridge
Designer: Pip Nash
Viola: Clare Perkins

The English Shakespeare Company, Notting-
ham Theatre Royal and tour: 1 November 1991–
Director/Lighting: Michael Bodganov
Designer: Claire Lyth
Music: Terry Mortimer
Viola: Jenny Quayle
A modern-dress production.

The London Shakespeare Group at the Ware-
house Theatre, Croydon and tour: 29 October
1991–
Director: Delena Kidd

THE TWO GENTLEMEN OF VERONA

The RSC at the Royal Shakespeare Theatre,
Stratford: 6 April 1991–

Director: David Thacker
Designer: Shelagh Keegan
Music: Guy Woolfenden
Valentine: Richard Bonneville
Proteus: Barry Lynch

THE WINTER'S TALE

The English Shakespeare Company tour continues. See *Shakespeare Survey 45*.

Leicester Haymarket Theatre Studio and tour of the Midlands: 21 January 1992–
Director: Simon Usher
Designer: Anthony Lamble
Music: Gavin Bryars
Leontes: Kevin Costello
Hermione/Perdita: Valeria Gogan
The interpretation of the role of Hermione considerably distorted the spirit of the play. A real statue was used in the final scene. Hermione herself hobbled on, with a wooden leg and smoking a cigarette.

The Salberg Studio, Salisbury Playhouse: 17 April–4 May 1991
Director: Deborah Paige
Designer: Moggie Douglas
Leontes/Old Shepherd: George Irving
Hermione: Helen Schlesinger
A modern-dress production which received good reviews.

The Young Vic, London: 12 September 1991–
Director: David Thacker
Designer: Shelagh Keegan
Leontes: Trevor Eve
Hermione: Rudi Davies
Autolycus: Barrie Rutter
Played in a sunken circular wooden arena.

Barebones Theatre, Bristol, at St Austell Arts Centre: 9 November 1991–
Director: Nick Benson
The company are described as part-time professional.

POEMS AND SONNETS

The Taking of Choice by Matthew Jones
Spiral Candle Theatre Company, Link Theatre, London: May 1991
Director: Trent Jones
A play set in the present day, based on *The Rape of Lucrece*, about a man who rapes his friend's wife through envy.

Sweet Sessions, devised by Paul Godfrey and Nancy Meckler. Tour: 15 March 1991–
Director: Nancy Meckler
Designer: Tim Hatley
Music: Peter Salem
A twentieth-century critic trying to solve the mystery of Shakespeare's sonnets acts out the feelings of love and jealousy which they describe.

MISCELLANEOUS

God say Amen
Excerpts from the history plays compiled by Michael Bogdanov and Michael Pennington.
The English Shakespeare Company, the Wyvern Arts Centre, Swindon and tour: 4 February 1991–
Director: Susanna Best
Huge cartoons of Saddam Hussain and Margaret Thatcher were used to relate the extracts from the history plays to modern politics.

Burbage and the Bard by Jonathan Milton and Stan Pretty
Travelling Light Theatre Company, Stratford, and touring: January 1991–
A comic two-hander.

Bill Shakespeare and Ben Jonson
Shakespeare Globe Museum: 17 April–2 May 1991
Andrew Tansey in a one-man show.

A little touch of Shakespeare
Pentameters Theatre Club, the Three Horseshoes, London: 4 June 1991–

Director/Designer: Tom Leatherbarrow

Me and Shakespeare
The Edinburgh Fringe Festival: 22–27 August
1991
Colin George one-man show giving a portrait
of Shakespeare as schoolboy and actor.

*An Evening with Shakespeare Kyogen and Tradi-
tional Kyogen*
The Izumi School of Kyogen, Japan at the
Shakespeare Globe Museum, London: 16 and

17 September 1991, Queen Elizabeth Hall,
Stratford: 20 and 21 September 1991
Extracts from *Twelfth Night, A Midsummer
Night's Dream* and *The Taming of the Shrew*.

Prospero's Children
The Orange Tree Theatre, Richmond, and
local tour: 4 November 1991–
Scenes from *A Midsummer Night's Dream,
Twelfth Night, Romeo and Juliet* and *The
Tempest*
Director: Peter Leslie Wild
Commissioned by the local education authority.

THE YEAR'S CONTRIBUTIONS TO SHAKESPEARE STUDIES

1. CRITICAL STUDIES
reviewed by DAVID LINDLEY

GENERAL STUDIES AND COLLECTIONS

Shakespeare criticism is under particular pressure at the moment. The clash of different critical perspectives has been a constant feature of these surveys, but Ivo Kamps' collection of essays, *Shakespeare Left and Right* (New York and London: Routledge, 1991), which begins with four papers originally presented at a Special Session of the MLA on 'The Role of Ideology', powerfully indicates the ways in which the internal squabbles of the academy have suddenly come to matter in the world outside. In Britain, the Conservative Government's co-option of Shakespeare in their attack on 'lefty' teaching in schools has an analogous effect in the focusing of critical minds, and to that challenge Lesley Aers and Nigel Wheale respond with their anthology *Shakespeare in the Changing Curriculum* (London and New York: Routledge, 1991). Whatever one might think of these collections, and both have a tendency to a strident querulousness, their effect is to superimpose upon familiar questions of the relationship between text and critic an urgent need to focus on the relationship of literary criticism to the audience for whom it is written. But one of the sharpest perceptions that come from attempting such a survey as this is a depressing sense of a fragmented landscape where critics call only to the like-minded, a feeling which becomes stronger as the volume of work continues to grow. (There is little sign of a world recession in Shakespeare criticism, and the plenitude of book-length studies has forced an even more restricted notice of critical articles in this year's survey.)

These issues are directly addressed in Alan Sinfield's *Faultlines: Cultural Materialism and the Politics of Dissident Reading* (Oxford: Clarendon Press, 1992) which puts the activity of the critic at the centre of a wide-ranging work, explicitly seeking to expose the contradictions and undecidabilities of texts and the politics of their reception. In chapters on *Macbeth* and *Henry V*, in discussions of character and subjectivity focusing on Desdemona, Olivia and Lady Macbeth, and in an exploration of the uncomfortable overlap between Senecan and Calvinist perspectives in Renaissance tragedy Sinfield pursues his announced purpose of 'contesting' the 'powerful cultural tokens' of Shakespeare's plays with learning, wit and subtlety. The last and longest chapter passionately argues for the necessity of resisting the appropriation of Shakespeare by the politics of the new right and the professionalization of the Englit industry through 'reversing the move away from subcultures of class, ethnicity, gender, and sexuality. We should seek ways to break out of the professional subculture and work intellectually (not just live personally) in dissident subcultures' (p. 294). The clarion-call to action is powerfully articulated, but runs a considerable risk of self-righteous exclusiveness. What, after all, is a white, heterosexual, middle-class and middle-aged male to do?

Terence Hawkes approaches issues related to those that animate Sinfield's book in his *Meaning by Shakespeare*. He claims, again and again, that 'Shakespeare's plays have no essential meanings, but function as resources which we use to generate meaning for our own purposes.' The essays have all Hawkes's usual wit in bringing together scraps of diverse information – *Coriolanus* and T. S. Eliot are allied one with the other through the mediation of Victor Sylvester (premier dance-band leader and war-time member of a firing-squad) in one essay, while another (more cogently, perhaps) examines the implications of the choice of *Coriolanus* as the play to be performed at the Stratford Festival in the year of the General Strike. It is possible to smile at the ingenuity of Hawkes's writing, to accede in part to his claim that Shakespeare 'exists' in readings and appropriations of him, while at the same time growing increasingly impatient at the abandonment of any possibility of claiming that Shakespeare's plays are significant in current cultural and political debate precisely because their actual richness and complexity as texts is what enables them to be fought over, and always to evade capture. Nigel Wheale complains justly that the Radical Academic (Hawkes himself) who in a TV programme refused to debate questions of the value of Shakespeare with the then Secretary of Education 'denying that Hamlet existed' left the ground for argument vacant, and a space for conservatism to occupy as it will.

As an apparent contrast to these highly politicized books come two long and weighty studies, René Girard's *A Theater of Envy* (New York and Oxford: Oxford University Press, 1991) and Ted Hughes's *Shakespeare and the Goddess of Complete Being* (London: Faber and Faber, 1992). Neither floats itself upon the raft of reference that the academy increasingly demands as sign of authority; both are engaged in reading Shakespeare from the perspective of a single idea; both claim that they are uncovering something that is 'there' in the texts. Girard sees Shakespeare as intensely and continuously preoccupied with what he terms 'mimetic desire'. In the comedies erotic desire is presented as always constructed out of emulation; in its simplest form the lover desires because the object is desired by someone else, or is forced to generate a mediator who will guarantee the lover's desire. *Troilus and Cressida* is the darkest version and Pandarus the embodiment of the essential mediator/creator of passion. In a wider context the scapegoat is generated as focus for the emulous envy of the crowd, and *Julius Caesar* becomes the play where 'the violent essence of theater and human culture is revealed' (p. 223). As a critical tool, Girard's concepts can yield local insights into the plays – in the case of the vertiginous switchings of the lovers in *A Midsummer Night's Dream*, or the 'foundational violence' of Caesar's murder, for example. But there is a very odd rhetoric at work in the course of the book. The few footnotes virtually all refer us to Girard's own earlier works; other critics are frequently berated, but almost never named or quoted; Shakespeare himself is imagined as appealing to an audience of 'initiates' able to recognize the truths of his analysis of mimetic desire, while palliating the 'groundlings' with plots that can satisfy their meagre capacities. The overall effect is one of hermetic closure and hermeneutic circularity, in which, ultimately, Shakespeare is patted on the back for anticipating the truths of Girard's anthropological theories.

Like Girard, Ted Hughes imagines that two dramas are being performed simultaneously, 'one for the public who wants to be entertained, and one for Shakespeare himself – and, it may be, a small circle of initiates' (p. 108). But unlike Girard, he claims to be disclosing Shakespeare's deployment of a mythic understanding of the world which was explicitly available, if only to certain spirits, at the time of his writing. His thesis is that in his two early narrative poems Shakespeare articulated a mythic combination subsequently explored in all the plays from *All's Well* to *The Tempest*. This combination, which Hughes calls the 'Tragic Equation', is of the Adonis who rejects Venus and then, gored by the Boar, becomes the ravisher Tarquin. The story of Shakespeare's work is the struggle to heal the double disabling of the male, a task only finally achieved in Prospero's defeat of the Boar, represented in Caliban. Upon this frame Hughes erects a work of high fantastic elaboration, syncretic in its absorption of mythic types, freewheeling in its quasi-allegorical treatment of the two stories of Venus and Adonis and the Rape of Lucrece (as the primal myths of Catholicism and Protestantism, or as the left and right hemispheres of the brain, for example) and permitting the absorption of some highly questionable biographical details. Hughes warns that 'everything depends on acquiring the simple polaroids that enable one to see through the surface glitter of the plot into the depth of the mythic plane' (p. 39). How far readers will be prepared to follow him depends entirely upon their readiness to don these particular spectacles.

Not the least important reason for the success of feminist criticism(s) has been the sense that such literary activity has a significant connection to the world in which students live. Several of this year's books testify to the variety and vitality of feminist work and to its continuous evolution. Of the critical approaches currently in vogue the psychoanalytic is normally that with which I make least contact. It is all the more surprising, then, that Janet Adelman's *Suffocating Mothers: Fantasies of Maternal Origin in Shakespeare's Plays* (New York and London: Routledge, 1992) should have proved the most compelling of all the 'big thesis' books I have encountered this year. Its central proposition is that *Hamlet* is the first major play in which the

mother 'occluded in [the earlier] plays returns with a vengeance' and that 'from *Hamlet* on, all sexual relationships will be tinged by the threat of the mother, all masculine identity problematically formed in relationship to her' (p. 35). She traverses Shakespeare's subsequent writing career, from *Troilus and Cressida* and *Othello*, seen as problematic rewritings of 'The Phoenix and the Turtle's' impossible desire for a perfect union from which sexuality is excised, through the increasing desperation of the problem comedies and later tragedies to a bleak climax as Timon's 'fantasy of male bounty' turns into extreme misogyny. Crucially, *Antony and Cleopatra* is able 'for one fragile moment ... to imagine the possibility of a maternal space that is neither suffocating nor deforming' (p. 191). The Romances conclude her survey, and while *The Winter's Tale* emerges as an 'astonishing psychic achievement' in which 'Shakespeare figures the loss and recovery of the world in the mother's body' (p. 235), *The Tempest* is barely discussed since it 'unmakes Paulina's female space ... reinstating absolute paternal authority with a vengeance' (p. 237). What makes Adelman's book so successful is the development of the central thesis through scrupulous attention to textual detail, and consideration not merely of the psychic identity of individual characters but of the shape and structure of each play. This means that, resistant though I am to the psychoanalytic motor, I find myself continually responding with delight to this very fine book.

There are connections between Adelman's book and Valerie Traub's *Desire and Anxiety: Circulations of Sexuality in Shakespearian Drama* (London and New York: Routledge, 1992), for she argues that the story of Hal's progress is one of displacing the grotesque maternal body, figured in Falstaff, in order to secure the sexual mastery displayed in the wooing of Katherine. Traub attempts to bring together psychoanalytic, historicist and feminist theories in her exploration of Shakespeare's expressions of sexuality. The first part of the book, 'Erotic paranoia', analyses the imprisonment of woman-as-object in *Hamlet*, *Othello* and *The Winter's Tale*, and explores the significance of syphilis in *Troilus and Cressida*. The second, and more novel section, 'Erotic possibility', begins with a substantial general essay seeking to unpick the cultural identification of sexuality, gender and desire one with the other, and is followed by an application of these ideas to 'the homoerotics of Shakespearian comedy', in which *As You Like It* 'is playful in its ability to transcend binary oppositions, to break into a dual mode, a simultaneity, of desire', whereas 'the homoeroticism of *Twelfth Night* ... is anxious and strained' (pp. 122–3). One of the attractions of this book is the sense it gives of the excitement of ideas in the process of being formed (an impression that is strengthened by the way in which earlier published work is substantially revised). At the same time, however, the comprehension-crushing clusters of abstractions suggest that not everything is yet fully worked out. But the valuable flexibility that Traub brings to the categories of sexual desire can be contrasted with Joseph Pequigney's 'The Two Antonios and Same-Sex Love in *Twelfth Night* and *The Merchant of Venice*' (*English Literary Renaissance*, 22, 1991, 201–21), which drives towards an assertion of a fundamental categoric difference between the undoubtedly homosexual attachment of Antonio and Sebastian in the first play, and the 'philia' of Antonio and Bassanio in the latter. He insists, however, despite interpretative and theatrical tradition, that both Antonios are actually integrated into their plays' ending.

Karen Newman, in *Fashioning Femininity and English Renaissance Drama* (Chicago and London: The University of Chicago Press 1991) asserts her purpose as being to move away from '"women" to ask instead how the category "femininity" is produced and deployed in early modern England' (p. xix). Between trenchantly written general chapters on the representation of the female body, on marriage, witchcraft, and fashion, are essays on *The Taming of the Shrew* (already something of

a classic study), *Othello* and *Henry V* (as well as Jonson's *Epicoene*). Her reading of *Othello*, where she argues that 'the union of Desdemona and Othello represents a sympathetic identification between femininity and the monstrous that offers a potentially subversive recognition of sexual and racial difference' (p. 86) is persuasive and challenging. If she is perhaps overly optimistic in seeing the cross-dressed heroine of *The Taming of the Shrew* or the linguistically disabled Kate of *Henry V* as sites of subversive possibility, Newman's arguments are forcefully presented and richly documented.

A collection of feminist essays, *In Another Country*, edited by Dorothea Kehler and Susan Baker (Metuchen, N.J. and London: The Scarecrow Press, 1991) includes substantial bibliographies of feminist criticism of Shakespeare and Renaissance Drama (welcome, but a sign in itself of the demarcation of territories within the scholarly world). Its own Shakespearian offerings include a reading of Isabella in *Richard II* by Jeanie Grant Moore, as 'a parallel to Richard' and 'a point of convergence for the mirror and perspective images', and an ingenious, if somewhat strained piece by Dorothea Kehler on 'Shakespeare's Emilias and the Politics of Celibacy', which enlists Paulina as an honorary Emilia, and tags on Emilia Lanyer for good measure. Its other pieces on Cleopatra (Mary Ann Bushman), on the relevance of the Jacobean woman controversy for *Measure for Measure* (Christy Desmet), on *Romeo and Juliet* and on *Macbeth* (Thomas Moisan and James Schiffer) are serviceable studies.

A critical approach perhaps less frequently invoked since its heyday in the work of Frye and Barber is given new life in two books. Linda Woodbridge and Edward Berry, the editors of *True Rites and Maimed Rites: Ritual and Anti-Ritual in Shakespeare and his Age* (Urbana and Chicago: University of Illinois Press) introduce the collection with a useful survey of the fortunes of 'that critical joint-stock company Myth and Ritual Criticism' in more recent years. Deborah Willis's discussion of the ceremony of Healing of the King's Evil, and Bruce W. Young on parental blessings are useful illuminations of Renaissance ceremonies. (Young's essay is also to be found in *Studies in Philology*, 89, 1992, 179–210). Pieces on the 'Rites of Rule' are workmanlike, but the collection is dominated by its most powerful essay, Michael D. Bristol's 'Charivari and the Comedy of Abjection in *Othello*', which represents the play as a 'ritual of unmarrying' conducted after the popular shaming practices of charivari, with Othello as the fool, Desdemona as the transvestite and Iago as the scourge of marriage. This reading attacks 'anaesthetic explanations' for the play's painfulness (a painfulness registered in the oft-repeated stories of attempts by spectators to disrupt the play's performance). It is an uncomfortable and challenging argument. A substantial related essay by one of the volume's contributors, Phyllis Gorfain, 'Toward a Theory of Play and the Carnivalesque in *Hamlet*', appears in *Hamlet Studies*, 13 (1991), 25–59. She uses Bakhtinian theory to 'help us appreciate *Hamlet*'s continuity with folk forms, marketplace and street performances'. This carnivalesque element, she argues, disrupts and complicates the linearity of tragedy.

François Laroque's *Shakespeare's Festive World: Elizabethan Seasonal Entertainment and the Professional Stage* (Cambridge: Cambridge University Press, 1991) is an expanded version, translated by Janet Lloyd, of a study which first appeared in French in 1988. A 'resolutely empirical' work, its first part, which provides a closely detailed account of festive customs and practices in Elizabethan England, synthesizes a great deal of scholarship and will be of enormous value, frequently consulted for many years. I have to confess, however, that when we turn to the plays, though there are many revealing details, the discussions do not often move substantially beyond a noting of similarities. In part this is because Laroque chooses not to consider 'these intellectual and artistic works as reflections of the social, economic and ideo-

logical conditions of the period'; in part it is because he does not often discuss, as Bristol does, for example, what the presence of festive elements means for the theatre audience (comparison of their essays on *Othello* reveals the strengths and weaknesses of each of their approaches). But perhaps most of all, the book seems itself complicit with the nostalgia with which it demonstrates festive rites enacted in Elizabethan society – as when he writes 'It is primarily because English popular culture of the Renaissance is so closely associated with festivals that it appears as a commitment to a joyous world and way of life' (p. 33).

'Subversion, subversion, no end of subversion' – but very definitely for us in this year's batch of criticism. In Richard Hillman's *Shakespearian Subversions: The Trickster and the Play-Text* (London: Routledge, 1992) almost every text in the canon receives some attention as the author charts a process by which the trickster (or the subversive spirit of which he/she may be the embodiment) is marginalized or demonized in the plays of the middle period, only to make a creative return from *Antony and Cleopatra* until *The Tempest*. Before the decisive moment of the death of Mercutio, Hillman argues, 'the textual impact of the trickster has not necessarily been measurable by his personal fate: silenced though they are, in different ways, Katherina, the Bastard, Aaron and Richard III transform their dramatic universes as thoroughly as do the fairies of *A Midsummer Night's Dream* or the ladies of *Love's Labour's Lost*'. There are stimulating passages in the book – especially the comparison of Portia and Prince Hal, and the discussion of the late plays, but the book suffers from its inclusive ambition; fewer plays more fully read might have made points more clearly and more forcefully.

Jack D'Amico also considers outsider figures in his *The Moor in English Renaissance Drama* (Tampa: University of South Florida Press, 1991). A long introductory section usefully sets out what the Elizabethans knew of the Moor and surveys a range of dramatic representations. In the second part of the book chapters on Aaron and Cleopatra, on the Prince of Morocco and Othello, and on Caliban explore the uses Shakespeare made of racial outsiders. His final conclusion is that through such characters the playwright forces his audience 'toward those imaginative encounters that open up the most basic questions of identity' (p. 217). Theorists of the post-colonial might well find some of this analysis rather under-powered, though the informed detail of the first section will prove valuable to scholars.

Marginal characters of a different kind are discussed in Martin Wiggins's wide-ranging and scholarly study *Journeymen in Murder* (Oxford: Oxford University Press, 1991). In it he traces the emergence of the figure of the hired assassin during the 1580s and 90s, its increasingly sophisticated use in the early seventeenth century, and a subsequent decline in the Caroline period. He provides a valuable context for discussion of assassins in *Richard III*, *Macbeth*, *Cymbeline* and other Shakespearian texts, though it is in Webster's plays that he locates the richest and subtlest uses of the types.

The remaining books in this section are of different kinds. Frances Teague's *Shakespeare's Speaking Properties* (Lewisburg: Bucknell University Press; London and Toronto: Associated University Presses, 1991) addresses itself to the contribution made by moveable props to the dramatic statement and effect of the plays. The commentary on the use of these objects is often rather leaden – 'A play that uses a mask is likely to be a comedy, while one that uses a crown is apt to be a history' (p. 79) – although the categorized list of all props called for in the canon will be useful.

The Show Within: Dramatic and Other Insets (Collection Astraea No 4, Université Paul-Valéry – Montpellier III, 1991) reprints papers from an International Conference at Montpellier in 1990. Its two volumes, and thirty papers, offer a variety of perspectives on the topic, though there is a good deal of overlap (the Mousetrap figures pretty frequently), and some essays which struggle to fit the theme. A more rigorous selection, and an invitation to some writers to extend their papers, would have produced a stronger collection.

Richard Hillman has had a productive year. In addition to his book on the trickster appears *Intertextuality and Romance in Renaissance Drama: The Staging of Nostalgia* (London: Macmillan, 1991). Its distinct chapters discuss the relationship of sundry plays to various other (mainly medieval) texts. In an anxious introduction Hillman insists that he isn't doing anything so old-fashioned as 'source study', but practising instead a much more fashionable 'intertextuality'. Despite the theoretical huffing and puffing, I'm not at all convinced that this makes much difference. I find his juxtaposition of Turkish texts with the Henriad more interesting than that of Chaucer's *Clerk's Tale* with *The Tempest* because the issues raised by the collocation are richer in implication.

If the short article which attempts to give an overview of an element in Shakespeare's works is always in danger of over-simplification, it can often be the more useful for undergraduates. Patricia Parker demonstrates delightfully the possibilities of the pursuit of a single idea in her 'Preposterous Events' (*Shakespeare Quarterly*, 43, 1992, 186–213). The 'preposterous', or placing first that which could come after, is pursued throughout Shakespeare's work from the linguistic trope of hysteron proteron, through sexual politics, scenic and plot structure. It's a sketch which is suggestive in itself, and makes one look forward to its fuller implementation at a later date. Of rather less ambitious scope, but nonetheless useful for students will be Steven Marx's 'Shakespeare's Pacifism' (*Renaissance Quarterly*, 45, 1992, 49–96), which sets out the humanist debate on war where 'the status of pacifist ideas oscillated between subversive and orthodox during the Renaissance', and suggests that Shakespeare's views shifted decisively between *Henry V* and *Troilus and Cressida*. If the suggestion that this coincided with the accession of the pacific James is much too simple an explanation it is nonetheless a valuable piece to set before undergraduates who so often assume that anti-war feeling was invented by Wilfred Owen. Students faced with the old chestnut of an essay-title on Shakespeare's use of disguise will find Susan Baker's 'Personating Persons: Rethinking Shakespearian Disguises' in *Shakespeare Quarterly*, 43 (1992), 303–16 useful if not unduly challenging.

COMEDIES

How far it is possible or profitable to consider Shakespeare's comedies as a whole is a question with a long pedigree. Two books attempt to provide a single perspective from which to view them. For Anthony J. Lewis they are plays which show us 'in affecting, compelling fashion, how a man comes to see the world and women aright'. In his *The Love Story in Shakespearian Comedy* (Lexington: The University Press of Kentucky, 1992) he treats all the comedies as versions of a basic plot matrix, where the fatherless male falls in love, then, impelled by contrary impulses, descends into misogyny, only to be rescued by the active–passive woman, and released into a new mutual recognition. Lewis is forced to concede that not all the plays fit his schema. *The Taming of the Shrew*, *A Midsummer Night's Dream* and *Measure for Measure* are exceptions, but their difference is not allowed to challenge the matrix. This is rather a benign (and male-centred) view of the comedies, although Lewis shows himself aware of recent feminist criticism, but it will be useful for undergraduates beginning to study the genre they tend to find most difficult.

Roger L. Cox proposes a more narrowly defined perspective from which to view the plays in his *Shakespeare's Comic Changes: The Time-Lapse Metaphor as Plot Device* (Athens and London: The University of Georgia Press, 1991). Transformation is the key element in the genre, but Cox's argument is that 'character transformation is to human personality as the pun is to word meaning' (p. 146). He suggests that we should not attempt to explain away the sudden changes that overcome characters in the plays, but accept the startling juxtaposition of radically different behaviours as being like the familiar 'duck/rabbit' image where alternative possibilities are held in suspension. Unlike a pictorial image, however, the plots of the plays offer us transformation over time, hence the 'time-lapse metaphor' of the title. Cox excludes three plays from consideration (*Comedy of Errors*, *Love's Labour's Lost* and *Twelfth Night*) because in his view they do not have 'transformational' plots; but he does include the *Henry IV* plays, and *Henry V*, as histories constructed to a comic matrix. I find the central idea much less persuasive than his discussion of *Merchant of Venice* in terms of biblical analogues and the problem of free will, and of *All's Well That Ends Well* as a rewriting of the Loathly Lady plot of medieval romance, neither of which need the hypothesis to sustain them.

A Midsummer Night's Dream is a dazzling, slippery and vertiginous drama. James L. Calderwood, in defiance of the declared aim of the Harvester New Critical Introductions series to provide analyses 'easily and immediately accessible to students', responds to the text with a fizzing, learned, playful exegesis founded on a psychoanalytic approach, but by no means restricted to it. Calderwood's study is impossible to paraphrase or pin down in brief review, though his discussion of the doubling of Theseus/Oberon and Hippolyta/Titania, of the signification of Puck's Door and Pyramus and Thisbe's Wall, or of Bottom as a 'half-assed metaphor' all offer moments of delight. After suggesting that the lovers' flight into the woods is 'a psychological journey from the lovers' cultural nature into what the Tzotzil Indians call *nagual* or animal nature', Calderwood smilingly observes 'Critics have been slow to recognise the influence of the Tzotzil Indians on Shakespeare' (p. 85). This is only just a joke;

throughout the study the boundaries of critical discourses are always under threat, and all but the most sophisticated undergraduate students are likely to find the experience as baffling as the Athenian lovers do their sojourn outside Athens.

John Powell Ward's volume on *As You Like It* in the same series (1992) seems much less ambitious. He makes clear from the outset that in his view the play is concerned entirely with a green/golden world from which politics and the rough-stuff of material existence are largely banished. (Louis Montrose doesn't even get a mention in the bibliography, nor are Corin's remarks on landowners discussed.) The book ends with the observation that the play is 'post-modern, feminine and green'. In between are over twenty short sections, on characters (including the suggestion that Rosalind may not have been a virgin), on language and on more general issues. But the whole is unfocused; the play is described as a 'bricolage', and the same term is appropriate to the discussion. Richard Wilson offers a violent contrast of perspective on the play in ' "Like the old Robin Hood": *As You Like It* and the Enclosure Riots' (*Shakespeare Quarterly*, 43, 1–19). In the context supplied by the subsistence crisis of the 1590s, he argues, 'no Shakespearian text transmits more urgently the imminence of social breakdown'. It does so, however, only to anaesthetize the revolutionary possibility contained in the forest world with its resonances of Robin Hood and of contemporary protests against enclosure. Wilson argues that instead 'the middling sort strangle protest ... and desert the dispossessed'. It is a powerful reading, but one which necessarily excludes a good deal of the play in its sour response to the 'implausibly romantic ending'.

It is unfortunate, perhaps, that the book which most nearly corresponds to the brief for the Harvester series is devoted to the play students are least likely to read. R. S. White's volume on *The Merry Wives of Windsor* (1991) seems to me an ideal introduction to the play in

that it is theoretically informed, but not burdened with jargon; lucidly argued but open-ended in its conclusion. Confronting the standard critical disappointment with the depiction of Falstaff in the play, he demonstrates the way its action foregrounds a contest between a carefully delineated bourgeois Windsor world and various dangerous outsiders. Falstaff, he argues, is a threat to the security of that world precisely because he mirrors its own values. White focuses on the questions the play raises about the place of women and suggests how the plotting of the play produces something akin to Brechtian 'alienation'. In a particularly suggestive chapter he analyses the language of the play as a contest between a plain style and variants upon it that 'opens up as a subject in itself the exhilaration of language' (p. 72). A concluding chapter deals briefly with operatic adaptations as 'readings' of the play. All in all it offers a model execution of the explicit aims of the series. The book is only marred by the bizarre choice of Frances Howard, the least merry of all Jacobean wives, to adorn its cover. (But then, why the sternly Puritan and warlike Prince Henry should figure on the cover of *A Midsummer Night's Dream* is equally a mystery.) A not very plausible footnote to this play is offered by Terry P. Morris in the suggestion that Shakespeare was aiming at Ben Jonson in his characterization of Slender (*Selected Papers of the Shakespeare and Renaissance Association of West Virginia*, 1992, 51–60). Derek Brewer suggests, in a rather generalized fashion, that jest-book material lies behind the play in 'Elizabethan Merry Tales and The Merry Wives of Windsor: Shakespeare and "Popular" Literature', an essay in the festschrift for Shinsuke Ando, *Chaucer to Shakespeare*, ed. Toshiyuki Takamiya and Richard Beadle (Cambridge: D. S. Brewer, 1992, 145–60).

Two articles in *Renaissance Drama*, 41, 1990, continue to give Duke Vincentio the hard time that is currently the fashion, M. Lindsay Kaplan by seeing his punishment of Lucio for slander as exposing his own defamatory practices, and

Janet M. Spencer by revisiting the question of pardon – juxtaposing *Measure for Measure* with the pardoning of Aumerle in *Richard II* to suggest that together they demonstrate the theatrical possibility of undermining state-controlled spectacle. A refreshingly different perspective is offered by Michael Flachmann in 'Fitted for Death: *Measure for Measure* and the *Contemplatio Mortis*' (*English Literary Renaissance* 22, 1992, 222–41). He claims that the play's comedic resolution of the pains of the contemplation of impending death would have seemed particularly potent in the plague-year of its original composition. It is a pity that this essay did not pursue the challenge it might offer to the currently dominant Foucauldian reading of the play. He remarks, but does not develop, the way that treatises of Holy Dying invited their readers to imagine that they were coming to execution – a parallel which might modify significantly the view that execution and the last dying speeches that attended them were always and only symbolic of the power of the state.

All's Well That Ends Well is seen by Tita French Baumlin as a play which 'represents, in comedic form, an essentially tragic vision of the role of language in the human community' with a struggle between a (largely) older generation which uses language as transparent sign, and the parasites who resort to a 'tragic' opacity (*Explorations in Renaissance Culture*, 17, 1991, 125–44).

Cynthia Marshall, in a compact study, *Last Things and Last Plays: Shakespearian Eschatology* (Carbondale and Edwardsville: Southern Illinois University Press, 1991), reads each of the four late romances against aspects of the period's contemplation of the last things. Cymbeline is seen as an Advent play, concentrating on death, judgement, and a communal reunion that figures the day of Resurrection, while *The Winter's Tale* negotiates with the idea of bodily resurrection. The dramatic structure of *Pericles* is seen as built upon the seven ages of the world. Ideas of the dissolution of time and of paradise are interrogated in *The Tempest*. While the general proposition that eschatological thinking is part of the intellectual and emotional furniture of these plays is persuasive enough, the specific correspondences seem less than compelling – and clarity of argument is not always aided by the intervention of Freudian psychology.

Boika Sokolova approaches the late plays through Brecht's dramatic theory in *Shakespeare's Romances as Interrogative Texts: Their Alienation Strategies and Ideology* (Lewiston, Queenston, Lampeter: The Edwin Mellen Press, 1992). In a rather angular style, each of the plays is subjected to a straightforward analysis which can sometimes descend into the commonplace.

Straightforwardness is emphatically not what H. W. Fawkner aims at. Deploying his 'hyperontological' theories, described as 'German Transcendentalism and new French Criticism Refashioned and Transmuted into a new Idiosyncratic Methodology', *Shakespeare's Miracle Plays* (Rutherford, Madison, Teaneck: Fairleigh Dickinson University Press; London and Toronto: Associated University Presses, 1992) argues that *Pericles* is the play which most rapturously celebrates the miraculous. Less completely present and less successfully treated in the next two plays, the miraculous 'from the hyperontological viewpoint' is entirely absent from *The Tempest*. A theory which requires one to see *Pericles* as the high point from which the later plays decline has the merit of novelty. Whether it is convincing is altogether different.

Two other essays on *Pericles* focus on the emblematic quality of its writing and stage pictures. Claire Preston, 'The Emblematic Structure of *Pericles*' (*Word and Image*, 8, 1992, 21–38), and Frederick Kiefer, 'Art, Nature and the Written Word in *Pericles*' (*University of Toronto Quarterly*, 61, 1991/2, 207–25) both stress the ways in which the audience is directed by the play's manner into acts of interpretation. (A similar approach to *The Merchant of Venice* is offered by Raphaelle Costa de Beauregard in

Cahiers Elisabéthains, 39 (1991), 1–16, where the sequence of emblems lead to a 'complex view of justice'.)

The ending of *The Winter's Tale* has become a locus classicus for dispute about Shakespeare's proto-feminism (or lack of it). David Schalkwyk approaches the topic through consideration of the play's treatment of the fact that only a woman's word can justify the legitimacy of the male bloodline. His '"A Lady's 'Verily' Is as Potent as a Lord's": Women, Word and Witchcraft in *The Winter's Tale*' (*English Literary Renaissance* 22, 1992, 242–72), is carefully and systematically argued to demonstrate the proposition that in the end 'the potency of female word and body, derided by witchcraft, is in fact appropriated by the patriarchal word that represented it as witchcraft in the first place'. As in many arguments of this cast it seems to me that concentration on what is *said* in the last act underplays the theatrical power of women in the final scene, where Leontes' efforts to re-establish control seem puny by comparison. Much more traditional is Soji Iwasaki's essay *Nature Triumphant: Approach to The Winter's Tale* (Tokyo: Sanseido, 1991), first published in 1984. He sets the play in the context of medieval and Renaissance views of Nature, which he finds Shakespeare's play celebrates in the restoration of its ending.

Caliban has, in recent years at least, been the central focus of a good deal of *Tempest* criticism. In their *Shakespeare's Caliban: A Cultural History* (Cambridge: Cambridge University Press, 1991) Alden T. and Virginia Mason Vaughan trace the possible origins of the play's character, and follow his subsequent fortunes in criticism, in theatrical performance, and in pictorial representation. Their work is detailed and comprehensive, and will be a valuable sourcebook. It is a pity therefore that the publishers should have chosen not to include a bibliography, nor the index to cite items referred to in footnotes. A by now very familiar 'colonialist' reading of Caliban and his dispossession takes on particular force in Martin Orkin's

'Shakespeare and the Politics of "Unrest"', delivered in Bloemfontein, and printed in *The English Academy Review*, 8 (1991), 85–97, where the context gives an urgency to his plea for readings that do not 'perpetuate conservatism and narrowness and that erase recognition of and respect for difference'.

Three substantial essays on the romances figure in Gordon McMullan and Jonathan Hope, eds., *The Politics of Tragicomedy* (London: Routledge, 1992). David Norbrook offers a complex view of *The Tempest* in his '"What Care these Roarers for the Name of King": Language and Utopia in *The Tempest*'. In a carefully modulated argument he suggests that 'the play is not overtly oppositional or sensationally "subversive"; but it subjects traditional institutions to a systematic, critical questioning'. Pointing out that the colonialist readings have largely left in place the assumption that the play is on Prospero's side, he offers a scholarly and forceful account of its multivalency. Erica Sheen draws attention to Seneca's *Hercules Furens* as both source for Innogen's misrecognition of Cloten's headless body, and subtext for what she takes to be the play's refusal to be co-opted into royalist ideology. Her essay is knotty, and ambitious. If in the end the move from the specifics of intertextuality to the large assertion that *Cymbeline* should be placed 'within the scope of the libertarian practices of the early seventeenth century' involves a leap of faith rather than compelling logic, the essay opens challenging possibilities. Finally Lois Potter offers a welcome essay on *Two Noble Kinsmen* (there is another by her in the proceedings of the Montpellier conference noted earlier), looking at three occasions of its possible performance to discuss the question of whether its meanings are truly political, or merely topical. In a final paragraph she wittily suggests that the play has been neglected in part precisely because the present 'politics of literary interpretation' has found difficulty in dealing with a play not only about, but by two 'contesting' authors.

HISTORIES

No critic has more vigorously focused his work on the history plays than Graham Holderness. His *Shakespeare Recycled* (Hemel Hempstead: Harvester Wheatsheaf, 1992) should perhaps be entitled 'Holderness Recycled' since it is an extensive rewriting of his own earlier *Shakespeare's Histories*. Holderness writes with commitment and usually with clarity; but he seems unwilling to grant that the same questions about the politicized reading of Shakespeare's texts which he addresses to Tillyard and the rest could, equally, be applied to his own celebration of '"a free Shakespeare", potentially a force for destabilizing (reactionary) culture and pushing it towards social transformation' (p. 232). He claims that 'conservative reproduction transmits an ideology, not a true vision'. Many readers will be less confident than he both of the 'truth' of his vision, and of the progressivist view of critical history that underlies his demolition job on earlier writers. It is symptomatic of a central anxiety in his thesis that his insistence on Shakespeare's awareness of the 'historicity' of his stories of late feudal society is coupled to an equally fervent belief that Shakespeare was not, in the reference to Essex in *Henry V*, for example, commenting directly on his own society. To admit this would, for Holderness, be to fall into the 'trap' of Tillyardism, of treating Shakespeare as a mere Tudor apologist. Such rigid disjunction is surely unnecessary – and unjustified.

No such questions trouble E. Pearlman in his survey *The History Plays* for the Twayne's English Authors Series (1992). The series is aimed explicitly at non-specialists, and this book is clearly and directly written – but even the general reader (if such a person exists) could surely be offered much more sense of the plays as controversial political statements both in their own time and in ours than emerges in this urbane commentary?

Character as a Subversive Force in Shakespeare looks at first sight like the title of a more radical redirection of the traditional tools of 'humanist' criticism, but Bernard J. Paris's book is ahistorical and apolitical. It is a companion to his *Bargains With Fate* (reviewed last year), and applies 'Third Force Psychology' to the decoding of the major characters in History and Roman Plays. The theories of Karen Horney are seen as simply 'congruent' with Shakespeare's methods, and fictional characters are neatly pigeon-holed into her pre-existing categories. The 'subversion' of the title arises because 'when we understand Shakespeare's mimetic characters in motivational terms, we find that they are "creations inside a creation" who tend to subvert the larger structures of which they are part'. It is not a thesis that I find persuasive.

A very different approach to the history plays is offered in W. F. Bolton's *Shakespeare's English: Language in the History Plays* (Oxford: Basil Blackwell, 1992). Essays on topics such as sound patterns, linguistic structure, rhetoric, pragmatics and linguistic variety are each focused on specific plays. Bolton claims that 'critical ideas about the development of Richard's character, for example, can arise from assumptions about segmental and supra-segmental phonology as well as from imagery or plot' (p. 19). There is no reason why this should not be so, but in the book at large critical insights are generally rather unexciting, and often buried beneath a welter of descriptive detail. One would share Bolton's belief that the study of rhetoric ought to be an illuminating guide for the reading of the *Henry VI* plays, for example. But though his chapter claims to focus on a single speech, his points are dissipated in an often confusing series of diversions. Perhaps the most suggestive chapters are those where he demonstrates the ways in which Hal, Falstaff and Hotspur 'share the view that to mimic another's idiolect is to conquer him' (p. 184), and a concluding chapter on 'Language and Nation in *Henry V*' where he traces the play's effort to bring a concluding resolution 'from the Babel of linguistic division'.

Idiolects are also the subject of David J. Baker's '"Wildehirissheman": Colonialist Representation in Shakespeare's *Henry V*' (*English Literary Renaissance*, 22, 1992, 37–61), where theorists of colonialist discourse are brought to bear upon the representation of Irishness in the play. In a rather repetitious argument, he seeks to distinguish his position from Greenblatt and Porter, maintaining that 'the discourse of the Other' is neither completely crushed by, nor completely outside imperialist discourse, but exists within that discourse as 'intimations of absent Otherness which can be neither traced nor effaced'.

Two essays in *Renaissance Drama*, 21, focus on the Henriad. Christopher Highley interestingly extends the frequently remarked importance of the Irish background for *Henry V* by arguing that *1 Henry IV* also draws upon the troubled state, transplanting it into Wales (91–114). Jonathan Crewe, in 'Reforming Prince Hal: The Sovereign Inheritor in *2 Henry IV*' (225–42), considers that critics have too easily perceived the second play as merely an extension or continuation of the first, rather than as a new attempt to render acceptable the reformation of the prince. He argues that the wildness of Hal is displaced to the dying King Henry and thereby buried with him. In *Works and Days 19* (10, 1992) Arthur Efron offers an anarchist reading of *1 Henry IV*, in an extended essay entitled 'War is the Health of the State'. He argues that the conflicts of King and Prince, of Prince and Hotspur betoken no conflict of values – merely a conflict of contention for control of the state for which warfare is a necessary precondition. Only in Falstaff is there real opposition, an opposition which Efron would characterize as 'anarchist'. Part of his argument is that anarchist theory provides a route that leads beyond New Historicism, and permits a fuller acknowledgement of what turns out to be a rather traditional empathy for the figure of Falstaff. Explicitly and unashamedly this study enacts the co-option of Shakespeare in a particular political interest –

although Efron wants to believe that his anarchist perception is also in part at least Shakespeare's.

TRAGEDIES

If generalizing about the comedies is problematic, the desire to produce general theses about the tragedies is, it seems, inexhaustible. Four books attempt the task this year, though Nicolas Grene's main aim in *Shakespeare's Tragic Imagination* (London: Macmillan, 1992) is to 'stress that Shakespeare's tragic imagination is not single but (at least) double. The tragedies do not conform to one pattern, do not support one view of the world' (p. 286). Instead, he proposes that there is a clear distinction to be drawn between a 'secular' and a 'sacred' tragic vision, embodied in the alternation between the tragedies of the classical world embedded in the historical perspectives enforced by their sources, and the others which, though often drawn from Holinshed, occupy a less historically defined space. By 'sacred' Grene does not mean specifically Christian, but rather a mythic or visionary mode. His comparative method largely eschews any placing of the plays in their Elizabethan or Jacobean context (he denies, for example, the importance of the Union debate to the opening of *Lear*, and the elements of *Macbeth* that might be designed to appeal to James are dismissed as a 'sideshow'). The book provides a series of readable accounts of the plays written in an accessible language that students will find stimulating, and suggestive in detail. The overall thesis, however, seems to me to be bought at the expense of emptying out rather too much of the specific cultural and political resonance of those plays Grene designates 'sacred'.

David Margolies operates from a very different set of premises in his *Monsters of the Deep: Social Dissolution in Shakespeare's Tragedies* (Manchester: Manchester University Press, 1992). From his Marxist perspective the tragedies document the collapse of a late-medieval belief in the social world before rampant individualism (this must be one of the few books in recent years that mention the Great Chain of Being with approval rather than anxiety). *King Lear* emerges as the most satisfactory of the plays because this struggle is fully embodied in its action, whereas in *Hamlet* issues are not fully defined, and the play too readily tempts us to focus on the psyche of the hero (through his undramatic (?!) soliloquies). In the later plays the increasing absence of any possibility of representing 'the social collective' marks out an increasing barrenness and despair. Like Grene, Margolies avoids almost any detailed documentation that might place the plays in their historical context. The rise of individualism is simply assumed to be the period's distinctive feature. How persuasive his readings will be will depend on the reader's readiness to accept his presuppositions as axioms.

Explicitly aimed at students is Michael Mangan's *A Preface to Shakespeare's Tragedies* (London: Longman, 1991). Only the Bradleian 'big four' tragedies are discussed. Very little sense is given of current critical approaches, though his accounts are clearly written for their audience. But a very boiled-down account of 'Shakespeare's England', a section on 'Shakespeare and the Theatre of his Time' only loosely connected to the plays, and seven pages given over to an arbitrary selection of biographies ranging from James I to Anne Hathaway, seem much less useful, even to the 'general reader', than would have been an extension of the discussion to the other major tragedies.

For me the most stimulating of these studies is Kent Cartwright's *Shakespearian Tragedy and its Double: The Rhythms of Audience Response* (Pennsylvania: The Pennsylvania State University Press, 1991). In a series of substantial essays he explores the ways in which the plays manipulate audience detachment from and engagement with characters and action. So, for example, he suggests that '*Hamlet* will shape the audience into something resembling Hamlet, just as he will behave as a critical observer of his

own tragedy', and notes that 'while *Othello* has innocent characters, it has no innocent spectators; we are always the audience who knew too much'. He develops the significance of the observers of the action in *King Lear*, and explores the implications of the ways in which *Antony and Cleopatra* presents a spectacle where 'all the major characters are watchers and interpreters, trusters and distrusters: "audiences" in themselves. Likewise, all are stage-actors, performing themselves before an audience, playing for trust.' Sensitivity to the ambiguity of an audience's response to staged action, coupled with a welcome gift for punchy formulations, makes this a continuously stimulating study.

Romeo and Juliet is the subject of Cedric Watts's contribution to the Harvester series (1991). It is at its strongest in discussing familial and sexual politics. He emphasizes the dialectical nature of the play, usefully contrasting the eighteenth-century suppression of the bawdy with the tendency in modern productions to miss out chunks of the elevated and courtly. As a whole, however, his volume seems unsure in its aim, and somewhat hastily put together, with a good deal of digression and very long quotations from critics. Compared with others in the series its Select Bibliography is extremely brief.

In another Harvester Introduction (1992) Vivian Thomas deals with *Julius Caesar*. In the preface the author explains that his discussion 'operates within the liberal humanist tradition'. He goes on to describe and to challenge more recent critical approaches, and then banishes them to the bibliography as he pursues his cogent, largely traditional reading of the play. Students will certainly find this a readable and responsible account, but one does wonder whether its right place is in a series which explicitly calls itself *New* Critical Introductions. It is the fifth of the series I have encountered this year, and though admirable aims are laid out clearly on the back cover, the execution of that brief is enormously varied. Without wanting uniformity, it does seem reasonable to ask whether there should not be a firmer editorial control.

In a short but suggestive book, *Otherworldly 'Hamlet'* (Montreal: Guernica, 1991), John O'Meara argues that the Lutheran insistence upon the fallenness of man embodied in his sexuality is what animates Hamlet's self-disgust, and that the search for an Otherworldly guarantee of that perspective is eventually validated at the end of the play.

Feminist criticism has often perceived the women in the tragedies as little more than pawns in patriarchal power-plays. A counter argument is offered in Evelyn Gajowski's *The Art of Loving* (Newark: University of Delaware Press; London and Toronto: Associated University Presses, 1992). She claims that 'the uniqueness of Shakespeare's representation of sexual relationships is his creation of females who are independent, yet relational human beings. Juliet, Desdemona, and Cleopatra are all endowed with a self-estimation that is independent of the estimations of the men in their dramatic worlds' (p. 125). Juliet and Cleopatra, by their constancy and 'true' understanding of love, educate both Romeo and Antony, revealing the inadequacy of their shifting, unstable masculine selves. The book's antipathy to any reference to seventeenth-century ideological systems means that it can teeter dangerously on the edge of sentimentality. To claim that Emilia's discussion of female sexuality in *Othello* 4.3.93–101 is a model of 'balance, reciprocity, and equality' which 'makes explicit the critique of male treatment of females' (p. 82), for example, requires one to put out of mind any question of the ambiguous response her words might have elicited from an audience familiar with the theatrical precedents for such a scene. Gajowski's is a view of the texts that sees their deepest resonances in what they have to say about human character, defined in terms of an individual's 'truth' to him or her self.

From the mass of *Hamlet* criticism in journals there is space only to note three articles which, like Gajowski's book, question the standard reading of the representation of Ophelia as the most terrible indictment of patriarchy. Nona Fienberg, in 'Jephthah's Daughter: The Parts Ophelia Plays', in *Old Testament Women in Western Literature*, ed. Raymond-Jean Frontain and Jan Wojcik (Conway: UCA Press, 1991, pp. 128–32) uses the association Hamlet makes between Ophelia and the biblical woman sacrificed to her father's promise to God as the springboard for a reading of her mad scene and Gertrude's elegy upon her as indicating a brief moment of womanly self-speaking. Ranjini Philip, in 'The Shattered Glass: The Story of (O)phelia' (*Hamlet Studies*, 13, 1991, 73–84) argues that her suicide was willed, and that 'Ophelia's story is one of nobility and heroism, of self-awareness and self-integration'. Michele Pessoni arrives at a similar end by seeing Ophelia as a Jungian Kore figure, and her story as one of specifically female initiation 'successfully completed' (*Hamlet Studies*, 14, 1992, 32–41). These articles are a tribute to feminist attempts to see from a different perspective, but their collective sense of optimism seems to me misplaced.

A collection of essays from the 1988 Shakespeare Association of America convention session on *Othello* is edited by Virginia Mason Vaughan and Kent Cartwright (Rutherford, Madison, Teaneck: Fairleigh Dickinson University Press; London and Toronto: Associated University Presses, 1991). It is a solid collection, with essays on language, staging and audience response. The most interesting items to me were B. A. Kachur's detailed account of Beerbohm Tree's 1912 performance, and Barbara Hodgdon's powerful 'Kiss me Deadly; or the Des/Demonized Spectacle' which considers the representation of Desdemona's death in Verdi's opera, and a number of films and stage performances both of Shakespeare's text and various adaptations of it. (At least three essays, by Gajowski, Teague and Cartwright, are versions of work also published this year in book form.)

The fool's puzzling line 'there was never yet

fair woman but she made mouths in a glass' is the starting point for Alan R. Shickman's 'The Fool's Mirror in *King Lear*' (*English Literary Renaissance*, 21, 1991, 75–86). He takes it to be an indication that the character carried with him an actual looking-glass, which he identifies as part of the standard iconology of the fool in various pictorial representations. One does not have to accept the physical actuality of this prop to find some of the resonances of the ambivalent looking-glass suggestive in the reading of the play. A largely traditional reading of Lear's progress to self-knowledge is proffered by Fumio Yoshioka in 'Beckoned By The Call of "Nothing": Lear's Odyssey in Quest of True Identity' (*Studies in English Literature*, Tokyo, 68, 1992, 207–25).

Essays on *Antony and Cleopatra* offer a conspectus of the variety of current approaches. Paul Yachnin, in '"Courtiers of Beauteous Freedom": *Antony and Cleopatra* and its Time', (*Renaissance and Reformation*, 15, 1991, 1–20) presents a simplistic political reading, identifying Cleopatra with Queen Elizabeth and Octavius with James, to suggest that the play is ambivalent about the reign of the peacemaker. Linda Charnes uses the play as a pretext to put the boot into Liberal Humanist Critics (always abbreviated throughout the article to 'LHCs') who insist on trying to read Transcendent Love as being above politics, whereas it is, of course, 'a monumental erection of the critical Phallus against any text that subversively insists on asking "what's love got to do with it"' (*Textual Practice*, 6, 1992, 1–16). Traditional readings are not much advanced by R. L. P. Jackson's 'Imagining Anthony[sic] and Cleopatra' (*Sydney Studies in English*, 18, 1992/3, 3–26) which speaks of the play's celebration of 'the creative and transforming power of the idealizing imagination'. Anthony Miller's essay in the same issue (29–47) pursues the influence of Ovid on the play, as does Paul Dean in '*Antony and Cleopatra*: An Ovidian Tragedy?' (*Cahiers Elisabéthains*, 40, 1991).

Is it not perhaps a coincidence, given the current political climate, that *Coriolanus* comes in for serious attention this year? In addition to Hawkes's essays already mentioned, three articles read the play in seventeenth-century contexts. Both Shannon Miller, in 'Topicality and Subversion in William Shakespeare's *Coriolanus*' (*SEL*, 32, 1992, 287–310) and Arthur Riss in 'The Belly Politic: *Coriolanus* and the Revolt of Language' (*ELH*, 59, 1992, 53–75) treat of its relation to the Midlands riots. In Riss's reading the play turns on the question 'who owns the rights to the body', and he argues that both Coriolanus and the plebs share an understanding of the concreteness of the individual body, as opposed to Menenius' cynical figuration of it in his speech of the belly. For Miller, Coriolanus figures James in his autocratic response to Parliament, and the allusion to the riots enables the play to 'expose the dangers of insisting upon the prerogative of rulers'. If this latter essay seems over-baldly to assert a quasi-allegorical reading of the play, Richard Wilson proposes an altogether more complicated strategy in his 'Against the Grain: Representing the Market in *Coriolanus*' (*The Seventeenth Century*, 6, 1991, 111–48). For him it is not the Midlands riots of 1608 which provide the context (he speculates that the play might have been earlier), but the corn famine of Stratford in the late sixteenth century and the contested election of Fulke Greville in 1601. *Coriolanus* is not a play about insurrection, but about 'an "addled election" with lethal repercussions', thereby raising questions about 'the epochal shift from collective values based on shared consumption to exchange values and private enterprise'. One is used to New Historicism's belief in the parity of texts of various provenance, but Wilson blurs completely any kinds of boundary, as the text of the play, atomized and fragmented, is used to supply the words equally for the burgesses of Stratford, or the Grevilles. As a rhetoric to compel a reader's assent to the proposition that the play is constituted out of the issues he supplies as its matrix it is striking; but in the process a good deal of the play's intricacy is inevitably lost, and important distinctions are collapsed.

COLLECTIONS OF REPRINTED ESSAYS AND OTHER REISSUES

The motivation for reissuing selections of articles and extracts from books is presumably a desire to make available for undergraduate students material they would otherwise find hard to locate. At the same time such anthologies can perform the task of presenting the claims of theoretical perspectives. Three new collections in the Longman Critical Readers series approach the task in rather different ways, and with varied success. Richard Wilson and Richard Dutton's *New Historicism and Renaissance Drama* is explicit in its theoretical focus. It is crisply introduced with an account of the growth of New Historicism by Wilson, and concluded by Dutton's brief account of its detractors. In between we encounter the familiar names – and some very familiar essays. Is this the sixth or seventh time that 'Invisible Bullets' have aimed themselves at the reader? Greenblatt, Dollimore and Belsey are each twice represented in the thirteen pieces (not all on Shakespeare) which make up the volume. Very few of the selections have not either already been reprinted at least once, or are not currently available in paperback books. It seems a missed opportunity. John Drakakis' selection for the volume on Shakespearian Tragedy arranges its essays under the headings of various different theoretical schools, from semiotics to post-structuralism. In a congested introduction the caricatured Other is, of course, 'liberal humanism', and the collection offers itself as a triumphal celebration of its dethroning. Inevitably in covering such a large field the selection must be to some extent arbitrary, though most of the essays earn their place.

There is a rather perfunctory two-page listing of further reading under the headings 'Theory of Tragedy' and 'Shakespearian Tragedy'. The most successful of these three collections is Gary Waller's selection on the comedies. The introduction is lucid, the essays are selected both to illustrate theoretical positions, and as specimen essays on each of the comedies, and the student is offered a sensibly arranged (and occasionally annotated) bibliography (as is also the case in Wilson and Dutton's volume).

By comparison with these determinedly contemporary collections, Thomas Wheeler's selection of essays on *The Merchant of Venice* in the Garland series (1991) is much more wide-ranging – from Hazlitt to Tennenhouse. The introduction recognizes the problematic nature of the play, but concludes with improbable optimism that 'the dark shadows of anti-Semitism may disperse ... *The Merchant* will continue to hold a unique place among the romantic comedies and future productions will find new ways to illustrate its power to delight and to disturb.' There is little sense overall of the urgency of what is at stake in the reading, representing and recuperation of this peculiarly fraught drama. The Casebook series is being revised, and the volume on *Antony and Cleopatra*, edited by John Russell Brown, inserts three essays published since 1968, by Michael Long, Leonard Tennenhouse and Kay Stockholder (London: Macmillan, 1991).

Two paperback reprints have been sent me: Stephen Greenblatt's *Learning to Curse*, and Vivian Thomas's *The Moral Universe of Shakespeare's Problem Plays* (both published by Routledge). Mannoni's influential essay, *Prospero and Caliban: The Psychology of Colonization*, is reissued in Pamela Powesland's translation (Ann Arbor: The University of Michigan Press, 1990).

2. SHAKESPEARE'S LIFE, TIMES, AND STAGE
reviewed by MARTIN WIGGINS

I

The quest for the sources of Shakespeare, as for that of the Nile, can develop into a fixation which outgrows its purpose. It is a scholarly activity which tends towards the production of catalogues like Jan Harold Brunvand's dry but valuable Indiana University doctoral dissertation documenting in detail the folktale origins of *The Taming of the Shrew*, which has finally reached print after thirty years.[1] It is sensible to proceed from making catalogues to using them, but all too often students of the subject have more limited horizons: preoccupied with the mere presence or absence of influence, without going on to consider its significance, they make source-hunting an end in itself, unconcerned with the critical responsibility of telling us something important about the plays.

This is the downfall of Charles and Michelle Martindale's *Shakespeare and the Uses of Antiquity* (London and New York, 1990), which seeks to demonstrate Shakespeare's debt to the classics. It is a workmanlike analysis, though occasionally over-reliant on shaky, negative evidence: it may indeed be unreasonable to suppose that Shakespeare was never exposed to certain Latin authors, but that is not in itself a *prima facie* case that they influenced his work, especially bearing in mind the vagaries of a schoolboy's memory and attention-span. On the whole, however, it is a competent if unimaginative restatement of the case for Shakespeare's classical knowledge. The problem is that this is taken to be the object of the exercise, and there is in consequence a curious dislocation between the Martindales' discussion of the sources and their analyses of the plays: because there is no sense of why it should *matter* whether or not Shakespeare read Plautus, or Seneca, or Ovid, the close readings are treated simply as evidence towards the conclusion that he did. The criticism and the scholarship never gel

together to produce interpretation, and all we are left with (besides the sensible recapitulation of what we already knew) is a clutch of sensitive close readings of individual passages.

There is an inevitability in the way that scholars who pursue sources for their own sake seem to end up grubbing in minutiae. Most of the major work has already been done and the texts made available (though a supplement to Bullough, covering *Edward III*, *The Two Noble Kinsmen*, and perhaps the putative sources of *Cardenio*, would be useful), and we are left, bar the odd lucky find, with details and with the sort of fine-tuning undertaken by Anthony Brian Taylor in work seeking to reassess the place of Golding's Ovid in the imagination of Shakespeare and his contemporaries.[2] Such research attends more to the construction of individual lines than of entire plays: the focus may be sharp, but the view is myopic.

How refreshing, then, is *Shakespeare and Classical Tragedy* (Oxford, 1992), a subtle and intelligent study of influence which eschews what its author, Robert S. Miola, calls 'the fallacy of misplaced specification' (p. 39). The search for parallels and attention to exact verbal constructions, he argues, can obscure rather than expose the workings of influence. Instead, he offers a broad analysis of Shakespeare's creative assimilation of Seneca's scenic forms, conventional devices, and subject matter. The

---

[1] Jan Harold Brunvand, *The Taming of the Shrew: A Comparative Study of Oral and Literary Versions* (New York and London, 1991).

[2] Anthony Brian Taylor, 'Arthur Golding and the Elizabethan Progress of Actaeon's Dogs', *Connotations*, 1 (1991), 207–23, and 'Shakespeare and Golding', *Notes and Queries*, 236 (1991), 492–9. Golding emerges as a rich source of allusion and phraseology, though Taylor also throws out a number of implausible identifications by previous annotators.

central, most influential feature of Senecan tragedy, he contends, is its concern with *scelus* – the atrocious crime to which the protagonist is impelled. From this derives the Elizabethan and Jacobean preoccupation with human evil: the revenge, tyranny, and uncontrollable passion which are 'the Styx within the human soul' (p. 33).

Seneca, then, is taken to be a determinant of the intense psychological interest of Renaissance tragedy, and this is well reflected in the book's discussions of revenge and *furor*. The weak link in this respect is the chapter on tyranny, which focuses especially on *Richard III* and *Macbeth*: here, Seneca's influence seems more apparent at the peripheries of the plays, with their wailing queens and manipulative, intellectual trickery, and an otherwise admirably sophisticated book slides back into the narrower, primarily technical concerns which it has criticized in its predecessors. Miola has little sense of the human Styx when its waters are least adulterated by finer feelings. His account of Richard avoids psychological considerations until the All Souls' Night speech, preferring instead the evasive obscurantism of phrases like 'the mystery of evil' (p. 87): his Richard is a hollow man, 'a master parodist' (p. 92) who is able brilliantly to ape established forms of behaviour, but who has an emptiness at his centre that leaves him little potential for self-understanding or tragic *anagnorisis*. Perhaps, in this case, the suppression of the villain's mental world is not crude or naive; but nonetheless one cannot help but feel that there is something seriously wrong with any account of *Macbeth* from which the play emerges, as it does from Miola's, as a set of rhetorical tropes curiously devoid of psychological insight.

A more fundamental limitation becomes apparent when Miola moves outside the charmed circle of the Shakespeare canon. Proper names are persistently misspelt: Agamemnon's wife was apparently called 'Clytemestra', and Nashe becomes 'Nash', courtesy, one supposes, of Gregory Smith

(there is no evidence that Miola has consulted the McKerrow edition). Non-Shakespearian plays, too, are often cited – the Bibliography notwithstanding – from unreliable nineteenth-century editions like Hazlitt's Dodsley, which is presumably why Miola uses, without explanation, the 1591 revision of *Gismond of Salerne* rather than the original (and in some respects more Senecan) 1560s text. This is more than just nit-picking: these and other errors of fact and scholarly procedure point to a general underestimation of the wider cultural context, which makes, in turn, for an unduly simple model of the process of influence.

Because the book concentrates so strongly on two chronologically distinct bodies of work, by Seneca and by Shakespeare, it implicitly posits a simple, one-way movement of content, from the classical to the Renaissance tragedian. Convincing though it is in identifying *scelus* as the focal point of the artistic contact between the two, it fails to consider the reasons for the sixteenth-century popularity of Seneca, and so, by omission, seems to advance his influence as an adequate explanation for Shakespearian tragedy's interest in criminality and evil. But great writers, even ones trained under Tudor educational principles, do not imitate established works merely through habit, or out of respect for their canonicity: a precondition for Seneca's influence on Shakespeare is Shakespeare's interest in Seneca, an interest predicated on a shared concern, whether personal or cultural, with human wickedness. Acknowledge that (Miola does not) and source-study becomes more than the tracing of literary family trees: a writer's selection of source texts (and non-selection of others) comes into question, and this is not always determined by purely aesthetic or literary factors.

In short, source-study has something to offer to historicist as well as to formalist students of Shakespeare: it can contribute to (and should in turn take note of) our sense of the plays as part of, or distinct from, a cultural context and a literary tradition. In this respect, another aspect of the ancients' literary legacy to the sixteenth century, examined in Neil Rhodes's informed and well-written but strangely disappointing book-length essay, *The Power of Eloquence and English Renaissance Literature* (Hemel Hempstead, 1992), provides a useful balance to Miola's very Senecan Shakespeare. Rhodes begins with a lucid synopsis of sixteenth-century attitudes to the English language, and to rhetoric in particular: the humanists' reading of Cicero and Quintilian had taught them that in eloquent speech was a practical power which they sought to harness by perfecting the vernacular. His central contention is that this concept of rhetoric went into retreat in the 1590s as literary fashion put writers' verbal facility in the service of scurrility and satire, and so subverted the lofty moralism of earlier proponents of eloquence; finally rhetoric becomes itself the object of satire.

This is, of course, the development which underlies the shift in fashionable prose style during the period, from Ciceronian verbosity to Senecan terseness. Rhodes constructs this as a movement from Marlowe through Harvey, Nashe, and Marston, to Jonson: from a dramatist of heroic speech to a satirizer of misplaced eloquence. This is evident even in the Marlowe canon itself: for Rhodes, the figure who strikes the keynote is not Tamburlaine but Mycetes, and subsequent plays present a series of heroes in recession from the Scythian's rhetorical achievement; Faustus, for example, is seen as more fool than scholar, and in this regard the relativity of humanist ideals is already imaginatively understood. Shakespeare (treated in a ten-page 'coda') is a marginal figure in this process, who resisted the anti-rhetorical, Senecan trend and so earned Jonson's condescension. The point is not that Robert Miola's account of Shakespeare is 'wrong' but that it is partial: by refusing him centrality (the bravest decision in a sensible but generally pedestrian book), Rhodes illuminates one field in which the influence of Seneca is conspicuously absent.

There is more than a grain of truth in the paradox that, for the historicist Shakespearian, the most useful studies are those which never mention Shakespeare. In this respect there is much to value in Michel Jeanneret's newly translated *A Feast of Words* (Chicago, 1991) and in Patricia Fumerton's lifelessly titled *Cultural Aesthetics* (Chicago and London, 1991). Jeanneret's topic is banquets and table-talk in sixteenth-century French literature, especially Rabelais, Erasmus, and Montaigne, while Fumerton deals with Renaissance court culture's fascination with apparently marginal and trivial things, from gilt nutmegs to Hilliard miniatures and their literary equivalent, sonnets. Neither book has much directly to say about Shakespeare, but each casts a great deal of collateral light. Fumerton argues, for example, that the sonnet form simultaneously exposed and concealed the innermost self, and goes on to demonstrate that the publication of such poems usually entailed obfuscation as well as exposure – a coy but ultimately disingenuous sense of privacy at once invaded and maintained. The 'mystery' of *Shake-Speares Sonnets* becomes a generic feature, not an historical conundrum to be solved by identification of the *poematorum personae*. From Jeanneret, meanwhile, we learn that the abstemiousness of the court of Navarre is even more ill-considered than Shakespeare leads us to believe: fat paunches did not make for lean pates in sixteenth-century France, for the banquet was a social occasion which unified the body and the mind, both of them feasting – on cates and on conversation respectively.

My point is the simple one that a book's utility in contextualizing Shakespeare is directly proportionate to the amount of contextual material it contains. An excellent example is F. David Hoeniger's enormous and clearly laid-out study of the period's medical knowledge, *Medicine and Shakespeare in the English Renaissance* (Newark, 1992). Shakespeare is far from absent here – Hoeniger is always punctilious about making applications where appropriate, and concludes with a detailed study of the medical aspects of *Macbeth*, *All's Well That*

Ends Well, and *King Lear* – but the wider subject is developed with patience and a painstaking scholarship which should make this the standard reference work. Of course, not all historicizing books have such aspirations: Richard F. Hardin's *Civil Idolatry* (Newark, 1992), for instance, is a contribution to an existing debate on kingship in the period, and so can afford to streamline its material somewhat as it offers its useful and cogent corrective to Kantorowicz's influential but Procrustean view of the sacred nature of monarchy in Renaissance political theory and in Shakespeare's plays.[3] Rather it is new lines of enquiry which are most debilitated by an author's swooping over-hastily to deal with major, canonical texts. That is why David C. McPherson's *Shakespeare, Jonson, and the Myth of Venice* (Newark, 1990) is such a frustrating missed opportunity.

Using a rich selection of source material, McPherson attempts to reconstruct English attitudes to Venice around 1600, and, following some recent historians, posits the existence of a 'myth' of Venice which credited the city-state with exceptional justice, wealth, and political wisdom. The breadth of scope of these opening chapters is misleading, however: the book's structure resembles a funnel as it closes in, chapter by chapter, on three individual plays. Of course, any book on this subject would have to give detailed consideration to *The Merchant of Venice*, *Othello*, and *Volpone*, and McPherson's analysis of the 'myth' as it influenced Shakespeare and Jonson is generally unexceptionable; but it is profoundly disappointing that there is no corresponding analysis (or even mention) of the Venetian settings and characters in, among others, Marston's *Antonio* plays and Shirley's *The Gentleman of Venice*, and that, in consequence, we must still await a properly comprehensive study of the 'myth' of Venice in English Renaissance drama.

It is not only unimaginative but also untimely to fetishize Shakespeare and other major texts like this: the literary canon has rarely been less stable than it is at the end of the twentieth century. This is not to say that Shakespeare is ever likely to cede precedence to Marston or Shirley, or, less humiliatingly, to disappear from the canon altogether, despite recent attempts to dislodge him: the staying-power of England's 'national poet' is apparent even in parts of the world where anti-colonial discourse has more urgency, as Laurence Wright has shown in a survey of his continuing influence in African curricula, theatre, and literature.[4] Even so, the upheavals in English studies over the past few decades have superseded the idea of a Great Tradition in which Shakespeare is Top Poet: that narrow concept of the canon excludes too many voices. If we accept that, for practical purposes, some form of canon will, like the poor, always be with us, then the restoration of those lost voices to the public ear must be one of the primary imperatives of non-Shakespearian editing today. In the field of sixteenth-century poetry, there can be few scholars better qualified to undertake this task than Emrys Jones.

The research that lies behind Jones's *New Oxford Book of Sixteenth-Century Verse* (Oxford, 1991) is nothing less than a systematic, comprehensive reconsideration of the period's surviving corpus of non-dramatic poetry: consciously superseding the original *Oxford Book of Sixteenth-Century Verse* (Oxford, 1932) by E. K. Chambers, Jones admirably reconstellates the Tudor and Elizabethan masterpieces which no such anthology can do without. The selection shows a new patience with the slower effects of narrative verse and a recognition of the period's variety of verse forms, from skeltonics to fourteeners, along with a corresponding shift of bias away from the pretty lyricism of poets like Thomas Lodge and Nicholas Breton, both of them less generously represented than in the volume's predecessor. The gainers are

---

[3] Ernst Kantorowicz, *The King's Two Bodies* (Princeton, 1957).

[4] 'Aspects of Shakespeare in Post-Colonial Africa', *Shakespeare in Southern Africa*, 4 (1990–1), 31–50.

writers whose style and subject-matter are more to our taste than that of Chambers-era readers: Marlowe's unexpurgated translation of Ovid now has its fair share of entries, and the 1590s verse satire movement benefits from the provision of far more representative selections from Hall and Marston, along with the new admission of Samuel Rowlands and, importantly, Donne. At the same time, Jones has reassessed a clutch of neglected minor figures, from Gascoigne to Harington, and from the Earl of Oxford to the Countess of Pembroke; some, like Robert Sidney, are included for the first time.

Jones's most eccentric decision is to include a few items of seventeenth-century origin. Given that he is acutely conscious of the lack of space, and that the merits of the poetry written before and after 1579 will make any sixteenth-century anthology bottom-heavy, the insisted-upon chronology which admits Donne should also debar extracts from, for instance, *Antony and Cleopatra* and *The Two Noble Kinsmen*, or Ralegh's verses written on the eve of his execution: Jones is readier to exclude the passages of Jacobean Dekker selected by Chambers than those of Jacobean Shakespeare, but greatness alone should be no passport into a volume such as this. That said, it is in every respect a better selection than its predecessor, and a better edition too: the poems are presented without the often sentimental titles affixed by Chambers, and some misattributions are now corrected.[5] Jones also offers the light annotation which is so essential to the general reader, though it is a pity that the volume perpetuates the user-unfriendly practice of indexing such anthologies by poem- rather than page-numbers, which places publishers' economics before ease of reference.

A more specialized Shakespearian context is offered in John Kerrigan's monograph-with-anthology, *Motives of Woe: Shakespeare and 'Female Complaint'* (Oxford, 1991). Kerrigan places 'A Lover's Complaint' – so convincingly vindicated in his New Penguin edition of the Sonnets (Harmondsworth, 1986) – in a tradition which stretches back to Anglo–Saxon times and forward to Pope and beyond: the plaintful female voice framed by an observing male reporter proves to be a recurrent poetic device in formal genres as diverse as lyric, satire, and prose epistle. Kerrigan surveys the development of the complaint in a dense, meaty introduction which is flawed only in the absence of a very necessary index.

The dramatic context is always harder to anthologize than the poetical: the days of Dodsley's *Old English Plays* are long gone, and the norm is now the smaller, topic-centred collections offered by series like the Revels Plays Companion Library, whose most recent entry, Peter Corbin and Douglas Sedge's *The Oldcastle Controversy* (Manchester and New York, 1991) pairs the less accessible of the three Elizabethan plays to feature Sir John Oldcastle. A radical but ultimately unconvincing alternative to this narrow focus is presented by David Mann in another specialized collection, *The Elizabethan Player* (London and New York, 1990).

Mann's unifying subject is the process by which, when an entertainment industry acquires institutional solidity, one of the things it starts to dramatize is itself: from *The Taming of the Shrew* and *Sir Thomas More* onwards, several plays included episodes featuring professional actors among the characters, a trend which reached its height during the period of competition between the adult and boy companies. Like *Motives of Woe*, Mann's book does double duty as a study of this phenomenon and an anthology of lengthy extracts to illustrate it; most of the ground is covered, though *A Mad World, My Masters* defies this selective approach, and Mann's failure even to mention *Summer's Last Will and Testament* leaves a significant lacuna. An edition of bits of plays will

---

[5] For example, 'His golden locks time hath to silver turned' (or, in the Chambers selection, 'The Old Knight'), which has been long an interloper in the Peele canon, is now given to Sir Henry Lee.

always be of fairly limited utility, but even for Mann's purposes the device does not serve its turn. The crucial difference from *Motives of Woe* is the structure: whereas Kerrigan keeps the monograph separate from the anthology, Mann tries to integrate them, and the result is a ceaseless switching of modes which interferes with the development of the argument. In each chapter, Mann introduces one of the texts with basic (but occasionally erroneous) information, and then places the extract before us without further comment. Every time, it is left up to us to draw our own conclusions, as if the provision of the evidence obviates further analysis by the author. Heap of broken fragments, and inconclusive excursus, *The Elizabethan Player* disappoints in both its functions.

If Mann's book is a fatal compromise between anthology and monograph, one cannot help but feel that *The Oldcastle Controversy* is a single-play volume straining towards the condition of an anthology. *Sir John Oldcastle, Part 1* is a play of great interest beyond its Shakespearian associations, and it is given an unexplained and unchronological primacy in the volume; *The Famous Victories of Henry V*, only loosely associated with the late 1590s 'controversy' over the historical interpretation of Oldcastle, seems almost to serve, along with some extracts from Weever's *Mirror of Martyrs*, as a makeweight. It would be churlish not to welcome this good modern edition of two rare plays, but it is an irksome feeling nonetheless that one of them may be there solely because Drayton, Hathway, Munday, and Wilson are not names to conjure with in a generally author-centric editorial market.

The survival of the author – part of Western culture's long hangover from Romanticism – means that the canon tends to remain an exclusive club, with anonymous or multi-author plays like *Oldcastle* or *The Witch of Edmonton* relegated to the margins, or at least to the Revels Plays Companion Library.[6] Obversely, editions of a playwright's Collected Works are prestige publications, irrespective of the often

varying merits of the plays which they contain. The 'Beaumont and Fletcher' juggernaut, now careering onwards without its originator, the late Fredson Bowers, but under the capable supervision of his former pupils Cyrus Hoy, George Walton Williams, and Robert Kean Turner, is a case in point. The most recent volume (VIII, Cambridge, 1992) offers six plays of the 1610s: in particular, reliable texts of *The False One* and *The Knight of Malta* are welcome, and Bowers's own edition of *Sir John van Olden Barnavelt* valuably complements the Malone Society's diplomatic transcript of the MS, though perhaps the Benny Hill fatuities of *The Custom of the Country* are less urgently required. It is regrettable that, having neither explanatory notes nor critical introductions, this edition gives the reader less help than it might; one can only hope that we shall not have to wait twenty years for the companion volumes, as we did with the Bowers Dekker.

For the same reason, teachers of Renaissance Women's Writing courses everywhere will give only two cheers for the reissue of the 1914 Malone Society edition of Elizabeth Cary's *Mariam* (Oxford, 1992): an unannotated diplomatic type-facsimile, though better than nothing, has its limitations as a seminar text. The Society can look to scholars and bibliographers for the third cheer, however, to greet the useful update which Marta Straznicky and Richard Rowland provide to A. C. Dunstan's original introduction.

Mariam is a rare instance of a play which has migrated from the corpus to the canon almost without editorial assistance, but it is fair to say that neither the Malone Society Reprints nor *The Dramatic Works in the Beaumont and Fletcher Canon* are series likely, even with more comprehensive annotation and introduction, to abet the process. The cutting edge of this aspect of the editorial project is where commercial and academic imperatives meet, and where ideals

---

[6] *Arden of Faversham* is an almost unique exception.

and realities make their compromise, in the main Revels series: since the time of Clifford Leech, the authority of The Revels Plays, combined with a concern to produce accessible and relatively cheap texts, has made the series the gateway to the canon. But such an entrance can easily be blocked: it may have seemed appropriately cautious to keep Middleton's name off the title page of Anne Lancashire's edition of the so-called 'second' *Maiden's Tragedy* (Manchester and Baltimore, 1978), but given the continuing commercial viability of authorship it was also a blunder which left an important play stuck in the gateway, half-in, half-out, and obstructing the admission of other 'risky' texts.

In this context, the general editors' decision to embark on a new complete Lyly, beginning with a volume (Manchester and New York, 1991) combining George K. Hunter's excellent edition of *Campaspe* with David Bevington's of *Sappho and Phao*, deserves more applause, for starting the reassessment of a significant body of work, than disappointment, for perpetuating the author fetish. A complete Revels Marston is probably not on the agenda – though perhaps *What You Will* and *Jack Drum's Entertainment* might make the Companion Library – but the only really conspicuous gap is *The Dutch Courtesan* now that W. Reavley Gair has provided a thorough basic edition of *Antonio and Mellida* (Manchester and New York, 1991), years overdue to pair his Revels edition of the sequel, *Antonio's Revenge* (Manchester and Baltimore, 1978). Both new volumes offer better texts than have previously been available: Bevington's *Sappho and Phao* is based on the recently identified first Quarto, and Gair's *Antonio and Mellida* mismatches his *Antonio's Revenge* in one far from regrettable respect in modernizing the spelling of the characters' Italian names for the first time – 'Matzagent' of the Quarto and the Revels *Revenge* becomes Mazzagent, and so on. Both could have done more in establishing these plays' claim on our (or our students') attention, however, by including some discussion of their subsequent influence, thus 'placing' them in relation to more familiar texts; a particularly notable omission is Gair's silence about *Twelfth Night*'s considerable debt to *Antonio and Mellida*.

If the state of the canon determines what we are able to teach, and the general reader to obtain, it is the state of the corpus which most excites diligent scholars. This year they have had that rare treat, two 'new' works of Jacobean drama. From C. E. McGee, we have an edition of 'The Visit of the Nine Goddesses' (1620–1), the only surviving late Jacobean country-house masque written for a cast of women.[7] The most likely author is Thomas Carew, making the masque an interesting precursor to his well-known *Coelum Britannicum* (1634). For the Shakespearian, however, the most welcome news is that *Tom a Lincoln* is at last generally available.

The manuscript containing the play (at least three leaves of which are missing) was discovered at Melbourne Hall in 1973, acquired quietly by the British Library in 1980, and is now published by the Malone Society in a diplomatic transcript by G. R. Proudfoot (Oxford, 1992).[8] The play is a very long and very episodic piece – the full text must have been as long as *Hamlet* – and one can well understand why the chorus-narrator, Time, repeatedly calls for the audience's patience and attention as the action takes the eponymous, illegitimate hero around the world: to jousting at the court of his father King Arthur, and thence on a punitive expedition to France, an excursion to fairyland where he is lusted after by the queen of the somewhat Amazonian fairies, and finally a visit to the court of Prester

---

7 '"The Visit of the Nine Goddesses": A Masque at Sir John Croft's House', *English Literary Renaissance*, 21 (1991), 371–84.

8 The MS also contains miscellaneous poetical and legal jottings, including one poem in Welsh, all of which associates the text with Morgan Evans of Gray's Inn, the copyist for more than half of the play. One Welsh characteristic of the passages in Evans's hand, not noted by Proudfoot, is the occasional use of *w* as a consonant in the word 'bwy' (i.e. 'buy'; lines 33, 1278).

John where he kills a dragon, finds a wife, and is the unwitting cause of a string of royal suicides.

There are divers things here that, in the commercial theatre, the length of the play would probably not bear in the presentment, and Proudfoot is convincing in linking it with a Gray's Inn Christmas entertainment of the 1610s. Nonetheless, its commercial-theatre associations are its most immediate point of interest. Generically it belongs with the romantic adventure dramas of Heywood and the Red Bull, so, as might be expected, its literary quality is extremely variable. Despite occasional gems, there is also a lot of bad verse to wade through: the stark sublimity of lines like 'We must go cope the dragon' (2040) stands out amidst fumblings and clichés. But such beautifications are often with Shakespeare's feathers: besides obvious plot similarities with *The Winter's Tale* and *Henry V* among others, the play is rich with verbal echoes from the Globe, including some plays not in print when it was written. Proudfoot's introduction sketches an outline – one can scarcely do more in a Malone Society Reprint – but there is still much scholarly work to be done on *Tom a Lincoln* and the evidence it offers of the early reception and assimilation of Shakespeare.

II

Stanley Wells is unusual amongst Elizabethan theatre scholars in that his work often envisages a direct, practical application for his conclusions about performance conditions. That application will take place on the stage of Sam Wanamaker's reconstructed Globe: 'We shall need', says Wells, 'to think in the closest practical detail about the staging requirements of the plays we want to perform in it, and about the performance styles that are appropriate.'[9] His recent thinking has been devoted to the staging of the supernatural, and in the First Annual Shakespeare Globe Lecture, delivered in March 1990 and now published, he offers a lucid analysis of the theatrical realization of appar-

ition scenes in four plays.[10] Though his text is scrupulously footnoted, Wells's tone is that of a well-judged public lecture rather than an entry in *Notes and Queries*: it is a study underpinned by deep scholarship rather than the direct expression of it. Only on one occasion does the lecture-room jocularity get out of hand, when Wells remarks, on the Spirit's Latinity in *The Contention, Part 1*, that 'Elizabethan dramatists seem to have assumed that characters consigned to the underworld spent their time in improving their classical education' (p. 8). The joke itself is an old one, cracked by Dover Wilson in 1928, and it obfuscates the real issue, the association of Latin with magic *via* Roman Catholic ritual.[11] In general, however, this pamphlet will be essential reading for directors seeking once again to affright the Globe with visitations from the nether world.

Most of the scholarship on Elizabethan playhouse practice that has accumulated over the years has been far less pragmatic in its aims, and it is perhaps in consequence that it has all too often been the pursuit of impractical men. A prime example emerges from David Bradley's book, *From Text to Performance in the Elizabethan Theatre* (Cambridge, 1992): the work of W. W. Greg on the seven surviving theatrical 'plots' reveals a strikingly deficient sense of the practicalities of theatrical performance. These documents, Greg theorized, were the Elizabethan equivalent of call-sheets: 'suspended on a peg in the wall', they served 'to get the actors on to the stage at the right point', and 'to remind those concerned when and in what character they were to appear'.[12] Though this explanation has

9 'Staging Shakespeare's Apparitions and Dream Visions', *The First Annual Shakespeare Globe Lecture* (London, n.d.), p. 3. The pamphlet itself is unpaginated.
10 See also his 'Staging Shakespeare's Ghosts', in Murray Biggs *et al.*, *The Arts of Performance in Elizabethan and Early Stuart Drama* (Edinburgh, 1991), pp. 50–69.
11 John Dover Wilson, 'The Schoolmaster in Shakespeare's Plays', *Essays by Divers Hands*, 9 (1930), 23.
12 W. W. Greg, *Dramatic Documents from the Elizabethan Playhouses* (Oxford, 1931), pp. 70, 77, 3.

become orthodoxy, most of it collapses under sustained critical scrutiny. It is a seriously under-rehearsed actor who needs reminding what part he is playing, and this latent underestimation of the period's theatrical professionalism is perhaps reflected in Greg's confident assumption that these occasionally confused documents, written in a crowded secretary hand and massing actors' entries into scene-by-scene paragraphs, could ever have been 'actually used in performance' for the purpose he suggests.[13]

Bradley's alternative hypothesis associates the plots with preparation rather than performance: documents which contributed to the play's transition from script to stage, and which are therefore an important source for any consider-ation of the theatrical logistics of the time. These logistics were, he sensibly asserts, an important factor in the composition of any play: the notion of an insouciant playwright, producing idealized, literary works without regard to the constraints of the loathed stage, pays too little attention to the realities of com-mercial scriptwriting. The book's analysis underlines the basic requirement that twelve, or sixteen, might easily act a play, with whatever help was needed from boys; given that doubling would usually be necessary, the actors would also need time between appearances to change their costumes, though Bradley does not con-sider the possibility of quick-change artists such as, for example, *The Gentleman Usher* seems to require in the role of Sarpego.[14] The plot was where the dramatist's prescience was tested against the human resources of the company, and the surviving examples reveal occasional miscalculations in instances of what Bradley calls the 'crucial scene', which calls for more actors than were available and enforces the co-option of miscellaneous tiremen, gatherers, and red-faced fellows.

At the core of the book is a case study of *The Battle of Alcazar*, the only play for which both plot and text survive. Bradley carefully matches the staging implicit in the plot to the demands of the text, and in the process sorts out a long-standing confusion over the doubling pattern, which had so foxed the bibliographi-cally minded Greg, by pointing out the obvious but hitherto overlooked fact that actors in black make-up are not available to double white characters. The analysis vindicates the Quarto text from Greg's charge, made in *Two Eliza-bethan Stage Abridgements* (Oxford, 1923), that it was a corrupt adaptation, and means that the play will now have to be re-edited, since the standard Yale edition is a 'reconstruction' based on Greg's conclusions.

The scholarly agenda should also include further thinking about the plots, for if Bradley's conclusions about staging are generally sound (except for an eccentric first chapter about entrances and stage doors), the finer points of his theory about the exact nature and purpose of the plots are not. The 'Plotter', he suggests, was not the lowly theatre functionary Greg assumed, but a powerful figure akin to the modern director, who planned the production and assigned the parts: the plot was his working paper, and was superseded by the prompt-book. The central failing of this thesis is that it undervalues the palaeographical dimension: Bradley gives too little weight to the evidence of the physical features of the plot manuscripts, or to the reasons for their survival. That these supposedly ephemeral documents were pre-served at all (and preserved with the prompt-book in the case of *The Seven Deadly Sins, Part 2*) is an anomaly in his theory, and the fact that they all have a hole cut near the top and are mounted on card (presumably for durability) suggests that at some point they were exhibited

---

[13] Ibid., p. 84. I owe some aspects of these observations not to Bradley but to a paper given by Anne Pickering at The Shakespeare Institute in 1990. I am grateful to Mrs Pickering for permission to draw on her work, which was conducted independently of Bradley's.

[14] In the first scene, Sarpego exits and, after only one line (I. I. 213 in the Regents edition), re-emerges in a different costume. (In the Holaday edition, Robert Ornstein makes him change on stage, but this would obviate the need for the exit marked in Q.)

for general company use. Such facts and inferences may not be fatal to Bradley's theory (though the indications of probable aural transmission in the plot of *The Dead Man's Fortune*[15] are harder to explain away), but they also admit the possibility that the plots remained necessary features of a production even after the prompt-book was drawn up, and that they were produced by a nominated member of the company recording collective decisions and discoveries made at the initial rehearsals. The case for the magisterial Plotter is not proven; the work of David Bradley has not solved a mystery, but opened a debate.

Five weeks after Bradley's study, the same publisher issued T. J. King's *Casting Shakespeare's Plays* (Cambridge, 1992); in fact, each book advertises the other on its dust jacket. The point is worth making because King writes in apparent ignorance of Bradley's ground-breaking work: theatrical plots, he asserts confidently, were 'posted backstage to remind the actors which parts they play' (pp. 6–7), and were drawn up from the scene-by-scene outline which, he claims, an author would invariably produce for the company before being commissioned to write the full script. We need not be too disappointed by this, however, for King's book has very little authority to lose by the inclusion of a few out-of-date ideas: that he should pass off Greg's theories and conjectures about plots as undoubted fact is, unfortunately, symptomatic of the tissue of often unsupported and usually highly questionable assumptions which makes up his study.

For example, King shows bizarre certitude, and not a shred of evidence, in his assertion that Forobosco in *The Duchess of Malfi* is 'a comic servant' (p. 53). Since Forobosco is a 'ghost' character who is mentioned but never appears in the extant text, this would seem rather difficult to prove, but the absence of data is never prominent amongst King's worries. As an account of theatre practice from 1590 to 1642, the book is alarmingly free with chronology: King has apparently never considered the possibility that some things might have changed in the course of fifty-two years, for evidence from late in the period is taken, without a trace of doubt or scepticism, to hold true for the whole. In contrast, where consistency might reasonably be expected, such as in his theorizing about casting practices for the smaller roles, it is in short supply. He explains the appearance of minor actors' names in some prompt-books by hypothesizing that they would typically have joined the company at the last moment, but this sits ill with his assertion (unsupported, but presumably from Gosson) that hired men received 'weekly wages' (p. 50): men on the payroll would have been available for rehearsal at any stage, and every actor knows the desirability of full-cast work early on.

Most of the book is taken up with a series of statistical tables analysing the distribution of parts in various plays: by establishing the length of each role scene by scene, King provides the evidence to determine their relative prominence and the possibilities for doubling. In most cases of plays with two or more substantive versions, the texts are dealt with separately, though F *Troilus and Cressida* is omitted, narrow-mindedly, on the argument that the casting requirements are the same as for Q: the possibility that the statistics might be useful for other purposes has evidently not been considered. In practice, that utility is further limited in that the tables go unlisted, while the absence of pagination in parts of the book makes them virtually impossible to find *via* the index. In this and most other respects, scholarship is ill-served by *Casting Shakespeare's Plays*.

In the present climate of revisionism, it is a shame that the work of both Bradley and King is still bound by the belief that boys invariably played the women's roles. Bradley, for instance, is altogether off-handed in his dismissal of the possibility that Cariola in *The Duchess of Malfi*

---

15 For example, in line 50, the word 'executioner' is preceded by a deleted 'x', and 'his' with deleted 'is'. Bradley reproduces the plot on pp. 92–3.

might have been played by a senior actor, which other scholars have bent over backwards trying to explain away: Robert Pallant, who had been acting since 1592 and is also listed as playing the Doctor, 'would hardly have doubled in the role of a waiting-woman' (p. 85).[16] In fact, as James H. Forse shows, this is an orthodoxy based on Restoration testimony which is at best ambiguous, and which is contradicted by some direct Jacobean evidence: as well as the cast list in the *Malfi* Quarto (which Forse fails to mention), the Ralph Crane manuscript of *Sir John van Olden Barnavelt* (1619) clearly assigns the part of Barnavelt's wife to Nicholas Tooley, who was probably in his forties and had been with the King's Men since 1605.[17]

Regrettably, Forse's article is in most respects a rather silly piece which will be easily discounted. He rightly attempts to discredit the theory of the 'exceptionally talented boy actor' for whom Shakespeare wrote his demanding female roles, but his argument is based solely on the recurrence of viragoes throughout the canon – a category which he takes to include, among others, Nerissa, Audrey, Gertrude, and the Countess of Rousillon. He might have done better to consider the extraordinary length and range of the part of Alice in *Arden of Faversham*, who has nearly twice as many lines as each of the principal male characters; far more than anything Forse has to offer, the play's textual status as one of the 'Pembroke group' of memorially reconstructed piracies dents the idea of the single, gifted boy who alone could handle such a part.[18] He is less interested in non-Shakespearian roles such as this because his overriding, almost obsessive concern is the eccentric notion that Shakespeare himself specialized in female roles, and created the part of at least one virago, Queen Margaret. Crackpot speculation it may be, but we should not overlook the genuine possibility the essay opens, however inadequately, of a less uniform practice than Bradley and King assume in the casting of women's parts on the Shakespearian stage.[19]

Most other developments in this field have

been, to steal a metaphor from the archaeologists, 'keyholes'. There is many an example in a collection edited by John Astington which is ambitiously and perhaps misleadingly entitled *The Development of Shakespeare's Theater* (New York, 1992). This is in fact an anthology of miscellaneous papers from a conference seminar, and has evidently been a long time in the press – one essay is supplied with a hurried postscript to take account of the Rose excavation of 1989. The book is most striking in its indication of a shifting centre of gravity in the subject: most of the contributors have turned their attention away from London to Norwich or Cambridge, away from the Shakespearian era to the early Tudor period and the 1630s, away from professional performances to amateur ones – even away from the stages of the London playhouses to their roofs and turrets. The same movement is apparent in the new volume of *Medieval and Renaissance Drama in England* (5, 1991), in which the commercial aspects of the playhouse business are almost as prominent as the aesthetic: for instance, Roslyn L. Knutson argues that Henslowe's Diary indicates that the Admiral's Men were expanding their commercial operation in 1599, which entailed substantial investment in new plays; and S. P. Cerasano considers the attempt in 1598 by Henslowe and Alleyn to acquire the Mastership of the Bears (an office which they were

---

[16] See Gerald Eades Bentley, *The Jacobean and Caroline Stage* (Oxford, 1941–68), vol. 2, pp. 519–20, for the standard explanation of the 1623 cast list. In fact, it would add an interesting slant to the character if she were seen as an older woman, played by Pallant senior, underlining in particular the desperation of her pretended pregnancy at the hour of her death.

[17] Bentley suppresses this information in his entries on the play and on Tooley: *The Jacobean and Caroline Stage*, vol. 2, pp. 601–2, vol. 3, p. 416.

[18] Why write, or pirate, a play which your company lacks the acting resources to stage?

[19] James H. Forse, 'Why Boys for (wo)Men's Roles? or, Pardon the Delay, "the Queen was shaving."', *Shakespeare and Renaissance Association of West Virginia: Selected Papers*, 15 (1992), 6–27.

eventually able to buy in 1604), and posits that their concern was not to gain control of the Bear Garden as a potential Hope Theatre but to branch out into bear-baiting as another lucrative entertainment business.[20] From architecture to accountancy, students of the English Renaissance theatre have acquired a new practicality.

This is not to say that these scholars seek to disestablish the artistic concerns which are the root of our interest in the Shakespearian stage; rather they offer a clearer sense of how such concerns are related to and often dependent on the practical considerations which were often despised or undervalued by earlier commentators. The connection is explicitly invoked by William Ingram in the first essay of Astington's collection: it was the acting companies' aggressively entrepreneurial approach which made possible the emergence of the theatre as a major Elizabethan art form. He suggests that this approach was, in turn, a consequence of the imposition of new and stricter licensing arrangements in 1559: censorship concentrates the business instincts wonderfully, so 'Regulation, restriction, and repression might well have been the best thing to have happened to Tudor stage players' (p. 27). As scholarship becomes less Platonic in its latent assumptions, so the material conditions for drama, censorship included, come to be perceived as relevant determinants, and no longer as contingent and therefore impertinent interventions in the timeless world of art.

Ironically, most of the cultural materialists' work on the state regulation of Elizabethan drama still follows the old idealist track, chafing at restrictions imposed, and so focusing, explicitly or by implication, on perforce unrealized plays; the underlying assumption is that works of art are separable from and corrupted by the means of their production. Richard Dutton offers an alternative point of view in his thorough and persuasive study, *Mastering the Revels* (Basingstoke, 1991), which exposes the *naïveté* of the conspiracy theory of theatrical censorship: the government did not, Dutton contends, impose repressive controls designed to gag dissent and subversion, nor did it (*pace* Jonathan Dollimore) 'harass' playwrights.[21] In fact, the normal relationship between the Master of the Revels and the acting companies was more likely to have been characterized by mutual co-operation than confrontation. Dutton argues that the arrangement whereby the Master should read over and, if necessary, censor plays came into being as an extension of his duties as supervisor of the Queen's entertainment, pioneered by Edmond Tilney at the end of the 1570s. In its early stages at least, it worked as an optional system of quality control: the Master's licence served much the same purpose as the royal crest on packets of cornflakes today, indicating that the play, like the cornflakes, was held to be good enough for the Queen. Probably many plays were licensed which never saw the royal presence, but for the companies it was nonetheless desirable to submit them for the Master's approval, in order to indemnify themselves in the event of subsequent official hostility: a play judged fit for performance before the Queen could scarcely then be judged seditious by her officers.

Dutton is obscure about when (or indeed whether) this system became compulsory, but it was probably another case of Revels Office empire-building by Tilney, who seems to have been just as entrepreneurial as the actors he dealt with.[22] The job brought successive Masters a

---

20 Roslyn L. Knutson, 'The Commercial Significance of Payments for Playtexts in *Henslowe's Diary*, 1597–1603', *Medieval and Renaissance Drama in England*, 5 (1991), 117–63; S. P. Cerasano, 'The Master of the Bears in Art and Enterprise', ibid. 195–209.

21 Jonathan Dollimore, *Radical Tragedy* (Brighton, 1984), p. 24.

22 Evidently a licence was a precondition for performance by Sir Henry Herbert's time as Master; he extracted a written apology when the King's Men jumped the gun with *The Spanish Viceroy* in 1624. Professor Dutton tells me privately that he believes compulsory licensing must have been established by 1592, when Henslowe's records begin.

tidy income, and this, along with the court context of power and patronage in which they operated, made their relationship with the players one of mutual self-interest. It is only when dramatists come to power and prominence (as they did in the 1950s) that censorship is seen as a purely repressive force; to acting companies, concerned as much with getting a show on and keeping out of trouble as with matters of state and subversion, the restrictions are balanced by the enabling effects of the system. But Dutton goes further than this: though some things were disallowed, from the political insolence of *The King and the Subject* to the 'foule and offensive matters' (p. 95) which so upset Sir Henry Herbert in the 1633 revival of *The Tamer Tamed*, 'there is no clear evidence of any Master of the Revels objecting to the *opinions, attitudes* or *doctrines* (as such) expressed within a play' (p. 89). His lucid and pragmatic analysis presents the Revels Office censorship as a means of establishing the boundaries of allowable discussion rather than of stamping out dissent, and so points the way forward for historicist and materialist analyses of English Renaissance drama.

All this makes W. R. Streitberger's edition of Tilney's *Topographical Descriptions, Regiments, and Policies* (New York and London, 1991) seem almost misconceived on occasion. The book is, in Dutton's phrase, 'an exhaustive diplomatic manual on Europe' (p. 54): a compendium of intelligence about the history, geography, and political arrangements of the nations of western Europe, a kind of personal guidebook for the ambassador or political operator, which Tilney compiled over many years, finally presenting a copy to James I. Streitberger has chosen to edit only the last three of the eight books, which deal with the British Isles, and has based his text on the King's presentation copy, now held by the University of Illinois, in preference to the Folger manuscript of an earlier version. In his introduction, however, Streitberger stresses the work's relevance to foreign affairs, and points out that, in spite of the dedication to James and

the revisions made in his copy, Tilney's approach owes more to the aggressive, anti-Spanish policies of the previous reign: '*Topographical Descriptions* stands as a monument to the age of Elizabethan, not to Jacobean, diplomacy' (p. xxxi). This being so, it is surely wrong-headed to choose the Jacobean rather than the Elizabethan version as copy-text. The extraction of the British section of the work is more defensible, though it contains much that Tilney gleaned from Holinshed, Harrison, Stow, and many others, and which is therefore already available in editions of those authors. What is no longer tenable is Streitberger's suggestion that the text may be used as an index of Tilney's political views, and so may help to determine the principles at work in his theatrical censorship: although it is never unhelpful to know the censor's political and personal sensitivities, it is also highly misleading to suppose that censorship is usually, or often, purely a matter of individual whim; now that Dutton's analysis has established that the issue is not what Tilney himself believed, so much as the range of different opinions he would tolerate, the utility of Streitberger's work is, in this respect at least, curtailed.

Dutton's study is also bad news for those who, like A. A. Bromham and Zara Bruzzi, seek for hidden political meaning in English Renaissance drama, for it will make it far more difficult to write books like their '*The Changeling*' *and the Years of Crisis, 1619–1624* (London and New York, 1990). For them, Middleton and Rowley's tragedy was actually a stalking horse, a vehicle for circulating heterodox political opinion in a climate of official repression. This it achieved by using a 'political code', indicated by the presence of topical references, recurrent words and imagery, and obscure specific allusions, which they set out to crack. That topical references, recurrent words and imagery, and obscure specific allusions are common features of the drama of the time seems not to have occurred to them – unless, of course, we are to expect a whole series of code-breaking books to follow.

Though the authors can be acute in their analysis of stage action, their discussion refuses to take anything literally: for example, a phrase which makes adequate sense in context, Vermandero's 'within are secrets' (1. 1. 166), becomes a topical allusion identifying the character as King James, and also an 'entry code' alerting the audience to allegorical 'secrets' within *The Changeling* itself. For all their considerable efforts to relate the details of the play (even those determined by sources)[23] to the Protestant radical politics of the early 1620s, all they can find, as they admit in their introduction, is 'an elusive inconclusiveness: suggestions of contemporary relevance are not obviously followed through' (p. 12). This might seem to make their speculations an untenable exercise from the start, but they do their best to muster conviction by offering shorter hypotheses about the possible political content of other plays and poems of the period; they are apparently unaware that this argument is a closed circuit, seeking to validate an assumption about one text by making it again about several more. Ultimately, their theory can never be absolutely refuted, but by the same token it can also never be satisfactorily proven – in which case, one may ask, why bother to advance it at all?

Of course, one cannot altogether banish Jacobean politics from *The Changeling*: the play's occasional affinities with the circumstances of the Essex divorce case have long been recognized. These are details which are, however, as explicable in imaginative as in political terms: the presence of topical references need not reflect the primacy of topical meaning, merely the 'seeding' of the creative mind by aspects of its contemporary context. That critics from Margot Heinemann to Bromham and Bruzzi have preferred the political option testifies to the continuing danger in some materialist criticism that a sense of history may engulf a sense of literature, a danger which is especially apparent

in Roger Sales's *Christopher Marlowe* (Basingstoke, 1991) in the Macmillan English Dramatists series.

Though the list of commissioned volumes indicates that the series is organized in traditional fashion around authors, Sales seems almost embarrassed to be writing a book about Marlowe: particularly in the early stages, his discussion is prone to spin off at tangents. Fundamentally, the book is a brief, introductory account of the five central plays in the Marlowe canon, concentrating especially on their tendency to promote marginal figures to centre stage; but Sales also feels the need for substantial excursions into aspects of the historical context, including an entire chapter retelling the story of the Babington conspiracy. Certainly it is a plausible undertaking to relate Marlowe's work to the shadowy world of Elizabethan intelligence, but in a single short, popular book, the threshold of explanation is too low: the undergraduate and general readership needs more of the basic historical material than can reasonably be accommodated in a volume which must also contain Marlowe and the argument linking the two.

The series' General Editor, Bruce King, remarks in his Preface on the need for each generation to reinterpret the culture and literature of the past in the light of its own interests. He would have done well to add that the reinterpretations will need to be scholarly, factually accurate, and true to the text. In all these respects, Sales's is a slipshod book. There is a garbled account of the two texts of *Dr Faustus*, but this seems more a gesture than a commitment, since the version he chooses to discuss is Roma Gill's conflation. His history is factually unreliable,[24] and there is a tendency to smother

---

23 For instance, the Spanish setting and, in a digression on *The Witch* (pp. 25–7), the cup made from a skull, are treated as independent, substantive features of the plays without reference to their origins in earlier texts.

24 Some of the smaller errors may be the fault of the proof-reading, which is execrable.

ideas with buzzwords – Spierenburg's 'spectacle of suffering' and Foucault's 'theatre of Hell' are irritatingly recurrent. He also wastes space on that well-known misreading of *Love's Labour's Lost*, 'the School of Night', and on conspiracy theories about Marlowe's death.

Facts are equally subordinate to theories in his discussion of the plays: for example, the suggestion that the original audience would construe the murder of Edward II as a public execution ignores not only the finicky precision of English attitudes towards the methodology of judicial murder, but also the text's insistence on its secrecy. What alone makes it public is its being enacted before spectators on a scaffold-stage, and in this and many another insistence upon the centrality of the medium in any interpretation, Sales seriously underestimates the theatre's power of enchantment which was so strong for contemporary commentators like Heywood and Webster. Muddle is paramount: Edward dies in earnest, but not privately. In the two halves of his point, Sales combines irreconcilables: on the one hand, acquiescence to the theatrical illusion, on the other, a materialism so dogmatic that it will scarcely even acknowledge the existence of the fiction it seeks to analyse. In the tensions of this botched compromise we can see, unresolved, one of the central problems of English studies today; for if a text is no more than a function of historical circumstance, as Bromham and Bruzzi, and sometimes Sales, assume, does not this make the need for modern reinterpretation, and so for the Macmillan English Dramatists series, rather less urgent than Bruce King suggests?

III

'Wipe them up and say no more about them.' So Andrew Lang, after Walter Shandy, about the 'doleful futilities' of Shakespeare's commentators, in a letter of 1899 to H. H. Furness.[25] Marysa Demoor has gathered Lang's side of this correspondence, along with other letters to America, and provided sparse and, regrettably, sometimes unreliable annotation.[26] In this she has rescued readers of *The Letters of Horace Howard Furness* (Boston and New York, 1922) from the frustration attendant upon hearing only one half of a conversation. It is an amiable exchange, the two men chatting about a range of subjects, from salmon-fishing to the anthropology of Borneo, but Shakespeare is their continual theme. As might be expected from his attitude to critics, Lang was an exponent of 'common sense' in the interpretation of the plays, but he was also happy, as an admirer of Joan of Arc, to entertain disintegration and throw out parts of *Henry VI, Part 1*. The larger assaults on the canon by 'the ignorant and impudent "Baconians"' (p. 182) infuriated him, however, and the letters document a growing impatience with this particular breed of Shakespearian futility that eventually resulted in his final, posthumous work, *Shakespeare, Bacon, and the Great Unknown* (London, 1912), which he dedicated to Furness.

Lang has never been alone in his feelings about the 'authorship controversy': it is a subject which arouses a kind of passionate frustration, with the result that polemical and satirical impulses can preclude serious consideration of it, not as an issue but as a phenomenon. This is nowhere better illustrated than in S. Schoenbaum's monumental *Shakespeare's Lives*, now available in an updated edition (Oxford, 1991) looking less like a large brick, and in a new jacket that is monumental only in its ugliness. In some respects it is more an augmentation of the 1970 edition than a thoroughgoing revision, and there are many lingering traces of the original: we are still 'almost a century' (p. 362) after Dowden's *Shakspere: A Critical Study of his Mind and Art* (1875), for example, and, rather

---

25 Marysa Demoor, ed., *Friends Over the Ocean: Andrew Lang's American Correspondents, 1881–1912* (Ghent, 1989), p. 160.
26 For example, the Baconian 'Dr Owen' (p. 166) is identified as one William Otway Owen, when Orville Ward Owen was surely intended.

unfortunately, William Urry remains alive and unpublished (p. 448). One of the casualties of the new edition, however, is part VI, the now abbreviated study of 'Deviations'.

Schoenbaum is an intelligent and perceptive critic, but he is also a bardolater. His prose and his thinking are marred by a lambent religious metaphor: for example, images of Shakespeare are not altered or vandalized but 'desecrated'. This obscurantist veneration sets a bourn how far to be judicious, outside which irrational intolerance takes over: for instance, dramatists who had the misfortune not to be Shakespeare are on the receiving end of a vigorous, peppery sarcasm in lieu of commentary. It is not surprising, then, that the same fate should befall the Baconians, Oxfordians, and other authorship controversialists – or 'heretics', as Schoenbaum distastefully dubs them in another manifestation of the religious metaphor. One can indeed sympathize with his irritation at having to read through the mounds of nonsense produced by anti-Stratfordians, but our sympathy cannot be compounded with relief that nobody else will have to do so: Schoenbaum's refusal to engage with the 'heretics' as anything other than laughable mental cases means that there is still a good book to be written about this particular byway of Shakespearian biography.

This aside, *Shakespeare's Lives* has, as ever, much to commend it: the research input is staggering in its quantity and scope, and few can beat Schoenbaum at his best for wit and urbanity. These qualities are especially evident in his account of the high road of Shakespearian biography from the seventeenth century through Malone to Dowden. Beyond the Victorians, however, as the volume of material increases, so the book fragments into a set of individual studies without any clear line of development; indeed, much of the updating for the new edition is little more than a string of book reviews. Schoenbaum offers not so much a study of Shakespearian biography this century, more a learned Michelin guide; perhaps we shall have to wait a while to see the wood for the trees.

The eighteenth century, in contrast, is a period in which we are starting once again to distinguish the trees: several of the Augustan Shakespearians have received individual scholarly attention. Richard Farmer, a man whom, according to Ritson, 'every lover of Shakespeare, literature, and truth must always regard with the utmost gratitude and respect', is the subject of a thorough biography from the experienced pen of Arthur Sherbo.[27] As well as documenting the published and unpublished revisions to the celebrated *Essay on Shakespeare's Learning*, the book establishes Farmer as an *éminence grise* of early Shakespeare editing – friend and adviser of Steevens, Reed, and Malone, whose work also prompted Johnson to reconsider several emendations. Taking for granted the now outmoded variorum philosophy of editing, Sherbo demonstrates, in relentless detail and with a perhaps unduly peevish tone, that Farmer's contribution to Shakespeare studies has not been properly acknowledged by his successors: the scholar who declared 'The rage of *Parallelisms*' to be almost over (a famous phrase not quoted in the book) turns out himself to have had a 'talent for parallels' (p. 137) which he put to lively use in annotation.[28]

Closer to the beaten track of editorial history, A. D. J. Brown and Edward Tomarken have investigated the work of Alexander Pope and Samuel Johnson. Tomarken's book, *Samuel Johnson on Shakespeare* (Athens, Geo. and London, 1991), treats the edition as an indivisible project rather than breaking it down into the traditional compartments of editorial practice and critical judgement, examining a number of Johnson's major concerns through detailed and sometimes unnecessarily repetitive studies of his work on eight major plays. In the

---

27 *Richard Farmer, Master of Emmanuel College, Cambridge: A Forgotten Shakespearean* (Newark, 1992). Ritson is quoted from p. 39.
28 Brian Vickers, ed., *Shakespeare: The Critical Heritage* (London and Boston, 1974–81), vol. 5, p. 261.

narrower confines of an article, Brown disputes the standard account of Pope as a neoclassicist obsessively trying to impose good sense on a recalcitrant Dead Poet: close attention to his version of a scene from *Romeo and Juliet* reveals an acute critical mind receptive to the virtues of bad sense for comic effect in the Nurse's dialogue.[29] Both authors expose the critical procedure implicit in the respective editions, and from Tomarken's book emerges forcefully a case for the inadequacy of the usual editorial procedures in presenting Johnson on Shakespeare: the Preface is often treated as a separate document rather than as the prelude to the practical criticism of the Notes, and an excessive regard for questions of authorship has led to the omission in otherwise complete editions of notes which, though composed by other hands, nonetheless represent Johnson's critical position in that he allowed them to stand with neither comment nor alteration.

Both studies share the same weakness: where Sherbo's biography of Farmer is so descriptive as to be at times fragmentary, Brown and Tomarken have the Augustan habit of prescriptiveness. Not content with the particularity of their topics, they offer grandiose proposals for the future of English: Tomarken feels that his work on Johnson points the way towards a new moralism in literary criticism, and Brown argues that Pope's 'poetical approach' is the proper one in editing corrupt texts (among which he includes Q2 and F *Romeo and Juliet*), which require not scholarly conservatism but 'major reconstruction by a craftsman with a sensitivity and skill comparable with Shakespeare's' (p. 149). Johnson said well when he remarked (of Warburton), 'Every cold empiric, when his heart is expanded by a successful experiment, swells into a theorist.'[30]

Johnson's long-suffering landlady, Hester Thrale, went on, after a second marriage, to become infatuated with a Shakespearian actor nearly fifty years her junior, William Augustus Conway. The story is told with evident sympathy by Conway's descendant, John Tearle, in *Mrs Piozzi's Tall Young Beau* (Rutherford, Madison, and Teaneck, 1991). Besides its obvious interest for historians of the early nineteenth-century theatre, the book is valuable as material for a case study of a *literata* of the period who is evidently steeped in Shakespeare: Tearle offers a generous but frustratingly undocumented selection from Mrs Piozzi's surviving correspondence and notebooks. It is hard, nonetheless, to shake off the feeling that a disproportionate amount of time has been devoted to a vain, silly, and insecure old woman's infatuation with a young, pretty, and, by most accounts, rather mediocre actor – who seems more than slightly bewildered by it all.

A more significant and substantial contribution to theatrical history is *The First English Actresses* (Cambridge, 1992), Elizabeth Howe's widely read, deeply informed study of the coming of professional actresses to the English stage during the Restoration. Howe deftly examines the impact of this new phenomenon on the construction and subject-matter of English drama after 1660, both in general terms and in the exploitation of the particular talents of individual actresses. Though the period's original plays rightly claim most of her attention, its Shakespeare adaptations frequently serve as a useful touchstone for the innovations which resulted from the professional and the physical presence of women. The professional factor led to a demand for roles, so that Restoration 'Shakespeare' introduced new female characters and expanded existing ones: Davenant's *Macbeth* provides an actress with more Lady Macduff than Shakespeare's, for example, and Cordelia becomes the central character of Tate's *Lear*. The physical, however, creates opportunities for sexual and quasi-pornographic devices ranging from the smutty innuendo

---

[29] 'The Little Fellow has Done Wonders', *The Cambridge Quarterly*, 21 (1992), 120–49.

[30] *Samuel Johnson on Shakespeare*, ed. H. R. Woudhuysen (Harmondsworth, 1989), p. 154.

of the Davenant-Dryden *Tempest* to the sadistic interest in rape apparent in several of Tate's adaptations. Perhaps, familiar as we are with feminist thinking, these are not especially surprising conclusions, but Howe sets them forth with clarity, wit, and a learning which combines admirable thoroughness with an engaging lightness of touch. It is bitterly to be regretted that we can expect no more such fine scholarship from the late Elizabeth Howe.

Two books are concerned, in different ways, with the relationship between modern actors and audiences. The broader, Martin Buzacott's *The Death of the Actor* (London and New York, 1991), is also the more perverse, a vigorous protest at the respect that Shakespearians currently afford the theatrical profession, which sees the actor as a sinister, usurping substitute for the authority of the dramatist, maintaining power through vulgar shock tactics. Depending on your point of view, it is either absurd or obscene to equate histrionics with the tyranny of dictators like Idi Amin and Ferdinand Marcos, but Buzacott's bleak view of human social intercourse allows no alternative: he takes every relationship to be inescapably and absolutely a power relationship, and this means that the only way he can talk about actors is in terms of oppressors and oppressed, turning handy-dandy somersaults as their social status is endlessly reassessed.

In contrast, Murray Cox has more sense of the liberating, therapeutic effects of performance. As a Consultant Psychotherapist at Broadmoor Hospital, he has been the driving force behind a series of actors' visits to the hospital to perform Shakespeare's tragedies for the patients and staff, and he has now edited an account of these occasions, *Shakespeare Comes to Broadmoor* (London and Philadelphia, 1992). Evidently many barriers were lifted, for performers as well as patients. A recurrent theme in the actors' contributions is the discontinuity between preconception and experience: they came with nervousness, not only at Broadmoor's dark but unfounded reputation,

but also that their portrayal of extreme psychological states might fail to convince an audience which had personal knowledge of similar emotional conditions; but they left having faced up to the human reality of rapists and murderers. The patients in turn had to face up to the reality of their crimes and the experience of their victims: although stage blood was not allowed, tragedy nonetheless made an effective Piracquo's finger to penetrate the closed consciousness; as one murderer told Mark Rylance after *Hamlet*, 'Until I saw you with that skull, I never really thought about the actual corpse' (p. 248). The book provides a valuable record of events and of an exceptional audience's reactions, along with broader thoughts about the role of drama in therapy, though the remorseless punning of Cox's prose style will not be to all tastes.

Two new Shakespearian volumes have appeared in Macmillan's Text and Performance series, on *Much Ado About Nothing* (Basingstoke, 1991) and *Romeo and Juliet* (Basingstoke, 1992), by Pamela Mason and Peter Holding respectively. Mason's is the more independent and ambitious of the two volumes: where Holding's discussion rarely strays far from his reading, her account of *Much Ado*, both as text and performance, contains many sensitive observations, and communicates genuine enthusiasm for the play. Neither volume is entirely free from careless factual error: for example, Sir Thomas Wyatt is renamed Andrew (*Romeo*, p. 19), and Leonard Digges, who died in 1635, is credited as the editor of Benson's 1640 collection of the *Poems*, to which verses of his were prefixed (*Ado*, p. 43). One may also query Holding's claim that the story of Romeo and Juliet would have seemed unlikely material for tragedy in the sixteenth century, given that Shakespeare's was not the first play on the subject.

Text and Performance has a long track-record of such mistakes, which an efficient general editor might be expected to remove;[31] but that is the least of the problems of this fundamentally misconceived series. Each volume has two sections, the first a straightforward critical account of the play as 'text', the second a set of shorter discussions of selected productions. The General Editor's Preface explains that this binary format was devised to promote the ongoing interaction between the two disciplines of Literary Criticism and Theatrical Production. The basis of that interaction, however, is surely overlap rather than separation: criticism cannot ignore the theatrical dimension of a play, and production can be the best form of critical interpretation. By sundering Text from Performance, the series directs attention more to the extremities than the shared common ground, and leaves a lacuna at the point where text becomes performance, and where theatrical interpretation takes place.

Both the most recent volumes address this difficulty, in different ways: where Holding speaks in terms of an 'ideal production' (p. 75), Mason takes a more controversially materialist approach, writing in her 'Text' section as if a play has no existence other than in specific performances – for example, in reading out the letter which arrives at the start of the play, she says, Leonato shares the news it contains 'with Hero, Beatrice and *frequently* other members of a household that is largely female' (p. 11, my italics). In Michael Goldman's pseudo-Aristotelian terms, this is to subordinate *praxis* to *poiesis*, allowing it no independence.[32] Holding's alternative, however, only brings up the perennial difficulty of performance-related criticism, the question of authenticity in interpretation.[33] This is the cleft stick in which the Text and Performance format catches its authors.

For all its faults and limitations, the series was timely when it was launched in 1983, when a long-standing antitheatricalism still dominated much school and some university teaching of Shakespeare; but the most recent contributions to the educational debate bear witness to the passing of this moment. A volume of essays

edited by Lesley Aers and Nigel Wheale, *Shakespeare and the Changing Curriculum* (London and New York, 1991), shows teachers and educationalists grappling with the problems and challenges thrown up by school Shakespeare. Performance is evidently a non-issue: the contributions in that area are less concerned with debating its relevance, which is taken for granted, than with exploring the implications of using workshops and videos in teaching.

Higher on the agenda are the modern theoretical approaches which have swept across the academy over the past twenty years. Most of the contributors combine a desire to take account of these new developments with a level-headed concern that the plays should be transmitted as works of art. It is on this ground that cultural materialism comes in for criticism from Fred Inglis: 'the institutionalist and externalist accounts of art, which purport to explain the significance of art by sociological or historicist accounts of its strictly social construction, fall by virtue of their failure to take account of art's special character' (p. 64). Feminist approaches seem to have more currency at school level, as several essays are concerned with hitherto underestimated presences in the plays – black and gay as well as female. Perhaps there is a degree of unimaginativeness in this, however: race and gender are the currently fashionable categories for this sort of activity, but others remain in marginal obscurity – the book has very little to say about class issues, for instance,

---

[31] A prominent earlier example is the first edition of Gāmini Salgādo's volume on *King Lear* (Basingstoke, 1984), written during his final illness and (on that account perhaps understandably) riddled with sometimes egregious errors.

[32] Michael Goldman, *Acting and Action in Shakespearean Tragedy* (Princeton, 1985), p. 12.

[33] H. R. Coursen addresses this problem in *Shakespearean Performance as Interpretation* (Newark, 1992), defending the value of productions both as stimulus and interpretation, paying particular attention to the kinds of reading favoured by the younger critical approaches, such as feminism and cultural materialism.

except in the rather obvious context of *A Midsummer Night's Dream*.

The most worrying feature of the book is a survey of thirteen-year-olds' preconceptions about Shakespeare (pp. 40–1). Here we learn (among other things) that he 'wrote many plays in the late eighteenth century', and that 'You need a degree in English and tonnes of A levels to be able to understand them'; his other accomplishments include paintings, the authorship of the Bible, and a 'Carling black label advert'. The greatest point of agreement is that Shakespeare is boring. Perhaps the best thing that one can say about the new Cambridge School Shakespeare series is that its users will be unlikely to share that opinion.[34]

These editions use the New Cambridge text of the 'scripts' (as they are not unreasonably but nonetheless over-insistently called), but that is their only link with the academic mainstream of Shakespeare editing. The very structure of each volume overturns editorial convention: the 'script' comes first, supplanting the critical account of its themes and style, which is relegated to the back of the book. These non-introductions are written to be suggestive rather than exhaustive, which is a disappointment for the breed of dull-witted schoolboys who compose their own essays by copying out the editor's, and a relief for the teacher wanting to encourage independent thought. Making pupils think for themselves is the central imperative of the series, but its corollary is the absence of explanatory notes: the editors seem unable to give the reader information above the glossarial level without basing an exercise around it. For example, a factual account of 'Mercutio's tragic ladies' in a passage of *Romeo and Juliet* (2. 3. 36–40) is not allowed to stand alone as a helpful piece of annotation: the reader is also asked to 'Work out a short mime showing all the love stories' (p. 72). Presumably the intention is to fix the information in pupils' minds, but the attendant risks are of giving undue prominence to often marginal facts, and, in some cases, of

relativizing those facts by asking readers to debate their relevance.

Most of the exercises call for direct engagement with the 'script' itself. Some offer for discussion such questions as 'Why does Mercutio have to die so early in the play?' (*Romeo*, p. 94), 'How did the Beatrice–Benedick feud start?' (*Ado*, p. 38), and 'Is Lorenzo a creep?' (*Merchant*, p. 102). Others attend to the language in performance, giving due attention to silences and explicating *double-entendres* with a pleasingly unembarrassed frankness. The poetic qualities of the language tend to lose out, however, except in Michael Clamp's *Richard II*, which is as unusual in its focus on imagery and key-words as it is in its general informativeness and the direct relevance of its exercises to the 'script'. The other volumes all too often use Shakespeare like a primary school topic, a focus for various creative activities as much as an object of study: to ask a pupil to 'Make a drawing or write a poem or story to show what the lines mean to you' (*Romeo*, p. 160) is to encourage naive impressionism in lieu of disciplined critical analysis. When the exercises involve improvisation, they usually direct attention away from the 'script': readers are asked to devise and perform versions of 'missing' scenes (but not, on the whole, to consider why they are missing), and to imagine what would have happened if events had not turned out as they do. There is certainly value in raising awareness of the plot as a series of choices which exclude alternatives, but too little is done to discourage 'what if' speculations as an end in themselves. By far the most frequent thing which readers are asked to do, though, is 'Insult

---

[34] *The Comedy of Errors*, ed. Richard Andrews; *King Richard II*, ed. Michael Clamp; *The Merchant of Venice*, ed. Jonathan Morris and Robert Smith; *A Midsummer Night's Dream*, ed. Linda Buckle and Paul Kelley; *Much Ado About Nothing*, ed. Mary Berry and Michael Clamp; *Romeo and Juliet*, ed. Rex Gibson; *The Taming of the Shrew*, ed. Michael Fynes-Clinton and Perry Mills (all Cambridge, 1992).

each other' (*Shrew*, p. 134).[35] If they learn nothing else from these exercises, at least they will know how to curse.

The Cambridge School Shakespeare is potentially very valuable to teachers: it offers a substantial quarry of teaching ideas, not all of them half-baked. For pupils, however, the more traditional approach of its main competitor in the educational market, the Oxford School Shakespeare, is also the more appropriate. The new series is so concerned to avoid the pedagogical and to make Shakespeare as

undaunting as possible, that it tacitly encourages a lack of humility in approaching his work. The tendency reaches its extreme in the edition of *A Midsummer Night's Dream*, which contains an exercise headed, 'Anything that Shakespeare can do, I can do' (p. 40); needless to say, this does not ask the reader to write an enduring classic of world literature.

---

[35] See also *Errors*, p. 66, *Dream*, p. 84, *Shrew*, p. 116, *Merchant*, p. 76.

3. EDITIONS AND TEXTUAL STUDIES
reviewed by H. R. WOUDHUYSEN

Five more volumes from the New Cambridge Shakespeare bring the series past the half-way mark. All the editions are worth having and represent an enormous amount of valuable editorial and critical work: some can for the moment claim their place as the best available edition.[1] The introductions are on the whole useful, even if some contain material which would be better suited to a periodical article rather than to an edition which undergraduates will buy and use. The textual introductions are rather good, but the handling of questions such as date and occasion is very patchy. Some editors go to great lengths to investigate the history of their play in the theatre, often turning up new and diverting information, but only Hattaway manages to use the history to illuminate the play itself.

The series also contains a number of minor but still irritating inconsistencies.[2] The asterisk in the commentary, used to indicate editorial emendation, appears to have been silently dropped: it is present in *2 Henry VI* but not in *Measure for Measure* (both published in 1991) nor in *The Poems* or *Henry V*. Use of the Oxford edition of the complete works is still sporadic.[3] Relined verse, verse set as prose, and prose as verse, are sometimes recorded fully and sometimes only occasionally: the same is true

for the recording of stage directions and of spelling variants. In the note on 2.4.186 Gibbons reports the *sententiae* marked by the Folio in *Measure for Measure*, but Roe ignores their presence in his collations and commentary to *Lucrece*. It is hard to make out what the series' editorial policy is for such thorny points as an/and/and't, enow/enough and such forms as knowst/know'st and so on. Hattaway usually inserts a space between th' and a consonant, the other editors do not.[4] It is also depressing to notice in several of these recent editions that the

---

[1] Ann Thompson with Thomas L. Berger, A. R. Braunmuller, Philip Edwards and Lois Potter, *Which Shakespeare? A User's Guide to Editions* (Milton Keynes, 1992), provide a useful and entertaining account of the current state of play.

[2] Full details of the New Cambridge editions are given in the notes below: *Two Gentlemen* in n. 5, *Measure* in n. 8; the *Poems* in n. 15; *2 Henry VI* in n. 23 and *Henry V* in n. 26.

[3] Hattaway, Gurr and Roe all refer to it, but Gibbons (p. 204 n. 2) makes only one passing reference to the *Textual Companion* in his textual analysis of the play.

[4] Even so doubts as to what is an error and what a silent emendation remain: in *2 Henry VI* 5.3.16 Hattaway prints 'By the mass' where F has 'By'th'Masse', in *Henry V* 3.3.55 Gurr prints 'i'the grund' for F's 'i'th | grund' and in *Measure for Measure* 5.1.86 Gibbons has 'i'th'wrong' for F's 'i'the wrong'.

spelling, typography, and punctuation of the collations are untrustworthy and that errors mar the text.

As Johnson said, *The Two Gentlemen of Verona* may not be one of Shakespeare's 'most powerful effusions', but it is a play full of interest and has its admirers in the study as well as on the stage. The last important single edition of the play was Norman Sanders' in the New Penguin series, issued over twenty years ago. Even before then its position in the canon had attracted some attention – not least because it has been claimed as Shakespeare's earliest surviving play or his first extant comedy. Kurt Schlueter[5] finds it 'more plausible' that Shakespeare began his comic career with *The Comedy of Errors* than 'the more original venture *The Two Gentlemen*, in which he found the basis of his own peculiar kind of comedy and to which he returned for devices to be reused and redeveloped in many of his maturer works' (p. 2), but remains agnostic about the order and dating of the early plays. Unwilling to speculate about this phase of Shakespeare's career, Schlueter is also determined to see *The Two Gentlemen* on its own merits, rather than as a convenient guide to what was to come. This approach allows him to make some interesting remarks about the play's handling of the themes of romance, education and male friendship. However, Schlueter's straight-faced critical introduction is too brief to allow enough room properly to handle important topics such as the play's indebtedness to Lyly, the actual audience or company which Shakespeare might have had in mind when writing the piece, or the play's use of language and parody. There are some good notes on its self-consciousness (see especially the commentary to 1.2.102–27) and the occasional sense it gives of presenting plays within the play.

This sketchiness is sometimes a little heavy-handed – 'The unresolved confusion of the dramatic identity of [Lance's] dog' he writes at one point, 'amounts to a metadramatic statement about the dangers of an over-optimistic expectation that a fellow creature should act as one's *alter ego*' (p. 15) – and contrasts noticeably with his long account of the play's stage history. He devotes some thirty-two pages to this as against barely seventeen for the critical part of his introduction. The play has a more interesting history in the English theatre and has been illustrated more often than has been generally thought. Schlueter documents both these aspects up to John Barton's 1981 production. It is good to be told about the 1821 Covent Garden operatic production which culminated 'in the appearance of Cleopatra's galley on the occasion of a carnival celebration on the "Great Square of Milan"' (p. 31). However, most accounts of productions shed only a faint and intermittent light on the play itself. Contemporary attitudes to its handling of male friendship and romantic love are touched on, most suggestively in the long caption to the plate of Holman Hunt's painting *Valentine Rescuing Silvia from Proteus*. Schlueter argues that this presented the height of the tendency to idealize Valentine, by putting him at the centre of the play's action; he goes on to criticize the figures in the picture for their 'totally unnatural control of emotion' (p. 34). One small detail which, interestingly, Schlueter does not mention is the way in which the disguised Julia plays anxiously with her ring. He also does not refer to the presence in the painting's background of Silvia's father, the Duke of Milan: generally, his introduction has little to say about the play's concern with parental authority and its effects on children.[6]

Schlueter provides a clear and straightforward account of the printing of *The Two Gentlemen* in F. The copy the compositors (here identified as (A)F and C rather than Oxford's D?(F?) and C) had in front of them was a manuscript prepared by Ralph Crane. His copy

---

5 *The Two Gentlemen of Verona*, ed. Kurt Schlueter (Cambridge, 1990), in the New Cambridge Shakespeare.

6 There is a good account of the picture in the catalogue of the 1984 exhibition *The Pre-Raphaelites* at the Tate Gallery, no. 36.

was not a theatrical manuscript, but 'an early draft' or 'an unfinished draft version' of the play (p. 151). Schlueter neatly argues that the characteristic signs of foul-paper copy in speech headings, stage directions, and punctuation were removed by Crane as part of his job. The fact that Shakespeare had not finished the play properly allows Schlueter to explain away several of its difficulties, especially about its geography, but he seems unsympathetic to the idea that whole scenes are missing.[7] His text and collations are accurate. As an editor he is conservative in all respects but one, rarely departing from F or the well-beaten tracks of other scholars: for example, he goes for minimum interference at 1.1.105–6 ('[*Nods*] Ay.') and rather less satisfactorily follows F at 3.1.269 with 'cate-log'. He allows himself a freer hand with names, and on the basis of the principle that F's Protheus should become Proteus, Panthino then becomes Pantino and Thurio becomes Turio; Launce is modernized to Lance, but Silvia does not become Sylvia. The commentary is at times a little thin, but there are some good notes such as one on why the gentlemen go by boat to Milan from Verona (1.1.54) and one on the use of 'you' and 'thee' in the play (4.2.87–8).

It is hard not to feel a slight sense of disappointment with Schlueter's edition: there is nothing actually wrong with it, but there is not enough in it to satisfy an inquisitive theatregoer, a scholar or a critic familiar with the work, or someone reading it for the first time. Schlueter's restrained enthusiasm for the play is attractive, but he seems too reluctant to press his case hard. In his commentary on Hunt's painting, for example, he writes of 'the grotesque compound of horror resolved in hilarity at which the play seems to aim' (p. 34): a fuller exploration of this pregnant remark would have been stimulating.

The unlikely combination of Holman Hunt and Ralph Crane comes together again in Brian Gibbons' edition of *Measure for Measure*,[8] which usefully reproduces Hunt's intense, brooding, serious-minded painting. Gibbons' is in all respects a good edition of this difficult and uncompromising play. Faced with some of the same problems as Schlueter he deals with them at greater length, paying particular attention to the setting and reproduction of short lines: on the whole, *pacè* Bowers, Gibbons preserves F's lineation where he can.[9] Crane's role in the transmission of the play's text is clear, but once again it is hard to determine whether he was working from foul papers or a theatrical manuscript. After a lengthy consideration of the point, Gibbons concludes that foul papers served as the basis of Crane's copy. The foul papers contained characteristic traces of authorial revision during composition, but not of post-composition revisions. Gibbons then goes on to elaborate his argument by suggesting: 'It is possible that some years after 1604 wear and tear of the playhouse "book" had led to a fresh copy being commissioned from a scribe, who supplemented this "book" by consulting the authorial draft; or it is possible that this is what Crane himself did' (p. 205). He also wonders, in relation to the absence of oaths in the play (p. 200), whether post-production changes were entered in Shakespeare's foul papers, perhaps 'taken over from the playhouse "book"', which may have been felt to be too valuable to be given to the scribe'. In other words, Gibbons could be accused of having his cake and eating it, except that indications of both kinds of copy – foul papers and promptbook – can be found behind F's text.

These difficulties are compounded by the fact that although aware of the arguments of the editors of the Oxford *Complete Works* in favour of Crane's working from a prompt-book, Gibbons does not reply directly to all of them.

---

7 See notes to 2.4.108, 2.4.177, 2.4.202, 2.7.86, 3.1.188 and p. 151.

8 *Measure for Measure*, ed. Brian Gibbons (Cambridge, 1991), in the New Cambridge Shakespeare.

9 Schlueter refers to this problem in his commentary on 2.1.109.

This is disappointing, but not in itself altogether surprising since Jowett and Taylor have not yet published their arguments about the play's theatrical adaptation by Middleton. The situation is further complicated in that where the editors of the Oxford *Complete Works* see adaptation, interpolation and non-Shakespearian work, Gibbons most decisively does not. He accepts as Shakespeare's the song at the beginning of Act 4 and the following dialogue (1–22), and consequently keeps the Duke's soliloquy 'Oh place and greatness' (56–61) at its position in F: 'it is psychologically plausible as a soliloquy' he suggests, 'in which the Duke's darker preoccupations ... now compulsively surface in his pause' (p. 201).

Similarly, Gibbons argues that the crowding in F at the beginning of 1.2 (on sig. F1ᵛ) was the result of a compositor's failure to notice that 1.2.71–7 were deleted in his copy text – a deletion which had been taken into account when the casting-off was done. Shakespeare was not responsible for this deletion, which was made for a revival or for publication. Anyway, the apparent repetitions of material from earlier in the scene in 1.2.71–7 'present no significant problem' in the theatre (p. 200). Furthermore, since 1.2.1–66 appear to allude to events of 1604, Gibbons argues that the lines were written then and therefore by Shakespeare. It follows from all this that Shakespeare meant Juliet to be included in the entry at 1.2.97 although she has nothing to say: 'her silent presence ... undoubtedly has an eloquent effect' (p. 198).

Gibbons is also untroubled by other stage directions which some have taken to be anomalous. The Justice has to make his one and only appearance in the play in 2.1 because, although the Provost could return from summoning the confessor for Claudio by the end of the scene and return in time to have his brief exchange with Escalus, the Provost would then have to remain on stage to begin the next scene. Following Lever's argument, Gibbons accepts that material relating to Lucio and Varrius was changed by Shakespeare in 4.3, which results in

their appearance in 4.5 and 5.1. These anomalies, as well as those in the play's time-scheme, especially Lucio's greeting 'Good even' at 4.3.141 when the Duke said 'Good morning' to Isabella under forty lines earlier, point to Crane's source being foul papers. Yet apart from its arguments for prompt-copy based on later non-Shakespearian adaptation, Oxford adduces three further types of evidence against foul papers. First, F's absence of oaths supposes some sort of post-1606 theatrical copy for Crane. Secondly, Oxford also points out three sets of stage directions – all containing the instruction '*Within*' – which suggest prompt-copy (at 1.4.6, 3.1.44/46 and 4.3.97) and thirdly, that in this play F favours 'oh' where Shakespeare preferred 'o': Gibbons does not address these last two issues.[10]

With the exception of one small slip, Gibbons' detailed handling of this complicated text is exemplary.[11] His critical introduction is long and carefully argued, repaying several readings. The stress throughout is on *Measure for Measure* as a tragi-comedy, 'an unstable, experimental kind of drama' (p. 48), which 'involved the bringing together of seemingly incompatible narrative materials and deliberately contrasting dramatic styles, which the dramatist would strive to combine in a design offering a spectacularly surprising conclusion' (p. xii). At first sight, Gibbons' conclusion that *Measure for Measure* is a '"problem"' play

---

10 For what they are worth the o/oh distribution figures for four Crane plays which derive from either foul papers or prompt-copy are as follows: *Tempest* 42:9; *Two Gentlemen* 12:33; *Measure* 7:56; *Winter's Tale* 31:26. Different compositors, of course may have affected these figures: A's hand has been detected in *Winter's Tale*, the other plays have been divided between B, C, D and F.

11 At 4.2.78 he prints 'Arrives' for 'Arise'; at 2.4.169 he silently emends F's 'the affection' to the more metrically regular 'th'affection'. He fails to note that F has an apostrophe before 'Save' at both 2.2.26 and 166 and before 'Pray' (2) and 'Please' (29) in the same scene; on the other hand, he prints ''Faith' at 5.1.497.

'dialectically presenting intellectual and moral issues in the casuistical tradition' (p. 49) may appear a little lame. But his argument goes further in seeking to connect the 'mystical adumbrations' of the tragi-comic playwright along with his 'rhetorical arts' to the equally manipulative role of the prince and 'the Duke's bizarre plotting' (p. 50). For Gibbons, while the audience may feel tempted to see things from the Duke's point of view, instead 'serious ironic criticism' comes from Juliet and Barnardine – an unexpected, even 'baroque' angle, which looks forward to Shakespeare's late plays.

Especially towards its end, the introduction is dense, almost heady stuff, and sometimes it is not immediately clear why a certain line is being pursued: in these respects it is not unlike the play itself. On the other hand, Gibbons handles questions of the play's date, sources, background and so on surely and concisely: he is particularly concerned with its links with *The Phoenix*, *The Malcontent* and *Sejanus*. His notes are full but not over-elaborate and he is quite willing to admit puzzlement or uncertainty over meaning or implication (see, for example, the commentary on 2.1.114 'lower chair', 2.2.127 'Would all themselves laugh mortal', 3.1.231 'refer yourself to this advantage', 3.2.236 'Making practice on the times' and 5.1.1 'cousin'). Yet Gibbons is on the whole unwilling to emend, even where F's meaning is otherwise hard to grasp or is metrically unusual.[12] For example, he retains F at 1.3.28 ('More' for Pope's 'Becomes more'), 2.1.22 ('knows'), 2.1.39 ('breaks of ice' for F's 'brakes'), 2.4.80 ('enshield'), 3.1.38 ('yet', despite the triple-repetition of the word), 3.1.93, 96 ('prenzie', perhaps a coinage 'fusing "princely" and "precise"?'), 3.2.130 ('dearer', a possible modernization of F's 'deare'). There are a few exceptions to this general practice, as at 2.4.9 where he prints 'sere' but is also willing to accept 'sear'd', 2.4.94 where he has 'all-binding' although he accepts that 'all-bridling' is also possible and 4.4.4 where he rejects 'reliver' for 'redeliver', although elsewhere, as he admits, he

prints 'Ignomy' (2.4.112) and 'disvouched' (4.4.1). Apart from removing a comma at 1.3.11, Gibbons' own emendations are confined to stage directions.

By coincidence N. W. Bawcutt's edition of the same play was published at about the same time as Gibbons' and allows a detailed comparison between the two editions to be made.[13] It has to be said that the two editions complement each other in unexpected ways. Where Gibbons worries over critical difficulties and textual problems Bawcutt tends not to. The Oxford editor is sceptical about most of the issues that so exercise the Cambridge one: Bawcutt refuses to pursue what he sees as the hares of contemporary allusions to King James and to other plays. He is an acute and careful observer, much exercised by the alleged lack of modern understanding of the nature of Claudio's sin. In the introduction he is at his best on sources and on the problems of successfully transferring the play to the stage, but he does not give the feeling that he is entirely at ease with the play and the modern responses it has provoked. This is perhaps appropriate for an editor of *Measure for Measure*, but it is not always helpful, as when he introduces his critical discussion by saying that the play 'is a complicated work of art, and its aim is to present a series of vivid dramatic situations, not merely to act as a vehicle for political and moral ideas which as some critics describe them sound like the most banal of platitudes' (p. 45), or when he ends his discussion of the Duke by saying that he is 'a collection of attributes which fail to coalesce' (p. 55). His commentary is often excellent: the notes are full of interesting and useful material and unlike many editors he draws freely on examples and quotations from other contemporary authors, particularly theo-

---

[12] At 2.4.94 and 3.1.93, 96 he uses 'orthographic' and 'orthographically' where he appears to refer to palaeography.

[13] *Measure for Measure*, ed. N. W. Bawcutt (Oxford, 1991), in the Oxford Shakespeare.

logians. Bawcutt and Gibbons differ on many occasions over meanings and interpretations in their commentaries, but the one often shows a need for annotation which the other has missed or skimped, and vice-versa (see, for example, Bawcutt on 1.4.64 'mice by lions', 2.2.98 'hatched', 2.3.28, 3.1.41 'makes these odds all even', 4.4.26 'should').

The most surprising aspect of Bawcutt's edition is the textual introduction. He has some new evidence – the three unusual 'Within' stage directions can also be found in two Crane transcripts (p. 66) – to confirm Crane's hand in the copy for F and tends to the belief that the scribe was working from uncensored foul papers. Conclusive evidence of authorial revision or of revision by another hand is simply lacking; equally, 'there is no decisive evidence for Fletcher's authorship' of the two stanzas of the song which appear in *Measure for Measure* and *Rollo* (p. 71). Furthermore, the dramatic inconsistencies which cause Gibbons and the editors of the complete Oxford edition such difficulty do not worry Bawcutt. Denying that the opening lines of 1.2 refer directly to contemporary events, he finds the two accounts of Claudio's arrest 'complementary rather than contradictory' (p. 73). Similarly, he argues that 'The silences in Act 5 are as much a critical as a textual problem' (p. 74) and that the confusions in the play can be put down to foul-paper copy or to deliberate obfuscation on the Duke's part: as he points out, an audience will barely notice them.

All of this is startlingly refreshing, but mildly puzzling. Bawcutt never directly engages with Jowett's and Taylor's theories about the play's authorship and textual history: the Oxford *Textual Companion* is not mentioned. The reader may be left wondering (not for the first time) about the relationship between the Oxford *Complete Works* and these one-volume editions, but also about whether Bawcutt has over-simplified the problems or brilliantly cut through them. The text he prints is remarkably clean and quite conservative; it is entirely accur-ate and keeps to the Folio wherever possible. Consequently almost all of Oxford's substantive emendations are rejected (apart from the past participle 'execute' for F's 'executed' at 2.1.34 and 'though', the reading of all the other witnesses to the song at 4.1.6, for F's 'but'). He also follows Oxford in having Act 3 in one long scene. Otherwise, like most single-volume Oxford editors he is mainly concerned with stage directions. He has only a few verbal emendations. Juliet becomes Julietta on the rather shaky basis that Isabella often is shortened to Isabel. The forms of F's 'Good'euen' at 3.1.470 and 4.3.147 and of 'pray'thee' at 1.2.61, behind which he detects Crane's hand, are contracted to 'Goode'en' and 'prithee' (and see also 3.1.4 'I'haue' in F, which becomes 'I've'). He holds that Crane may have been responsible for F's 'yond' at 4.3.87 which he expands to 'yonder', but equally it may have been cut short by the compositor (compositorial error is also detected behind Folio readings at 2.4.75 'crafty', 3.1.38 'yet', 3.1.248–9 'time...place' and the speech-prefixes at 4.2.41–4 and 4.3.62; foul-papers error is implicated at 1.2.111 'Thomas tapster', the speech prefixes at 4.2.100 and 4.2.120, and 4.3.126 'his confessor').

Comparing Bawcutt's text against Gibbons' reveals a slight fondness on Gibbons' part for capitalizing abstract nouns. Bawcutt adopts emendations at 1.3.27 'Becomes more', 2.2.58 'back', 2.4.75 'craftily', 3.1.38 'in' for 'yet in', 3.1.306 'Free from' and 4.4.24 'so' on metrical grounds where Gibbons is content to let short or awkward lines in F stand. One important moment where the editions diverge occurs at 2.3.40, where Bawcutt emends the Folio to have Julietta exclaim 'O injurious law', supplying 'a richer meaning' and Gibbons has Juliet say 'Oh, injurious love', which 'goes to the heart of the situation'. There are a few spelling variants (the Oxford reading and location are given first), such as 1.2.62 'Signor'/'Signior', 1.2.128 'raven'/'ravin', 2.2.134 'advised'/'avised', 2.2.151 'sicles'/'sickles', 4.2.64 'travailer's'/ 'traveller's' and 4.3.12 'Dizzy'/'Dizie'. Like

Gibbons, Bawcutt prints 'Save' for F's "Save" and retains F's puzzling 'prenzie' at 3.1.95 and 98, but he resorts to upper-case at 5.1.412 for the Duke's pointed 'Measure still for Measure', signals a hiatus in the Duke's speech at the end of 3.1 and opts for 'brakes of vice' at 2.1.39 and 'unshifting' at 4.2.89.

Despite the textual and critical differences of approach between the two editions, both have a great deal to offer: Gibbons is perhaps finally more generous to the play than Bawcutt, but he in turn is often sharper-eyed. It is paradoxical that the Cambridge editor engages to such an extent with the Oxford *Complete Works*' textual theories, which the single-volume Oxford editor dismisses – more by his silence than by explicitly addressing them. The issues cannot really be satisfactorily opened up until Jowett and Taylor publish their account of the play's authorship and textual history in full. Clearly, these questions about *Measure for Measure* far from being settled are ripe for further investigation.

Crane's vital role in the transmission of copy for F is reconsidered in a useful and provocative article by Trevor Howard-Hill.[14] He is mainly concerned with the scribe's treatment of Middleton's *A Game at Chess*, but his larger argument is that Crane acted as editor (in the sense in which we would understand the term) for F until old age forced him to relinquish the task. Howard-Hill is particularly keen to show to what extent Crane interfered with the texts he copied and considers his various scribal characteristics, such as 'how deftly Crane used parentheses' (p. 119) and that he 'apparently did not approve of swearing of any kind' (p. 122). In a footnote Howard-Hill puts forward two admittedly limited types of evidence concerning the presence of Crane's hand in F *Cymbeline* and *Twelfth Night*: the frequency of parentheses in F lines and of hyphenated prefixes in some words both suggest that the copy-text for F *Cymbeline* might have been transcribed by Crane but that *Twelfth Night* probably was not. Crane played a crucial part in the transmission

of many dramatic works of the period and Howard-Hill's researches into his scribal habits in play texts are remarkably thorough and clear sighted: further investigation of Crane's career, which took his large amount of non-dramatic work into account, might modify the picture of his practices which has been so painstakingly built up.

After wrestling with Crane, revision, rewriting and the Folio, the copy-text for an edition of the *Poems* is much more straightforward – or at least appears so at first sight. There are however textual problems of one kind or another with all the poems. First of all an editor must decide which poems to print. In his New Cambridge edition John Roe includes *Venus and Adonis*, *The Rape of Lucrece*, *The Phoenix and the Turtle*, *The Passionate Pilgrim* and finishes his volume with *A Lover's Complaint*.[15] His rationale for separating the last work from its companion-piece the *Sonnets* is partly generic – it 'stands interestingly' between the two longer narrative poems (p. 2) – and partly based on the way that there is no reference to the *Complaint* on the title-page of the 1609 volume, no direct cross-reference from the *Sonnets* to it and that the Cupid sonnets (153 and 154) formally close off the sequence and do not act as a bridge to the following work (pp. 63–4). Roe admits that the case against separating the two works is not closed, but his decision will still cause some unease. His appeal to the negative evidence of the poem's absence from the *Sonnets*' title-page is not very convincing and it could be pointed out that there is one possible cross-reference between the two works, with the mention in the *Complaint* of 'deep-brained sonnets' (line 209).

If *A Lover's Complaint* seems wrenched from

---

14 T. H. Howard-Hill, 'Shakespeare's Earliest Editor, Ralph Crane', *Shakespeare Survey* 44 (1992), 113–29.

15 *The Poems: Venus and Adonis, The Rape of Lucrece, The Phoenix and the Turtle, The Passionate Pilgrim, A Lover's Complaint*, ed. John Roe (Cambridge, 1992), in the New Cambridge Shakespeare.

its context, Roe gives perhaps too much context for Shakespeare's poems in *The Passionate Pilgrim*. Here each poem, whether by Shakespeare or not, is collated against some (but not all) contemporary texts and generously annotated. It would be churlish to complain about being given edited versions of poems by Barnfield, Griffin and Marlowe, but Roe's examination of *The Passionate Pilgrim* as a volume (especially in relation to *Venus and Adonis*) contrasts markedly with his unyoking of *A Lover's Complaint* from the Sonnets and with his reluctance to print any of the other poems which have been attributed to Shakespeare. He is 'not persuaded' that 'Shall I die', the 'various slight funerary verses', 'other epitaphs and the like verses' are by Shakespeare (pp. 2–3).[16] Roe may well be correct when he proposes that Shakespeare did not write these poems. Additionally, he has something of a point in arguing that 'The danger of including works of dubious attribution is that habit builds on habit' (p. 2). On the other hand, these poems have to a certain extent entered the field of public interest and a reader might well expect to find a fuller account of them than Roe gives here;[17] there is, moreover, nothing to stop editors from consigning the poems in question to appendices of dubious, attributed or possible poems.

What Roe does print is reproduced accurately and with some thought: there is one significant slip, in *Lucrece* at line 911 where he has 'hath' for 'have'.[18] He is conservative about questions of modernization: 'alablaster' and 'verdour' are retained in *Venus* (lines 363, 507), 'Ætna' in *Lucrece* (line 1042), while 'vaded' and 'vadeth' are defended in *The Passionate Pilgrim* 10 and 13. Especially in *Lucrece* he is peculiarly keen to print hendecasyllabic lines which result from feminine rhymes and to accent final '-èd': he defends the practice (see p. 74), but it may well offend some readers as intrusive.[19] They may also find his fondness for capitalizing abstract nouns in the same poem equally annoying. Roe proposes no new substantive

emendations of his own to any of the poems, but suggests that *Venus* line 275 'scornfully glisters' is 'metrically awkward' and may have been accidentally reversed by the compositor. Of the two press variants in outer forme I of *Lucrece*, he prints the one at line 1182 'for him' from what is usually called Qa as against Qb's 'by him', but against this he substitutes Qb's 'blast' for Qa's 'blasts' at line 1335. He emends poems in *The Passionate Pilgrim* from manuscripts and early prints.[20] In Roe's view the texts of Sonnets 138 and 144 which appear in *The Passionate Pilgrim* are not early versions of the poems which later were published in 1609, but are

---

[16] Some further, circumstantial evidence that Shakespeare might have written the Stanley epitaphs is supplied by Alan Dilnot in 'Shakespeare, the Stanley Epitaphs, and Sir William Dugdale', *Notes and Queries* NS 38 (1991), 499–501.

[17] Although he refers to some of the published debate over 'Shall I die', Roe only mentions the version in the Rawlinson MS, of which he rather confusingly says 'Following the poem in the same scribal (Secretary) hand appears the signature "William Shakespeare"' (p. 2).

[18] Other minor errors include *Venus and Adonis* line 95, where 'flint-hearted' needs an opening rather than a closing quotation mark; 999 'Whenas' for 'When as' (cp *The Passionate Pilgrim* 8.12); in collations: 873 'twin'd' for 'twined'.

[19] The difficulty of the accented '-èd' endings is also brought out by Gibbons' and Bawcutt's disagreements over it in their editions of *Measure for Measure*. Bawcutt omits the accent in 'blessed' 2.3.3, 3.1.34 and 5.1.137 where Gibbons prints it; he prints it in 'thick-ribbed' at 3.1.126 where Gibbons omits it. Given the Cambridge series' frequent metrical laxity, it is odd that editors should retain the accent; equally, its presence in the Oxford series, where ''th'' is regularly expanded 'the' (at least in Bawcutt's edition) is perhaps unnecessary.

[20] At least one of Oxford's and of J. Q. Adams's collations differs from his (*The Passionate Pilgrim* 4.4). Rather annoyingly he refers to all Folger manuscripts by their old call-marks, a decision he does not justify until poem 18. Roe does not record the presence of poem 7 in Victoria and Albert Museum Dyce MS 44, nor – more strangely – of the many manuscript versions of poem 19. He might also have noted Katherine K. Gottschalk's 1979 article in *Modern Philology* on Harley 6910: the manuscript has a text of poem 17.

memorially contaminated – he does not indicate the possibility that they might be both. The three poems which come from *Love's Labour's Lost* may have been taken from the quarto of 1598 or from manuscript copies: Roe offers no firm opinion about the matter and does not mention the possibility that they might come from a lost, earlier quarto.

All of this is well done in practice, but the theoretical approach of the 'Textual Analysis' is less satisfactory. Roe's accounts of the poems' printing histories (strangely, there is nothing here on *The Phoenix and the Turtle* or *A Lover's Complaint*) betrays some unusual assumptions, as well as including several minor errors and confusions, especially about later editions. It would have been improved (as would his note on *The Passionate Pilgrim* 12.0) if Roe had consulted the revised *Short-Title Catalogue*. This slightly casual treatment of later editions is a curious aspect of how Shakespeare's poems are usually edited: play editors will give detailed accounts of productions of plays up to modern times, but the poems' editors rarely have much to say about their later histories. Roe does not mention any of the manuscript quotations from the poems which survive, nor, apart from Meres' allusion to the *Sonnets*, does he refer to any of the contemporary references to them.[21] Although he writes about the surmised biographical backgrounds to the poems, Roe's account of their origins is uncontroversial and he sticks to what is generally accepted: Honigmann's theories about the origins of *The Phoenix and the Turtle* are reasonably set to one side with no more than the raising of 'a quizzical eyebrow' (p. 48), but it is a pity that he does not mention the fact that Richard Field, the printer of the two earlier works, came from Stratford. He believes that Jaggard assembled *The Passionate Pilgrim* from a commonplace book or from various manuscript sources, without meaning to deceive purchasers into believing they were getting Shakespeare's *Sonnets* (pp. 56–7). The author himself probably did not have much to do with any of this, but may

have been displeased when the (enlarged) volume was reprinted in 1612 (pp. 58–60). Roe has little to say about the date of *A Lover's Complaint*.

Roe's approach to the *Poems* in the introduction and in his commentary reveals his belief in the influence of Neoplatonism on Shakespeare: it is hard to feel warmly towards this line of criticism. He is generally sympathetic to the poems, strong on their genres and interesting on Shakespeare's debts to Sidney: he does not speculate as to how the dramatist may have had access to what must have been a manuscript of the *Apology* (see the note on *Lucrece* 1324–7). His commentary is very full – perhaps over-full in parts – and constantly nudges the reader towards taking Roe's larger view of the *Poems*. He pays a good deal of attention to formal rhetorical devices and questions of metre, but not of stanza form. Some notes may puzzle the reader a little or give pause for thought.[22] Roe's edition is certainly useful and complements Maurice Evans' unpretentious volume for the New Penguin Shakespeare, but a firmer (general) editorial hand might have improved some of the less satisfactory aspects of Roe's edition.

The real question about Michael Hattaway's remarkably rapid journey through the Henry

---

[21] In an exemplary account of 'Unrecorded Extracts from Shakespeare, Sidney and Dyer', *English Manuscript Studies*, 2 (1990), 163–87, Hilton Kelliher notes the presence of lines 229–40 of *Venus*, copied before the end of 1596, in a Cambridge University Library manuscript.

[22] Sonnets 1–17 are dated to the period of *Venus* at 129–32; dictation is suggested as playing a part in the typesetting of *Lucrece*, see line 24; there may be a contradiction between what is said about lead coffins at line 124 and at *The Passionate Pilgrim* 20.24; 'Night's black bosom' is described as 'mammary darkness' at line 788. On the other hand 'drops' in *A Lover's Complaint* line 300 are simply glossed as 'teardrops', ignoring John Kerrigan's argument that they have medicinal associations. Kerrigan reaffirms his belief that they are 'liquid drugs' in his old-spelling edition of *Complaint* included in his valuable anthology *Motives of Woe: Shakespeare and 'Female Complaint': A Critical Anthology* (Oxford, 1991).

VI plays is whether he edited the plays in the order in which he believes they were written: the passage in the Preface to *2 Henry VI* (p. xi) in which he alludes to his undertaking is ambiguous.[23] It seems logical, however, to accept that he worked on them as a planned trilogy following what he calls 'the order of history'. He despatched *1 Henry VI* in 1990 and his *2 Henry VI* was published in 1991. Having kept his nerve about so many matters – not least the play's title – it is a pity that this latest instalment shows evident signs of haste and does not maintain the high level of accuracy achieved in *1 Henry VI*. There are 9 slips in the text – many quite unnecessary – as well as errors in the collations and rather a lot of signs of poor copy-editing.[24] There is also a slight feeling of a decline in editorial enthusiasm for the task in hand; much less attention is paid in *2 Henry VI* to problems of staging and to the work of Shakespeare's contemporaries than in *1 Henry VI*. Despite some rather good notes – in particular on Shakespeare's supposed knowledge of Greek at 3.2.89, on the deliberately fustian style at the beginning of 4.1, comparing Suffolk with Othello later in the scene (lines 132–8) and on Shakespeare's legal knowledge at 4.7.23 – the commentary is at times rather brief, often limiting itself to one- or two-word glosses where a reader might expect and occasionally need a little more.

Nevertheless, Hattaway's edition still has much to offer, not least in his assessment that *2 Henry VI* is 'without doubt, a major play', 'a fine, important, and undervalued play' (pp. xi, 1). He continues his arguments about the sort of secular, realist history which Shakespeare was writing in the Henry VI trilogy, has interesting things to say about Cade and carnival in this second part and pursues this argument far enough to invoke Shakespeare's radicalism (in a fairly strict sense), but also suggests that he 'may be underlining divisions in society that are deep enough to be called class divisions' (p. 24). His well-illustrated account of the play's usually mutilated stage history makes for quite painful

reading for those who believe in the play's dramatic integrity.

With the exception of one paragraph and one sentence, Hattaway reprints the text of the section on 'Date and occasion' which had appeared in his edition of *1 Henry VI* (pp. 34–41). The new material (on p. 66 – there are also some revisions in the footnotes) relates mainly to the significance of Q1's title *The First Part of the Contention*. Essentially, Hattaway argues that the quarto represents a memorial reconstruction of London performances in which the play, especially in its last act, had been revised. Since there is no way of knowing whether these revisions were made with or without Shakespeare's approval, and since there is 'no compelling argument that allows a

---

23 *The Second Part of King Henry VI*, ed. Michael Hattaway (Cambridge, 1991), in the New Cambridge Shakespeare.

24 In the text at 1.4.72 he prints 'go' for 'goes' (the correct reading is given in the note); at 2.3.91 'enemies' for 'mine enemies'; at 2.4.83–4 Pope's relining cited in the collation has not been carried out in the text; at 3.1.0.3–4 he has '*and* QUEEN' for '*and the* QUEEN'; at 3.2.332 'turn' for 'turns' (both the collation and the note are consequently muddled); at 4.1.60 'thus' for 'this'; at 4.2.115 'this:' where the collation demands Theobald's emendation 'this: –'; at 4.4.43 'hate' for 'hateth' and at 4.10.27 'whatsoever' for 'whatsoe'er'.

From among the collations, at 2.1.157 he has 'them' where F (TLN 909) clearly reads 'thē'; at 2.3.59 Pope's reported emendation to the SH is unnecessary since F (TLN 1120) reads '1.*Neighbor*'; at 2.3.87 SD.1 he prints '*Alaums*' for '*Alarums*'; at 4.1.0 he has 'Alarmes with' for 'Alarmes within'; at 4.1.117 '*Maxell*' for '*Maxwell*'; at 4.2.82 Q1 (TLN 1612) reads 'that' not 'y''; at 4.4.49 he has 'hath almost' for 'haue almost'. Elsewhere, there are further minor errors and inconsistencies in reporting Q's readings in Appendix 2; the author of *Early Modern England: A Social History, 1550–1760* is called J. A. Sharpe on p. 5 n. 5 but becomes Kevin Sharpe ten pages later (p. 15 n. 4) where ten years are also lopped from the end of the volume's coverage; in the List of Characters Jack Carde makes a surprising appearance; there are a few slips in the commentary, such as at 4.4.43 'hate' for 'hateth' and unfilled cross-references on pp. 114 and 183; and in the table of contents three of the five page references to sections in the Introduction are wrong.

modern editor to decide whether the author's second thoughts are to be preferred over his first' (p. 217), he takes his text almost entirely from F, but draws on Q from time to time, mainly for stage directions. He believes that F was set up from foul papers (or a scribal transcript of them), but with some reference to a quarto text, probably Q3, where the manuscript copy was illegible or – when it came to showing Cade at his most triumphant – had been censored. The question of possible censorship here perhaps deserves further investigation. In Appendix 2 he prints passages from Q1 which do not appear in F (some because of possible censorship), further passages from Q1 which reveal echoes of other Strange's or Pembroke's Men plays and Q3/Q1 variants which show that the later quarto was based in part on a supplementary report (cp. p. 215).

Hattaway's account of the text is brisk and efficient. He does not agonize over questions such as the identity of the reporter or reporters, whether Q's departures from F are the result of censorship or of revision, or whether F's copy was a scribal transcript or Shakespeare's foul papers. This results in a straightforward text which rejects most of Oxford's emendations and particularly its use of Q. Despite his belief that Q's stage direction about Gloucester's murder at the beginning of 3.2 'presumably records details of the staging of the scene's opening in a London playhouse' (p. 146), he nevertheless prints F's admittedly 'ambiguous' direction. The traditional scene divisions at 4.8 and in 5.2 are retained. Hattaway is particularly and probably rightly concerned to keep what he sees as Q's theatrical gags out of his text (see for example the commentary on 1.3.28, 2.1.40, 2.3.85, 4.2.100 and 4.7.47) and avoids its Clerk of Chatham for Chartham. On the other hand, he is prepared to suggest that some Q passages may preserve authorial revision (see the commentary on 3.1.319ff. and Appendix 2 1.9 on 5.2.31–65.) Hattaway is less certain about 4.7.93, which may report a phrase, 'to the Standard in Cheapside', 'omitted by F's compo-

sitor, or, less probably, due to authorial revision', but which Hattaway still does not print. He attributes most of the errors which he detects in F to eye-skip or contamination from the surrounding text; this is perhaps overdone, as when he suggests F's 'Duke' at 2.2.28 for Cairncross's emendation 'Duke of York' can be justified partly 'on the grounds that it was probably caused by eyeskip from "-ke", to "-ke"'.

If Hattaway is sceptical about most of Oxford's emendations (for example, he sticks to Saunder Simpcox at 2.1.128 on the grounds of 'the association of "sand" with blindness' and rejects 'wame' for 'way' at 2.3.90, 'its' for 'his' at 3.2.393 and 'health' for 'help' at 4.7.76), he offers no substantive emendations and few conjectures of his own.[25] His questioning of the potential value of the 'bad' quarto is refreshing. After all there is no logical reason why actors who misreport dialogue and speeches should *necessarily* remember stage directions and theatrical business correctly. Hattaway has a clear and purposeful view of the difficult editorial task he has in hand and, despite its errors, his edition should help to refocus attention on the Henry VI plays.

Andrew Gurr's edition of *Henry V* is equally full of interest.[26] The critical part of his introduction has some sharp and helpful things to say about the King's 'opaque self' (p. 12), about the coerciveness of the Chorus, about the play's concern with kinship and social rank and about its staging. But too much space is perhaps given up to the question of the materials which went into the play, its sources, especially Shakespeare's additions and omissions. Gurr writes at length about two important elements in the play's make-up. First, there is the question of Salic law, which he relates to John Stubbs' 1579

---

[25] He attributes 'baiting-place' at 5.1.150 to '*This edn*' although this is what Sanders and Cairncross, among others, print.

[26] *King Henry V*, ed. Andrew Gurr (Cambridge, 1992), in the New Cambridge Shakespeare.

tract written in opposition to Queen Elizabeth's proposed marriage with the French king's brother, the Duc d'Alençon. Secondly, he turns to the military propaganda of the 1590s which he examines against the context of the Oxford jurist Alberico Gentili's *De Jure Belli*, 1589. He is also naturally much concerned with *The Famous Victories*, Holinshed's *Chronicles* and rather more surprisingly Richard Crompton's *The Mansion of Magnanimitie*, 1599, to each of which he devotes an appendix. Much of his account of these works and their relation to Shakespeare's play is very interesting, but some readers may feel that getting through it is rather hard work.

Gurr's commentary is excellent, always full, clear and to the point: he is particularly interesting about the play's use of syllepsis ('the same word with different senses' as he describes it at 1.0.13), for example in 'for many a thousand widows / Shall this his mock mock out of their dear husbands, / Mock mothers from their sons, mock castles down . . . ' (1.2.284–6). From an editorial point of view, Gurr's most challenging decision is to question the origins of the first quarto of the play, published in 1600. He begins by drawing on unpublished work by Peter Blayney, arguing that although the famous staying entry of 4 August 1600 in the Stationers' Register refers to *HENRY the FFIFT*, this was in fact a reference to *2 Henry IV*. This is plausible, not least because the title-page of Q1 of *2 Henry IV* includes a mention of the '*coronation of Henrie / the fift*' and because two of the other plays stayed at the same time were subsequently published in 'good' quartos. The players were therefore not trying to block the publication of *Henry V*, and the transfer of rights in the play to Thomas Pavier on 14 August was quite regular. Gurr's next step is more conventional, for he accepts that the first quarto is a memorial text assembled by Pistol, along with Exeter and Gower, but he then proposes that Will Kemp was the actor who played Pistol and betrayed the company which he left late in 1599.

This is an intriguing possibility, which Gurr pursues further. There is no way, he argues, of determining why the cuts in Q were made, but because they do not reflect theatrical practice – at three points characters leave the stage at the end of one scene, only to come on again immediately in the next – it follows that the quarto was designed not for acting, but for reading. If this is the case (although the absence of the Choruses might argue powerfully against it), then awkward questions about the casting for Q disappear, but there remains the issue of the nature of its copy. On the basis of 'the three exits with immediate re-entries' and of a 'progressive loss of closeness in the correlation between F and Q' (especially at 4.8.72, where Q assigns Exeter the whole of the list of the dead), Gurr argues that Q was compiled from a London performance 'with more regard for readability than performance', for sale to printers rather than for provincial touring companies (p. 223). Yet it would seem that compared to the labour involved in compiling a memorial reconstruction, the profit gained from selling it to a publisher cannot have been very great.[27]

Gurr's account of the origins of Q means that he is cautious about using it to emend F: in other words his conclusions about the texts of the play run quite counter to Gary Taylor's and those of the Oxford Shakespeare. He is also strongly aware that F's text, set from foul papers, is by no means clean. He detects 'unresolved hesitancy' on Shakespeare's part 'about what to do with the Dauphin's role in the play' (p. 225) and that the author was 'unsure which venue the play would eventually appear at' (p. 43). Furthermore, Macmorris and Jamy 'seem to be late inserts in the manuscript which was used to print' F (p. 4), as may be the scene in which Katherine and Alice rehearse their French (p. 58). All of this goes to show that F's text 'was the product of discontinuous

---

[27] Gurr is aware both of Werstine's recent, sceptical view of memorial texts and of Irace's computer analysis of Q (for an account of which, see *Shakespeare Survey 45*, 1993, 198–9).

composition, and possibly some imperfect revisions' (p. 60) – a position not so far removed from Gibbons' view of *Measure*. He also argues strongly that the Oxford editors are wrong to detect the influence of Q3 on F; instead he maintains that in its printing Q3 drew on the same manuscript which was used by F – 'This of course devalues Q3 as an authority independent of F and destroys the Oxford case for Q contaminating F through Q3' (p. 216).

Despite errors and slips, the text itself is generally handled with great authority and good sense.[28] Much attention is paid to the rendering of the French – which he believes Shakespeare might have learned from Richard Field's wife (see pp. 27, 61) – and the regional accents. Gurr's defence of 'Ancient' as against 'Ensign' Pistol is a good one: he seems slightly less happy with his own decision to modernize 'Fluellen' to 'Llewellyn' (p. 63). Elsewhere he is cautious about modernization, retaining Pistol's distinctive 'mervailous' at 2.1.40, Bourbon's 'prescript praise' at 3.8.42, printing 'gemelled' at 4.2.49; but at 3.2.41 'handkerchiefs' is silently changed from the Folio's 'Hand-kerchers'. Gurr's major departure from F is in the role of the Dauphin, who is replaced by Bourbon in 3.8, 4.2 and 4.5, thus resolving Shakespeare's apparent hesitancy in favour of Q's theatrical text. He carefully rebuts Taylor's arguments about the staging of the end of 4.6 (also pointing out the discrepancy between Henry's motive for the deed and Gower's interpretation of it) and does not have the French prisoners killed in front of the audience. Above all, while he uses Q judiciously to emend F, he rejects the very large number of Q readings which Taylor and the Oxford edition introduced: some of these are considered in detail, such as the question of Warwick and Westmorland in 4.3 and the rearrangement of 4.5. But he is not unwilling to resort to Q where he feels it is necessary. Taylor's and Oxford's emendations are followed on only a few occasions, as at 2.0.32 'force perforce' for 'force', 2.4.57 'mountant' for 'Mountaine' and 4.7.17 'e'en Macedon' for

'in *Macedon*'. Disappointingly, he has little to say about Q's 'leno' as against F's 'pander' at 4.5.15. Gurr's own substantive emendations include adopting Blayney's emendation of 'when' for 'till' at the end of the Chorus to Act 2 in order to resolve the problem that the act's first scene is set in Eastcheap not Southampton. He has no new solution to Theobald's version of Falstaff's last moments, but he does propose one plausible solution to a difficult and important passage: at 4.6.34 he prints 'wilful eyes' for F's 'mixtfull', suggesting that the manuscript had 'willfull' in it which, he claims (not altogether plausibly), 'most nearly suits the range of possible readings in the handwriting'.[29]

It is extremely valuable to have an edition of *Henry V* which complements and challenges the Oxford/Taylor account of the play. Gurr still follows the new editorial orthodoxy when he writes that the 'target text for this edition is what we might loosely call the play-script, the text of the play as it was originally performed'

---

[28] At 2.3.11 he prints 'e'en at the turning o'the tide' for Folio's 'eu'n at the turning o'th'Tyde'; 2.4.57 'Whilst' for 'Whiles'; 3.0.11 'the invisible' for 'th'invisible'; 3.4.57 'we will' for 'will we'; 3.7.50+ Llewellyn's words 'Very good.' have been omitted; 4.1.118 'honorable' for 'honourable'; 4.7.35 'I speak out' for 'I speak but'.

The following are some of the errors from among the collations: 1.0.17 Taylor does not suggest the emendation 'So'; 1.2.115 Taylor does not conjecture but emends to 'those'; 2.1.58 Taylor prints F's reading 'Couple a gorge', but conjectures 'Coupe' (not 'Coup') 'la gorge'; 2.1.83–4 'wonne' for 'woon'; 2.2.26 Taylor conjectures 'one' but does not print it; 3.5.53 'de count' for 'de con'; 3.8.7 '(Burb.)' for '(Burbon.)'; 4.1.278 Taylor does not conjecture but emends to 'ill'; 4.5.16 'Who least' for 'Why least'; 4.7.3 F reads 'offert in', which affects the note on the punctuation of this passage; 4.7.12 the collation should refer to 'great' in line 13; 5.2.84 F reads 'Clarence', Q simply has 'Lords' for all the nobles the King summons: Gurr has silently emended 'Clarence' to 'Bedford' to accord with the SH at the beginning of the scene; 5.2.174 '(meilleus)' for '(melieus)'.

[29] His argument is not helped by misreporting F's reading as 'mixt-full'. The collocation of tears and 'wilful' eyes is not found elsewhere in Shakespeare's work.

(p. 56) and like Hattaway he makes judicious use of the quarto in trying to arrive at this. Some of the questions which arise from this approach are coming in for close attention with recent work, mainly on the first quarto of *Hamlet*. A new reprint of this document has appeared in a series, edited by Graham Holderness and Bryan Loughrey, which intends to provide readers with 'editions of early modern play-texts whose literary and theatrical histories have been overshadowed by editorial practices dominant since the eighteenth century' (p. 1).[30] The volume has a brief introduction, a reasonably accurate old-spelling text and very brief explanatory notes: act and scene divisions, as well as line numbers are not supplied. A far more elaborate three-text edition of the play has also been published.[31] This offers a completely plain text of Q1, Q2 and F spread across three columns of each opening with the fourth column reserved for Q1's transpositions. While there is through-line-numbering for only Q1 and F, as well as the typographical arrangement of the three texts as far as is possible in parallel, each Q1 and Q2 line has the equivalent F TLN added where this can be done. Although the volume is not nearly as sophisticated as Warren's two-text *King Lear*, it is extremely convenient: apart from abandoning the long s, the edition aspires to absolute fidelity to the originals, even down to typographical arrangement (see, for example, its treatment of the outer forme of signature F in Q2).

The appearance of these two editions coincides with the publication of a whole book devoted to the 'Origins, Form, Intertextualities' of Q1.[32] The enterprise is an interesting one with some good contributions to the subject. Unfortunately, the book cannot be said by any stretch of the imagination to hang together. Its enthusiastic editor, Thomas Clayton, knows this and rather hopes that disagreements between contributors will sharpen the debate, but the reader is more likely to feel irritated than stimulated. For example, Kathleen Irace applies some of the techniques she developed in her analysis of Q1 of

Henry V to examine Q1 of *Hamlet*: she pays particular attention to confirming the usual identification of Marcellus as the play's reporter, either doubling his role with, or being aided by, Voltemar and Lucianus. Her conclusion is that Q1 represents a memorial reconstruction, which was then abridged (possibly for a provincial tour), of the London version of the play preserved by F. Irace predicates her analysis on the close relationship which is usually perceived as existing between Q1 and F. Yet the piece before hers in the volume by G. R. Hibbard specifically sets out to cancel that relationship and to argue, quite powerfully, that Q1 preceded F and should rather be considered in relation to Q2. Similarly, at the end of a discussion between those involved in two productions of Q1, Bryan Loughrey appends a cast list for the Orange Tree production in which the actor who played Voltemar doubled the part with Lucianus, but also played the Ghost, the Gravedigger and Osric. Still later in the volume Scott McMillin has a characteristically original account of casting the *Hamlet* quartos in

---

[30] *The Tragicall Historie of Hamlet Prince of Denmarke*, ed. Graham Holderness and Bryan Loughrey (Hemel Hempstead, 1992). Also in this series of *Shakespearean Originals: First Editions*, Holderness and Loughrey have published *The Taming of a Shrew* and *The Cronicle History of Henry the Fift*.

[31] *The Three-Text Hamlet: Parallel Texts of the First and Second Quartos and First Folio*, ed. Paul Bertram and Bernice W. Kliman, AMS studies in the Renaissance: No. 30 (New York, 1991). Working from the Scolar Press facsimile of the British Library copy of Q2 the editors correctly claim to have found three apparently unrecorded press variants on sig L1ʳ.

[32] *The Hamlet First Published (Q1, 1603): Origins, Form, Intertextualities*, ed. Thomas Clayton (Newark, London and Toronto, 1992). Eric Sams joins the fray about Q1 armed with his cosh and knuckle-duster in a short piece, 'Assays of Bias', *Notes and Queries*, NS 38 (1991), 60–3. In 'The Mute Voltemar: Q1 Hamlet, 5.2', *Shakespeare Quarterly*, 43 (1992), 70, Sidney Thomas seeks to explain Voltemar's entry with the English Ambassadors by noting that ambassadors had to be escorted into the court: the quarto reporter simply identified the usher as the actor who played Voltemar.

which he argues that in addition to being Lucianus, the actor who played Voltemar was also Montano.

This sort of disagreement about fundamental matters is not so much bracing as confusing. In his essay McMillin suggests that Shakespeare's company made it a rule that every London play they put on had to be capable of being performed by no more than eleven actors when plague made the Company leave town. He poses radical questions and comes up with an equally radical solution to them, but his piece looks positively sedate in comparison with Giorgio Melchiori's. *Hamlet*, Melchiori believes, originally circulated in manuscript at Oxford and Cambridge and this closet version was made more generally available in Q2. Q1 represents a memorial version of the play as restructured by Shakespeare for the London stage, and F stands midway between the two. Such extreme views can be found again in the volume's concluding piece by Steven Urkowitz. He has some excellent, detailed passages in which he seeks to cancel the printer's use of Q1 in the setting of Q2. These are convincing as far as they go, but he plays down the correspondences between the ornamental title-pages of the two quartos and common-sense which suggests that a printer or publisher embarking on a second version of a text already in print would more likely than not look at the earlier work – the case of the two 1591 quartos of *Astrophil and Stella* provides an interesting parallel. To bolster his case that Q1 represents an early draft and should be studied as a theatrical document in its own right, Urkowitz looks at several passages in detail and if he does not find much of real merit in them, he seeks to show how their confusions could have arisen. Against these views, Sidney Thomas's brief but robust and sceptical account of how bad much of Q1 is appears persuasive.

The trouble with *The Hamlet First Published* is that although there are some good and careful pieces – Philip C. McGuire on Fortinbras in the three texts, Marga Munkelt on the (often

unacknowledged) use editors have made of Q1 – the book as a whole does not stand up. Furthermore, despite the close attention paid to Q1, few of the contributors have anything very interesting to say about it either in relation to the familiar conflated *Hamlet* or as a dramatic document in its own right. There will no doubt be other examinations of Q1 – further bibliographical work on it remains to be done – but they need to be animated by more than a desire to perplex and astonish. This is perhaps not as easy as it once was, since there is a growing trend among those who write on so-called 'bad' quartos to argue that they are early authorial versions of the plays. Few will be persuaded by Yashdip Singh Bains' assertions to this effect about Q1 of *Romeo and Juliet*.[33] Similarly, while Eric Sams has a point when he draws attention to the discrepancies between the *OED*'s and the Oxford edition's dating of the works, all the usual suspects – including 'bad' quartos as 'first versions' – are once again rounded up for what turns out to be a very cursory interrogation.[34] Leah S. Marcus does not go quite so far as these writers, but while calling for 'a thorough rethinking of textual practice toward all of Shakespeare's plays' (p. 169), she concludes that '"bad" texts can readily be shown to be "good" if we suspend our need to rank them hierarchically' (p. 178).[35] Drawing mainly on *The Merry Wives of Windsor*, she argues that quarto and Folio texts which differ do not always do so because of corruption, but because they were directed at different sorts of audiences – 'a middle-class urban public' for the first and 'the court itself' for the second (p. 177).

If Marcus is right, and her admittedly speculative essay heralds what she wittily calls 'the

---

[33] 'The Bad Quarto of Shakespeare's *Romeo and Juliet* and the Theory of Memorial Reconstruction', *Shakespeare Jahrbuch*, 126 (1990), 164–73.

[34] 'Shakespeare and the Oxford Imprint', *The Times Literary Supplement*, 6 March 1992, p. 13.

[35] 'Levelling Shakespeare: Local Customs and Local Texts', *Shakespeare Quarterly*, 42 (1991), 168–78.

mobilization of a holistic, New-Critical inter-
pretive method (somewhat leavened with historicism)' (p. 178), then editors will have to
adopt new approaches to their traditional task.
Two such approaches can be found in a volume
of essays in honour of James T. Boulton.[36] In
'Towards a Mobile Text', the late Philip Brockbank touches on some of his anxieties about
Philip Edwards' edition of *Hamlet* for the New
Cambridge Shakespeare – of which Brockbank
was then general editor. To counteract the
exclusivity of printed editions, he imagines
what an 'interactive optical video *Lear*' (p. 99)
on CD-ROM or WORM (Write-Once-Read-
Many) might contain: to which the answer is
more or less anything and everything. Charles
Whitworth who has been editing *The Comedy
of Errors* for the Oxford edition considers 'Rec-
tifying Shakespeare's *Errors*: Romance and
Farce in Bardeditry'. He gives some advance
notice of his handling of a few of the cruces in
the play (he intends to print 'Luce' not 'Nell',
'Epidamnus' not 'Epidamium' nor 'Epidam-
num', 'Porcupine' not 'Porpentine' and so on),
but the textual part of his essay is also influenced
by his involvement in Phyllida Lloyd's 1989
Bristol Old Vic production. Whitworth's argument returns to the way that editors favour
performance texts, labour over minor and
major problems and yet that 'In performance,
almost anything can be said and no one will
blink' (p. 125). Since, he argues, plays only
come into their true existence in the theatre
where actors and directors do all sorts of things
to their texts (including usefully emending
them) which audiences may not even register, it
is only the fixity of print that gives editors
trouble. Consequently, editors 'can only edit
texts, finally, not plays, not authors' (p. 133). If
this is not, as Whitworth admits, a very revolutionary view, it is at least a bracingly sobering
one to set besides the extravagant claims of
first-version enthusiasts. On the other hand, it
produces very narrow practical and theoretical
limitations for editors, scholars and theatre
directors.

These claims are symptomatic of a larger
anxiety about the nature of Shakespeare's
dramatic practice and about the handling of his
texts by modern editors. Grace Ioppolo has
written the first book entirely devoted to
presenting an account of a *Revising Shakespeare*.[37] She argues that the growing awareness
of the dramatist as a constant and careful reviser
of his own work has created 'an economic crisis
for publishers and consumers as well [as] a
theoretical crisis among literary and textual
critics' (p. 17). Her own book is designed to add
fuel to the fire by 'reporting on the new
revolution' of a revising Shakespeare, 'and
defending its constitution by placing it in a
much broader historical, theatrical, textual, and
literary context' (p. 4). There is no doubting her
enthusiasm for the task. She sails through the
previous debates about the question and argues
vigorously that authorial revision was the norm
in the theatre, drawing on four detailed 'Case
Studies' – *The Malcontent*, Bale's *King Johan*,
The Gypsies Metamorphosed and *A Game at
Chess*. Turning to Shakespeare, she acknowledges that censorship and altered performing
conditions may have necessitated changes to his
plays, but that the author himself could or
would have been responsible for these. She
illustrates Shakespeare's mainly artistic motives
for revision by a brief examination of *Romeo and
Juliet* and *Love's Labour's Lost* in their quarto and
Folio texts. Her account of these two early plays
contains new material and leads her on to
challenge the orthodoxy that Shakespeare's
heavy revising only began after 1596. The last
two chapters of *Revising Shakespeare* are devoted
to the well-known 'two-text' plays, *Hamlet*,
Troilus and Cressida, *Othello*, and *King Lear*

---

[36] *The Theory and Practice of Text-Editing: Essays in Honour
of James T. Boulton*, ed. Ian Small and Marcus Walsh
(Cambridge, 1991). The volume also includes a piece by
Russell Jackson on 'Victorian Editors of *As You Like It*
and the Purposes of Editing'.

[37] *Revising Shakespeare* (Cambridge, Mass., and London,
1991).

in which she pays particular attention to the role of Cordelia. Her concluding arguments concern the theory and implications of revision, especially from the point of view of editorial practice and of modern views of Shakespeare's artistry. She rightly dismisses the view of editors who believe that by choosing theatrical texts they are choosing the ones which Shakespeare finally wanted: 'there is no evidence that any of the texts presents Shakespeare's "final" form, only a *later* form' (p. 186).

Revising Shakespeare shows great energy and a single-minded determination to prove the author's thesis: all is grist to Ioppolo's mill, including rather a lot of John Dover Wilson's slightly musty grain. Yet the evidence on which so much of her argument is built – title-pages, manuscripts, quartos of one kind and another and their differences from the Folio – is often either capable of being interpreted in different ways, or is simply untrustworthy. Ioppolo pays special attention to two practical aspects of revision, which may well provoke some scepticism: first, she relies heavily on printers' setting of uncancelled passages (which should have been deleted) and their setting of passages marked for cancellation; secondly, she argues that hypermetrical lines sometimes contain evidence of authorial revision. The implications of her revisionary arguments for constructing a stemma for each of Shakespeare's plays are not always worked out. Editors and critics will no doubt turn to Ioppolo's book and find much of interest there. Yet even though at times she overstates her arguments, for some tastes her account of Shakespeare's revisions will be based on too narrow an approach to be quite convincing. The revising Shakespeare turns out to have been concerned, as far as she can tell, with perhaps two or three thousand lines out of

about a hundred thousand and he seems mainly concerned with intricate changes to character and plot, occasionally to the 'themes' of the plays. The question of the possibility of local revision within the *Sonnets* is not addressed.

There may well be a crisis within editorial theory and practice at the moment, as Ioppolo and others claim: all sorts of material and categories as well as ways of handling and presenting them, have been questioned in the past few years. Even the revolutionary approach of the Oxford Shakespeare will no doubt in time look outmoded. But it is perhaps worth bearing in mind G. K. Chesterton's proposition (*mutatis mutandis*) that when people cease to believe in God, they become willing to believe in anything.[38]

---

[38] Among other books and articles which have been received, the ninth, concluding volume of Giorgio Melchiori's edition of Shakespeare's plays, *I Drammi Storici* volume three, for Arnoldo Mondadori (1991), contains parallel, modernized texts of *King John*, *Edward III*, *Sir Thomas More* and *King Henry VIII*: the second of these will be of particular interest to Shakespeare scholars. In 'The Authorship of *The Raigne of King Edward the Third*', *Literary and Linguistic Computing*, 6 (1991), 166–74, M. W. A. Smith applies some stylometric tests which he has developed and concludes that the play, which he dates to around 1590, should be included in the Shakespearian canon. There are further articles on *Pericles* by MacD. Jackson in the same issue of the journal and by Smith, on 'The Authorship of *Timon of Athens*' in *TEXT*, 5 (1991), 195–240, in which he detects hands other than Shakespeare's but not specifically Middleton's.

The Japanese journal *Shakespeare Worldwide: Translation and Adaptation* (Tokyo, 1991) has reached its thirteenth volume and is largely devoted to *Othello*, with essays on Italian, German and Finnish translations of the play: there is also a text of Kuniyoshi Munakata's *Noh Othello* of 1986, which reduces the play to one or two hundred lines performed by Othello, Desdemona and a Chorus.

BOOKS RECEIVED

This list includes all books received between September 1991 and September 1992 which are not reviewed in this volume of *Shakespeare Survey*. The appearance of a book in this list does not preclude its review in a subsequent volume.

Barker, Francis, Peter Hulme, and Margaret Iverson, eds. *Uses of History: Marxism, Postmodernism and the Renaissance*. Manchester and New York: Manchester University Press, 1991.

Berry, Herbert, ed. *The Noble Science: A Study and Transcription of Sloane MS 2530, Papers of the Masters of Defence of London, Temp. Henry VIII to 1590*. Newark: University of Delaware Press, 1991.

Bradley, A. C. *Shakespearian Tragedy*, 3rd edn, new intro. by John Russell Brown. Basingstoke: Macmillan Education Ltd., 1992.

Buchman, Lorne M. *Still in Movement: Shakespeare on Screen*. New York and Oxford: Oxford University Press, 1991.

Clemen, Wolfgang. *Interpretationen zur englischen Literatur*. Bonn, 1992.

Dessen, Alan C. *Titus Andronicus*, Shakespeare in Performance. Manchester and New York: Manchester University Press, 1989; paperback edition 1992.

Dietrich, Julia, ed. *'Hamlet' in the 1960s: An Annotated Bibliography*. New York and London: Garland Publishing Inc., 1992.

Freund, John. *Broken Symmetries: A Study of Agency in Shakespeare's Plays*. London and New York: Peter Lang Publishing Inc., 1991.

Newell, Alex. *The Soliloquies in 'Hamlet': The Structural Design*. Cranbury, N.J., London, Ontario: Associated University Presses Inc., 1991.

Pilkington, Ace G. *Screening Shakespeare from Richard II to Henry V*. Newark: University of Delaware Press, 1991.

Ronberg, Gert. *A Way with Words: The Language of English Renaissance Literature*. London: Edward Arnold, 1992.

Udall, Joanna. *A Critical, Old Spelling Edition of The Birth of Merlin (Q1662)*, MHRA Texts and Dissertations, vol. 31. London: MHRA, 1991.

INDEX

Listing within the alphabetical sequence of titles of books and plays indicates that the books, or editions of the plays, are considered in the review articles.

INDEX

INDEX

INDEX

INDEX

ALSO PUBLISHED BY CAMBRIDGE UNIVERSITY PRESS

DRAMA AND THE MARKET IN THE AGE OF SHAKESPEARE

DOUGLAS BRUSTER

Douglas Bruster's provocative study of Engish Renaissance drama explores its links with Elizabethan and Jacobean economy and society, looking at the status of playwrights such as Shakespeare and the establishment of commercial theatres. He identifies in the drama a materialist vision which has its origins in the climate of uncertainty engendered by the rapidly expanding economy of London.

Cambridge Studies in Renaissance Literature and Culture 1

1992   0 521 41664 7   Hardback

THEATRE AND GOVERNMENT UNDER THE EARLY STUARTS

Edited by J. R. MULRYNE *and* MARGARET SHEWRING

This is a collection of newly commissioned essays by established scholars, responding to recent critical debate on political theatre of the turbulent early years of the seventeenth century. Addressing a wide range of theatre tests from the period between the accession of James I and the Civil War, the authors draw on criticism by both new historicists and cultural materialists.

Contributors: J. R. MULRYNE, SIMON ADAMS, RICHARD DUTTON, GRAHAM PARRY, MARTIN BUTLER, JAMES KNOWLES, JULIA GASPER, KATHLEEN MCLUSKIE *and* MARGOT HEINEMANN.

1993   0 521 40159 3   Hardback

HAMLET VERSUS LEAR

Cultural Politics and Shakespeare's Art

R. A. FOAKES

This book focuses on the two plays of Shakespeare that have generally contended for the title of 'greatest' among his works. *Hamlet* remained a focal point of reference until about 1960, when it was displaced by *King Lear*, a play which at the same time ceased to be perceived as a play of redemption and become a play of despair. Foakes attempts to explain these shifts by analysing the reception of the plays since about 1800, an analysis which necessarily engages with the politics of the plays and the politics of criticism.

1993   0 521 34292 9   Hardback

PLAYERS OF SHAKESPEARE 3

Further Essays in Shakespearean Performance by Players with the Royal Shakespeare Company

Edited by RUSSELL JACKSON *and* ROBERT SMALLWOOD

Contributors: ROGER ALLAM, SIMON RUSSELL BEALE, BRIAN COX, GREGORY DORAN, PENNY DOWNIE, RALPH FIENNES, DEBORAH FINDLAY, PHILIP FRANKS, ANTON LESSER, MAGGIE STEED, SOPHIE THOMPSON, HARRIET WALTER *and* NICHOLAS WOODESON.

1993   0 521 36320 9   Hardback

SHAKESPEARE AND THE GEOGRAPHY OF DIFFERENCE

JOHN GILLIES

In this engaging book, John Gillies explores Shakespeare's geographic imagination, and discovers an intimate relationship between Renaissance geography and theatre arising from a shared dependence on the opposing impulses of taboo-laden closure and hubristic expansiveness.

Cambridge Studies in Renaissance Literature and Culture 4

1994   0 521 41719 8   Hardback
        0 521 45853 6   Paperback

BIT PARTS IN SHAKESPEARE'S PLAYS

M. M. MAHOOD

'This is a wittily written, elegantly thought out, wonderfully original work that abounds in new ideas. It will be rewarding to all readers and actors of Shakespeare, first for its multitude of details about bit parts, and secondly for the rich possibilities for performance that the author uncovers.'
Andrew Gurr, *The Times Literary Supplement*

1993   0 521 41612 4   Hardback

SHAKESPEARE'S PROFESSIONAL CAREER

PETER THOMSON

Shakespeare was a supremely successful accommodator. The story of his career as actor and playwright, which this book tells, shows the accommodation of his remarkable talents to the circumstances of his time: the social, political and professional life of Elizabethan and Jacobean England. There are numerous illustrations gleaned from museums, libraries and great houses to illustrate the theatrical and social context of Elizabethan and Jacobean England.

1992   0 521 35128 6   Hardback
1994   0 521 46655 5   Paperback

LOOKING AT SHAKESPEARE

A Visual History of Twentieth-Century Performance

DENNIS KENNEDY

This book describes the relationship between scenography and international Shakespeare performance in the twentieth century. Dennis Kennedy discovers how the visual element relates to the use of Shakespeare on the stage and how it conveys both textual meaning and cultural overtones. The numerous and varied illustrations (173 in all, with over 20 in full colour) document and illuminate the commentary.

1993   0 521 34655 X   Hardback

FOREIGN SHAKESPEARE

Contemporary Performance

Edited by DENNIS KENNEDY

This is the first collection to offer a considered account of contemporary Shakespeare performance in non-English-speaking theatres.

Contributors: DENNIS KENNEDY, JOHN RUSSELL BROWN, DOMINIQUE GOY-BLANQUET, AVRHAM OZ, LEANORE LIEBLEIN, RON ENGLE, LAWRENCE GUNTER, PIA KLEBER, SPENCER GOLUB, IRENA R. MAKARYK, JARKA BURIAN, MARVIN CARLSON, WILHELM HORTMANN, ANDREA NOURYEH *and* PATRICE PAVIS.

1993   0 521 420253   Hardback

SHAKESPEARE AND MULTIPLICITY

BRIAN GIBBONS

Brian Gibbons presents the idea of multiplicity as a way of understanding the form and style of Shakespeare's plays: composed of many different codes, woven together in a unique pattern for each play, rather than variations on fixed notions of Comedy or Tragedy.

1993   0 521 44406 3   Hardback

THE NEW CAMBRIDGE SHAKESPEARE

General Editor: BRIAN GIBBONS

Associate General Editors: A. R. BRAUNMULLER
and R. C. HOOD

Aimed at senior school students and undergraduates, *The New Cambridge Shakespeare* offers modern, freshly edited texts. Each volume provides an extensive treatment of the theatrical qualities of the play by means of a substantial and detailed critical introduction, a wide range of informative illustrations, and detailed footnotes.

'Introduction, text, and apparatus are all highly legible, and blessedly footnotes really are footnotes, not endnotes tucked away somewhere else in the volume. Attractive illustrations range from title pages and appropriate historical material to production photographs.'   *The Times Educational Supplement*

ALL'S WELL THAT ENDS WELL
Edited by RUSSELL FRASER

ANTONY AND CLEOPATRA
Edited by DAVID BEVINGTON

THE COMEDY OF ERRORS
Edited by T. S. DORSCH

HAMLET PRINCE OF DENMARK
Edited by PHILIP EDWARDS

JULIUS CAESAR
Edited by MARVIN SPEVACK

THE SECOND PART OF KING HENRY IV
Edited by GIORGIO MELCHIORI

KING HENRY V
Edited by ANDREW GURR

THE FIRST PART OF KING HENRY VI
Edited by MICHAEL HATTAWAY

THE SECOND PART OF KING HENRY VI
Edited by MICHAEL HATTAWAY

THE THIRD PART OF KING HENRY VI
Edited by MICHAEL HATTAWAY

KING HENRY VIII
Edited by JOHN MARGESON

KING JOHN
Edited by L. A. BEAURLINE

KING RICHARD II
Edited by ANDREW GURR

MEASURE FOR MEASURE
Edited by BRIAN GIBBONS

THE MERCHANT OF VENICE
Edited by M. M. MAHOOD

A MIDSUMMER NIGHT'S DREAM
Edited by R. A. FOAKES

MUCH ADO ABOUT NOTHING
Edited by F. H. MARES

OTHELLO
Edited by NORMAN SANDERS

THE POEMS
VENUS AND ADONIS · THE RAPE OF LUCRECE
THE PHOENIX AND THE TURTLE
THE PASSIONATE PILGRIM · A LOVER'S COMPLAINT
Edited by JOHN ROE

ROMEO AND JULIET
Edited by G. BLAKEMORE EVANS

THE TAMING OF THE SHREW
Edited by ANN THOMPSON

THE TRAGEDY OF KING LEAR
Edited by JAY L. HALIO

TWELFTH NIGHT *or* WHAT YOU WILL
Edited by ELIZABETH STORY DONNO

THE TWO GENTLEMEN OF VERONA
Edited by KURT SCHLUETER